ROYAL COMMISSIONS AND PUBLIC INQUIRIES

Government, Policy and Politics Series

A partnership between Connor Court Publishing and Griffith University

Royal Commissions and Public Inquiries – Practice and Potential edited by Scott Prasser and Helen Tracey, is part of the **Government, Policy and Politics Series**, a joint initiative of Connor Court Publishing and the Institute for Ethics, Governance and Law (a joint initiative of the United Nations University, Griffith University, ANU, QUT and OP Jindal Global University headquartered at Griffith). The series explores past, present and future developments in Australian government, policy and politics.

Series Editor: Dr Scott Prasser

Books in the Series:

Gary Johns, *Right Social Justice – Better Ways to Help the Poor* (2012)

Graeme Starr, *Carrick: Principles, Politics and Policy* (2012)

Ian Hancock, *Greiner: A Political Biography* (2013)

Kate Jones and Scott Prasser, *Audit Commissions: Reviewing the Reviewers* (2013)

Scott Prasser & Helen Tracey, (eds), *Royal Commissions and Public Inquiries – Practice and Potential* (2014)

ROYAL COMMISSIONS & PUBLIC INQUIRIES

Practice & Potential

Edited by
Scott Prasser and Helen Tracey

Connor Court Publishing Pty Ltd

PO Box 224W

Ballarat VIC 3350

sales@connorcourt.com

www.connorcourt.com

ISBN: 9781925138245 (pbk.)

Cover design by Ian James

Printed in Australia

CONTENTS

Section 3: What inquiries do and how they do it?

Section 4: What is there to show for it? Assessing inquiry effectiveness

Section 5: Other countries' inquiries

Section 6: Conclusion

Preface

Public inquiries play a significant, if not particularly visible, role in Australia's political system and public life. A public inquiry, in its many forms – royal commission, committee of inquiry, taskforce, to name but a few – is a versatile instrument available to government when it needs to investigate an event or action or to delve deeply into a complex policy area.

Governments value ad hoc, independent inquiries for their capacity to marshal information, views and evidence as a basis for formulating policy, as a way of meticulously investigating the causes of an accident or disaster, or as a means of gaining a clear understanding of the facts involved in a public controversy or scandal. At their best, public inquiries are a tool for rational policymaking and for achieving accountability and integrity in public life. As a result of their work, our political decision-makers are better informed and better equipped to develop good policy, assign responsibility and take remedial action. Ultimately, public inquiries have the potential to raise the quality of governance and public policymaking and as a result, generate greater confidence and trust in government.

For a sceptical public however, the establishment of a public inquiry is often seen as an exercise in political expediency, a device to delay decision-making, a way to avoid taking action, a ploy to pacify interest groups and a waste of scarce resources.

The contributors to this book, writing variously from practical and academic experience, reveal both sides of the public inquiry coin in their exploration of the distinctive role inquiries have played in Australian public life. From the perspective of their own direct involvement in and knowledge of inquiries, the writers examine the standing and value of public inquiries in the past and present. They throw light on the reasons why governments continue to choose the independent inquiry instrument when they have access to so many alternative avenues for developing policy, launching an investigation into misconduct or clarifying the causes of a catastrophic event.

The contributors explore the potential of inquiries to have a significant impact on policy and administration, the kind of outcomes they have produced in practice, and factors in the form and make-up of inquiries that make them more or less effective. The book also includes commentary and analysis on the development and use of the public inquiry instrument in the United Kingdom, New Zealand, Canada and the USA. The concluding chapter draws on the insights of the earlier chapters to assess why the public inquiry has remained such a relevant and useful part of our political system.

A deep and abiding interest in public inquiries is not a common affliction among public policy academics, but hopefully the writings in this book will encourage other researchers to pay greater attention to this small but significant feature of government processes. It would be worth the effort. In all their variety, public inquiries make an important contribution to the business of government in Australia and they are here to stay.

Scott Prasser and Helen Tracey

All chapters in this book were blind refereed. Special thanks to the referee panel:

- Professor Neal Ryan, previously Pro Vice Chancellor of Southern Cross University and Executive Director (Publications and Research) of the International Research Society of Public Administration, currently Adjunct Professor at Curtin and Southern Cross universities.
- Professor Geoff Cockfield, School of Commerce, Faculty of Business, Education, Law and Arts of the University of Southern Queensland.
- Tony Harris, former New South Wales Auditor-General, Deputy Secretary of the Immigration Department and Commissioner of the Industry Commission.

Also acknowledged is Michael Gilchrist of Connor Court for preparing the text for publication and Susan Prior, editor at Write-now (www.write-now.com.au), for checking the proofs.

Section 1

History, trends and key issues – the story so far . . .

Scott Prasser and Helen Tracey

Public inquiries have a long history in Australia, dating back to the period between colonial settlement and federation when numerous inquiries, mostly in the form of royal commissions, were appointed by Australia's six states. The *Royal Commissions Act 1902* (Cth) was one of the first acts passed by the new Commonwealth Parliament, laying the foundation for over a century of royal commissions at the national level. At the same time, the states have continued to appoint royal commissions, under their own legislation.

The first investigative royal commission answerable to a Commonwealth minister, appointed on 12 August 1902, two weeks before the passage of the *Royal Commissions Act*, was required to inquire into and report upon the arrangements made for the *Transport of Troops returning from service in South Africa in the S.S. Drayton Grange and the Circumstances under which Trooper Harold Burkitt, 2nd Australian Commonwealth Horse, who was in a serious condition of health, was not landed at Adelaide from the S.S. Norfolk.* Like so many royal commissions in the century that followed, the Drayton Grange commission was set up in response to public outrage, in this case over the conditions on board the troop ship S.S. Drayton Grange bringing soldiers back from the Boer War and the 17 deaths which occurred as a result of the voyage. The *Royal Commissions Act* was hastily put together to provide the powers deemed necessary for the Drayton Grange inquiry, enabling it to call witnesses and compel evidence. The commission, which reported in the space of two months, on 9 October 1902, found that several different authorities were responsible for the overcrowding of the ship, defects in accommodation, lax discipline on board and the poor medical response, although no legal action followed. It was certainly not the last time a royal commission's report was labelled by the press as a whitewash.

This first investigative commission was followed soon after by the first policy royal commission, the Kirkpatrick *Royal Commission on Sites for the Seat of Government of the Commonwealth*, which reported to the Minister of Home Affairs in July 1903. After considering nine potential sites for the national capital, the Commission came out in favour of Albury and Tumut as preferred sites, setting an early precedent for the Commonwealth government to ignore the recommendations of a public inquiry. The site of Canberra was not settled until 1908, after several years of further political and parliamentary debate.

Up to the time of writing, some 132 royal commissions have followed at the national level.[1] Many of these have served to resolve a contentious issue, explain a catastrophic event, uncover corruption or provide the substance of new public policy. Others have had little impact on public life. The number of royal commissions however is dwarfed by the more than 600 public inquiries appointed at the Commonwealth level not under statute but by ministerial authority over the same period. The powerful and prestigious royal commission is the minority form of a public inquiry. The great majority of public inquiries are appointed without a legislative base, by executive government seeking independent advice on a policy matter or to review and explain an event or action.

Both inquiry forms share some distinctive characteristics. In the first place, they are temporary, ad hoc bodies appointed by executive government to provide advice or to investigate some issue, against specific terms of reference. Once the specified task is completed, the inquiry disbands, and has no further role in advice, implementation or administration. The essence of an inquiry or commission is that it is public – it responds to public terms of reference, its proceedings are public, community input is sought through public submission and consultation, and reports are publicly released. Members are drawn from outside government and the bureaucracy and are chosen generally for their special expertise. Although an inquiry may be serviced by a departmental secretariat, it operates independently of the government that appoints it. Inquiries and commissions are funded entirely by government, often at significant cost.

Over the history of the Commonwealth, there has been considerable cross-over between royal commissions and public inquiries, with both varieties of the instrument used for matters of high public importance as well as for less significant, more narrowly defined matters. From time to time, a government decision to set up a royal commission has been regarded as a disproportionate response, exceeding the needs of the particular circumstances. Likewise, a decision to set up an official inquiry rather than a royal commission has also at times been regarded as inadequate, lacking the necessary powers to investigate the situation properly.

In the former category, where the government's response was regarded as heavy-handed, were the Howard Government's *Royal Commission into the Building and Construction Industry* (Cole 2001) and the 2004 appointment of a second royal commission into the Centenary House Lease (Hunt), to investigate the findings of an earlier royal commission. Both these inquiries were criticised at the time of their establishment for being intensely political, aiming to embarrass the Opposition or being ideologically motivated.

The latter category, where a government decision to appoint an inquiry rather than a royal commission was regarded as inadequate, includes the Howard Government's establishment of a non-statutory inquiry rather than a royal commission into the immigration detention of Cornelia Rau (Palmer 2005) and the Rudd Government's *Inquiry into the Case of Dr Mohamed Haneef* (Clarke 2008), both of which were criticised for lacking the necessary powers to investigate the situation properly, to collect evidence and to grant immunity to essential witnesses.

The trend towards the appointment of non-statutory based inquiries rather than royal commissions has accelerated over the past few decades. The two royal commissions appointed in 2013 – the *Royal Commission into Institutional Responses to Child Sexual Abuse* (McClellan), appointed in January by the Gillard Labor Government, and the *Royal Commission into the Home Insulation Program* (Hanger), appointed in December by the newly elected Abbott Coalition Government, were the first royal commissions appointed by the Commonwealth since 2005 under the *Royal Commissions Act 1902* (Cth). Most often now, royal commissions are used as investigative or inquisitorial instruments on matters regarded as of great significance rather than for policy advice or review. Their appointment is most likely to be triggered by significant issues of corruption or maladministration, by a serious accident or disaster, or as in the case of the McClellan Commission, by a failure of a long run of other types of investigation to resolve matters to the public satisfaction.

Different governments have taken quite different approaches to the appointment of public inquiries. Some steer clear of them as much as possible and prefer to use the mechanisms that are available to them within the apparatus of government. These include parliamentary inquiries, Commonwealth-state working groups and task forces as well as existing Commonwealth bodies such as the Ombudsman and the Productivity Commission. Others, particularly reformist governments with a commitment to evidence-based policy, are wont to appoint a number of inquiries – sometimes too many to handle. This was the case with the Whitlam Labor Government (1972-1975) which was something of a watershed in the history of inquiries in Australia. In less than three years, some 70 non-statutory, mostly policy public inquiries were appointed, along with 13 royal commissions. Near the end of the Whitlam years, as this proliferation of inquiries produced copious recommendations for change involving substantial investment from the Commonwealth, at a time when Treasury coffers were running dry, the attraction of comprehensive evidence-based policy reform had waned. Many reports were shelved, at least for the short term.

Speaking subsequently as Opposition leader in the House of Representatives, Whitlam defended his government's reliance on the inquiry instrument:

> The Labor Government found that the scarcest commodity after 23 years of conservative rule was information. In whole areas of public policy – schools, health, the environment, industrial conditions, the national estate, social welfare, local government – no body of facts or evidence existed … There was no core of information on which federal or state governments could take decisions. (24 February 1976)

This information gathering function has always been at the heart of the public inquiry's value and contribution. Historically, governments needed to appoint ad hoc independent bodies because no entity existed within the public administration with the functions, powers or expertise to marshal the facts and data needed for soundly based government decision-making. Since the 1970s, the machinery of government at both national and state levels has matured and expanded, to the point that most issues that warrant thorough investigation can now find a suitable home in an already established body. Despite this development however, governments to varying degrees continue to use the inquiry instrument to provide accountability, to allow wide public participation and to enrich the process of public policymaking. Arguably, as policy issues become more complex and the reach of government extends further into everyday lives, the need for this kind of help from outside the bureaucracy will only increase.

This then is the historical setting for the two chapters in this Section which review the legal underpinnings of the public inquiry mechanism in Australia. In chapter 1, Rosalind Croucher, Professor of Law and President of the Australian Law Reform Commission (ALRC), explains the evolving use of public inquiries, both statutory and non-statutory, and their institutional positioning, from the earliest inquiry in colonial times through to the present. Fittingly her point of reference is the review of the *Royal Commissions Act* undertaken in 2009 by the ALRC. This inquiry into inquiries, conducted by a government agency rather than as an independent review, examined the various forms of inquiry available to government, with a view to making sure that the legal underpinnings and administrative arrangements for inquiries continued to meet contemporary needs for pursuing matters of public importance.

Croucher draws out the major distinctions between statutory and non-statutory inquiries, particularly in relation to powers of investigation and protection, and discusses the reasoning behind the ALRC's recommendation of a two-tier statute to provide a legislative framework for royal commissions on the one hand and official inquiries on the other. The proposed new Act would confer coercive powers on both levels of inquiry. While maintaining a higher level of information-gathering and investigatory powers for royal commissions, it would for the first time bestow a limited degree of coercive powers on official inquiries, to enable them to require the production of information and the attendance of witnesses and gather documents. As Croucher explains, the ALRC's proposals acknowledged the enduring value of public inquiries as an instrument of accountability and transparency. They were directed at giving the different kinds of inquiry a firm foundation in law, and addressing some of the perennial concerns about public inquiries, such as independence, implementation and costs.

Following Croucher's broad overview of the inquiry scene, Nicholas Aroney, Professor of Constitutional Law at the University of Queensland, turns the spotlight onto critical constitutional issues that can affect the conduct of royal commissions and challenge their legitimacy. Questions of the legal authority for a commission, the separation of powers between the executive and judiciary, and the powers of the Commonwealth in a federal system of government have been significant for the establishment and operation of royal commissions in the past, and are important considerations for future royal commissions. The rule of law applies to inquiries of all kinds, not least to the far-reaching coercive powers of royal commissions. Aroney's discussion of how the courts have from time to time interpreted the law as it applies to the appointment and operation of royal commissions is a reminder that even these powerful instruments of executive government are bound by constitutional principles and subject to ongoing legal scrutiny.

In this sense, while the inquiry instrument is an inheritance of our colonial past, it has adapted to the unique constitutional framework of the Australian federation and continues to evolve alongside other institutions of government to play a significant part in the decision-making practices of modern government.

Endnote

1 This includes the 2007 *Equine Influenza Inquiry* which was appointed under the *Quarantine Act 1908* (Cth) which gave the inquiry comparable powers to a royal commission.

1

Towards a common legislative base for inquiries

Rosalind Croucher

Introduction

Public inquiries have a long history in the British Commonwealth. They were initiated when William I sent his royal commissioners throughout his new realm of England in 1085 to undertake a thorough inventory and produced the *Domesday Book* as a record of property holdings across the land (see chapter 17: Starr). The numerous public inquiries since that time have taken many forms, from committees, task forces, working parties and reviews, to the most prestigious form of all, royal commissions. As the name suggests, royal commissions are a delegation from the Crown or, in former British colonies, the Queen's representative. Royal commissions are authorised in Australia at the national level by the Governor-General and across the states by the respective governors. Other public inquiries are initiated by ministers rather than the Crown, and have become *de rigueur* "the new consumer item of modern government" (Prasser 2006: 1).

The public inquiry mechanism came to Australia early in its colonial history. In 1819, John Thomas Bigge was appointed by the Secretary of Colonies, Earl Bathurst, as special commissioner to report on the state of the colony of New South Wales and the administration of Governor Lachlan Macquarie, and specifically on the effectiveness of transportation as a deterrent to felons (Bennett 1966). Bigge's three reports prompted the insertion of clauses in the *New South Wales Act 1823* to set up limited constitutional government through a Legislative Council, to establish

Van Diemen's Land as a separate colony, to enable extensive legal reforms, and to make new provisions for the reception of convicts from England. From that time, public inquiries were used regularly by each of the colonies after they became self-governing and they have come to perform an increasingly important function in Australian government.

Not all public inquiries have a legislative base. If coercive powers are warranted at a national level, they must be set up under statute, either under the *Royal Commissions Act 1902* (Cth) or under other legislation. This was a reflection of the clear delineation of the limitations on the royal prerogative in the wake of the English Civil War during the 17th century (Clokie and Robinson 1937: 44). Other public inquiries are mostly ad hoc, without statutory foundation, and are established to provide advice or develop policy on a diverse range of matters, or to conduct investigations.

Given the array of different models and approaches for conducting inquiries and their extensive use, in January 2009 the Australian Law Reform Commission (ALRC) was asked by the Attorney-General in the first Rudd Government to review the appropriateness of the alternative forms of executive inquiry available to the Commonwealth. The Rudd Government's concern was to ensure that the forms of inquiry available to it to pursue matters of public importance were effective and efficient, and in keeping with contemporary requirements. The ALRC was asked to consider whether there was a need to develop an alternative form of inquiry, with statutory foundations, to provide more flexibility, less formality and greater cost-effectiveness than a royal commission, and whether the existing legislation, the *Royal Commissions Act 1902* (Cth) remained current and appropriate.

This inquiry by the ALRC was the first major review of the *Royal Commissions Act* since its introduction. In its report, *Making Inquiries: A New Statutory Framework*, released in October 2009, the ALRC recommended that the *Royal Commissions Act* be refurbished into a single inquiries statute as a foundation for both levels of independent inquiry

– investigative-inquisitorial, and policy investigation-review. These two tiers were to be defined and distinguished by differences in their powers. The ALRC also proposed that an *Inquiries Handbook* be produced to provide practical guidance on the establishment and conduct of inquiries, and recommended public reporting on government action on inquiry reports in order to improve accountability and increase public confidence in their value. To date, there has been no response from the Commonwealth government to these proposals. The value of the ALRC review therefore lies in its comprehensive analysis of the institutional framework underpinning public inquiries in Australia and issues that have arisen in their use over time.

Commonwealth public inquiries

The *Royal Commissions Act* provides the Commonwealth government with a statutory framework for establishing public inquiries with coercive information-gathering powers. Under the Act, the scope of the power to establish a royal commission is very broad. The *Royal Commissions Act* provides that the Governor-General, by Letters Patent, may issue a commission, "which relates to or is connected with the peace, order and good government of the Commonwealth, or any public purpose or any power of the Commonwealth". Other statutes, such as defence or quarantine legislation, also incorporate powers and protections similar to the *Royal Commissions Act.* To all intents and purposes, commissions of inquiry appointed under this kind of legislation have the powers and standing of a royal commission and are indistinguishable from them. Before the announcement of the *Royal Commission into Institutional Responses to Child Sex Abuse* in November 2012 (Letters Patent were not issued till 2013), the most recent Commonwealth inquiry appointed under the *Royal Commissions Act 1902* (Cth) was the Cole *Inquiry into Certain Australian Companies in Relation to the UN Oil-for-Food Programme* (2005) (see chapter 12: Bartos). Other inquiries, however, including the Callinan *Equine Influenza Inquiry* – the 2007 inquiry into the outbreak of equine flu in eastern Australia – had comparable powers derived from the *Quarantine Act 1908* (Cth).

A major focus of the ALRC's remit was to consider whether forms of public inquiry other than royal commissions needed a statutory base and, if so, what statutory model would be appropriate. The number of non-statutory inquiries and investigations far exceeds statutory-based inquiries. In this category are policy reviews such as the 2004 *Inquiry into Australian Intelligence Agencies* (see chapter 10: Flood), and the 2008 *National Human Rights Consultation* (see chapter 8: Brennan); and investigative inquiries such as the bushfire inquiries (see chapter 6: Wettenhall); and inquiries, mostly royal commissions, into political wrongdoing or maladministration (see chapter 4: Ransley).

Alternative instruments of inquiry and review exist within the machinery of government, including parliamentary inquiries and permanent bodies, such as the Commonwealth Ombudsman, who has powers to consider and investigate complaints about Commonwealth government departments and agencies; the Inspector-General of Intelligence and Security, who has the power to inquire into the activities of intelligence agencies; and the Productivity Commission, which has a statutory function to conduct public inquiries as part of its policy advisory responsibilities. These mechanisms were outside the scope of the ALRC review but demonstrate the diverse and diffuse nature of the inquiry mechanisms available to government, to which the ALRC sought to bring greater clarity.

Pressures for change

As an Act of 1902, the *Royal Commissions Act* was very much of its time. It was modelled on a United Kingdom Act, the *Witnesses (Public Inquiries) Protection Act 1892 (UK)*, was only eight provisions long, and was, as noted by Justice Kirby, "expressed with high compression" (Kirby 2007: 36). Not surprisingly, it has been amended 23 times with the result that its "seams" are showing, as seen in the variety of drafting styles. Some amendments have been of a minor, technical nature. Others have been more significant, addressing deficiencies in the legislation identified by particular royal commissions. For example, the Act was amended in 1982 to empower a royal commissioner to apply for a search warrant, in response to a request by the Costigan *Royal Commission on the Activities of the Federated Ship Painters and Dockers Union.*

Given that the focus of the ALRC's review was the legislative base for Commonwealth executive inquiries, comparative models were naturally relevant. Could there be a tidier way to provide the foundation for public inquiries in Australia?

Canada's *Inquiries Act 1985* was instructive. Most federal public inquiries in Canada are appointed under this legislation (d'Ombrain 1997: 90; see chapter 19: Hoole), which allows for two types of inquiry with coercive powers to be established, categorised as either a "public inquiry" or a "departmental inquiry". A public inquiry is established by the Governor-in-Council, and a departmental inquiry by a minister with responsibility for a federal government department. The public inquiry in this model is like a royal commission in Australia, while the departmental inquiry is like a ministerial inquiry, without statutory foundation.

At the time of the ALRC's report, the New Zealand Law Commission's (NZLC) work on its *Commissions of Inquiry Act 1908* also provided a useful resource. The NZLC recommended a new statute providing for two tiers of inquiry: "public inquiries" and "government inquiries". The first tier would take over the ground of royal commissions and commissions of inquiry and would be for "big and meaty issues that are of high level concern to the public and to ministers – the occurrence of an accidental disaster or the devising of a comprehensive new policy framework for a particular topic". The second tier would be for "smaller and more immediate issues where a quick and authoritative answer is required from an independent inquirer" (NZLC 2008: 5). At the time of writing, legislation to put this proposal into effect is still working its way through the parliamentary processes in New Zealand (see chapter 18: Simpson).

The ALRC also looked at Ireland and the work of the Law Commission of Ireland (LRC of Ireland 2005), and at Singapore. The suggestion of Tom Sherman (see page 78) for the enactment of a general inquiry statute in Australia was also influential (Sherman 1997).

The need for a new statutory framework in Australia

The ALRC identified a number of shortcomings with the current arrangements for public inquiries in Australia. The lack of a legislative foundation for non-statutory inquiries was seen as an inherent weakness. This meant they lacked the powers that might be needed to investigate matters comprehensively, to provide adequate legal protection to inquiry members and staff, or to require public input. The result could be a lack of public confidence in their findings, if it was considered there had not been access to all the information necessary to make the best recommendations.

The ALRC received overwhelming support from stakeholders for retaining the highest statutory form of public inquiry, the royal commission, as an essential aspect of accountable and transparent government. The *Making Inquiries* report agrees with several submissions that, because of their public nature and independence, royal commissions "enhance Australian democracy" (ALRC 2009: 94) and that the "robust public scrutiny" of governments that may be undertaken by royal commissions "has become increasingly critical in the context of expanding executive power" (ALRC 2009: 94). In addition to retaining this prestigious first tier of public inquiry, the ALRC saw a need for a statutory base to empower second-tier inquiries to operate in the same legalistic way in order to determine all the facts:

> First, many non-royal commission forms of public inquiry need access to coercive information-gathering powers, such as compelling a person to appear and provide answers to an inquiry, to ensure the efficient investigation of a particular issue or event.

> Secondly, legal protections are necessary to ensure that the way information is collected in an inquiry reflects an appropriate balance between the need to determine the facts and protecting the rights of individuals involved with, or affected by, the inquiry. Finally, legal protections can help to prevent inquiry members and staff from suffering detriment through being appointed to, or employed by, an inquiry. (ALRC 2009: 96)

A new legislative basis for public inquiries could also address some confusion about the standing, powers and protections of both statutory and non-statutory inquiries not called "royal commissions".

Should this mean that all statutory public inquiries should be brought under the *Royal Commissions Act*? The ALRC did not think this was the right policy answer: "Royal commissions fulfil particular functions, and it would not be desirable to 'dilute' their perceived importance or prestige by commencing all public inquiries as the 'highest' form of executive inquiry" (ALRC 2009: 96). The ALRC also pointed to the reticence of the Commonwealth government to establish royal commissions and observed that they were frequently lengthy and expensive. Other forms of public inquiry are often preferred because they are a more flexible, expeditious and cost-effective option.

But would the standing of royal commissions be diminished by the introduction of another form of statutory inquiry? The ALRC thought not – on the basis that the executive "regularly establishes non-royal commission forms of inquiry and there is little evidence that these inquiries diminish the importance of royal commissions" (ALRC 2009: 96). The ALRC, therefore, concluded that there should be a new framework, one that accommodates both royal commissions and other public inquiries, to provide "a cohesive framework with respect to: inquiry hearings and other procedures; the review of decisions; and consistent government responses to inquiry recommendations" (ALRC 2009: 97).

Two tiers of public inquiry

The ALRC recommended that the *Royal Commissions Act 1902* (Cth) should be totally refurbished and given a new name, the Inquiries Act. The essence of the remodelling was to provide for two tiers of public inquiry, similar to the approach taken in other jurisdictions.

The ALRC kept the title "royal commission" for the higher tier, reserving it for an inquiry established to look into matters of substantial public importance and requiring a degree of coercive power and abrogation of privilege. While some stakeholders suggested the word "royal" should not be used, the ALRC decided to keep it, on the basis that "royal commission" is well recognised as denoting an inquiry of singular importance – "unquestionably the most ancient and the most dignified of the various kinds of inquiry" (Clokie and Robinson 1937: 24-25) or the "heavy artillery" of the inquiry framework (NZLC 2008: 4). Keeping "royal" also indicates that the inquiry is established by the Crown, namely by the Governor-General. The ALRC considered it appropriate that the head of state should continue to be responsible for establishing the highest form of public inquiry in Australia.

For second-tier inquiries established by a minister to look into matters of public importance, the ALRC suggested the term "official inquiries".

Inquiry powers

In addition to the way the inquiry is established, the key distinction between a royal commission and official inquiry would be the degree of coercive powers and abrogation of privilege. The question of powers and protections was central to the ALRC's review and it looked for guidance in other countries' arrangements. In 1966, the *Royal Commission on Tribunals of Inquiry* (Salmon Royal Commission) in the United Kingdom recommended that the use of coercive powers by inquiries should be limited to "matters of vital public importance concerning which there is something in the nature of a nation-wide crisis in confidence"

(Salmon 1966: 16). In 1977, the Law Reform Commission of Canada took a similar view, concluding that commissions should be armed with coercive powers only when they were undertaking investigatory inquiries of major importance.

In its 2008 report, the NZLC considered the option of a menu of powers, procedures and immunities that could be applied to each inquiry on a case-by-case basis. It decided against such a process on the basis that it was not always possible to determine what powers would be required by an inquiry and if commissioners had to refer back to government to seek additional coercive powers, it may undermine the independence of a commission and be open to "politically motivated horse-trading and litigation" (NZLC 2008: 44). The NZLC concluded that it is preferable that all inquiries have recourse to statutory powers should they be needed. Their existence "acts as a carrot", encouraging cooperation of those involved with an inquiry, even though coercive powers "are rarely relied on by commissions of inquiry" in New Zealand (NZLC 2008: 44).

The ALRC did not like the "menu" approach either, nor the "politically motivated horse-trading" that it might generate. While flexibility is important, this should not be the overriding consideration when determining the powers available to an inquiry. Since enhancing clarity in the arrangements for establishing and conducting public inquiries was one of the main aims in designing a new statutory framework, the solution proposed by the ALRC was to delineate in the legislation the powers to be available to each tier of inquiry, leaving it to the executive to determine which form of inquiry should be established on the basis of the powers required in the particular circumstances, and leaving it to the chair of the inquiry to control the use of the powers made available by statute. Each inquiry would then have the necessary tools to carry out its investigations without inappropriately infringing on the rights of persons involved with, or affected by, its processes.

Conferring coercive powers on both forms of inquiry would ensure that inquiry members have access to all the information necessary to make informed findings and recommendations. However, only a royal commission would have the ability to exercise powers to authorise the application for entry, search and seizure warrants, for the issue of warrants for the arrest of those who fail to appear before it when called, partially to abrogate the privilege against self-incrimination and, if set out in the Letters Patent, to abrogate client legal privilege.

This higher level of coercive information-gathering and investigatory power for royal commissions reflects the ALRC's view that royal commissions would be more likely to investigate major events or problems, while official inquiries – policy inquiries in the main – would be established to inquire into less significant events and be conducted in a more informal setting.

In summary, the ALRC recommended that both royal commissions and official inquiries should have the power to:

- require the production of documents and other things;
- require the attendance or appearance to answer questions (on oath or affirmation if so directed by the inquiry); and
- inspect, retain and copy any documents or other things.

A royal commission, but not an official inquiry, should have the power to:

- apply to a judge for an entry, search and seizure warrant, or a warrant for the apprehension of a person who fails to appear or attend; and
- exercise concurrent functions and powers under Commonwealth and state and territory laws.

Finally, only a royal commission should have the power to abrogate client legal privilege or the privilege against self-incrimination.

Inquiries handbook

One focus of the ALRC's recommendations for reform was to capture the "institutional knowledge" about how inquiries work. A strength of the public inquiry mechanism is that it is specific to the issue or problem it is addressing, but this ad hoc nature is also a weakness if there is no formal process by which the institutional knowledge of those that have established, conducted and administered inquiries can be passed on. To overcome this weakness, the ALRC recommended the development of an *Inquiries Handbook* containing information for those responsible for establishing and administering inquiries, inquiry members, inquiry participants and members of the public.

Such a publication was intended to streamline and guide the operation of both levels of inquiry. It would provide practical guidance and information on the establishment of inquiries, the appointment of members, administration, powers, protections and procedures, and the use and protection of national security information. Given the infrequency of royal commissions, such a guide would be a welcome repository of good practice, and an important resource for the effective and efficient conduct of an inquiry. It would ease the establishment process, clarify issues around operation and provide useful advice on management and administrative matters.

It would not, however, have statutory force or circumscribe the manner in which a particular inquiry is conducted. As a supportive tool, the *Inquiries Handbook* would be designed to give flexibility so that each inquiry could strike its own balance between the degree of importance of the issue and the powers needed to pursue investigations, within the new statutory framework.

Accountability

Independence

A key aspect of the integrity of public inquiries is the extent to which they are perceived to be independent, "a discrete activity, with leadership at 'arm's length' from the executive and policy departments in particular" (Banks 2013: 3; see chapter 7: Banks). The NZLC observed that "[t]he principle that justice should be done and be seen to be done applies to inquiries as well as courts" (NZLC 2008: 53). Hence, it concluded that an inquiry's independence "should be made clear, rather than simply inferred", and recommended that the new NZ Act state that public inquiries "have a duty to act independently in the exercise of their functions, powers and duties". The ALRC agreed with this approach, believing it would "help to ensure public confidence in the independence of the inquiry" (ALRC 2009: 142), and made a similar recommendation in relation to the proposed Inquiries Act.

Tabling

The ALRC considered that requiring royal commission reports to be tabled was an important accountability mechanism. While this has tended to be the practice, there is no statutory tabling requirement. The ALRC recommended that the Inquiries Act should contain a presumption that reports of both royal commissions and official inquiries will be tabled by government within 15 sitting days of receiving the inquiry's final report, the same tabling requirement that the ALRC itself operates under. In general, the tabling requirement would extend to the whole of an inquiry report, but there may be occasions for example, when an inquiry report contains classified or security sensitive information, when the whole report should not be tabled. The ALRC, therefore, recommended that if the government decided not to table the whole report of an inquiry it should table a statement explaining why. This flexible approach, the ALRC considered, would preserve the accountability of the executive to parliament.

Implementation

Implementation of recommendations is one important measure of the effectiveness of public inquiries, given their many and varied functions. The *Royal Commissions Act* does not oblige the Commonwealth government to provide updates on implementation of royal commission recommendations, although parallel state legislation, for example the *Commissions of Inquiry (Children in State Care and Children on APY Lands) Act 2004* (SA), does require the responsible minister to provide ongoing reports to parliament on the implementation of inquiry recommendations. While not a statutory requirement, the Commonwealth government often provides ad hoc updates on the implementation of recommendations made by public inquiries, as it did for a period following the report of the *Equine Influenza Inquiry* (2007).

The significant investment of resources in any public inquiry, without any established means of accountability for this investment, led the ALRC to propose that action on those inquiry recommendations accepted by government should be recorded in public reports, and an update on progress with implementation published within 12 months of the release of the inquiry report. This reporting would cover only those recommendations government had accepted, allowing implementation to be monitored without intruding on government decision-making powers.

Costs

Knowing the costs of an inquiry is another dimension of public accountability. There is no statutory requirement for government, a royal commission or other public inquiry to provide information or report on the predicted, ongoing or final cost of an inquiry. While some royal commissions have included information on costs in their reports, more often the difficult task of collating information on costs, which has to be done by accessing a range of public sources, is left to others.

To increase transparency and address concerns about the high costs of inquiries, the ALRC recommended that the Inquiries Act should require the Commonwealth government to publish summary information about the costs of completed royal commissions and official inquiries within a reasonable time after the inquiry has concluded.

Conclusion

Despite action in other jurisdictions to place the different kinds of public inquiry on the solid foundation of a statutory base, and the ALRC's proposal for an Inquiries Act that would provide a coherent and layered, but also flexible, framework for the establishment and operation of public inquiries in Australia, inquiries continue to operate here without an appropriate legislative foundation. If the Commonwealth moves in this direction it will bring greater clarity, transparency and accountability to processes that have become an integral part of public policy development in Australia, as the chapters that follow in this book clearly demonstrate.

Public inquiries mentioned in chapter

(in chronological order by year of appointment, with name of chair)

Australia

Royal Commission on the Activities of the Federated Ship Painters and Dockers Union (Costigan: 1980)

Inquiry into Australian Intelligence Agencies (Flood: 2004)

Inquiry into Certain Australian Companies in Relation to the UN Oil-for-Food Programme (Cole: 2005)

Equine Influenza Inquiry (Callinan: 2007)

National Human Rights Consultation (Brennan: 2008)

Royal Commission into Institutional Responses to Child Sex Abuse (McClellan: 2013)

United Kingdom

Royal Commission on Tribunals of Inquiry (Salmon: 1966)

References

Australian Law Reform Commission, (ALRC), 2009, *Making Inquiries – A New Statutory Framework*, Report 111, Canberra: Commonwealth Government

Banks, G., 2013, "Public Inquiries, Public Policy and the Public Interest," *Inaugural Peter Karmel Lecture in Public Policy*, Canberra: The Academy of Social Sciences in Australia in conjunction with Australian New Zealand School of Government

Bennett, J.M., "Bigge, John Thomas (1780-1843)," in *Australian Dictionary of Biography,* Melbourne: Melbourne University Press, Volume 1, 1966, online edition http://adb.anu.edu.au/biography/bigge-john-thomas-1779 at 1 July 2013

Callinan, I., 2008, *Equine Influenza Inquiry Report*, Canberra: Commonwealth Government

Clokie, H.M., and Robinson, J.W., 1937, *Royal Commissions of Inquiry: The Significance of Investigations in British Politics*, Stanford: Stanford University Press

Kirby, M., 2007, in *X v Prudential Regulation Authority (2007), 226* CLR 630

Law Reform Commission of Canada, 1977, *Commissions of Inquiry*, Working Paper 17, Ottawa: Ministry of Supply and Services, Canada

Law Reform Commission of Ireland, 2005, *Report on Public Inquiries, Including Tribunals of Inquiry*, Dublin: Law Reform Commission

New Zealand Law Commission, (NZLC), 2008, *A New Inquiries Act*, Report 102, Wellington: New Zealand Law Commission

d'Ombrain, N., 1997, "Public Inquiries in Canada," *Canadian Public Administration*, 40(1), Spring, 86-107

Prasser, S., 2006, *Royal Commissions and Public Inquiries in Australia*, Sydney: LexisNexis Butterworths

Salmon, C., 1966, *Royal Commission on Tribunals of Inquiry Report*, London: HMSO Command 3121

Sherman, T., 1997, *Executive Inquiries in Australia: Some Proposals for Reform*, Law and Policy Paper No 8, Canberra: Centre for International and Public Law, Faculty of Law, Australian National University

2

The constitutional first principles of royal commissions

Nicholas Aroney

Introduction

The institution and conduct of a royal commission – strictly speaking, a document by which the Queen or her representative appoints a person to a position – is an act of the executive. The purpose of a royal commission, like other public inquiries, is to investigate and report on a specified matter or matters considered appropriate by the government. These matters are defined in the terms of reference in the letters patent used to establish the commission. When establishing a royal commission, the executive exercises historical powers recognised by the common law as being vested in the Crown. These powers have been confirmed and supplemented by parliamentary statutes, but the power to inquire itself is executive in character.

There have been three major constitutional issues that have arisen in relation to royal commissions.

The first concerns their legal foundations. How is the establishment and conduct of a commission authorised by law? What is the proper source of law that authorises its establishment? Questions such as these, although of theoretical interest to lawyers, can also have important practical consequences. This is because the fundamental principle of the rule of law is at stake. The rule of law means that all persons – the executive included – are subject to the law. Just because it is the executive government that acts does not mean that its actions are not subject to legal control and regulation, or that any special powers it exercises must not be legally authorised. So, if the executive seeks to establish and empower a royal commission, this establishment and empowerment must be authorised by, or at least consistent with, the law. Thus, the first constitutional question confronting a royal commission is this: what is the legal authority upon which it is established?

The second set of questions concerns the relationship between royal commissions and the administration of the law by the ordinary courts. Here, the principles of separation of powers and independence of the judiciary are especially relevant, for it is a fundamental principle of our constitutional system that there must be a separation between executive and judicial power. Noting that royal commissions are often composed of sitting judges, and that they are sometimes established to undertake forensic inquiries into what has occurred and whether any law has been breached, at what point does a royal commission unconstitutionally interfere with the administration of justice and the integrity of the court system? Can a royal commission determine, for example, whether a person is guilty of a crime?

The third set of questions concerns the kinds of matters that a royal commission established by the Commonwealth – as distinct from the states – may be authorised to investigate. Because Australia is a federation, the powers of the Commonwealth are limited. Does this mean that the Commonwealth is limited in the matters on which it can establish a public inquiry? Moreover, it is a well-established legal principle that the conferral of coercive powers on royal commissions – such as the power to summon witnesses and to require them to answer questions on oath and to produce documents – is not an inherent aspect of the executive power itself, but must be specifically authorised by law, that is, by a statute enacted by parliament. Is there any limit to the matters on which such powers of inquiry can be conferred upon a royal commission by a Commonwealth statute?

For each of these sets of questions, there is an established body of law that is explored in this chapter.

Constitutional background and legal foundations of royal commissions

As mentioned, the institution and conduct of a royal commission of inquiry is an act of the executive and an exercise of executive power. Constitutionally, the executive power of the Commonwealth and states is vested in the Queen and exercised by the Governor-General and state governors respectively (see Section 61 of the Commonwealth Constitution). According to the conventions of responsible parliamentary government, these executive powers are normally exercised on the advice of the Prime Minister or state Premier and other ministers of the Crown. Thus, when a royal commission of inquiry is established by government, it is formally appointed by the Governor-General or state governor in the name of the Crown, but the decision to establish the inquiry is taken on the advice of the executive government of the day.

While the institution and conduct of a royal commission is an exercise of executive power, the source of the power to establish the inquiry is the law, and the content of the law is not determined by the executive. The legal power to establish a royal commission has long been recognised by the common law, but there have been two theories about the exact nature and source of the power. One theory is that the government's power to conduct an inquiry is nothing more than the capacity to ask questions and receive answers as a means of obtaining information, a capacity that the government (technically, the Crown) has in common with ordinary, natural persons. Sir Samuel Griffith, the first Chief Justice of the High Court of Australia put it this way: "in accordance with a fundamental principle of the common law, we are all free to do anything that is not specifically prohibited; one of the things we are all free to do is ask questions of others and to receive their answers, provided that we do not coerce them into answering; and this capacity to ask questions and receive answers is something which applies alike to both the Crown and to ordinary citizens" (*Clough v Leahy* (1904) 2 CLR 139, 156-7). We can all ask questions and receive answers essentially because there is no law against it. There is no difference between the government and ordinary citizens as far as the fundamental principles of the common law are concerned. The basic assumption is that we are all subject to the same body of law, and we all alike enjoy the same fundamental liberties under the law.

But this common law liberty to ask questions and receive answers does not include the power to coerce people into listening to us and answering our questions. Ordinary citizens cannot force people to provide them with information, and governments cannot do so either, unless there is some specific law which authorises them to do so. This principle is fundamental to the rule of law. The most basic assumption of the law is that the government only has the freedoms and powers that the law specifically grants it. The government is not at liberty to use coercion without legal warrant.

That said, it is well known that royal commissions do, in fact, exercise far-reaching powers of coercion. They compel people to attend, they compel them to give evidence under oath, and they compel them to produce documents. However, the only reason why they can do this lawfully is because the Commonwealth and state parliaments have enacted statutes granting them these special powers, such as the *Royal Commissions Act 1902* (Cth) and the *Commissions of Inquiry Act 1950* (Qld). The legitimate power of royal commissions to exercise coercive powers is based on these statutes and cannot lawfully extend beyond them.

The second theory about the source of the power of governments to establish royal commissions is that it is a part of the historic "prerogatives" of the Crown that are recognised by the common law. In other words, when the government appoints a royal commission, it is not merely exercising a capacity to ask questions and receive answers, a power it has in common with ordinary citizens, but, rather, it is exercising a special power of government, vested (technically) in the Crown. Sir Owen Dixon, one of Australia's most distinguished High Court judges, was of this view (*McGuiness v Attorney-General (Vic)* (1940) 63 CLR 73, 93-4). His emphasis, unlike that of Griffith, was that when the Crown establishes a commission of inquiry, it issues a commission that authorises particular individuals (commonly called commissioners) to conduct the inquiry, and the very act of commissioning is an exercise of a prerogative power.

These two views are not necessarily inconsistent. Griffith's emphasis was on the act of asking questions and receiving answers; Dixon's was on the commission issued by the Crown authorising individuals to conduct an inquiry on behalf of the Crown. As Sir Ninian Stephen later pointed out, the "command" that is issued by the Crown to a commissioner to undertake an inquiry could properly be regarded as an aspect of the prerogative, whereas the consequence of a delegate of the Crown asking questions and receiving answers would be no different "were some private person to choose to inquire of his own motion ... and then inform the executive of his conclusions" (*Victoria v Australian Building and Construction Employees' and Builders Labourers' Federation* (1981-82) 152 CLR 25, 68).

While there are other statements in the case law that are not so easy to reconcile, a recent decision of the High Court appears to reject the idea that the Crown possesses the ordinary capacities of a natural person, with the possible implication that the power to initiate and conduct commissions of inquiry must be considered to be part of the prerogative and not a capacity that the Crown has in common with natural persons (*Williams v Commonwealth* (2012) HCA 23). This could possibly have consequences for how the legal foundations of royal commissions are understood as a matter of law, but what seems clear is that while the Crown can undoubtedly establish commissions of inquiry, it cannot grant commissioners coercive powers except to the extent that this is authorised by a statute enacted by parliament. Nothing less than the rule of law is at stake in this principle.

The separation of powers

A second vital constitutional principle relevant to the conduct of royal commissions is that they must not interfere with the regular administration of justice by the courts. This principle is fundamentally about the separation of powers. During the 17th century, early Stuart kings sought to use their executive powers to establish and empower special "commissions" (eg the High Commission) and "prerogative courts" (eg the Star Chamber) with a capacity not only to inquire into matters, but to exercise coercive powers, to determine guilt and to sentence the guilty to punishment. It took a series of extraordinary constitutional enactments and, indeed, a civil war in England to put an end to the use of the Crown's prerogative to establish such courts.

There remained, however, the fine point whether the executive might nonetheless be able to establish an inquiry merely to inquire into whether a crime had been committed, without also possessing the power to pronounce guilt and sentence the convicted person to punishment. In New Zealand, the executive cannot, without statutory warrant, establish an inquiry that has as its main purpose the investigation of the guilt or innocence of a particular individual. However, in Australia, the principle is more modest: a royal commission cannot interfere with the administration of justice insofar as doing so would constitute a contempt of any court before which a person has been charged and is being tried (*Victoria v. Australian Building and Construction Employees' and Builders Labourers' Federation* (1982) 152 CLR 25; *Hammond v Commonwealth* (1982) 152 CLR 188).

Even though a royal commission cannot be empowered to make conclusive determinations of guilt and impose sentences, its interrogation of witnesses and its findings of fact can certainly have very significant adverse consequences for people's reputations. For this reason, among other things, the High Court has held that the possibility of injury to reputation requires that an inquiry accord procedural justice to a person who is the object of its inquiries (*Ainsworth v Criminal Justice Commission* (1992) 175 CLR 564).

Governments sometimes decide to appoint sitting judges as royal commissioners to draw on their forensic skills, political independence and public respect, but some Australian jurisdictions tend to avoid this because of the potential threat it poses to the separation of powers, especially at a federal level.

Federalism

The third major constitutional question concerns the capacity of the Commonwealth to establish and empower royal commissions in fields outside its legislative competence. While the executive power of the Commonwealth can be used to establish an inquiry, legislation is required to confer coercive powers. However, the legislative power of the Commonwealth is in principle limited to the topics that appear in Sections 51 and 52 of the Constitution. Can the Commonwealth – using both its executive and legislative powers – empower inquiries outside of these limits? It seems not.

The *Royal Commissions Act 1902* (Cth) provides a statutory basis for the appointment of royal commissions of inquiry in relation to "any matter … which relates to or is connected with the peace, order, and good government of the Commonwealth, or any public purpose or any power of the Commonwealth". Other sections of the Act confer the power to summon witnesses, to require the answering of questions under oath and the production of documents, and to apply for search warrants, while others provide for the imposition of penalties and other forms of enforcement. On the face of it, the potential subject matter of an inquiry under the legislation is very broad, and is not limited to matters on which the Commonwealth has power to legislate under the Constitution. Is the provision constitutionally valid?

In *Attorney-General (Cth) v Colonial Sugar Refining Co Ltd* (1913) (17 CLR

644; [1914] AC 237), the Privy Council, on appeal from a split decision in the High Court could not validly give generic statutory authorisation for the conduct of a royal commission exercising coercive powers in relation to any topic lying outside the Commonwealth's legislative powers. The *Royal Commissions Act 1902* (Cth) was therefore considered to be ultra vires, and void to the extent that it purported to provide royal commissions with general authority to compel answers to questions, production of documents or compliance with requests. In order to have a constitutionally valid operation, the Act had to be interpreted so as only to authorise and empower the conduct of inquiries within the legislative powers of the Commonwealth, and it was upheld specifically on this basis. As a consequence, the relevant section of the Act has since been interpreted as merely giving statutory force to the pre-existing common-law power to issue a commission for an inquiry, and as only authorising the establishment of an inquiry in relation to matters where the Commonwealth has constitutional power.

However, the *Colonial Sugar Refining* case has an interesting status in Australian constitutional law for several reasons. First, it involved a split decision within the High Court. Second, it was appealed to the Privy Council on the only occasion that a certificate has ever been issued by the High Court to allow an appeal on a matter involving the powers between the Commonwealth and the states. Third, having been decided prior to the High Court's watershed decision in the *Engineers' Case* (*Amalgamated Society of Engineers v Adelaide Steamship Co Ltd* (1920) 28 CLR 129), *Colonial Sugar Refining* contains reasoning based on the now reviled "state reserved powers" doctrine. Does it therefore still represent good law?

The split decision of the High Court in *Colonial Sugar Refining* involved judgments by Justices Griffith and Barton on one hand, and Isaacs and Higgins on the other.

Griffith and Barton reasoned that the distribution of legislative powers between the Commonwealth and the states is fundamental to the federal compact on which the Australian Constitution is founded, and that the Commonwealth cannot legislate in a manner that intrudes into what Griffith called the "large sphere of action reserved to the States by the Constitution" (*Colonial Sugar Refining* (1912) 15 CLR 182, 194-5). While Griffith and Barton affirmed that the Commonwealth does have an incidental power to legislate to provide for the conduct of compulsory inquiries into matters where the Commonwealth has power to make laws, this does not extend to matters that are "reserved" to the states and therefore lie outside the Commonwealth's legislative powers. Their decision, therefore, rested in part on the "state reserved powers" doctrine, pursuant to which the powers of the Commonwealth are read *subject to* those reserved to the states.

Isaacs and Higgins, by contrast, considered that the Commonwealth's "incidental" power to legislate includes the power to authorise compulsory inquiries into matters that might be the object of a constitutional amendment, and that the subject matter of any such constitutional amendment was, in principle, unlimited. Their reasoning was that the power to amend the Constitution is, in essence, a "legislative" power of the Commonwealth, even though under the Constitution any proposed amendment must be first approved by the voters of the Commonwealth and the states in a referendum. It therefore followed that the Commonwealth has incidental legislative power to make provision for the establishment and conduct of compulsory inquiries into virtually any matter at all, whether or not it falls within the ordinary legislative powers of the Commonwealth.

These two views were based on fundamentally different perspectives about the nature and grounds of the Constitution itself.

According to Isaacs and Higgins, the Constitution is essentially a statute enacted by the British Parliament that provides for the exercise of legislative power by the Commonwealth Parliament, including the power of the British Parliament itself to amend the Constitution. On this view, the power to amend the Constitution is regarded as nothing more than an ordinary capacity to make laws that happens to be subjected to a special procedural requirement (ie approval at a referendum). And, as Isaacs reasoned, it is not for the courts to question the exercise of such constitutional powers by the Commonwealth Parliament and executive on the basis that such powers might be abused, for where the text of the Constitution explicitly grants a power, the text is conclusive.

In Griffith and Barton's view, on the other hand, the Constitution is, in substance, a federal compact by which the states agreed to the conferral of certain powers on the Commonwealth while reserving to themselves ultimate control over any amendments to the Constitution that the Commonwealth might propose. In other words, the power to amend the Constitution is an aspect of the constitutive power to establish the Constitution in the first place; it is a power that is distinct from the ordinary power to legislate. Thus, Barton pointed out that the framers of the Constitution did not regard the power of constitutional amendment to be a legislative power of the parliament in the ordinary sense of the term, but rather a special capacity to "amend the fundamental law by popular vote" (*Colonial Sugar Refining* (1912) 15 CLR 182, 207). Such amendments, he noted, could result in either an expansion or a contraction of the powers of the Commonwealth, for it was the states – from which the federal compact originally derived – that continued to possess the necessary plenary powers of inquiry into such matters.

On appeal, the Privy Council endorsed the conclusions of Griffith and Barton. The Council considered the Australian Constitution to be "federal" in the "strict sense of the term", meaning one in which "self-contained states" agree, not only to delegate some of their powers to a common government, but "in the main continue to preserve their original Constitutions" and "reserve" all powers not delegated to themselves. Given that the "scheme" of the Australian Constitution was thus to create a "true" federation, the Privy Council considered that the "burden" lay on the Commonwealth to show that the *Royal Commissions Act* was constitutionally valid. Although the Constitution is clearly contained in an Imperial statute, the Privy Council pointed out that it was the "people of Australia" who chose to *prevent* the Commonwealth Parliament from making any changes to the "compact" without a referendum.

Griffith, Barton and the Privy Council thus referred to the Constitution as being the result of a federal compact granting strictly limited power to the Commonwealth and otherwise reserving to the states their originally plenary powers. However, in the well-known *Engineers' Case* decided in 1920, a differently composed High Court overturned the state reserved powers doctrine on which much of the reasoning in *Colonial Sugar Refining* had rested. Is the result in *Colonial Sugar Refining* still to be regarded as good law?

Certainly, ever since the *Engineers' Case* state reserved powers reasoning has been regarded as a kind of constitutional "heresy" (Aroney 2008). Case after case has interpreted federal powers just about as widely as the language used can possibly sustain. However, there are several reasons to think that *Colonial Sugar Refining* still represents good law. In the first place, the decision has been subsequently approved and has never been specifically questioned, let alone overruled. Second, although there are problems with the state reserved powers doctrine in its "extreme" and "absolute" form, there is good reason to support a more moderate "interpretive" version, in which the scope of federal powers is read in the light of the federal scheme of the Constitution as a whole. Third, the view advanced by Isaacs and Higgins rests on a conception of the Australian Constitution as being nothing more than a statute of the imperial parliament that conferred on the Commonwealth Parliament a power of constitutional amendment. However, there are good reasons to see the Constitution, especially since the British Parliament abdicated power to legislate for Australia in 1986, as a document that rests on the agreement and consent of the people of the Australian states, which can only be amended with the consent of the people (Aroney 2009). The High Court's recent decision in *Williams v Commonwealth*, with its emphasis on the parliamentary and federal features of the Constitution, only serves to reinforce the importance of interpreting the Commonwealth's powers in relation to royal commissions as subject to constitutional limitations, in the interests of the parliamentary and federal features of the Australian Constitution.

Conclusions

The power to establish and conduct a royal commission is a significant one. Armed with powers of compulsion, royal commissions can force individuals to appear before them, to answer questions on oath and to produce documents. While the institution of royal commissions may be considered necessary in order to uncover information and investigate serious problems, it is important, in the interests of the rule of law, the separation of powers and preservation of the federal system of government, that they are subjected to constitutional scrutiny. The rule of law requires that the executive only establishes and conducts inquiries in a manner that is legally authorised. The common law recognises the capacity of the Crown to make inquiries, and it could now well be that the High Court is committed to the view that this power of inquiry is not to be considered merely as a capacity that it has in common with ordinary persons, but as an aspect of the unique prerogatives of the Crown. While such a conclusion is not altogether free of conceptual and practical problems, it at least has the virtue of emphasising that when the executive undertakes an inquiry, it does so as a government possessing a monopoly over the use of force in the community. There is, therefore, every reason to be vigilant in ensuring that the establishment and conduct of such inquiries occurs in a manner that is properly authorised by pre-existing law.

It is also very important that a proper separation of powers is maintained. While it may be accepted in Australian law that a commission of inquiry has the power to inquire into whether a criminal offence has occurred, it is of vital importance that commissions of inquiry are not allowed to interfere with the independent administration of justice by the ordinary courts, which alone ought to have the responsibility of making determinations of guilt and of imposing criminal sanctions.

Lastly, the Commonwealth of Australia is for good reason constituted as a federation of states, and it is a consequence of the federal nature of the Australian Constitution that the executive and legislative powers of the Commonwealth are limited. This means that the capacity of the Commonwealth executive to undertake inquiries, as well as of the Commonwealth parliament to grant compulsive powers to commissions of inquiry must be limited to matters where the Commonwealth has the constitutional authority. If the Commonwealth wants to initiate an inquiry into a matter that falls outside its constitutional powers, then it must do so in cooperation with the states. Although this principle was recognised by the High Court and the Privy Council a whole century ago, the principle remains a vital one, for all of the reasons why federalism remains a good idea for Australia generally (see Twomey and Withers 2007).

References

Aroney, N., 2008, "Constitutional Choices in the Work Choices Case, or What Exactly is Wrong with the Reserved Powers Doctrine?," *Melbourne University Law Review*, 32(1), 1-43

Aroney, N., 2009, *The Constitution of a Federal Commonwealth: The Making and Meaning of the Australian Constitution*, Cambridge: Cambridge University Press

Twomey, A., and Withers, G., 2007, *Federalist Paper 1 Australia's Federal Future: Delivering Growth and Prosperity*, A Report for the Council for the Australian Federation, April

Section 2

An inquiry by any other name . . . types of public inquiry

Scott Prasser and Helen Tracey

Public inquiries come in a variety of shapes and forms and go by a number of different names – royal commissions, special commissions, commissions of inquiry, committees of inquiry, independent inquiries, inquiries, panels, reviews, taskforces, and working parties. The nomenclature of judicial inquiry, used frequently in everyday parlance, is the least apt label, implying as it does that the inquiry is positioned within the justice system. The main thing that inquiries by any name have in common is that, in our system of separation of powers between the legislature, the executive and the judiciary, they sit squarely in the executive arm of government. They are not part of the judiciary, even though they rely heavily in their staffing on judges, former judges or senior legal professionals, and even though their procedures are often quite legalistic.

The common characteristics of public inquiries are that they are temporary ad hoc bodies appointed by the executive to provide advice or to investigate some issue, with specific terms of reference and with members drawn largely from outside government and the bureaucracy. They follow public processes, they generally seek community input, they report to the responsible minister and, except in rare cases, governments publicly release their reports. They have only advisory powers and cannot action their own proposals. Excluded from this definition are parliamentary committees and inquiries, permanent government advisory bodies, and inquiries initiated by government bodies such as ombudsmen, anti-corruption bodies and departments.

There the generalisations come to an end. The form of the inquiry mechanism can vary considerably and rarely is the title a sufficient pointer to the significance of the issue being addressed, the processes the inquiry will follow or whether the primary orientation of the inquiry is investigative or advisory. Only in the case of "royal commission" does the title designate an important aspect of the type of inquiry being undertaken, signalling that it has a statutory base. While the main statute at the Commonwealth level is the *Royal Commissions Act 1902*, other legislation such as the *Quarantine Amendment (Commission of Inquiry) Act 2007* (for the *Equine Influenza Inquiry*, Callinan: 2007) and the *Public Service Act 1922* (for the *Inquiry into Allegations of Corruption within the Australian Federal Police,* Harrison: 1996 and the *Commonwealth Paedophile Inquiry,* Hunt, then O'Neil: 1996) may be used as the statutory base for an inquiry which, for all intents and purposes, has all the powers of a royal commission. The legislation gives an inquiry powers such as the ability to call and cross-examine witnesses and obtain evidence, and rights of entry and phone-tapping and also provides protection to witnesses and inquiry members from legal action such as defamation. The majority of public inquiries however have no such legislative base.

In general, an inquiry will be primarily either inquisitorial, investigative or advisory, although some inquiries have elements of all three. An inquisitorial or investigative inquiry sits at one end of the spectrum of formality and consequence. Inquisitorial inquiries are tasked with examining allegations of impropriety or maladministration or a catastrophic event of some kind – often a major accident or natural disaster. The main focus of these inquiries is to find the facts behind an allegation or incident. To do this, they will generally rely on legalistic processes. They differ from an investigative inquiry mainly in their scope. Where inquisitorial inquiries have a broad canvas, an investigative inquiry tends to be more narrowly focused on a particular action or incident that a government feels impelled to examine through a public and legalistic process.

In this Section, in chapters 3 and 4, Geoffrey Davies and Janet Ransley describe the inquisitorial and investigative forms of public inquiry through different lenses. A retired Queensland judge, Davies chaired the 2005 *Queensland Public Hospitals Commission of Inquiry*, which was tasked with inquiring into the role and conduct of the Queensland Medical Board in relation to the registration of overseas trained doctors, with a particular focus on Dr Jayant Patel and his employment by Queensland Health. The Davies Commission took over from the *Bundaberg Hospital Commission of Inquiry* (Morris 2005) which was shut down following a Supreme Court finding of a "reasonable apprehension of bias" on the part of Commissioner Morris, a rare example of a public inquiry interrupted as a result of legal challenge. From his experience chairing the Davies Commission and his close knowledge of other Queensland inquiries, Davies identifies five requirements he considers essential, or at least highly desirable, if an inquisitorial inquiry is to be effective in meeting its purpose of uncovering all the evidence, without prejudice or political interference, in a way that is fair to all parties and also serves the public interest. This is a big ask, and Davies shows where certain inquiries have failed, through a want of independence, a lack of openness about evidence and findings, insufficient powers of investigation, a constrained approach to the inquiry or the absence of procedural fairness.

Janet Ransley, from the perspective of a law academic with a special interest in commissions of inquiry, and as a Queenslander who has had more than a fair share of the available opportunities to observe inquisitorial and investigative inquiries into political wrongdoing, shows how public inquiries have proven to be an important supplement to the criminal justice and court systems for investigating political misconduct. Using examples from all jurisdictions, she paints a picture of the immediate and longer-term systemic impact of political inquiries and explains why some are effective and some are not.

As Ransley notes, in recent years, governments have been reluctant to appoint inquisitorial inquiries unless there is no viable alternative. Most jurisdictions now are able to call on a range of alternative mechanisms for dealing with allegations of impropriety and maladministration within the machinery of government. Mechanisms such as anti-corruption bodies, integrity commissioners and ombudsmen – often themselves set up on the recommendation of a commission of an inquiry – now exist to offer governments an expert, in-house, more controllable and probably more expeditious and less costly avenue for investigation when one is needed. If advice is required on a matter of wrongdoing, the first port of call these days is more likely to be an existing body with relevant responsibilities within government than an independent inquiry.

A reluctance on the part of governments to establish an independent inquisitorial inquiry is well founded, given the number of state and Commonwealth governments whose political fortunes have waned as a consequence of inquiry findings. But as Ransley points out, while an independent public inquiry may be an institution of last resort, there is a point where it is more damaging politically for a government to continue to resist appointing an inquiry than to run the risks of adverse findings, and in the right context, an independent review has certain advantages over permanent investigatory bodies and the legal system itself.

In chapter 5, Charles Sampford, a senior law academic and barrister, reviews the role of royal commissions vis-a-vis other elements of government integrity systems such as specific anti-corruption bodies. His background of research into integrity systems and involvement in the establishment of Queensland's comprehensive ethics and integrity regime in the 1990s leads him to support the creation of a standing royal commission, similar to the Electoral and Administrative Review Committee (EARC) that was created in the state following the Fitzgerald Commission of Inquiry's report in 1989 (*Commission of Inquiry into Possible Illegal Activities and Associated Police Misconduct*). While conceived by the Fitzgerald Commission as a permanent body, the EARC was disbanded in 1993. Sampford considers that ad hoc royal commissions would continue to have a place within an integrity system, but the main business of promoting integrity and reducing corruption should fall to an integrated set of standing bodies.

From a public administration background, Roger Wettenhall, in chapter 6, explores a different kind of investigative inquiry, the independent inquiry that often follows a catastrophic event, accident or disaster. Governments are likely to gain public approval through the appointment of a commission of inquiry after such an event, to investigate what happened and why, to see who might have been responsible and to suggest how to avoid similar disasters in the future. Governments signal the importance they attach to the event and show themselves in a positive light by taking quick action at a time when the public is looking for explanations. The establishment of both the *Victorian Bushfires Royal Commission* (2009) and the *Queensland Floods Commission of Inquiry* (2011) quickly after the immediate crises reflected well on the state governments at the time. This kind of investigation is intended to establish accountability and responsibility, to reach a clear understanding of what happened, to provide catharsis or reconciliation for those involved, to avert the worst consequences of similar events in the future and to rebuild public confidence in the capacity of government to respond appropriately when disaster strikes.

Wettenhall examines the inquiries held in the aftermath of arguably Australia's most frequently occurring and life-threatening natural disaster, the summer bushfire. With particular reference to the firestorm in Canberra at the height of an exceptionally hot summer in 2003, he contrasts the style and impact of the two different post-fire inquiries: first, the fact-finding, more technocratic investigation by the McCleod *Inquiry into the Operational Response to the January 2003 Bushfires in the ACT* which reported six months after the firestorm; and second, the more legalistic, adversarial, blame-seeking coronial inquiry led by Coroner Maria Doogan, which reported three and a half years later. In Wettenhall's analysis of the two approaches lie valuable lessons for future responses to disaster.

A different, by no means lesser and much more common form of public inquiry, the policy advisory inquiry, is the subject of chapter 7 by Gary Banks, formerly long-time head of Australia's Productivity Commission. Frequently used as a non-statutory mechanism to provide advice, information, research and options to government about complex policy problems, policy inquiries constitute by far the bulk of public inquiries in Australia.

As for investigations, governments have many other options for securing policy advice, but the inquiry instrument continues to have a number of advantages over the alternatives. Keeping a distance between policy advice and the political process is one attraction of an independent expert inquiry. A degree of separation from government means that the evidence is more likely to be seen as objective and untainted by political bias. Policy inquiries have the further advantage that they are able to marshal particular expertise, and they are resourced so that they can gather information in a variety of ways, call in the assistance of specialists and undertake stakeholder and public consultation at arms length from government. Not only does this have the potential to bring benefit to the public, in the form of solid, evidence-based policy development framed by a concern for the public interest, it also has a number of political benefits.

Banks draws on his extensive knowledge of policymaking in the Commonwealth government, particularly from the standpoint of his leadership of the government's own inquiry instrument, the Productivity Commission, to explore the way well-conceived and well-conducted public inquiries add value to public policymaking. Their primary contribution to the workings of government is to produce the evidence on which to base new policy. The best public inquiry reports will inform new policy directions and will be called on over time to vindicate policy directions. As long as the evidence the inquiry produces is sound, it will support policies that are in the best interest of society.

Banks is able to pinpoint the important success factors for an effective public inquiry, highlighting the potential for inquiries to continue to contribute to successful public policies, as they have done in the past.

3

Some reflections on commissions of inquiry

Hon Geoffrey Davies AO

Introduction

This chapter discusses what I consider to be five highly desirable and, in some cases, essential requirements of a commission of inquiry with a particular focus on that most singular of inquiries, the inquisitorial statutory commission, the successor to a royal commission. In summary, at the outset, those requirements are that it:

1. be and be seen to be independent of government;
2. be conducted in public and that its report be made public;
3. have and exercise the power to compel witnesses to give evidence on oath or affirmation, tested by cross-examination, and to compel the production of documents;
4. be and remain throughout investigatory and inquisitorial in nature; in that respect being unlike a judicial proceeding between parties; and
5. accord procedural fairness to all those likely to be adversely affected by any decision, report or recommendation of the inquiry.

In the discussion that follows, I explain why I think each of these requirements is essential or at least highly desirable, in some cases with examples of some adverse consequences of failing to adhere to that requirement.

Requirements for a commission of inquiry

1. *That an inquiry be, and be seen to be, independent of government*

It has long been the view of the Supreme Court of Queensland and of the Bar Association of Queensland (and at least some equivalent bodies elsewhere)[1] that sitting judges should not be asked to conduct commissions of inquiry. One reason for this is that the absence of a judge for what may be a prolonged period tends to disrupt the business of court, to delay court proceedings and, consequently, to delay justice.

But another reason, more relevant for present purposes, is the possibility of conflict between duty and self-interest or, just as important and much more likely, the possibility of a public perception of that conflict. Because, generally, a commission of inquiry is established when something is perceived to have gone wrong in a public or semi-public body, the likelihood is that the commissioner may be required to make findings or reach conclusions as to the integrity or competence of some other arm of government, or of one of its emanations or officers. The public perception of a conflict in those circumstances, between interest and duty, is understandable. All judges have some prospect of advancement: District Court judges to the Supreme Court; Supreme Court trial judges to the Court of Appeal; all judges to Chief Justice; and even the Chief Justice to some higher public position. The risk of that perception is an important reason why judges should not be placed in this position.

It is equally important that the person appointed to conduct a commission of inquiry should not be someone whom the public might understandably perceive will not, for fear of harm or hope of reward, make any finding or reach any conclusion that would unduly favour or embarrass the government, or the political party in power.

Once a commissioner has commenced upon an inquiry there should not, other than in exceptional circumstances, be any further communication between the commissioner and persons in the political arms of government. That may seem self-evident to some, but it is not to all. When I embarked on my inquiry (*Queensland Public Hospitals Commission of Inquiry*, henceforth the Davies Commission) in 2005 I found, to my great surprise, that both the Premier and the Leader of the Opposition expected regular, separate, meetings with me. They produced some precedent for this. Both, however, readily accepted my explanation for refusing to follow this precedent: the public perception that any such meetings could lead or be seen to lead to political influence on findings or conclusions of the inquiry.

One obvious exception to this principle is where a commissioner, during the course of the inquiry, reaches the view that the terms of reference or powers of the commissioner should be expanded or clarified, or the duration of the commission be extended. However, any communication between the commissioner and the government in this respect should be in writing and be made public.

2. *That an inquiry be conducted in public and that its report be made public*

There is an underlying assumption in the *Commissions of Inquiry Act 1950* (Qld), the legislation governing commissions of inquiry in Queensland, that a commission established under it will be conducted in public. Although the commissioner is given the power to prohibit publication of any evidence and to exclude the public from any hearing that power is rarely exercised. However, there is no similar assumption about the publication of the commission's report. On the contrary, though the relevant minister may table the report in parliament there is no obligation to do so.

In my opinion, other than in the most exceptional circumstances, both the report and the evidence on which it is based should be made public, especially when adverse findings are made, or conclusions reached, against a person or body, or against some practice or conduct of either. Because a commission of inquiry is established in the public interest, it must, with few exceptions, be also in the public interest to publish its findings and conclusions and the evidence on which these are based. Otherwise justice cannot be seen to be done.

If the government perceives that it is in the public interest that the practices or conduct of a public body requires investigation it is difficult to see either how an inquiry that requires the evidence be given in public or that the report be made public can be justified. Yet by establishing such an inquiry, not pursuant to the legislation but merely by executive act, with no coercive information-gathering powers and no protection of evidence given by witnesses, nor protection for those conducting the inquiry, this sometimes occurs.

Nor is justice seen to be done if, when a report is published, the evidence on which the report is based is not. That is what occurred in the 2012 *Independent Advisory Panel to Review the Crime and Misconduct Act and Related Matters* in Queensland[2] with the consequence that neither the Crime and Misconduct Commission (CMC) nor the public could see whether findings and conclusions adverse to the CMC were justified by the evidence.

Neither is justice seen to be done if the evidence before the inquiry is made public, but the report, or part of it, is not published. When asked by the Premier of Queensland to conduct the *Queensland Public Hospitals Commission of Inquiry*, I was presented with the terms of reference on which the previous *Bundaberg Hospital Commission of Inquiry* had been conducted. Although they required that the inquiry be open, they were silent on the publication of a report. One of a number of additional terms which, at my request, was added was "that the report transmitted to the Honourable the Premier and Treasurer be made public upon its transmission ... "

3. *That an inquiry have and exercise the power to compel witnesses to give evidence on oath or affirmation, tested by cross-examination, and to compel the production of documents*

I start with some self-evident truths. The first of these is that almost all commissions of inquiry of an inquisitorial nature are established because the government has perceived that something has gone wrong in some public or semi-public body and the commission is tasked with finding whether that is so. And if so, what it is that went wrong, including whose fault it was, and how that may be avoided in the future.

The second is that the instinct for self-preservation, which we all have, is likely to lead to witnesses who were in any way involved in what went wrong seeking to absolve themselves of blame, and this may well include blaming others.

And the third is that it is much easier to shift the blame onto others with impunity if telling untruths, failing to tell the whole truth, or failing to disclose relevant documents is not visited with any penalty. Though for most people the swearing of an oath no longer carries with it the fear of damnation, the risk of criminal prosecution for perjury remains a powerful incentive to tell the truth. So also is the risk of cross-examination.

Obtaining evidence in some informal way, free of the risks of prosecution for perjury and of cross-examination, also risks a miscarriage of justice. Not only is there the possibility that one person involved will seek to pass the blame to another, and give evidence accordingly, there is also a risk that even an innocent, well-motivated witness may have a preconceived belief as to what went wrong or whose fault it was. This witness may give a version of events more in accordance with that preconceived view than in accordance with the objective facts. In litigation, reconstruction can replace recollection and witnesses unconsciously tend to take sides. Both factors affect the reliability of evidence. This tendency is greatly increased when what takes place is not made public, where the questioning is informal, or where there is no risk of prosecution for perjury.

4. *That an inquiry be, and must remain throughout, investigatory and inquisitorial in nature, in that respect being unlike a judicial proceeding between parties*

Judges in proceedings *inter partes* have no right to travel outside the issues contested or evidence adduced by the parties; commissions of inquiry, by their nature, embark upon an independent search for the truth concerning the matters that are the subject of their inquiry. In that, they are not restricted by the rules of procedure and of evidence which apply in litigation.

A commission of inquiry is generally established when something is perceived to have gone wrong in a public or semi-public body, and it may find fault with a person or system or practice of that body. This, in turn, may lead witnesses to seek to absolve themselves of blame, or to place blame on others. Consequently, contemporaneous documents and objective evidence of the surrounding circumstances are of the utmost importance in getting to the objective truth. These can often cast doubt on or even give the lie to what appears, otherwise, to be convincing oral evidence. It is therefore important for the inquirer to search out and examine any contemporaneous objective evidence. Until that has been done, the oral evidence of all witnesses should be approached with some reservation.

Two examples, one from my own inquiry, the Davies Inquiry, and one from the *Queensland Floods Commission of Inquiry* appointed in 2011,[3] illustrate the importance of this approach.

In my inquiry, the evidence of some medical practitioners working in public hospitals tended to blame non-medically qualified hospital administrators for the poor quality of surgical and medical services in those hospitals. The standard of surgical and medical care had been compromised, they said, by the failure of those administrators to provide sufficient medical and surgical staff and sufficient up-to-date equipment. However, further evidence showed that those administrators were very limited in what they could spend on staffing or equipment, and that some of those who had yielded to the demands of staff doctors and exceeded those limitations had been dismissed. Consequently, while administrators were not free from blame, the poor quality of staffing or equipment was caused, principally, by the limited budgets that had been imposed by government.

In the *Queensland Floods Commission of Inquiry*, the evidence of those in charge of the release of water from the Wivenhoe Dam in the period immediately prior to the flooding was that they had performed their work in accordance with established protocols. They had also been praised for their work by the media and by political leaders. Those responsible for leading evidence in the inquiry seemed to assume the correctness of this view.

However, documentary evidence found, unfortunately, only late in the inquiry, tended strongly to contradict this. It is possible that this early assumption that procedures and protocols had been followed correctly was responsible for the failure to find this documentary evidence sooner, notwithstanding that it was among the documents in the possession of the inquiry.

These examples illustrate the danger of accepting without reservation the oral evidence of witnesses, particularly where self-interest or preconceived views may be involved, without first searching for and carefully examining all relevant documentary evidence and objectively ascertainable facts. To fail to be alert to this danger is to lose sight of the inquisitorial nature of the proceeding.

5. *That at all times an inquiry accord procedural fairness to all those likely to be adversely affected by a decision, report or recommendation of the inquiry*

A preconceived view about a person or entity involved, or about some conduct of that person or entity, appears to be one cause of a failure to accord procedural fairness. Another related reason appears to be a premature judgment before all relevant evidence has been given, about what went wrong and who was responsible. It is possible to see examples of these in the two Queensland cases where public inquiries were terminated because of ostensible bias and led to legal proceedings (see *Carruthers v Connolly* (1998) 1 Qd R 339) and *Keating v Morris* (2005) QSC 243).

The Carruthers case concerned the 1996 *Connolly-Ryan Inquiry into the*

Future Role, Structure, Powers and Operations of the Criminal Justice Commission, established under the *Commissions of Inquiry Act 1950* (Qld) to inquire into, in effect, the establishment and conduct of an earlier, but still continuing inquiry established by the Criminal Justice Commission under its statutory power. That earlier inquiry, the *Carruthers Inquiry*, was appointed by the then Criminal Justice Commission, Queensland's anti-corruption watchdog, to examine, among other things, whether a cabinet minister in the state Borbidge Coalition Government had been guilty of a criminal offence. The chairman of the later inquiry, Mr Peter Connolly QC, had, before his appointment as inquiry chair, given an opinion to the Minister to the effect that he had not committed any such offence and that opinion had been tendered to the Carruthers Inquiry. Consequently, both the Carruthers Inquiry and the Connolly-Ryan Inquiry had political implications.

Both before the commencement of the Connolly-Ryan Inquiry, and during it, Mr Connolly, by his words and conduct, demonstrated opinions favouring the Coalition side of politics, represented by the Minister. He made comments denigrating both Mr Carruthers and the Criminal Justice Commission, and made it clear that he retained the opinion that he had earlier given to the Minister. He implied that the Carruthers Inquiry was a waste of time and money. Some of these words and conduct were outside his inquiry and some occurred in the inquiry, including in Mr Connolly's own questioning of witnesses.

In those circumstances the Judge in *Carruthers v Connolly* applied the test laid down by the High Court: whether the circumstances were such as would give rise, in the mind of a fair-minded and informed member of the public, to a reasonable apprehension that the decision maker's mind is so prejudiced by conclusions already formed that those conclusions would not be altered irrespective of the evidence or arguments put forward. His Honour concluded that this was established here.

This was a case in which it was held that the decision maker's political prejudice and preconceived views about the conduct of the Minister, the need for the Carruthers Inquiry and the performance of the Criminal Justice Commission appeared to preclude him from bringing an unbiased mind to the task.

The Keating case involved the *Bundaberg Hospital Commission of Inquiry*, chaired by Anthony Morris QC, established to investigate, relevantly, the treatment of patients by Dr Jayant Patel, a surgeon employed at Bundaberg Hospital and the consequences of this including the appropriateness of actions taken by Dr Darren Keating, the Director of Medical Services of Bundaberg Hospital, and Mr Peter Leck, the District Health Manager.

Early in the *Bundaberg Hospital Commission of Inquiry*, and without allowing them sufficient time to complete written statements, apparently contrary to the commission's own Practice Direction, the commission chair called both Keating and Leck to give evidence. He questioned them himself without having them first questioned by counsel, again apparently contrary to the commission's Practice Direction; and, according to the Supreme Court judge to whom Keating and Leck had appealed, treated them contemptuously and dismissively, in stark contrast to his treatment of other witnesses. By this conduct, the judge said, the commission chair had shown ostensible bias against each, warranting termination of the inquiry (*Keating v Morris and Ors*, (2005), Qd R, para 158).

Thus it was the commission chair's treatment of these witnesses that gave rise, in the mind of a fair-minded and informed person, to a reasonable apprehension that the commissioner was already committed, irrevocably, to a conclusion adverse to them.

While there is no excuse for a failure to accord procedural fairness, it is not always easy to reconcile the need to pursue a diligent, even vigorous investigation with the need to accord procedural fairness.

It is not sufficient, in order to ensure procedural fairness, for a commissioner to refrain from forming a premature opinion adverse to a party to the inquiry. He or she should also ensure that any such party is fully informed of any likely adverse decision, report or recommendation, and is given the opportunity to answer the facts on which that might be based. In many cases that will occur during the course of the inquiry. However, in my own inquiry, at the conclusion of evidence, I had sent, in confidence, to each party against whom I might make adverse findings a summary of those possible findings and the facts on which they might be based, giving each party an opportunity to respond. That is by no means always necessary but in a long inquiry or one involving multiple issues I think that such a course is desirable.

Conclusion

As the outset, I suggested that these five requirements are highly desirable and in some cases essential.

I believe that the first requirement, that a commission of inquiry be, and be seen to be independent of government; the fourth, that it be investigatory and inquisitorial in nature; and the fifth, that it accord procedural fairness, are essential without any exceptions.

It is possible to find exceptions to the second requirement: that a commission of inquiry be conducted in public and report publicly. The risk that disclosure of information might endanger national security is an obvious one. And in some other cases it may be necessary to balance the public's right to know against other rights such as the maintenance of trade secrets or even the right to privacy.

It is also possible to find exceptions to the third requirement: that all evidence be subject to the risk of prosecution for perjury or contempt. One is to permit informal proof of uncontroversial facts.

But the exceptions to these requirements are few. And when an exception to either of them is permitted it should be identified and explained.

Public inquiries mentioned in chapter

(in chronological order by year of appointment, with name of chair)

Inquiry into the Future Role, Structure, Powers and Operations of the Criminal Justice Commission (Connolly and Ryan: 1996)[4]

Bundaberg Hospital Commission of Inquiry (Morris: 2005)[5]

Queensland Public Hospitals Commission of Inquiry (Davies: 2005)[6]

Queensland Floods Commission of Inquiry (Holmes: 2011)

Independent Advisory Panel to Review the Crime and Misconduct Act and Related Matters (Callinan: 2012)

Other inquiries mentioned in chapter

Investigation into a Memorandum of Understanding between the Coalition and the Queensland Police Union of Employees and an Investigation into an Alleged Deal between the ALP (Australian Labor Party) and SSAA (Sporting Shooters Association of Australia), in March 1996 (Carruthers: 1996)[7]

Endnotes

1 This was most explicitly stated in 1922 by Mr Justice Irvine, Chief Justice of the Victorian Supreme Court who prohibited members of the Victorian Supreme Court participating in commissions of inquiry and is known as the Irvine Doctrine (see G. Fraser, (ed), 1986, *Judges as Royal Commissioners and Chairmen on Non-Judicial Tribunals*, Melbourne: Victorian Law Foundation, 11).

2 The *Independent Advisory Panel to Review the Crime and Misconduct Act and Related Matters* was appointed in November 2012 by the newly elected Liberal National Party (LNP) Queensland Government following concerns during the March state elections when the outgoing Labor government referred, on the eve of the election, a number of matters concerning the family business arrangements and his activities as Lord Mayor of Brisbane of LNP leader Campbell Newman to the Crime and Misconduct Commission.

3 Appointed by the Queensland Government in January 2011 following disastrous floods in south-east Queensland that caused 33 deaths, $5 billion damage to homes and infrastructure, and affected 78 per cent of the State.

4 As this inquiry was terminated by order of the Supreme Court there was no final report.

5 As this inquiry was terminated by order of the Supreme Court there was no final report.

6 This inquiry was appointed in September 2005 and reported in November 2005.

7 This inquiry was established by the Criminal Justice Commission with Ken Carruthers QC as chair. He resigned from the inquiry in October 1996 and was replaced by R.W. Gotterson QC and B.W. Butler SC who reported in December 1996.

4

Public inquiries into political wrongdoing

Janet Ransley

Introduction

How can politicians, their conduct and the conduct of those closest to them be appropriately investigated? While criminal behaviour is clearly the province of police, crime and corruption commissions, and prosecutors and criminal courts, the boundaries between criminality and moral, ethical or political misconduct are not always clear-cut. The closed and powerful nature of the political decision-making process especially that of ministers, cabinet and party structures makes investigations difficult and fraught for police and prosecutors. There is often a need for more powers, protections and political will to break through the barriers to proper investigation.

Australian governments have a long and sustained history of appointing public inquiries, especially royal commissions and commissions of inquiry, to examine issues of political wrongdoing. Most jurisdictions have legislation governing the establishment, powers and conduct of formal inquiries, whether they are called royal commissions, commissions of inquiry, special commissions of inquiry, or boards of inquiry.[1] Inquiries have a political context when they investigate governments, politicians, or the public servants they are responsible for, in order to determine criminal, civil, disciplinary, or moral culpability for various failings. Inquiries into political wrongdoing are almost always inquisitorial or investigatory in nature, armed with extensive coercive and intrusive powers. Once appointed, they are beyond most formal accountability and control mechanisms. They have proved an important supplement to the criminal justice and court systems because of their capacity, in some circumstances, to investigate criminal or quasi-criminal issues in a more complete and effective way than other parts of that system.

Despite criticisms, the inquisitorial political public inquiry, especially in the form of a royal commission, continues to be popular with Australian governments. Since the 1970s the majority of royal commissions have been of the inquisitorial type (ALRC 2009), with many having a political context. This is despite the plethora of specific anti-corruption agencies with equivalent or even greater powers that have been established since 1988, namely, the Criminal Justice Commission (CJC) in Queensland, replaced in 2002 by the Crime and Misconduct Commission (CMC); the Independent Commission Against Corruption (ICAC) and the Police Integrity Commission (PIC) in New South Wales; the Corruption and Crime Commission (CCC) in Western Australia; the Integrity Commission in Tasmania (IC); the Independent Broad-based Anti-Corruption Commission (IBAC) in Victoria; the Independent Commissioner Against Corruption (ICAC) in South Australia; and the Australian Commission for Law Enforcement Integrity (ACLEI) and the Australian Crime Commission (ACC) at the Commonwealth level. Many other administrative agencies also have ancillary inquiry functions, including human rights commissions and ombudsmen.

This chapter examines the continued use of ad hoc inquisitorial public inquiries such as royal commissions to investigate political wrongdoing, addressing two key questions:

- Why and how are public inquiries used for this role?
- What factors make the ad hoc inquiry model most effective for investigating political wrongdoing?

To answer these questions, this chapter examines the range and nature of inquiries into political wrongdoing that have been appointed in Australia, and takes a more detailed look at some prominent examples. It considers criticisms of the ad hoc public inquiry model and possible alternatives, before analysing why public inquiries continue to be appointed. Finally, this chapter suggests the factors and characteristics that are necessary for public inquiries into political wrongdoing to be effective.

What are public inquiries into political wrongdoing?

A typical reaction to some political scandal or failing, at both federal and state levels, is to call for a royal commission. Over the years since federation, governments have appointed commissions of inquiry with varying degrees of enthusiasm, with the 1980s and early 1990s being perhaps the high point of such inquiry activity. In the last decade, at the Commonwealth level, public inquiries in the form of royal commissions have examined the lease of Centenary House by an entity owned by the Australian Labor Party in 2004 (Hunt) and inquired into the actions of certain Australian companies in relation to the United Nations Oil-for-Food Program in 2005 (Cole; see chapter 13: Bartos). At the state level, in Queensland alone, recent public inquiries into political wrongdoing have examined the appointment of overseas doctors to public hospitals in 2005 (Morris and Davies inquiries; see chapter 3: Davies), the actions of public officials leading up to and during the 2011 floods (Holmes) and the failure of the Queensland Health Department's payroll system in 2013 (Chesterman).

These public inquiries are political because they focus on the conduct, actions, decisions and failings of political figures or the public entities for which they are responsible. Such inquiries are appointed because of a belief that in times of public crisis they can act as a catalyst for addressing larger, more systemic issues underlying the crisis, which cannot be addressed by conventional mechanisms. In this respect, public inquiries are seen as contributing to the securing of government accountability, as well as investigating individual moral culpability.

Impacts

In Australia, over a long period of time, specific political inquiries have had far-reaching systemic effects. This may have been through their impact on political institutions (including parliament, government, political parties, and individual politicians), on political processes generally, or on other relevant bodies (such as the courts, police or government instrumentalities). While the intensity of these effects varies, some Australian public inquiries have had a profound impact on political events and processes, including contributing to the fall of governments. For instance, at the Commonwealth level, the Costigan *Royal Commission on the Activities of the Federated Ship Painters and Dockers Union* (1980) adversely affected the electoral standing of the Fraser Coalition Government and contributed to its loss of office in March 1983.

At the state level, the Fitzgerald Commission into police corruption caused the fall of the National Party government in Queensland when it reported in 1989, ending 32 years of non-Labor rule. In Western Australia, the 1991 Kennedy Royal Commission inquiring into the questionable business dealings of members of government and government agencies (known as WA Inc) caused the Labor government to lose office in 1992. Indeed, such public inquiries have gone beyond mere examinations of misconduct of individuals, or even particular institutions like the police, to contribute to major changes in the institutional framework and practices of government (Finn 1994).

Inquiries often reflect adversely on the personal conduct of members of the government. Although inquiries cannot themselves mete out punishment or penalties, their recommendations frequently lead to legal or other action. For example, evidence given to the Fitzgerald Commission in Queensland led directly to the criminal prosecution of a former premier (resulting in a mistrial) and three former ministers (who were all convicted). Similarly, prosecutions of two former premiers followed on from the Kennedy Royal Commission into WA Inc, while also in Western Australia, the Marks Royal Commission, concerning improper or inappropriate use of executive power (1995), led to the trial of a former Labor premier, Dr Carmen Lawrence and a backbench parliamentarian over perjury at the royal commission. Although the prosecution against Dr Lawrence failed, the process effectively destroyed her political career, forcing her to stand down as federal Health Minister in the Keating Government, and also undermined the Keating Government on the eve of the 1996 federal election which it subsequently lost (see Peachment 2006 for an overview of these Western Australian inquiries).

Some inquiries do not result in prosecutions, but nevertheless lead to the standing aside, dismissal or resignation of premiers or ministers. In Tasmania, Robin Gray resigned as premier in 1991 because of investigations into his personal conduct by the Carter *Royal Commission into the Edmund Rouse Bribery Affair*. In New South Wales, Premier Neville Wran stood aside for the duration of an inquiry in 1983 by the Street *Royal Commission into Certain Committal Proceedings Against K.E. Humphreys*, in which his involvement in attempting to influence a legal process was under investigation. In South Australia, Premier John Bannon resigned at least in part because of the findings concerning his conduct, and that of his government, reached by the 1991 Jacobs *Royal Commission into the State Bank of South Australia*.

Examples of the political effects of royal commissions can be found even further back in the history of Australia, particularly in state governments. Before federation, seven Queensland inquiries were appointed to investigate the conduct and alleged corruption or conflicts of interest of prominent politicians and officials, and were major political scandals of their time (Clark 1962). In the 1930s, investigations by the Campbell Royal Commission into mining rights allocations for the Mungana-Chillagoe mines forced the resignation of then federal Treasurer and former Queensland Premier R.G. Theodore (Kennedy 1978). The 1956 Townley Inquiry into allegations of corruption in land administration caused the resignation of the Queensland Minister for Lands, Tom Foley. In Victoria, a minister resigned because of the 1977

Gowan Board of Inquiry into allegations of corruption in the allocation of state housing.

As well as affecting government members, public inquiries have also had a political impact by reflecting adversely on aspects of government administration or the conduct of senior appointees or associates. Such findings call into question the administrative capacity or effectiveness of the government. For example, the Fitzgerald Commission in Queensland, in addition to a focus on members of parliament, investigated the conduct of two judges, the Police Commissioner, and numerous police and business identities close to the then government, and drew attention to the government's failure to properly administer public affairs and supervise public administration. The various inquiries into collapsed state enterprises – such as the WA Inc Royal Commission, the 1990 Victorian Woodward *Royal Commission into the Tricontinental Group of Companies*, and the 1991 South Australian Jacobs *Royal Commission into the State Bank of South Australia* – all brought into question the economic management abilities of the respective governments. In each case, there was a clear link between the inquiries and the subsequent fall of those governments.

Inquiries also have a political impact because that is the government's intention in appointing them — to achieve clear vested political objectives. For instance, it has been argued that the Menzies Coalition Government announced the *Royal Commission on Espionage* (Petrov Commission) in 1954 just weeks before an election was due in order to bolster flagging electoral support by generating distrust of the Labor Party (Whitton 1994), although this view is hotly contested (Manne 1987; Martin 1995; Nethercote 1995).

The Queensland National Party Government, while subject to intense pressure from the Fitzgerald Commission in 1989, appointed the Cooke Commission to inquire into the activities of particular Queensland trade unions. Adverse findings would have diverted attention from the National Party and reflected badly on the Labor Party, with which the unions were affiliated. And the 1995 Marks *Royal Commission into the Use of Executive Power* in Western Australia was established by the Court Coalition Government at least partly to affect adversely the career of former Labor premier Carmen Lawrence, who had become federal Health Minister, and thus damage the Keating Labor Government in Canberra.

Why are public inquiries into political wrongdoing appointed?

From these examples, it is clear that public inquiries into political wrongdoing have been common in Australia. But their use is not without criticism. This ranges from the often very large costs and time delays associated with some inquiries to their potential impact on the civil liberties and privacy of individuals investigated, and their potential to adversely affect any criminal proceedings against those individuals (see Gilligan 2002). Sometimes inquiries are criticised for not leading to enough prosecutions because of their focus on systemic reforms (see Toohey 1990). Other criticisms are that the inquiries are appointed for partisan purposes to undermine political opponents. The idea that the Marks Royal Commission was purely a political "witch-hunt" was taken up in no uncertain terms by Prime Minister Paul Keating (1995) when the report was released. He described the inquiry as:

> ... conceived as an act of political malevolence by the Court government … basic principles of natural justice were ignored ... the terms of reference were deliberately narrow … drawn up to put Dr Lawrence and the Labor Party on trial … the establishment of the Royal Commission was unique and uniquely disreputable. It will stand as an example of the lack of principle, propriety and decency of the Court Government . . . (Statement by the Prime Minister, 14 November 1995)

Alternative investigatory bodies

The principal alternative to ad hoc public inquiries is the traditional criminal investigation and trial, led by police and prosecutors. However, the goal of that process is to determine the legal culpability of an individual, or individuals, and to impose sanctions on those found guilty. This mechanism is not well-suited to investigating broader system issues or failures. Additionally, the criminal standard of guilt requires the proof of allegations beyond reasonable doubt. This high standard is hard to meet for "hidden" offences, such as corruption and misconduct, which occur behind closed doors often where all the observers are complicit and have something to lose by exposing the behaviour. Police and public prosecutors have considerable discretion in determining whether to act on allegations, or to require further evidence before taking any action. In exercising this discretion they will be conscious of possible reactions to any politically unpalatable investigation, whether in the form of active hindrance, or more subtle pressures. Even if they decide to investigate, police lack the powers and freedom of procedure often needed to uncover hidden and secret crimes such as corruption. And the jurisdiction of police and prosecutors is defined by whether the allegations concern criminal, as opposed to ethically wrong conduct.

Another barrier for some investigators is that they have competing responsibilities and a finite budget. Faced with other, less problematic, investigations, overtly political inquiries may receive less priority. This may be because of the complex nature of political inquiries, or because of concern as to how governments will react to their conduct being examined. Also, some matters are complex and large-scale, requiring specialised expertise, a multi-disciplinary or cross-jurisdictional approach, or coercive powers exceeding those of a normal criminal investigation. Further, what happens when those complained about are involved in the investigation, such as in cases of alleged police, prosecutor, or judicial misconduct or negligence? And finally, as Van Harten (2003) argues, sometimes criminalisation is not the right or sufficient answer to difficult social problems and what is needed is a broader type of response.

As highlighted at the beginning of this chapter, Australia now has a multitude of permanent investigative agencies, including standing crime and corruption commissions, ombudsmen and human rights commissions, many of which have a continuing brief to review alleged misconduct of parliamentarians, police, and public officials. Many of these arose out of public inquiries that were appointed in the 1980s and 1990s. Additionally, many of these new integrity bodies have a much greater mix of resources, expertise and powers than was previously available to traditional police and prosecutors.

When these permanent bodies exist specifically to investigate wrongdoing, it is difficult to understand why ad hoc public inquiries continue to be appointed. Queensland's Crime and Misconduct Commission, for example, has a standing brief to investigate alleged misconduct in almost all aspects of the public sector, including among politicians, public servants and police. It is Australia's most powerful all-in-one anti-corruption body. Yet, since its establishment in 2002, and the creation of its predecessor body, the Criminal Justice Commission in 1989, ad hoc commissions of inquiry have continued to be called for and appointed.

The permanent agencies are well suited to investigating individual criminality or administrative wrongdoing, but their position becomes fraught when they are called on to investigate matters close to the political arm of government, particularly ministers and their advisers. This is at least in part because of the constitutional position of such agencies, which allows them to circumvent notions of Westminster accountability to make ministers and their officials answer for their conduct other than through parliament. The end result has often been tension between the corruption commissions and the government of the day. Agencies such as the CMC and ICAC in NSW have a vested bureaucratic interest in securing their own continued existence and resourcing, which can lead to perceptions of them limiting investigations so as to forestall political criticism or retribution.

The CJC experience in Queensland (1989-2002) provides a clear example of direct government retribution against an agency because of its political investigations. In 1996 the new Borbidge Coalition Government appointed the Connolly-Ryan Inquiry to investigate the powers, organisation and personnel of the CJC itself. This was a response to a CJC activity that had severely embarrassed the former leader of the National Party and former premier, Russell Cooper, who had become Police Minister in the Borbidge government. Ultimately, the Connolly-Ryan Inquiry was shut down by the Supreme Court, following a finding of actual bias (see chapter 3: Davies).

The capacity for agencies to apply their own limits to their investigations, so as to deflect political criticism or retribution, is also demonstrated by the CJC. In 1993, the CJC established an investigation, the so-called Cape Melville affair, into allegations that advisers to Premier Wayne Goss had attempted to interfere in a police inquiry. Following past government criticism of its public inquiries, the CJC decided to hold its investigation in private. When the investigation recommended that no charges be laid, somewhat inevitably the investigation was derided by the Opposition as a cover-up (see Lewis 1997).

Another potential barrier for anti-corruption agencies investigating political wrongdoing is their jurisdictional limits. All are statutory agencies and therefore delimited by their statutory jurisdiction. For ICAC, and the CJC or CMC, this has meant barriers to the investigation of conduct of politicians that falls short of criminality. Both agencies are barred from investigating disciplinary matters or ethical misconduct by politicians, and it was for this reason that the findings of a 1992 ICAC investigation into the role of NSW premier Nick Greiner in the appointment of a former Liberal MP, Terry Metherell, to a senior public service position, were subsequently overturned by the Court of Appeal (*Greiner v ICAC* (1992) 28 NSWLR 125). Various parliamentary travel rort scandals at both federal and state levels have shown that there is considerable scope for conduct that is not criminal because of the lack of precise guidelines and rules, yet which is publicly regarded as immoral. This was the case with a 1991 CJC investigation into the misuse of travel entitlements by members of parliament between 1986 and 1989, which found that about 50 past and present members of the Queensland Parliament had "abused" their parliamentary entitlements. However, the lack of clear rules about the use of those entitlements combined with evidentiary difficulties meant no criminal action could succeed, and the CJC's jurisdictional limitations meant it could take no other action against elected politicians (Lewis 1997).

In addition to these structural conflicts, another reason why ad hoc public inquiries are often called for, even though permanent agencies already exist, is the perception that royal commissions, in particular, are a superior type of investigation. For some commentators, only royal commissions have the powers, independence and investigative capacity to unravel complex issues. Independence is the key criterion here, for the problem with permanent bodies is that they become associated with the status quo. Royal commissions are seen as non-partisan, and this is enhanced when they are headed by judges or former judges. Oppositions call for such inquiries to call attention to alleged government failings, often supported by media interest in scandalous stories in a public forum (Tiffin 1999).

Another traditional means for investigating political wrongdoing has been through parliament itself, either by raising allegations in public debate, where the government is required to respond, or by parliamentary committee investigation. Neither of these measures has proved adequate for addressing the conduct of governments, ministers, or those close to them. Public debate in the parliament is a particularly blunt and toothless weapon. While parliament, as a venue for free speech, theoretically seems ideal for the airing of serious allegations, the reality of Australian parliaments is that lower houses at least are subject to tight government control. Governments set the parliamentary timetable and control debates, through techniques such as the guillotine, gag and the rulings of partisan speakers. Even where matters are raised in debate, governments have no obligation to act on them, or even to respond to the detail of the allegations. Even when governments do not have absolute control, for example in the Senate, the mere raising of an issue in parliament of itself achieves nothing. On occasion, frequent parliamentary criticism has contributed to the establishment of an investigation, as, for example, in the cases of the WA Inc Royal Commission and the 1994 Wood *Royal Commission into the New South Wales Police Service*, set up to investigate corruption and misconduct within the state police force. However, in both these cases, rather than the mere parliamentary debate, it was the combination of parliamentary criticism with an unstable government, caused in one instance by the crumbling of its reputation and solidarity, and in the other by its dependence on support from independent MPs that led to the inquiry (Ransley 2001).

Parliamentary committees are also a less than adequate means of investigating political wrongdoing. While popular in the last decades of the 1800s and up until World War II, their viability as independent investigators declined concurrently with the rise of the two-party system and strong party discipline, which saw committee members bound to vote in the interests of their party, regardless of the facts uncovered by their investigation. This occurred in Britain as well as Australia, and led to the enactment of the *Tribunals of Inquiry (Evidence) Act* 1921 (now repealed) solely to enable the appointment of tribunals to investigate serious political wrongdoing. In Australia, the reaction instead was to make increased use of the ad hoc royal commission to conduct such investigations (Hallett 1982). While the lack of government control in the Senate has occasionally seen the appointment of investigative Senate committees, they tend to involve majority and minority reports divided on party lines, and the political reception of their recommendations is also dominated by party factors. They are also subject to strong criticism for their processes, given the limited rights and protections for those investigated or appearing before them as witnesses. Finally, Senators and other members of parliament are not always trained investigators or cross-examiners, and for as long as parliamentary practice limits the use of advisers for research and preparatory roles, the committees will be hindered by a lack of practical skills.

The conclusion to be drawn from this discussion is that regardless of the meaning or limits of political wrongdoing, it cannot generally be adequately dealt with by any of the normal, permanent investigative agencies. Police and prosecutors suffer from defects of powers and processes, and many of the other statutory agencies from defects of jurisdiction. All permanent institutions face potential conflict from the need to preserve their own bureaucratic interests while actively investigating and possibly discrediting the government that controls their budget and their future. Parliament and its committees are unsuited to such investigations because of their lack of investigative resources and experience, but particularly because of the inevitable politicisation that results from the priority given to promoting party interests in any investigation.

From this conclusion, it follows that only ad hoc inquiries such as royal commissions are capable of overcoming these limitations and adequately investigating political wrongdoing. Royal commissions in all jurisdictions possess powers lacked by normal police and prosecution agencies, particularly the power to force the giving of self-incriminating evidence and the production of documents. Some jurisdictions now go well beyond this basic power and equip royal commissions with many other investigative and detection type powers, but even the basic ability to require answers to questions exceeds the normal powers of police. Also, royal commissions possess the freedom to adopt flexible processes that advantages their investigations over normal criminal justice procedures, particularly in their ability to conduct hearings not bound by the rules of evidence and to generally act as inquisitors rather than as part of the adversarial system.

What makes a public inquiry effective?

How then can political misconduct best be investigated? Investigations of political wrongdoing face particular barriers that make the task difficult.

The first is the diffuse and changeable nature of concepts of political wrongdoing. While criminal conduct will always be regarded as wrong, the extent to which less than criminal conduct is seen as morally or ethically objectionable will depend on circumstances, particularly the prevailing political climate. A government with only a narrow grip on power, perhaps reliant for support on independents or a minor party, will face more pressure to act on alleged wrongdoing than one comfortably ensconced in office. Thus, the NSW Wood Royal Commission into Police was appointed because of pressure applied by independent MPs holding the balance of power in the lower house. The WA Inc Royal Commission was forced on an unwilling government after sustained pressure from the Opposition, media and public groups. Sometimes governments face internal pressures that cause action to be taken, such as the divisions within the Queensland branch of the Liberal Party that led Prime Minister Malcolm Fraser, in 1978, to appoint the McGregor Royal Commission into electoral redistribution in Queensland, to investigate whether then Minister for Finance and senior Liberal powerbroker in Queensland, Eric Robinson had interfered in the 1977 electoral redistribution. Similarly, jockeying within the Queensland National Party for positioning as heir to the Bjelke-Petersen premiership was, at least partly, the motivation for the appointment of the Fitzgerald Commission.

Also, the boundaries of unacceptable conduct change from time to time. The idea of political patronage in appointments to the public service was anathema during the 1960s and earlier, when the accepted concept of the public service was that it was apolitical, at least in the party sense. By the 1980s, however, that concept had changed to the extent that it was common for incoming governments to make their own appointments at chief and senior executive level. Therefore, when ICAC investigated Premier Greiner's appointment of Terry Metherell to a senior public service position, it was caught between applying outdated concepts of public service neutrality and recognition that values and practices had in fact changed. ICAC's judgement in this case was founded on its determination of those values when it became clear that no law had been broken in the appointment. While the decision was overturned on a point of law, much of the criticism of ICAC was because it had reached its moral judgment based on wrong or superseded values.

But neither their powers nor their flexible processes are the real crux of the difference between ad hoc royal commission inquiries and other investigative agencies. After all, the standing bodies possess considerable, if not superior, powers to ad hoc commissions, as well as the same freedom from adversarial procedure. The real advantage possessed by royal commissions is their independence from government control, and in particular, the public perception of that independence that leads to a legitimacy and degree of political support for the work of the commission. This independence is not absolute, and royal commissions are all subject to various forms of outright and subtle pressures from government, ranging from the ability to withdraw the commission or manipulate the terms of reference, to imposing budgetary and other resource constraints. Even more significantly, governments may simply reject or not act on commission recommendations.

Those royal commissions that are affected by government manipulation are failures, except in so far as they can be regarded as succeeding by fulfilling the government's agenda. Thus, the Petrov Royal Commission may be judged to have failed if it was designed to uncover a major Soviet spy ring in Australia, and no one was charged as a result of its investigations, but it did have the effect of winning political support for Prime Minister Robert Menzies. Similarly, the 1963 Gibbs Royal Commission in Queensland failed to uncover systemic police corruption in the state, largely because of the Commissioner's strict interpretation of his narrow terms of reference, but it did succeed in the government's objective of taking police corruption off the public agenda for the next 25 years.

In addition to narrow terms of reference, governments can also manipulate public inquiries through tactics including ignoring their findings, attacking the report or the inquiry chair, bureaucratising the response to recommendations or reviewing the role of inquiries (Prasser 1994: 13). On occasion governments seek to control inquiries by requiring them to observe special procedures in their investigations, as was the case with the Costigan Royal Commission, although in effect that technique failed on that occasion (see Ransley 2001). The Gibbs Royal Commission was also affected by the limited resources it was provided with by government, forcing it to rely on police to investigate other police (Fitzgerald 1990). The Cooke Inquiry, established by a National Party government in Queensland to examine alleged misconduct in unions connected to the ALP, was denied extra resources and an extension in its reporting time by an incoming ALP government (Ransley 2001). And, of course, governments appoint the members of inquiries, and can attempt to keep control by seeking compliant commissioners (or those expected to be compliant). In the royal commission into the conviction of Rupert Maxwell Stuart, two of the three commissioners were judges who had been involved in the criminal cases where justice was alleged to have been denied to Stuart. Not surprisingly, they found no error in the legal proceedings they had presided over (Whitton 1994).

Given this potential for manipulation, to succeed as investigators of political wrongdoing royal commissions and other public inquiries need more than their powers and flexible procedures. They need to maintain their independence from government influence, and they need to preserve the public perception of that independence. That is, they have to develop and maintain their own pool of public support in a politically contentious environment. Recent successes among inquiries have done this first by being seen to have serious matters to investigate, rather than simply being tools for political point-scoring. Thus the Fitzgerald, Wood and WA Inc inquiries all investigated matters of serious corruption or crime, while the Costigan Royal Commission entered this category when its focus shifted from union malfeasance to the lack of action taken against widespread tax evasion. On the other hand, inquiries into matters of purely political or moral judgement, such as the Marks Royal

Commission, have less public support and are often criticised as not justifying their expenditure.

Inquiries can maintain public support through active manipulation of the media, by encouraging reporting of their activities to promote continued public interest. Thus, the Fitzgerald and Wood inquiries carefully staged the exposure of evidence of great public interest early in their processes, both to prove the importance of what they were investigating and to show the success of their strategies. They established an image of successful investigation that had both operational and public relations benefits. This relationship with the media continued throughout the inquiries.

A strong commissioner or chair, who is willing to take on governments where necessary, also strengthens the perception of independence. Thus, Fitzgerald made no secret of calling in the leaders of the political parties to extract implementation agreements from them when the politically unstable environment looked as though it might threaten the outcome of his inquiry. This strength is also made apparent when various commissioners have approached governments seeking and obtaining extensions of their terms of reference, even where those extensions might seem to threaten the political position of the government. But commissioners need to tread warily and maintain their independence, or they risk perceptions of bias. In Queensland, the first *Bundaberg Hospital Commission of Inquiry* chaired by Tony Morris QC was successfully challenged in the Supreme Court for bias, on the basis of questions and comments made by the Commissioner during the evidence given by two witnesses (*Keating v Morris & Ors* [2005] QSC 243).

Royal commissions as public inquiries are able to maintain a perception of their independence when other continuing agencies cannot, largely because they are seen as having no long-term bureaucratic interests to push. Commissions and commissioners are not seen as having careers to promote, budgets to enhance, or empires to increase, and hence they appear less likely to pander to government interests. Inquiries that depart from this model because they continue for too long, or appear to engage in empire building, may lose the benefits of the perception of independence. An example here is the Costigan Royal Commission which, its tax investigations more or less complete, moved into new and only marginally related areas of investigation, leading to accusations of empire building.

In addition to public support, it is also essential for inquiries to maintain a degree of political support, both from the government and other important players in the political environment. Commissions that lack political support cannot succeed – they will either be shut down or ignored. The Costigan Royal Commission was established with the Fraser Government's support to investigate unions. It achieved strong public support when it exposed the bottom-of-the-harbour tax schemes, but lost both public and political support, particularly after a change in government, when its investigations continued on into the more arcane areas of bureaucratic reorganisation and law reform (see Gilligan 2002).

Conclusions

Hence, while royal commissions and equivalent public inquiries are equipped with the powers, flexible processes, and independence to investigate wrongdoing, some will succeed at this task and some will not. Those that do succeed are likely to be investigating real and substantive wrongdoing, have a strong inquiry chair able to extract procedural and administrative support from a sometimes unwilling government, and take an active role in the management and presentation of information about their activities rather than leaving their work to stand for itself. The main impediment to the effectiveness of a royal commission is political manipulation by the government, and the self-imposed constraint of an unduly legal and inquisitorial style of inquiry. Despite these impediments, the royal commission model still has value and will continue to be used to investigate issues of political wrongdoing.

Public inquiries mentioned in chapter

(in chronological order by year of appointment, with name of chair)

Commonwealth:

Royal Commission on Espionage (Petrov Inquiry) (Owen: 1954)

Royal Commission of Inquiry into Matters in Relation to Electoral Redistribution Queensland, 1977 (McGregor: 1978)

Royal Commission on the Activities of the Federated Ship Painters and Dockers Union (Costigan: 1980)

Inquiry into the Centenary House Lease (Hunt: 2004)

Inquiry into Certain Australian Companies in Relation to the UN Oil-for-Food Programme (Cole: 2005)

State and territories:

New South Wales

Royal Commission of Inquiry into Certain Committal Proceedings Against K.E. Humphreys (Street: 1983)

Royal Commission into the New South Wales Police Service (Wood: 1994)

Northern Territory

Royal Commission of Inquiry into Chamberlain Convictions (Morling: 1986)

Queensland

Royal Commission Appointed to Inquire into Certain Matters Relating to Mungana-Chillagoe Mines (Campbell: 1930)

Royal Commission into Allegations of Corruption Relating to Dealings with Certain Crown Leaseholds in Queensland (Townley: 1956)

Royal Commission into Alleged Police Activities at the National Hotel (Gibbs: 1963)

Commission of Inquiry into Possible Illegal Activities and Associated Police Misconduct (Fitzgerald: 1987)

Commission of Inquiry into the Activities of Particular Queensland Unions (Cooke: 1989)

Inquiry into the Future Role, Structure, Powers and Operations of the Criminal Justice Commission (Connolly-Ryan: 1996)

Bundaberg Hospital Commission of Inquiry (Morris: 2005)

Queensland Public Hospitals Commission of Inquiry (Davies: 2005)

Queensland Floods Commission of Inquiry (Holmes: 2011)

Queensland Health Payroll System Commission of Inquiry (Chesterman: 2013)

South Australia

Royal Commission into the Conviction of Rupert Maxwell Stuart (Napier: 1959)

Royal Commission into the State Bank of South Australia (Jacobs: 1991)

Tasmania

Royal Commission into the Edmund Rouse Bribery Affair (Carter: 1990)

Victoria

Royal Commission to Investigate the Failure on the 15th October 1970 of Portions of the Westgate Bridge (Barber: 1970)

Board of Inquiry into Certain Land Purchases by the Housing Commission and Questions Arising Therefrom (Gowan: 1977)

Royal Commission into the Tricontinental Group of Companies (Woodward: 1990)

Western Australia

Royal Commission into Commercial Activities of Government and Other Matters, Western Australia (WA Inc Royal Commission) (Kennedy: 1991)

Royal Commission into Use of Executive Power (Marks: 1995)

References

Atkins D., 1999, "After the acquittal of Dr Lawrence," *The Courier-Mail*, 24 July

Australian Law Reform Commission, (ALRC), 2009, "Making Inquiries: A New Statutory Framework," Report 111, Canberra: Commonwealth Government

Centa, R., and Macklem, P., 2001, "Securing Accountability through Commissions of Inquiry: a role for the Law Commission of Canada," *Osgoode Hall Law Journal*, 39, 117-160

Clark, C.S., 1962, "Royal Commissions of Queensland 1859-1901," *Australian Law Journal*, 36, 131-137

Gilligan, G., 2002, "Royal Commissions of Inquiry," *Australian and New Zealand Journal of Criminology*, 35(3), 289-307

Finn, P., 1994, "The Significance of the Fitzgerald and WA Inc Commissions," in Weller, P., (ed), *Royal Commissions and the Making of Public Policy*, Melbourne: Macmillan Education, 32-39

Fitzgerald, R., 1990, "Judicial Culture and the Investigation of Corruption: A Comparison of the Gibbs National Hotel Inquiry 1963-64 and the Fitzgerald Inquiry 1987-89," in Prasser, S., Wear, R., and Nethercote, J., (eds), *Corruption and Reform: The Fitzgerald Vision*, St Lucia: University of Queensland Press, 61-80

Grove J., 1999, "Court hits out on Easton," *Western Australian*, 28 July

Hallett, L.A., 1982, *Royal Commissions and Boards of Inquiry*, Sydney: Law Book Company

Keating, P., MP, 1995, *Press Release*, "Marks Royal Commission," 14 November

Kennedy, K.H., 1978, *The Mungana Affair: State Mining and Political Corruption in the 1920s*, St Lucia: University of Queensland Press

Lewis, C., 1997, *Civilian Oversight of Complaints Against Police: External Relationships and Their Impact on Effectiveness*, PhD thesis, School of Politics and Public Policy, Griffith University

Lewis, C., 2010, "Crime and Misconduct Commission: Moving away from Fitzgerald," in Lewis, C., Ransley, J., and Homel, R., (eds) *The Fitzgerald Legacy: Reforming Public Life in Australia and Beyond*, Bowen Hills: Australian Academic Press, 57-80

Manne, R., 1987, *The Petrov Affair: Politics and Espionage*, Sydney: Pergamon

Martin, A.W., 1995, "New Light on the Petrov Affair," *Quadrant*, June, 46-50

Nethercote, J.R., 1995, "The Timing of the 1954 Election," *Quadrant*, June, 50-52

Peachment, A., 1995, "The Royal Commission into WA Inc," in Peachment, A., (ed), *Westminster Inc: A Survey of Three States*, Sydney: Federation Press, 67-80

Peachment, A., (ed), 2006, *The Years of Scandal: Commissions of Inquiry in Western Australia 1991-2004*, Perth: University of Western Australia Press

Prasser, S., 1994, "Royal Commissions and Public Inquiries: Scope and Uses," in Weller, *Royal Commissions and the Making of Public Policy*, 1-21

Prasser, S., 2003, *A Study of Commonwealth Public Inquiries*, PhD thesis, School of Politics and Public Policy, Griffith University

Prasser, S., 2006, *Royal Commissions and Public Inquiries in Australia*, Sydney: Lexis Nexis Butterworths

Ransley, J., 2001, *Inquisitorial Royal Commissions and the Investigation of Political Wrongdoing*, PhD thesis, Law School, Griffith University

Ransley, J., 2010, "Fitzgerald: A Model Investigative Inquiry?," in Lewis, Ransley, and Homel, *The Fitzgerald Legacy*, 57-80

Ransley, J., and Homel, R., "Fitzgerald: A Model Investigative Inquiry?," in Lewis, Ransley and Homel, *The Fitzgerald Legacy*, 22-38

Tiffin, R., 1999, *Scandals: Media, Politics and Corruption in Contemporary Australia*, Sydney: UNSW Press

Toohey, B., 1990, "Fitzgerald: How the Process Came Unstuck" in Prasser, Wear, and Nethercote, *Corruption and Reform*, 81-88

Van Harten, G., 2003, "Truth before Punishment: A Defence of Public Inquiries," *Queen's Law Journal*, 29, 242-282 http://papers.ssrn.com/sol3/papers.cfm?abstract_id=1582963

Whitton E., 1994, *Trial by Voodoo: Why the Law Defeats Justice and Democracy*, Sydney: Random House Australia

Endnotes

1 But note that in Victoria only, powers and offences are governed by the *Evidence (Miscellaneous Provisions) Act 1958* which also applies to Boards of Inquiry, and that NSW has both the *Royal Commissions Act 1923*, and the *Special Commissions of Inquiry Act 1983*. Some other inquiries have had their own establishing legislation, eg the *Royal Commission on Espionage* (Petrov Inquiry) in 1954, the *Royal Commission of Inquiry into Chamberlain Convictions* in the Northern Territory, and the Victorian royal commission into the West Gate Bridge collapse in 1970.

5

Royal commissions and integrity systems

Charles Sampford

Introduction

In 1989, Queensland awaited the report from what was possibly the most dramatic and influential commission of inquiry in the state's, if not the nation's, history, the Fitzgerald *Commission of Inquiry into Possible Illegal Activities and Associated Police Misconduct* (henceforth the Fitzgerald Commission). The two major parties had attempted to outdo each other in promises to fully implement the Fitzgerald Commission's recommendations, torturing their thesauruses to find ways to circumvent mathematical inevitability that there is no way to go beyond 100 per cent. Queenslanders were keen to find out what had gone wrong in the public life of the state. They were also very keen to find out what Commissioner Tony Fitzgerald thought they should do about it. It was the proposals for institutional change that were the lasting legacy of the inquiry.

Fitzgerald did not recommend the then fashionable Hong Kong model of an integrity system, comprising a strong anti-corruption law and a strong Independent Commission Against Corruption (ICAC) with permanent royal commission powers to enforce it. He did not think Queensland should rely on anti-corruption laws and institutions alone. Many other reforms were needed, but he did not set out to prescribe them all. He did not claim to have all the answers, but he had a very good idea of what the governance questions were and the processes for answering them. The system of reforms he recommended, led by an independent Electoral and Administrative Review Commission

(EARC), has not been bettered in any other jurisdiction. The EARC had a number of features, in its personnel, processes and positioning, that bolstered its effectiveness. It was chaired initially by a lawyer with wide experience beyond the law, Tom Sherman, a former Commonwealth Crown Solicitor and Australian Government Solicitor, and later by David Solomon, one-time press secretary to Gough Whitlam (Labor Prime Minister, 1972-75), founder and editor of *The Legal Reporter* (1981-2003) and then contributing editor with *The Courier-Mail.*

The EARC's processes for addressing the 27 issues before it involved in-depth study with the assistance of expert consultants, the publication of issues papers, public submissions, public seminars and hearings, a response to public submissions and a final report to parliament. Its recommendations resulted in the formation of a parliamentary committee (PEARC) which received further submissions, commissioned further papers and delivered its own report to parliament before the normal legislative process began. While it was appropriate for parliament to form its own conclusions, the recognition by all major parties that reform was necessary, the quality of EARC's work and the inclusiveness of its processes meant that most of its proposals were accepted.

The EARC had the benefit of looking at the whole system of governance in Queensland and a good understanding of the way existing institutions operated, where new ones might fit and how they might interact. The system that resulted was an integrated set of norms, laws and institutions that would improve governance in Queensland, promote integrity and reduce corruption. Because of the strong ethical foundation of EARC's proposals and the prominence given to public sector ethics, I call it an ethics regime; the Organisation for Economic Co-operation and Development (OECD) also adopted the system but changed the name to "ethics infrastructure"; Transparency International called it an "integrity system", the term that has enjoyed the widest usage.

Ironically, two kinds of institution were not included in EARC's remit and are generally not considered as part of an integrity system:

one is a royal commission or commission of inquiry; the other is a standing governance reform commission such as the EARC itself. This is possibly because studies of integrity systems tend to concentrate on bodies that are more or less permanent, whereas royal commissions are intended to conclude with the delivery of their final report. The EARC, which Fitzgerald recommended be an "enduring" body, was terminated after five years. Also, the Fitzgerald Inquiry and EARC were intended to be solutions to long-standing governance problems within existing Queensland institutions so it would have seemed counterintuitive for them to be studied. In addition, EARC was more or less unique to Queensland and so does not figure in studies and assessments of integrity systems (see Doig and McIvor 2003; KCELJAG and TI 2005; Sampford *et al* 2005; Schacklock *et al* 2007). And finally, it would not have been appropriate for EARC to review itself.

However, if we look at integrity systems as a whole, royal commissions can fulfil a number of important functions and interact with other institutions to improve governance outcomes. Some integrity functions may be taken on by standing anti-corruption agencies such as Queensland's Criminal Justice Commission (CJC), which later became the Crime and Misconduct Commission (CMC), and other functions by standing governance reform commissions.

This chapter examines the role royal commissions may play within integrity systems and the circumstances in which integrity functions are best exercised by standing bodies, and when a short-term inquiry by a royal commission is a better approach.

Royal commissions as adjuncts to integrity systems

Royal commissions serve a number of purposes, take a number of forms, and produce a range of different outcomes. Some are engaged in investigating disasters, either natural disasters such as the Queensland floods and the Victorian bushfires (see chapter 6: Wettenhall) or man-made crises, such as the financial collapse of HIH insurance group and the corruption examined by the Gibbs, Fitzgerald and Wood commissions (see chapter 4: Ransley), or a mixture of natural disaster exacerbated by human decisions or action. Some investigate widespread, systematic or significant wrong doing, for example, the 2005 Cole Commission inquiring into Australian companies in relation to the UN Oil-For-Food program (see chapter 13: Bartos). These do not directly determine guilt (a clearly judicial function), but engage in systematic investigation as to what went wrong. Their recommendations, backed by evidence, may lead to the prosecution of individuals, or simply a better understanding of what went wrong. Sometimes the latter is more important. Royal commissions generally privilege finding the facts over prosecution, a function they share with Truth and Reconciliation commissions, which trade full knowledge for immunity from prosecution for those who confess all. A third form of royal commission is one that is engaged mainly in fact finding about issues of perceived public importance, for example, the current *Royal Commission into Institutional Responses to Child Sexual Abuse*. A final category is an inquiry into major areas of policy reform, such as the 1974 Coombs *Royal Commission into Australian Government Administration* (see chapter 12: Gourley) and the Finkelstein *Inquiry into the Media and Media Regulation* (see chapter 9: Tiffin).

The functions of investigation and proposals for reform can often be performed by other institutions within an integrity system. Indeed, one would hope that investigations and policy analysis do not have to await the appointment of an ad hoc royal commission. However, a royal commission can generally investigate a broader set of issues than a police investigation. It can mix and match executive powers that are not usually found within the one institution. The dedication of resources, the appointment of commissioners and senior staff who can singularly devote themselves to the task and the existence of a high level panel of great prestige with a range of mutually complementary knowledge and skills are all features that add to its value.

A further advantage of a royal commission is its flexibility. No integrity system will be perfect for all time and all eventualities. As unexpected problems emerge, or as old problems that were not completely resolved re-emerge and become more pressing, ad hoc commissions have an important role. To some extent, the establishment of a royal commission is intended to show that a government takes a matter seriously (whether or not it actually does); however, it also reflects on other institutions within the integrity system and their perceived ability to handle the issue at stake.

As they are created by the executive and exercise executive power, royal commissions are often seen as part of the executive. In a pure tripartite division of power, that is the only alternative. However, they are more like "fourth arm" institutions than standard elements of the executive. Several of the critical elements within integrity systems, such as ombudsmen, departments of public prosecution, auditors-general, some inspectorates and anti-corruption commissions operate with a high degree of independence from the executive. While the agency heads are generally appointed by the Governor or Governor-General on the advice of ministers, they have terms that extend beyond the life of a parliament, and they can generally only be dismissed for cause and by a vote of parliament. Although they have delegated executive power, they are not directed, controlled or generally accountable to the executive for its exercise. Many integrity agencies do not report to the executive but to the legislature. They are generally established by statute and are often entrusted with coercive powers (such as the power to compel testimony and documents) that have been largely stripped from the executive. The standing of those appointed to senior positions in integrity agencies and the long terms of appointment mean there is limited temptation to give way to the wishes of the executive. The degree of independence is such that integrity agencies can be seen as part of a loose "fourth arm" of government.

Ad hoc royal commissions share many of these features of "fourth arm" institutions. They are appointed by the Crown and are not easily dismissed. There is great emphasis on their independence and they are commonly headed by judges or former judges, a practice designed to secure legitimacy for the process and to imply that the degree of independence is greater than it is. They are not subject to direction and are sometimes even more independent than intended, as demonstrated by the Costigan *Royal Commission on the Activities of the Federated Ship Painters and Dockers Union* (1980) and the Fitzgerald Commission into police corruption in Queensland (1987) (see chapter 4: Ransley). It is very difficult for government to close them down, though the Bjelke-Petersen Government tried with the Fitzgerald Commission (Whitton 1989: 137-139).

Limitations of royal commissions

However, royal commissions do not have the same degree of effective independence as other integrity agencies. One limitation is that it is the government that determines what is considered by a royal commission and when it is considered, by setting specific terms of reference and timelines, whereas other integrity agencies deal with issues and complaints as they arise. While they have to meet criteria set down in legislation, integrity agencies investigate the issue or complaint as they interpret it.

Government is also influential in the choice of royal commissioners. They can choose someone who is biased towards the government's view, but in the main the wisdom of choosing someone who appears to be independent and fair minded prevails. Generally, government will have a notion of a potential commissioner's views on the matters to be investigated. This can be particularly useful if the individual is not widely seen as a sympathiser, but on this issue has a principled stand that is congenial to government.

The relatively short term of royal commissions and the fact that many commissioners become serial appointees to inquiries might be seen to encourage them to provide the kind of reports that are wanted. Those who conduct tame inquiries do not generally seem to suffer in later public life. Harry Gibbs, who conducted an inquiry into corruption in the Queensland police force (1963) and failed to discover the widespread corruption that was suspected at the time and later definitively proven, was subsequently appointed to the High Court, and finally to the highest judicial office in Australia.

There is a great deal of interaction between royal commissions and other institutions within an integrity system. In the first instance, one-off royal commissions necessarily rely on expertise developed in other institutions. They depend on the skills of barristers and counsel assisting, on staff generally seconded from the public service, and on the commissioners themselves. Apart from the dissemination of knowledge (whether from documents tabled and testimony before open hearings or contained in their published reports), the effects of royal commissions can only be realised through other bodies – public prosecution services and courts for legal proceedings, the executive for policy and legislative support, parliamentary counsel and the legislature for new legislation.

Advantages and limitations of other integrity agencies

A number of other bodies have the power to consider the kind of issues that come before royal commissions, each with its own advantages and limitations. It is a feature of most integrity systems that there is more than one institution that can perform a particular integrity function. Citizens can raise matters with their local member who can ask questions in parliament, although often neither the citizen nor the MP has enough knowledge or information to frame the question in the right way, and governments can avoid giving a full answer.

Ombudsmen

An ombudsman (appropriately called "parliamentary commissioner" in many jurisdictions) is an updated institutional version of asking questions in parliament, with the power to investigate complaints or concerns about process. An ombudsman review can often stimulate genuine improvements in public administration.

Parliamentary committees

Parliament can also instigate its own inquiries, with the same powers as a royal commission to compel the production of documents and testimony. Parliamentary committees in Australia are, however, wary of exercising those powers and rarely take up the opportunities open to them for investigation. Given their resourcing and inclination, this is not surprising. Parliamentary committees and parliamentary debates can, however, be instrumental in establishing a royal commission – as was the case when Edward St John, a Liberal member in the Commonwealth Parliament, criticised the conduct and findings of the first 1964 *Royal Commission into the Loss of HMAS Voyager* and successfully called for a second royal commission into this disaster that was established in 1967 (see Frame 1992 for a detailed account of these royal commissions).

Courts

The judiciary is, of course, responsive to complaints that take legal form. However, the courts are restricted to matters brought before them, the arguments litigants choose to raise, and documents the parties seek to discover and put before the court. Parties can always settle something which is at the heart of the common law, but which can have unfortunate consequences where government actions are being litigated. If a court action is likely to reveal government wrongdoing, parties can use government resources – ie taxpayer funds – to settle the matter, thus preventing taxpayers gaining access to information.

While elements in all three branches of government can engage in royal commission-style investigations, the executive can deflect most attempts. They can stonewall in parliament. They can settle in court. Or they can decide against establishing a royal commission, whatever the pressure. Where the pressure is overwhelming, the choice of commissioner and the framing of the terms of reference mean that government can defuse the situation and defer consideration until well into the future when the public might be concerned with other matters, or possibly when another government has to take responsibility.

The terms of reference for a royal commission are set by the government of the day, leaving open the potential for conflict of interest if there is a concern that the government, or a previous government, may have had some responsibility for what happened. There is a temptation to set terms of reference in such a way as to block the royal commission uncovering such responsibilities. Since large sums of money and a good deal of public time and debate are devoted to a commission, succumbing to such a temptation could be seen as an abuse of power. If the abuse of power is for personal or party political gain, it falls within Transparency International's definition of corruption although more often, the problem will merely be that a government will be seeking to minimise the distraction from the positive things they want to do, and the positive message they want to project.

In such cases, the choice of commissioner is important. One would hope that commissioners would insist on varying the terms of reference if they perceived such a restriction *ab initio*. One would also hope that they would seek expanded terms of reference if evidence indicated the need. Some of the most important and successful royal commissions have involved significant extensions of time and subject matter, including both the Costigan and Fitzgerald inquiries. The latter started as an inquiry into "possible illegal activities and associated police misconduct" and then had added to its remit "any other matter or thing appertaining to the aforesaid matters". The Costigan Inquiry was probably the most notorious case of extension. It started with hooliganism and contract violence, uncovered massive tax evasion and then moved on to even murkier issues. The most controversial case of non-extension is the Cole *Inquiry into Certain Australian Companies in Relation to the UN Oil-for-Food Programme* (see chapter 13: Bartos). Australians were unsurprisingly shocked when it was discovered that the Australian Wheat Board was paying bribes to secure deliveries of Australian wheat to Iraq, potentially providing funds for weapons that could later be used against Australian soldiers. The Cole Commission's terms of reference covered breaches of law by Australian companies, but no other forms of wrongdoing in breach of our UN obligations, such as those involving elected and appointed officials, were covered.

Conversely, there is the danger that a royal commission might feel that the matters it is investigating are of such importance that more and more time and resources (including, sometimes, very substantial fees) should be devoted to them. A commitment to the public interest the commission is intended to serve could lead to a desire to address a whole raft of inter-related problems in a complex legal, political and economic environment.

So, we have two potential conflicts, one between a government that will not want a royal commission exploring areas where they might face embarrassment or worse, and the other where a commission is on a crusade.

Proposals for reform

How should such conflicts of interest be handled? The solution is to look to a neutral party. I would suggest that this could be found in other areas of the integrity system. The judiciary should not get involved in an executive or "fourth arm" decision; the legislature will be divided along party lines; in my view, the best solution would be for decisions to be taken by a small committee of the leaders of integrity agencies – perhaps the ombudsman, auditor general and one or two others, such as an integrity commissioner or chair of an anti-corruption body.

Of course, if the terms of reference can be changed, governments might be reluctant to establish a royal commission in the first place. Should the decision be taken by another body? In one sense, this may seem a foolish question. Royal commissions are so called because they are established by the Crown. I would still be in favour of this being the normal route. But perhaps the body suggested above, with the Attorney-General chairing it and the Shadow Attorney taking part and being heard, might be able to establish a royal commission.

Another alternative would be for relevant parliamentary committees to decide on the establishment of a royal commission, perhaps as an option if a committee finds an issue before it is too extensive or too political.

A final alternative is the establishment by parliament of Standing Royal Commissions. These would be extremely limited in number, perhaps two in total: a broad ICAC-style body, and a broad governance reform commission like EARC. Where issues of a particular nature are likely to recur, there is much to be said for having a standing body available to address them, with commissioners and staff who are used to working together and can form effective teams. While such activities could be carried out by other bodies (police, coroner, a public service commission, and a department of state), a standing royal commission can offer something beyond the traditional standing bodies. Costigan recommended the establishment of an Australian Crime Commission (ACC). Fitzgerald proposed two ongoing commissions – the Criminal Justice Commission (CJC), to investigate and research corruption, and the EARC, to research and propose governance reforms. There was much to be said for recommending both. Unfortunately, despite Fitzgerald's recommendation that EARC be an "enduring" body, it did not continue. As Peter Forster[1] (1993: 18-19) stated:

> Although it was always envisaged that the list of priorities identified by the Fitzgerald Inquiry would be satisfactorily investigated and reported within the first few years, the Commission could have an ongoing mandate to monitor the impact of reform and address what it thought appropriate or were brought to its attention. The concept of a part time Chair with the capacity to call the

> Commission into action when and if required was the enduring model envisaged.

Integrity systems with standing commissions of this kind are less likely to need ad hoc commissions of inquiry. An independent standing body such as EARC could play a role in reviewing the performance and effectiveness of other integrity agencies, protecting them from self-interested political attack and revealing any inadequacies or failures of the agency itself or the integrity system as a whole. Such reviews could consider the functions the integrity agencies are intended to perform, how well they perform them, and how well they assist other integrity agencies in performing their functions.

An advantage of an enduring body is that it would develop expertise in the operation of the integrity system and its agencies – including strengths, weaknesses, gaps, overlaps and co-ordination problems. This would help address systemic problems as well as look at issues generated by individual agencies.

The Queensland Crime and Misconduct Commission (CMC) established in 2002, and which replaced the CJC and the Queensland Crime Commission (QCC), for example, is subject to triennial review by a parliamentary committee. However, the skills, resources and time available to the committee make this task difficult and, like most parliamentary committees, it is liable to split along party political lines. A standing body like the EARC, in contrast, would have the necessary resources to review the operation of anti-corruption bodies to ensure they are not abusing their powers or using them over enthusiastically, nor being subjected to government interference. A provision for appointments to the EARC to have bipartisan approval would go a long way to ensuring that its advice would be genuinely independent and non-partisan. It could report to the relevant parliamentary committee.

Royal commissions report to the executive. The executive is under pressure to release the report, but is generally not under a legal obligation to do so. Many of the other more prominent integrity agencies report directly to parliament. Consideration should be given to making the reports of a royal commission go directly to parliament – possibly with a week's embargo during which the government could consider its response. The argument for this approach is that parliament has authorised extraordinary powers, and often considerable expenditure, on a matter of great public importance, which warrants public disclosure and a government response.

Governance and reform commissions: the Queensland model

The experience of the EARC in Queensland, set up as a result of the Fitzgerald Report, is an example of governance reform that was not only effective, but inspiring. The EARC produced 21 issues papers and 23 reports and created an integrity system that became the global gold standard. Indeed, the OECD's concept of an "ethics infrastructure" and Transparency International's concept of a "national integrity system" were derived from the set of institutions put in place by EARC.

I am not engaging in nostalgia for a past that seems better now than it ever was then nor am I ignoring the special dynamics of the time when anger at corruption led to an extraordinary degree of political collaboration in, and commitment to, root and branch reform when I commend the EARC approach and lament its loss. The legitimacy secured by the EARC would have enabled it to make a continuing contribution to the review, reform and development of the Queensland integrity system. This legitimacy should not have been squandered and I believe it was institutionally reckless to do so.

The task of reform is never complete. Anyone who thinks an integrity system has been perfected is ignoring the giant banana skin in their path. In Queensland, following a collaborative research project led by the Key Centre for Ethics, Law, Justice and Governance (KCELJG) at Griffith University, an Office of the Integrity Commissioner was established in

1999 with bipartisan political support. A proposal for the leaders of the main integrity agencies to meet on a regular basis was rejected by the government, but this occurred informally at state and later federal levels. The investigation, conviction and jailing of two Queensland ministers in 2009 who had not taken the governance arrangements seriously was, in part, an endorsement of the effectiveness of the integrity system, but also a shock, leading Premier Anna Bligh to initiate a review of the state's integrity and accountability arrangements which resulted in a number of proposals to strengthen the system (Queensland Government 2009).

None of the new measures proposed, however, involved comprehensive and ongoing reform with a dedicated independent body like EARC. Even if EARC were not resurrected, there are a number of ways in which its functions could be continued. David Solomon, the current Queensland Integrity Commissioner and I were disappointed that our proposals for an "EARC lite", costing so little that even a razor gang would smile, were rejected by successive Labor governments that were otherwise well disposed to our work and our proposals for reform.

It is important that governance reform commissions are not merely law reform commissions. As I have argued elsewhere, governance reform involves a combination of ethical standard setting, legal regulation and institutional reform (Sampford and Wood 1992), and requires the input of ethicists, lawyers, political scientists and economists (Sampford 2010). Legislation should not be the first resort, and alternatives should always be considered. In governance reform, legislation is often a part of the answer but is rarely the whole answer.

Conclusion

Royal commissions can fulfil important functions within an integrity system. However, they have not been studied as part of integrity systems because they are short-lived and generally ad hoc. While exercising delegated executive power, they are best seen as part of the "fourth arm" of government, reporting but not being accountable to government. Governments are able to constrain what short-term commissions can do, in the way they set and approve changes to terms of reference and make appointments. While Fred Daly's view that "a government should never set up a royal commission unless it is certain of the outcome" (Downer 1986) is a little cynical for today, it represents a real problem. I have suggested some ways of dealing with the problem, including handing decisions to a committee of the chairs of key integrity agencies and the establishment of some standing commissions. Those standing commissions should include an anti-corruption commission such as ICAC and CMC and a governance reform commission like EARC. The latter is a key part of an integrity system that is "beyond best practice" and would ensure that the integrity system is subject to continuous improvement rather than gradual erosion.

Public inquiries mentioned in chapter

(in chronological order by year of appointment, with name of chair)

Commonwealth:

Royal Commission on the Loss of HMAS Voyager (Spicer: 1964)

Royal Commission on the Statements made by Lieutenant-Commander Cabban and matters incidental to the HMAS Voyager Royal Commission (Burbury: 1967)

Royal Commission on Australian Government Administration (Coombs: 1974)

Royal Commission on the Activities of the Federated Ship Painters and Dockers Union (Costigan: 1980)

Royal Commission of Inquiry into HIH Insurance (Owen: 2001)

Commission of Inquiry into Certain Australian Companies in Relation to the UN Oil-for-Food Programme (Cole: 2005)

Independent Inquiry into the Media and Media Regulation (Finkelstein: 2011)

Royal Commission into Institutional Responses to Child Sexual Abuse (McClellan: 2013)

State and territory:

New South Wales

Royal Commission into the New South Wales Police Service (Wood: 1994)

Queensland

Royal Commission into Alleged Police Activities at the National Hotel (Gibbs: 1963)

Commission of Inquiry into Possible Illegal Activities and Associated Police Misconduct (Fitzgerald: 1987)

Queensland Floods Commission of Inquiry (Holmes: 2011)

Victoria

Victorian Bushfires Royal Commission (Teague: 2009)

References

Doig, A., and McIvor, S., 2003, "The National Integrity System: Assessing Corruption and Reform," *Public Administration and Development,* 23(4), October, 317-32

Downer, A., 1986, "McClelland Royal Commission," *Quadrant,* 30(3), 33-38

Fitzgerald, T., 1993, "An Opposition View of EARC," in Prasser, S., (ed), *Was EARC Worth It?,* Brisbane: Royal Institute of Public Administration (Qld Division), 113-15

Foster, P., 1993, "Establishing EARC," in Prasser, *Was EARC Worth It?,* 17-23

Frame, T., 1992, *Where Fate Calls: The HMAS Voyager Tragedy*, Sydney: Coronet

Hughes, C.A., 1993, "A Reform Program: Time and Methods," in Prasser, *Was EARC Worth It?,* 72-80

Key Centre for Ethics, Law, Justice, and Governance (KCELJAG) and Transparency International, 2001, "Australian National Integrity System Assessment," *Queensland Handbook*, Brisbane: KCELJAG and Transparency International

KCELJAG, 2005, "Chaos or Coherence? Strengths, Opportunities and Challenges for Australia's Integrity Systems," Brisbane: KCELJAG and Transparency International

Lewis, M., Shacklock, A., Connors C., and Sampford, C., 2013, "Integrity Reforms in Developing Countries: An Assessment of Georgia's Integrity System," *Public Integrity*, 15(3), 243-64

Nolan, The Right Hon Lord, 1995, *Standards in Public Life: First Report of the Committee on the Standards in Public Life*, London: HMSO

Preston, N., Sampford, C., and Connors, C., 2002, *Encouraging Ethics and Challenging Corruption*, Sydney: Federation Press

Queensland Government, 2009, *Response to Integrity and Accountability in Queensland*, Brisbane: Department of Premier and Cabinet, November

Ransley, J., 2001, *Inquisitorial Royal Commissions and the Investigation of Political Wrongdoing*, PhD thesis, Law School, Griffith University

Sampford, C., 2010, "From Deep North to International Governance Exemplar: Fitzgerald's Impact on the International Anti-Corruption Movement," *Griffith Law Review*, 19(3), 560-75

Sampford, C., 2010, "Adam Smith's Dinner," in O'Brien, J., and Macneil, I., (eds), *The Future of Financial Regulation*, Oxford: Hart Publishing, 23-40

Sampford, C., Smith, R., and Brown, A.J., 2005, "From Greek Temple to Bird's Nest: Towards a Theory of Coherence and Mutual Accountability for National Integrity Systems," *Australian Journal of Public Administration*, 64(2), June, 96-108

Sampford, C., and Wood, D., 1992, "The Future of Business Ethics? Legal Regulation, Ethical Standard Setting and Institutional Design," *Griffith Law Review*, 1(1) 56-72.

Shacklock, A., Saldadze, M., Connors, C., Lewis, M. and Sampford, C., 2007, "An Assessment of Georgia's National Integrity System: Final Report," Tbilisi: IEGL, Tiri and Caucasus Institute for Peace, Democracy and Development

Whitton, E., 1989, *The Hillbilly Dictator: Australia's Police State*. Sydney: ABC Enterprises

Endnotes

1 Peter Forster held senior positions in the Queensland Treasury and then established the private consultancy firm, The Consultancy Bureau. He was employed as consultant to the Fitzgerald Commission and was then appointed to lead the Implementation Unit recommended in the Fitzgerald Report. He continues as Director of The Consultancy Bureau.

6

Inquiring into disasters: contrasting styles and forms

Roger Wettenhall

Introduction

Australia is no stranger to natural disasters. The floods, cyclones and bushfires keep coming. They are especially prevalent during the summer months, and are complemented by the occasional earthquake and land slip. And each such "event" generates much investigating and reporting activity, as the community seeks to find out the causes of the disaster, the extent of damage caused, and what might be done to prevent future disasters of the same kind, or, if that cannot be done, to lessen their impact.

This chapter has two main aims. First, it offers a general introduction to the area of disaster investigating and reporting. Second, and in more depth, it directs particular attention to a division of investigating and reporting practice between two major styles: the one more legalistic and seeming mostly concerned to apportion blame for assumed errors, the other more technocratic, primarily fact-finding with a view to recommending system improvements that might reduce the impact of future disasters. The two approaches are illustrated mainly through responses to the destructive firestorm in Canberra in mid-January 2003, Canberra's own natural disaster. Since my own disaster research experience relates mostly to bushfires, my other examples come mostly from that field, although the reporting experience is likely to be fairly common across the various categories of natural disaster.

In this as in other writings about disasters as social phenomena, several matters of definition need attention. First, it is generally understood that the disaster is what happens to a settled community in all its effects; the fire, flood or cyclone is itself the disaster agent. Second, the disasters I am concerned with here are normally referred to as "natural disasters", distinguishing them from "man-made disasters" (although there may be human contributions to them like planning inadequacies or arson) and differentiating them in important ways from industrial explosions, riots and the like. And third, the full disaster experience can be quite drawn-out: for research and study purposes, it is now conventional in disaster studies to see that experience as being divided into the seven stages of warning, threat, impact, inventory, rescue, remedy and recovery. As a vital ingredient of this experience, investigating and reporting begin with inventory and continue through the following stages.

A complex accountability exercise

Investigating and reporting on disasters, like so much other investigating and reporting, has to be seen as an exercise in accountability. A useful framework for the discussion in this chapter comes from a study of political leadership in crisis events that cause major community disruption, with natural disasters providing a leading example of such events. As this study by Boin, 't Hart and colleagues notes, "the search for solutions" after such an event is inevitable and usually highly complex, and poses a huge challenge for the political leadership (Boin *et al* 2005: 2-3). The investigating-reporting-accounting process is expected to begin almost immediately after the disaster agent has struck, and it goes on through all the subsequent stages of the disaster experience. The disruptive event:

> sets in motion extensive follow-up reporting, investigations by political forums, as well as civil and criminal judicial proceedings. It is not uncommon for public officials and agencies to be singled out as the responsible actors for prevention, preparedness and response to the crisis at hand. The crisis aftermath then turns into

> a morality play. Leaders must defend themselves against seemingly incontrovertible evidence of their incompetence, ignorance or insensitivity. (Boin *et al* 2005: 8)

Consideration of a variety of such events leads to this proposition:

> Two types of reaction modes compete for dominance in the public arena. The debate may highlight the need to learn from past mistakes and induce organizations and policies to improve accordingly. Or it may zoom in on questions of responsibility and guilt. (Boin *et al* 2005: 101)

The first mode is seen as a way of optimising social abilities to prevent and absorb extreme circumstances and, through professional and technical debriefings and the like, to focus on organisational and system learning. Since it progresses using "more or less routinised organisational and political protocols, it can perform a sanitising function", and help to bring closure to the sense of community crisis. This positive effect can, however, be seriously threatened where inquiry activity and associated public debate is more combative and adversarial, more concerned to discover who is responsible and to attribute blame. This second reaction mode features "interaction between actors who are out to protect their self-interests rather than to serve the common good" (Boin *et al* 2005: 101-103).

Other contributions to this literature relate a concern with these inquiry modes to the basic questions whether to have an inquiry at all and, if so, what form of inquiry. There is no space here to offer a literature review, but other disaster researchers (eg Elliott and McGuinness 2002; Brändström and Kuipers 2003; Sulitzeanu-Kenan 2010; McConnell 2011) conclude similarly that the two modes are usually present. In a commentary published about the time a royal commission was reporting on Victoria's 2009 firestorm (further discussed below), Boin and 't Hart (2010: 357) made this further real-life application:

> The search for culprits was on, as well as the search for lessons to prevent the recurrence of such runaway fires as well as to improve

> the robustness of emergency management systems more generally. The Bushfire Royal Commission, which reported in June 2010, was the chief vehicle for this dual quest.

Whether to have an inquiry at all is a first question for governments. It is suggested here that with natural disasters of the Australian variety – notably major floods, cyclones and firestorms – they have little choice. They would be perceived as utterly derelict if they did not establish some sort of inquiry, so the only question for them is: what sort of inquiry? Moreover, since the law requires coronial investigation where there are (multiple) deaths, this is really taken out of a government's hands, although a big question remains: how is this investigation to relate to the primary inquiry?

From this brief review of the expectations created by the literature, it seems likely that the two modes will be present in all such inquiry exercises. Whether they emerge within a single inquiry mechanism or find separate "champions" is likely to depend on the structure of the particular inquiry process.

Canberra's January 2003 firestorm

While the major Australian bushfire disasters have mostly attracted inquiry by royal commissions, this did not happen in the Australian Capital Territory (ACT). The ACT never has, in its whole history as a self-governing jurisdiction, appointed a royal commission, and was not about to start now.

Major bushfires occur in extreme weather conditions – high temperatures and strong blustery winds – and usually have several points of origin, with causes varying between lightning strikes, self-combustion in overheated forest litter, wind-driven spotting from other fires, sparks from malfunctioning overhead power lines and, occasionally, arson. The usual pattern is that several initially small fires join together to create vast fire fronts. In the case of the destructive southern Tasmanian firestorm of February 1967, for example, careful investigation showed that there were about 110 individual outbreaks, many of which came together as they advanced on the suburbs of Hobart and neighbouring towns and rural properties (Wettenhall 1975).

Our firestorm of January 2003 was one that affected two jurisdictions, New South Wales as well as the ACT, and so engaged the fire protection services of both. Investigation showed that a core fire began with a lightning strike in a rugged part of NSW, just west of the ACT border, but there were many other initially separate fires in both jurisdictions that joined together to create massive fire fronts, one of which entered the western suburbs of Canberra. There were four deaths and many injuries; 501 houses were destroyed and many others severely damaged. There was also much industrial damage, such as the loss of the Mt Stromlo solar observatory and most of the pine plantation estate. The emergency was not limited to the ACT and neighbouring areas of NSW: the stormy weather that generated our firestorm also generated other fires in the NSW alpine country and Victoria, resulting in a plethora of investigating and reporting activity.

Investigating and reporting: mode-one

The fire that did most damage in Canberra reached the perimeter of the city on 18 January 2003. Just over a month later, on 20 February, ACT Chief Minister Jon Stanhope announced the establishment of an official inquiry and issued its terms of reference: in short, it was "to examine and report on the operational response to the bushfires". The principal investigator was named as Ron McLeod AM. After a long and distinguished career in the Commonwealth Public Service (Public Service Board and Department of Defence), McLeod had moved in the 1990s to roles and positions involving high-level investigating and reporting activity. He headed a major review of the *Public Service Act*, became Inspector-General of Intelligence and Security, and was appointed Commonwealth Ombudsman in 1998.

McLeod's was the first of the major investigations into the firestorm, producing one of the two substantial reports memorialising the Canberra experience, this one drawing particularly on professional and technical resources. A small team assisted McLeod in the inquiry, which considered more than 130 written submissions – including detailed submissions from all the official bodies involved and interviews with many of their personnel – and undertook inspections and visits of fire-damaged properties and related operational facilities. The final 272-page report was available after five months, at the end of July 2003, satisfying the ACT Government's desire that it should be available in time for the suggested operational changes to be considered and if necessary implemented before the next fire season. It contained 61 recommendations spread over operational and educational matters such as fuel management; fire tracks and trails; forestry settlements; aerial operations; vehicles and equipment; incident command and control; fire control manuals; the evacuate (your home) or stay issue; training and development of firefighting personnel; occupational health and safety; public information and education, and the expressed need for a more unified and independent emergency services organisation.

Significantly for the comparisons in this exploration, it seems this inquiry was fairly well insulated from the legalistic styles that lean towards the blame-seeking approach, making it a fairly clear example of mode-one at work. However, a coroner's inquiry had commenced before McLeod had completed his remit, and people whose firestorm-related activities were in some danger of being seriously questioned had a second exposure in another connection in which legal representation featured heavily. Mode-two would surface here rather than in the McLeod Inquiry.

Investigating and reporting: mode-two

The second of the major reports resulted from the rather more prolonged investigation by Coroner Maria Doogan. Clearly this investigation connected with many of the same professional and technical sources that McLeod had used, but its progress throughout was overlaid by heavy legal argument and legal posturing. In the ACT, as in most Australian jurisdictions, a coroner's remit runs both to conducting inquests into the deaths of victims of a disaster, and investigating and reporting on the circumstances of the disaster that caused those deaths. There is a coroners' roster in the ACT, and Doogan was on duty when the firestorm struck, thus acquiring responsibility for the coroner's part of the investigation. She viewed the fire damage on 19 January 2003, one day after the major strike, opened the formal inquiry on 16 June 2003, and began hearing evidence on 7 October 2003. But it was not until the final submissions by counsel were heard, in late July 2006 that the final report could be submitted in December 2006, ie 3½ years after the McLeod Report had been presented to government.

In the Coroner's own words, the report was "based on a very large quantity of exhibits, evidence and submissions by counsel ... the inquiry generated documents running to more than 10,000 pages". The two volumes of the report ran to 839 pages. There were several counsel assisting the Coroner, some in the role of "contradictors", to challenge submissions made by other counsel. There were 37 witnesses and entities represented by counsel, and 61 other witnesses not represented by counsel. With or without counsel, 23 residents of burnt or damaged properties gave evidence, and several fire behaviour experts assisted, generating much controversy about their evidence.

Another factor operated here to make this a virtual inquiry caricature. Sensing that the process was more likely to result in support for the critics of official behaviour than for the officials who had had to cope with the fire and its aftermath, the ACT Government itself and nine leading officials sought to secure the disqualification of the Coroner on the grounds of perceived bias. She refused to disqualify herself, so the proceedings moved to the Supreme Court of the ACT in September 2004. There was a unanimous judgment in her favour on 4 August 2005, allowing the suspended inquiry process to resume.

The Coroner's inquiry would always have been a slower process than the mode-one McLeod Inquiry, but this interrupting litigation made it very slow, and for a year or more the community was rife with debate about "who was responsible", doing much damage to the reputations of people who had worked strenuously and conscientiously in an effort to protect the city during the fire period. Chief Minister Jon Stanhope had been feted as a minor hero when it was revealed that he was one of two men who had dived into a water storage lake to rescue the pilot of a helicopter that had crashed while trying to refill its tanks for dumping on the fires. After the release of the Coroner's report, however, he had to face a no-confidence motion in the Legislative Assembly based on what *The Canberra Times* (1 March 2007) described as "scathing criticisms". Some who lost homes became vociferous supporters of the by-now-assumed anti-government position of the Coroner, and some even formed a new political party to contest the next ACT election.

This exercise thus exhibited the mode-two category of inquiry to the full. But two questions arise: was it necessary that it should be so? And do all coronial inquiries have this effect? I come back to these questions in considering the experience of some other Australian firestorm disasters below. But it is relevant here that Coroner Doogan herself had some awareness of the problems. In her report she noted that "some counsel conducted themselves throughout the inquiry as if they were engaged in adversarial litigation", adding: "I did not find this helpful in seeking the truth – a coroner's inquest is not an adversarial process but an inquisition designed to ascertain the facts." However, her many recommendations included observations approaching constitutional significance, including difficulties for a branch of the judiciary (as she saw herself) gaining resources from the executive government when not treated as a budget entity in its own right. Probably the most commented-on judgment was the report's strong criticism of the way the Emergency Services Bureau was managed by its senior officers during the fire period. The Coroner supported the recommendation of the McLeod Inquiry that the Bureau should become an autonomous statutory authority. Reporting so much later than McLeod, she was able to complain that, while done briefly, reversion had already occurred.

Insights from reporting on other Australian firestorms

In a study of Australian disaster experience commenced soon after the southern Tasmanian firestorm of February 1967, it was possible to assert that, although disaster planning may then have been in its infancy, a set of disaster-related administrative arrangements that had emerged from experience in past disasters was likely to guide responses when new disasters occurred. These arrangements included: the conduct of rescue work; the establishment and management of a citizens' relief appeal; speedy availability of state financial assistance for disaster victims and to facilitate reconstruction projects; and "enquiry and reform". Thus, away from bushfires, the Tasmanian government appointed a royal commission very quickly after a mine disaster in 1912 to probe the circumstances of that disaster, and the episode helped consolidate a pattern for later inquiries: the lessons learned have been overwhelmingly technical and organisational in nature, and many of the resulting recommendations are adopted – even if sometimes fairly slowly (Wettenhall and Power 1969: 270-271).

A classic earlier example of a bushfire inquiry, one frequently remembered today because of the magnitude of the disaster and the thoroughness of its report, was the royal commission investigating the firestorm that took 71 lives and burned 2,000,000 hectares in south-eastern Australia in the 1938-39 summer. Headed by Judge Leonard Stretton, this inquiry in the form of a royal commission (Stretton 1939) and the resulting report is remembered, among other things, as having "led to major changes in forest management ... such as the construction of fire towers and access trails ... and the creation of a regime of supervised burning, which still exists today" (Wikipedia 2013). In reflecting on this report from the vantage point of Victoria's 2009 firestorm, Griffiths wrote of the "enduring wisdom forged" by it and of its literary quality, and commended the strength shown by Judge Stretton in maintaining the position that his was "not an inquisitorial commission" and that he did not "represent any punitive or detection arm of the law", and his readiness to "excoriate (any) who threatened his search for the truth" (Griffiths 2012: 166, 178).

In the southern Tasmanian fires of February 1967, the fourth most devastating of all the Australian bushfire experiences – with 62 deaths, 1400 major buildings destroyed, massive stock losses and damage to rural properties – there were two inquiries, both reporting in the year of the disaster, with senior members of the legal profession again playing prominent roles (Wettenhall 1975: 222-226). Notwithstanding the input of the legal profession in the 1939 and 1967 firestorm disasters, however, the *modus operandi* in both cases fitted the mode-one inquiry style well. Although some official mistakes and errors may have been recorded, this was with a view to proposing remedies for future occasions rather than as a forum for indulging in blame-seeking like the mode-two inquiry in the Canberra case.

My own experience in living through and observing the investigating and reporting of the Tasmanian and ACT disaster events led me to inquire why Canberra had generated both mode-one and mode-two inquiries, whereas Tasmania had seemingly needed only mode-one. A check back in my book on the Tasmanian firestorm showed that I had not even bothered to index a coroner's inquiry! Had I missed something of major importance in the Tasmanian experience? And, if not, then how to explain this major difference between the two response styles?

I then corresponded with Australian National University Law College expert Hugh Selby, who provided me with an excellent brief education about coronial systems. "The move," he informed me, "for coronials to be 'socially responsible, disaster preventive inquiries' is a late 1970s, early 1980s phenomenon," and it was likely that in Tasmania in the 1960s coronials were strictly limited to manner and cause of death. The formal coronial exercise would take just a few moments for each person who died in the fires (necessary so that estates could be finalised), the exercise could be conducted by clerks of courts, and it would not therefore provide a platform for the adversarial behaviour that came to mark the coronial inquiry in Canberra (Selby 2007a).

By the time of the Canberra firestorm, the role of the coroner in the Australian states had evolved to the extent that, at least in some jurisdictions, he or she could conduct a much more wide-ranging inquiry and comment on many facets of the administrative process involved in events causing death (see Freckelton 1999; Freckelton and Ranson 2006). Thus, when another firestorm struck a rural area of South Australia in January 2005, another coroner was very blunt about what he saw as a series of errors in the handling of the disaster (Schapel 2007). His report was widely publicised, attracting much anti-government sentiment and leading to demands for the dismissal of the Chief Officer of the South Australian Country Fire Service.

Victorian Bushfires Royal Commission 2009–10

How did the public inquiry generated by the 7 February 2009 firestorm in Victoria – with 173 deaths, Australia's most calamitous bushfire disaster – reflect on these earlier experiences? The centrepiece of the inquiry exercise was undoubtedly the *Victorian Bushfires Royal Commission* appointed on 16 February 2009. This royal commission was headed by experienced investigating judge Bernard Teague (henceforth known as the Teague Royal Commission), and included Ron McLeod, fresh from leading the mode-one Canberra firestorm inquiry, and Susan Pascoe, an experienced senior executive within public and private sectors in Victoria.

In the report submitted after an 18-month inquiry, the Teague Royal Commission gave attention to the extent of its work. It had held consultations in 14 disaster-affected communities, received almost 1700 public submissions, heard 434 witnesses, and dealt with tenders of more than 1000 articles and more than 20,000 pages of transcripts.

There was also an internal research program. This was undoubtedly a major exercise in mode-one reporting, the inquiry doing a great deal to trace the progress of the fires, and the planning and management of the rescue and recovery effort. There were many important suggestions for improvements in the planning for, and handling of, future disasters.

A distinguishing feature of the Victorian inquiry was that, in appointing the royal commission, the Victorian Government separately appointed a "senior counsel" who saw himself as having a special role to protect the public interest. Considerable use was made of professional legal assistants, called "counsel assisting", who led and tested evidence given before the commission by witnesses, managed the commission's investigations, reviewed the material generated by them, and determined the evidence to be brought forward in open hearings. Their role, and relationship to the commission itself, were addressed in an important post-inquiry assessment by Susan Pascoe, one of the commissioners, who noted that they were all barristers formally engaged by the Victorian Government Solicitor after consultation between the commission chair and the senior counsel, who selected his own team, and they were supported by a contracted firm of solicitors (Pascoe 2010: 395-396).

The Teague Royal Commission became a virtual two-headed exercise, with Senior Counsel, Jack Rush QC, appearing at times to challenge the commissioners. The commission acknowledged the substantial support from counsel assisting and the legal team, but there were obvious tensions. The final report acknowledged "robust" discussion between counsel assisting and the commission on many procedural matters. Aggressive questioning of key officials, especially of the then Police Commissioner, by counsellors assisting contrasted with the more conciliatory tone of the final report in criticisms of perceived performance failures of other senior officials, and was also at odds with the commission's publicly declared intention at the outset that it was not embarking on a witch-hunt but focusing on lessons that could be learnt for the future.

What of the coronial input? The Teague Royal Commission quickly established a close and positive association with the Victorian Police, who were responsible for finalising the disaster casualty list, and with the coronial service, whose responsibility was to certify deaths and clear estates. The commission's process of having individual hearings for each death was described in Pascoe's commentary (2010: 397) as a "unique feature" of its work. This satisfied most of the families about the last movements and circumstances of the deaths of their loved ones, allowing the coroner to exercise discretion not to undertake individual or collective formal coronial inquests. This represents a significant improvement in the manner of dealing with multiple tragedies, in contrast with the duplication and overlap following the Canberra fires. It is significant that the counsel assisting played no role in these hearings. A separate lawyer was engaged by the commission to answer any questions from families that involved legal considerations. This worked well, and many families expressed their gratitude to the commission for the ease of access to the material, the competent and thorough way the police witnesses presented their evidence, and the sensitive atmosphere that prevailed.

Commissioner Pascoe's post-commission assessment implies that the technocratic and legalistic sides of this inquiry had operated harmoniously. She argued not only that a royal commission was the only form of inquiry that "would have satisfied the need to forensically investigate the causes of and response to the fires", but also that the innovative approaches it adopted in dealing with expert opinion and community consultation meant that it won bipartisan support and "reduced the legalism [usually] associated with these sorts of inquiries" (Pascoe 2010: 400). However, a conflicting view from a senior South Australian official who observed the Victorian disaster closely, drew attention to what he saw as "the adversarial approach of the Counsel Assisting," and preferred "a more considered and respectful approach" (Holmes 2010: 389).

In his survey published several years after the Victorian fires,

Griffiths reviewed several items seen as its "literary legacy". He noted commentary that "contemporary Australia responds to the dilemma of fire ... with lawyers" and that it is hard "for a profession whose primary function is to find somebody guilty or innocent not to be drawn into the blame game". He concluded that, while the Teague Royal Commission had demonstrated some significant strengths it was "less successful in guiding the adversarial legal style of the courtroom away from the pursuit of personal blame" (Griffiths 2012: 167-8, 177-8).

Is there a "best way"?

This exploration has noted the fairly widely held view that there is a division of disaster investigating and reporting practice between two modes: mode-one that is mostly fact-finding, policy-advising and technocratic in orientation; and mode-two that is far more legalistic, responsibility-attributing and blame-seeking in orientation. The experience of the 2003 Canberra firestorm illustrates the distinction, with the two modes represented by separate inquiry mechanisms. A snippet from the coroner's report on South Australia's 2005 Eyre Peninsula fires adds further support, as does commentary on Victoria's 2009 firestorm royal commission, which suggests that while the two modes were present, mode-two was somewhat modified in the sharpness of its effects because, notwithstanding tensions produced by a strong legal presence, essentially they operated within a single inquiry mechanism.

These experiences provoke the question: is there a one best way to structure and conduct these sorts of inquiries? Reporting in 2004 to the Council of Australian Governments (COAG), the *Inquiry on Bushfire Mitigation and Management* observed that inquiries such as that of the ACT Coroner were "problematic" for several reasons, including the "legalistic and potentially adversarial approach" that so often develops, the "significant periods of time" taken, and the "enormous stress" created for many individuals involved in a variety of ways in the disaster event (Ellis 2004: 233-4). Seeking a way forward, a *communiqué* issued by a National Bushfire Forum in 2007 reported:

> [W]e need a new process for inquiries, one that is effective and fair. Some of the coronial processes have become tortuous and unproductive. The Stretton report into the 1939 fires [in Victoria] was completed in three months. Four years [for these inquiries] is an excessive time and the nature of the inquiries is likely to discourage good people from pursuing careers in fire and land management. (O'Loughlin 2007: 47)

In a persuasive commentary, Selby (2007b) argues that the expertise required in investigations of disaster and emergency events is that of specialists in the relevant area of disaster and emergency, people who know what questions to pursue, with power to compel those being questioned to answer those questions, and all this "in interview rooms and at the scene of the tragedy ... not in the glare of public hearings". And that those being questioned must have an assurance that their answers cannot be used against them in criminal, disciplinary or civil proceedings – all vastly different from what happens in an inquiry process which "assumes that a lawyer is the best person to take charge of the inquiry", and "puts a confusing inquisitorial gloss over an adversary process".

Clearly contrasting inquiry styles are evident in Australian firestorm experiences. The cumulative record abundantly confirms the proposition that two modes are likely to be in operation, but it also shows that the balance between the modes has varied considerably between particular experiences. My conclusion is that, as Selby has argued, we need to do all we can to reduce the sort of legalism in which blame-seeking thrives, and that our own Canberra experience did not provide a good example to follow. This is of course a judgment on one part of the reporting process, not on the total response to the firestorm. It is instructive to consider how the more recent Victorian experience has stacked up in this context, with the two modes present but somewhat ameliorated in their opposed effects by being embraced in a single inquiry mechanism.

Perhaps a more detailed review of that inquiry and reporting experience is needed to discover just what valuable lessons it can offer.

Notes

My thanks to Ron McLeod AM for discussing with me his experiences in reporting on the 2003 Canberra and 2009 Victorian firestorms, and to Hugh Selby of the ANU College of Law for support in several ways, not least in giving me a quick course on coronial systems (and for his suggestion that I use the term "technocratic" for an operating mode that embraces professional, technical and bureaucratic elements and applies to inquiries that aim to be evidence-based in their processes). However, I accept full responsibility for all that is written.

Public inquiries and coronial inquiries mentioned in chapter

(in chronological order by year of appointment, with name of chair)

Royal Commission to Inquire into the Causes of and Measures Taken to Prevent the Bush Fires of January 1939, and to Protect Life and Property and the Measures to be Taken to Prevent Bushfires in Victoria and to Protect Life and Property in the Event of Future Bushfires (Stretton: 1939)

Inquiry into the Operational Response to the January 2003 Bushfires in the ACT (McLeod: 2003)

The Canberra Firestorm: Inquests and Inquiry into Four Deaths and Four Fires between 8 and 18 January 2003 (Doogan [Coroner]: 2006)

Inquest into the Deaths of Star Ellen Borlase, Helen Kald Castle, Judith Maud Griffith, Jody Maria Kay, Graham Joseph Russell, Zoe Russell-Kay, Trent Alan Murnane and Neil George Richardson (Schapel [Deputy State Coroner]: 2007)

Victorian Bushfires Royal Commission (Teague: 2009)

References

Boin, A., 't Hart, P., Stern, E., and Sundelius, B., 2005, *Politics of Crisis Management: Public Leadership Under Pressure,* Cambridge: Cambridge University Press

Boin, A., and 't Hart, P., 2010, "Organising for Effective Emergency Management:

Lessons from Research," *Australian Journal of Public Administration,* 69(4), December, 357-71

Brändstrom, A., and Kuipers, S., 2003, "From 'Normal Incidents' to Political Crises: Understanding the Selective Politicization of Policy Failures," *Government and Opposition,* 38(3), 279-305

Cary, G., Lindenmayer, D., and Dovers, S., (eds), 2003, *Australia Burning: Fire Ecology, Policy and Management Issues*, Collingwood, Victoria: CSIRO Publishing

Clack, P., 2003, *Firestorm: Trial by Fire*, Milton: Wiley

Elliott, D., and McGuinness, M., 2002, "Public Inquiry: Panacea or Placebo?," *Journal of Contingencies and Crisis Management,* 10(1), 14-23

Ellis, S., 2004, *National Inquiry on Bushfire Mitigation and Management Report,* Canberra: Council of Australian Governments

Freckleton, I., 1999, "Coronial Law: The Evolving Institution of the Coroner," *Alternative Law Journal,* 24(3), 156-7

Freckleton, I., and Ranson, D., 2006, *Death Investigation and the Coroner's Inquest,* Melbourne: Oxford University Press

Griffiths, T., 2012, "Remembering," in Hansen, C., and Griffiths, T., *Living with Fire: People, Nature and History in Steels Creek,* Collingwood, Victoria: CSIRO Publishing, 159-85

Holmes, A., 2010, "A Reflection on the Bushfire Royal Commission: Blame, Accountability and Responsibility," *Australian Journal of Public Administration,* 60(4), 387-391

Hyland, A., 2011, *Kinglake-350,* Melbourne: Text Publishing

McConnell, A., 2011, "Success? Failure? Something in-between? A Framework for Evaluating Crisis Management," *Policy and Society,* 30(2): 63-76.

Nairn, G., MP, 2003, House of Representatives Select Committee into the Recent Australian Bushfires, *A Nation Charred: Report on the Inquiry into Bushfires,* Canberra: Commonwealth Parliament

O'Loughlin, K., 2007, "Are big fires inevitable?," *Fire Australia,* Winter, 44-7

Pascoe, S., 2010, "The 2009 Victorian Bushfires Royal Commission: Lessons for the Conduct of Inquiries in Australia," *Australian Journal of Public Administration,* 69(4), December, 392-400

Selby, H., 2007a, Personal communication, 9 January

Selby, H., 2007b, "Inquiries too costly and time-consuming," *Canberra Times*, 22 January

Sulitzeanu-Kenan, R., 2010, "Reflecting in the Shadow of Blame: When do Politicians Appoint Commissions of Inquiry?," *British Journal of Political Science*, 40(3), 613-34

Taylor, J., and Webb, R., 2005, *Meteorological Aspects of the January 2003 South-East Australian Bushfire Outbreak*, Melbourne: Bureau of Meteorology

Wettenhall, R., 1975, *Bushfire Disaster: An Australian Community in Crisis*, Sydney: Angus and Robertson

Wettenhall, R., 1976, "Natural Disaster: Australia's Summer Fate," *Current Affairs Bulletin*, 52(11), 4-12

Wettenhall, R., and Power, J., 1969, "Bureaucracy and Disaster – 1," *Public Administration*, (Sydney), 28(4), December, 263-77

Wikipedia, 2013, "Black Friday (1939)," viewed 13 May 2013, http://en.wikipedia.org/wiki/Black_Friday_(1939)

7

Making public policy in the public interest – the role of public inquiries

Gary Banks

Introduction

It is a good time to be reflecting on the role of public inquiries. In recent years, we have seen them established in unprecedented numbers, yet, arguably, there has never been a time when there has been so much contention and division about so many important public policy issues, and so little trust in government to produce effective policy solutions.

This current situation stands in contrast to the era of economic reform in the 1980s and 1990s, when public inquiries preceded most of the major policy change, yielding large and enduring benefits – the 1979 Campbell *Committee of Inquiry into the Australian Financial System*, the 1993 Hilmer *Independent Committee of Inquiry into National Competition Policy* and the 1991 Industry Commission report on *Energy Generation and Distribution*, to name just three.

What has changed? Have public inquiries lost their ability to foster successful public policies: policies that not only do good, but are accepted as such? If so, does it matter? And what, if anything, can be done? These are some of the questions I address in this chapter, drawing on my years at the Productivity Commission and its predecessors, as well as my involvement in independent reviews such as the 1997 West *Review of Higher Education Policy* and the Prime Minister's *Taskforce on Reducing the Regulatory Burden on Business* appointed in 2005.

What is a public inquiry?

The essence of a public inquiry (by any name) is that it takes place as a discrete activity, with leadership at arms length from the executive and the bureaucracy. A public inquiry is appointed by, and provides recommendations to, government, but has no power or role in relation to implementation or subsequent administration. In other words, a typical inquiry provides policy-relevant information and advice at the front end of the policy cycle, on a take-it-or-leave-it basis. A key feature of that advice is its "publicness", responding to public terms of reference, drawing on public submissions, and, ultimately, reporting publicly.

The broad definition I use goes beyond the standard scholarly definition (Prasser 2006: 15) to include reviews conducted by the Productivity Commission, a standing body within the machinery of government. The inquiries that the Productivity Commission conducts share the ad hoc and once-off character of royal commissions and other public inquiries into important policy issues, and they have made a major contribution over the years to public policymaking. My definition, however, does not extend to parliamentary inquiries, which, though relevant, are birds of a different feather.

How can a public inquiry add value?

It seems self-evident from the extensive use of public inquiries that governments see considerable value in them. The motivation to undertake an arms-length review, from a policy perspective, generally falls into one or more of three categories. They seek to either:

1. vindicate or substantiate a policy course already being followed or intended (eg the 2010 Orgill *Building the Education Revolution Implementation Taskforce* [see chapter 14: Makin and Humphreys] or the 2010 *Fair Work Act Review Panel*);
2. determine how preferred policy directions should be framed or designed (eg the Productivity Commission's

2009 *Paid Parental Leave: Support for Parents with New Born Children* and 2011 *Disability Care and Support* reports); or

3. help establish what the policy approach in a specific area should be, whether by reviewing existing policies (eg taxation) or addressing a "new" issue (eg greenhouse or population ageing).

It is sometimes suggested that governments can be motivated more by the desire to avoid having to take policy action, or at least defer the need for it. Such intent is no doubt real, but it can be subsumed within other motives. No action effectively means supporting the policy status quo (first motive); and deferring action, which though maligned is often a beneficial strategy all round, is merely about the timing of all three. Similarly, the occasional attraction of public inquiries as a means of showing concern for an issue of (temporary) importance to the public without having to do anything substantive about it, would fall into the first category, if it succeeded.

My principal interest, however, is not just in how inquiries can help governments get what they want, but rather in how they can help obtain better outcomes for society. Ultimately, if Harry S. Truman's dictum that "good policy is good politics" is correct, as I believe it is, there should be little difference, though it appears that currently, this is not widely believed.

The question of how public inquiries contribute to achieving better policy outcomes for society is best answered by considering separately two dimensions of the policy challenge: the *technical* – determining what to do; and the *political* – getting it agreed. There is a third dimension, getting it *implemented*, which is just as important, but outside the bounds of this chapter.

Technical support

Contrary to popular opinion, few solutions to policy problems are self-evident or can be lifted from a textbook, or even from another country's practice. Some analysis of the specific nature of the problem and likely impacts of different options, including their interaction with existing policies, is generally required. For the bureaucracy, this policy work is core business, but, depending on the issue, there will not always be the necessary skills on tap, especially if more specialised or in-depth research is required, or the capacity and latitude to undertake necessary public consultations. Policy problems that cut across different portfolios or jurisdictions, or are new or highly contentious, particularly need this outside help.

Arguably, in recent years the need for independent technical advice has grown. For one thing, the analytical capacity of the bureaucracy appears to be in decline. Few departments today have in-house research units, and generalists have been displacing specialists at key levels in the public bureaucracy. This development goes some way to explaining why the Productivity Commission has been able to extend its influence into areas of policy that in earlier years would have been jealously guarded by responsible departments, and why departments increasingly rely on external consultancies, even for core policy development activities.

Budgetary pressure impacting on training and research is one factor that goes part of the way to explaining this shift. Other more fundamental contributors have been the shift to an ethos of responsiveness (read "passivity" and "reactiveness") in the public service, the related power shift to ministerial offices, and the consequently reduced attractiveness of a public service career for smart analysts – compounded no doubt by the rise in alternative sources of employment.

At the same time, the scope for public servants to engage externally in the development and design of policy appears to be more circumscribed. There have been a number of policy mishaps in recent years with unintended consequences that even cursory consultation with business would have helped avoid, such as the ill-fated initial changes to tax rules for employee shares schemes, announced ahead of the Productivity Commission's 2009 inquiry into *Executive Remuneration in Australia.*

In this context, public inquiries provide a means of marshalling dedicated expertise as well as enabling public consultation on policy options to occur without exposing government politically. For an incoming government, which may feel uncertain about the capability or inclination of incumbent bureaucrats, they offer the further advantage of providing some control over who does the job.

Political benefits

While public inquiries can help address technical challenges in policy development, their ability to improve the *politics* of policy change can be even more important. There are multiple dimensions to this:

- first, a policy initiative based on the advice of credible outside experts will generally be easier to sell to the public and parliament (eg the 1993 Hilmer *Inquiry into National Competition Policy*);
- second, and a closely related consideration, is that public inquiry processes can serve to educate and inform the public and help build broad support for policy change (eg the Productivity Commission's 2011 *Disability Care and Support* report);
- third, public inquiries can diminish the credibility and influence of special interest groups, by exposing self-serving arguments and demonstrating adverse impacts on the community (eg Productivity Commission's 2011 *Gambling* report);
- fourth, they can enable a government to credibly defer taking action in response to an emerging issue, allowing time for some of the heat or fuss to subside, as well as enabling a more considered response (eg the Productivity Commission's 2009 review of *Executive Remuneration in Australia)*;

- fifth, public inquiries can provide an opportunity for government to observe the behaviour of different interest groups and how they react to different policy proposals, leading to better informed political judgements (eg the Industry Commission's 1998 *Private Health Insurance* inquiry);
- finally, in helping governments deliver policies that work and that demonstrably benefit the community, public inquiries can engender public support for genuine reform and promote trust in government itself.

A potential downside, politically of course, is that, once in train, public inquiries can make it harder for a government to avoid adopting the policy options recommended (eg the 2005 *Taskforce on Reducing the Regulatory Burden on Business*, the various gambling inquiries by the Productivity Commission and Ross Garnaut's first *Climate Change Review* released in 2008).

For an incoming government, public inquiries can have further distinct political advantages. They can provide a plausible pretext for modifying problematic parts of a policy platform developed in Opposition. They can also provide an authoritative base for dismantling a policy introduced by a government's predecessors, in circumstances where this may otherwise be contentious or interpreted as merely ideological. In this way, they may lead to policy outcomes that are not only in the public interest, but also are less vulnerable to reversal with the next change of government. A current example is in the field of industrial relations, where the Coalition has signalled that it will ask the Productivity Commission to undertake a thorough review of the existing regulatory framework, on the strength of which it would take any substantive reform proposals to the subsequent election.

What connotes success?

It follows that, to be judged successful from a public interest perspective, an inquiry needs to achieve more than having an impact on policy; it needs to have an impact that is likely to lead to better outcomes.

Various examples come to mind of inquiries, or at least key recommendations, that managed to pass the first test, leading to policy change, but failed the second test, improving outcomes in the public interest. A recent case is the 2008 parliamentary inquiry into coastal shipping which led to legislative changes that may benefit Australian ship making and the local marine workforce, but at significant net cost to the Australian economy and community.

By the same token, there have been many review recommendations that would have passed the second test, but did not clear the first hurdle. The Productivity Commission has a long list, including its 2010 inquiry into restrictions on book imports; its 2011 recommendation for a public interest test in anti-dumping processes; and, from the Howard Government era, its 2000 broadcasting inquiry; and its 2007 inquiry recommending an end to freight-equalisation subsidies for Bass Strait shipping.

Occasionally, a public inquiry will fail on *all* counts, its recommendations neither being taken forward by government nor likely to benefit the community in the long term. A very recent example is the Finkelstein Inquiry recommendations relating to freedom of the press (see chapter 9: Tiffen).

Increasing the prospects of inquiry success

So what are the preconditions for an effective inquiry? There are at least six determinants of success that are within the control of government.

Selecting the right topic

Public inquiries generally involve considerable set-up costs and extensive public participation. The use of this mechanism for policy advice therefore needs to be reserved for issues that warrant the effort. Generally, inquiries are best suited to issues that are technically complex and politically contentious, and where there is much at stake for society in getting it right. Complexity alone is unlikely to provide sufficient justification, as experts can always be called in without the need for a full-blown inquiry. However, an issue that is not technically complex, but is highly contentious or has the potential to create winners and losers could still warrant an arms-length review if the gains from getting the policy right are potentially large. Tariff protection is a case in point, an area where reforms in the national interest confront strong and politically influential resistance from sectional interests. Inquiries have enabled claims to be publicly scrutinised, faulty arguments exposed, and the benefits and beneficiaries from specific reforms to be identified and quantified.

Scanning the large number of reviews that have taken place during the past decade, it is hard to find many that involved no political sensitivity at all. Most reviews address issues or topics where the benefits from improved policy outcomes would more than outweigh the costs of the review. However, the stakes for the public interest vary greatly. This is true even for Productivity Commission reviews, where significant effort is devoted to screening and selecting topics. In recent years, the Commission has, at one end of the scale, undertaken reviews on topics as diverse as private health insurance, consumer policy, electricity network regulation and broadcasting; and, at the other, battery egg sales in the ACT and reviews of local government exemptions from Section 20 of the *Trade Practices Act*.

Perversely, the sheer number of reviews at any one time will diminish their contribution, even when there is no doubt about the significance of the policy issues. For example, early in the first Rudd administration, major reviews were simultaneously underway for higher education, health and hospitals, taxation, defence, climate change, innovation, quarantine, 457 migration visas, national infrastructure, and assistance to the car and textiles industries. This is aside from several important inquiries by the Productivity Commission covering consumer policy, paid parental leave, and drought policy, and many other reviews of less important matters.

The failure of some of these inquiries to realise their potential can be attributed, at least in part, to the inability of government to give them the attention they needed, particularly at the crucial response and implementation stage. Arguably, advancing tax reform or health system reform alone on the scale envisaged could have fully occupied the first term of even the most ambitious government.

Asking the right questions

The old saying about "ask a silly question" is apt for public inquiries. The potential of an inquiry to contribute to good policy depends heavily on what is expressly asked of it. An inquiry has to be directed by the commissioning government. It cannot be allowed to become a happy hunting ground or loose cannon. However, if it is directed in its brief to do unproductive things, or is excluded from doing certain things that, from a public interest perspective, should be examined, then the inquiry is predestined for failure, or at least to making a lesser contribution.

The Productivity Commission has two procedural protections against "silly questions". One is the convention that terms of reference for a prospective inquiry are first given in draft form. This is principally intended to ensure that the task is comprehensible and feasible, but also serves to elicit comments on scope and utility that can help avert later problems. The second protection is the provision in the Commission's enabling legislation that permits it to consider any matters relevant to the task at hand, even if these are not specifically mentioned in the terms of reference. This has helped ensure that the Commission can address issues that are important to a good outcome, but which may only emerge in the course of public consultations or research.

In some cases, government may wish to exclude some part of the policy terrain from a review. While this is procedurally legitimate, and indeed understandable, to avoid debilitating the inquiry, the excluded issues need to be "separable" and not integral to the main thrust of the review.

In the Industry Commission's 1998 *Private Health Insurance* inquiry, the rest of the health system was ruled out of scope because at that time the government was responding to a more narrowly targeted community concern about price rises for health premiums. While this veto was respected, the Commission felt it necessary to consider different possible reform directions for the health machine as a whole, to ensure that recommendations to improve this one "cog" would be complementary.

The Henry *Australia's Future Tax System Review,* set up in 2008, was presented with a much bigger obstacle in seeking to reform Australia's tax system without being able to recommend changes to the GST. This was not a "separable" matter and, while the Henry Tax Review came up with an alternative proposal for putting more weight on the consumption base, its report was handicapped and its value diminished. The issue, of course, has not gone away. Indeed, momentum has been gradually building over the past couple of years for the GST to be restored to the tax policy agenda. However, this will now require new policy foundations to be laid and valuable time has been lost.

The *Fair Work Act Review Panel* appointed in 2010 contained no explicit exclusions, but its terms of reference were framed to ensure a focus on legalistic aspects of the Act's implementation, rather than broader impacts on industry and the economy. This was justified on the basis that it was merely a post-implementation review, triggered by the failure to undertake a regulation impact statement when the regulations were being formulated. However, as the Productivity Commission has argued, a post implementation review should be as wide in scope as the regulation impact statement for which it is effectively a substitute. The final report of the panel was welcomed by unions and many of its recommendations were accepted by government. However, business groups expressed disappointment that the review had not addressed their substantive concerns, arguing that the inquiry should have been conducted by the Productivity Commission. A member of the review panel defended the report by asserting that the Commission could have done no better given the same terms of reference, ignoring the Commission's economy-wide analytical framework and its statutory ability to look at related matters.

Getting the timing right

In the art of comedy, timing is everything. The same could be said about public inquiries. While provoking laughter may not be as positive a sign for an inquiry as it is for comedy, timing can make the difference between success and failure.

Choosing the right time to hold an inquiry is a first rule for success – "the right thing at the wrong time is the *wrong* thing." For example, if the political obstacles to desirable change in some policy areas vary inversely with business conditions, it will generally be better to tackle such areas when business conditions are good. It was ironic, for instance, that the long-awaited National Competition Policy *Review of Australia's Anti-Dumping and Countervailing System* (which protects imports from "unfairly low" prices) was finally sent to the Productivity Commission in 2010 when an appreciated dollar was placing extra competitive pressure on local manufacturers. The predictable outcome was rejection of the Commission's key public interest recommendation and the recasting of the anti-dumping regime to make it more receptive to an industry's complaints about imports.

For similar reasons, it is not wise for an inquiry on a sensitive matter to report near the time of an election. Regardless of its merits, the report will inevitably become a political football. This was no doubt part of the story with the Henry Tax Review, compounded in that case by the government having had the report for six months before releasing it and then choosing to respond only to the politically most contentious recommendations, in isolation from other balancing proposals.

There have been plenty of examples over the years of Productivity Commission reports being rejected, or responses to them distorted, because of a looming election, to the point where in later years, the Commission found pretexts for delaying the completion of a number of its draft reports, knowing that they would be better received and more influential if released after the election.

Conversely, there can be a political gain in initiating an inquiry in the lead up to an election. A government is thereby seen to be taking an issue seriously, while ensuring that no action will be necessary until the next term, which will possibly have to be undertaken by the other side. At the Productivity Commission, the arrival of a pork inquiry (an industry that spans key electorates) invariably heralded a looming election.

Another important consideration is duration – the time allowed for an inquiry. If consultation is to be more than a token gesture, it is hard to complete a public inquiry in less than six months. There are, of course, plenty of examples of reviews meeting tighter deadlines (see chapter 10: Flood), but they are not heavily represented among the success stories.

A short sharp review can help government get the answer it needs in a politically convenient timeframe, depending on who undertakes it. But in most cases, lack of consultation will rebound on a review's credibility and reduce its political value. It can also make it hard to get the right answer where complexity is a factor. These sorts of issues clouded the public's reaction to such reports as the Howard Government's 2007 review of carbon abatement policies and the Gillard Government's 2011 review of population policy.

Selecting the right people (in the right settings)

The contribution an inquiry can make often comes down to who does the job and what incentives or disciplines they face. Getting either the personnel or the settings wrong can predestine failure against at least one of the dual tests of "influence" and "outcome". Controversy around appointments makes it hard for an inquiry to develop the public credibility it needs. Over the years, a number of major inquiries have started off badly in this respect, including the 2006 Warburton-Hendy *International Comparisons of Australian Taxes Review*; the 1997 West *Review of Higher Education*; the 2008 Bracks *Inquiry into the Automotive Industry*; the 2010 Orgill *Building the Education Revolution Implementation Taskforce*; and the 2012 McCallum *Fair Work Act Review Panel.*

The qualities of the people involved in an inquiry and the governance arrangements under which they operate are interconnected, and some trade-offs between them may be possible, depending on the topic under review.

The minimum requirement for personnel could be expressed as "competence without conflicts". Desirable additional qualities are integrity, openness of mind, and independence of spirit. Admittedly, these are demanding requirements, and people with all of these are not in abundant supply.

Governments will often be torn between their natural inclination to appoint a person they trust and the desirability of that person having wider credibility.

There will generally be scope to find such people if a government tries hard enough. "Trying hard" is important as such appointments typically receive intense scrutiny from interested stakeholders. They will rightly see the qualities and connections of an appointee as having an important bearing on their chances of at least getting a good hearing, if not the outcome they want. A review that cannot withstand such scrutiny will struggle to get broad participation in its processes, and for its recommendations to be accepted as being in the public interest.

Equally important are the governance arrangements of an inquiry. Arguably, the more independent the institutional setting, and the more rigorous and transparent its procedures, the less reliance needs to be placed on the qualities of the appointees heading it. A secret of the success of the Productivity Commission and its predecessors in producing consistently good reports, notwithstanding the unavoidable variation in the abilities of the outside appointees to specific inquiries, lies in the quality of its processes and the dedication of its core support staff.

Many public inquiries are supported by departmental secretariats. This has pros and cons, depending on the topic and the department. Central agencies have generally performed better than line agencies, reflecting their broader responsibilities. The 1993 Hilmer *National Competition Policy Review* is a good example, contrasting with the 2004 Hogan *Review of Pricing Arrangements in Residential Aged Care*. The 2005 *Rethinking Regulation Taskforce* was allocated a secretariat drawn from several departments, with representation also from the Productivity Commission. This proved challenging to manage, but was ultimately very effective.

A recent development is the appointment of departmental heads alongside external appointees to lead policy reviews. In 2007, Peter Shergold, Secretary of the Department of Prime Minister and Cabinet, chaired the *Prime Ministerial Task Force Group on Emissions Trading*. A year later Jeff Harmer, Secretary of the Department of Families, Housing, Community Services and Indigenous Affairs, led the *Pension Review*. And the Secretary of Treasury, Ken Henry was appointed in 2008 to chair the *Australian Future Tax System Review Panel*. This approach benefits from the undoubted policy skills and experience of agency heads, but deprives a government of the benefits to be gained from "deniability" and policy learning at one step remove. And there will always be suspicions that the inquiry's findings and recommendations have been discussed with government ministers in advance. This is an understandable concern, one from which even arms-length reviews are not immune.

Such considerations may have been behind former Prime Minister Rudd's use of the term "commission" in his early references to the Henry Tax Review. The fact that the Review did not have the independence commensurate with that terminology made it hard to persist with the title. The lack of separation from government also made it hard for the review to issue preliminary recommendations for public scrutiny and debate. If it had, much of the subsequent political fallout might have been averted.

Ensuring transparency

Transparency is a key dimension of a successful inquiry and a key source of the value an inquiry can add to public policy development.

Public servants, despite their title, are neither trained nor encouraged to be open with the public, at least not when it comes to policy matters. Their main connection to the public is through their minister. Ministers vary in attitude and inclination, but most do not want their departments to be out consulting publicly on sensitive policy matters. For one thing, anything revealed or said by departmental officials is likely to be interpreted as the minister's or government's own views.

For another, an arms-length review enables findings to be tested and policy options floated without implicating government itself. It is an opportunity to learn about likely reactions to different courses of action without incurring the political pain of actually experiencing them. Moreover, the public testing of preliminary ideas can serve to reveal unintended potential consequences while there is still the opportunity to avert them, and to do so on the front foot.

Transparency amounts to more than mere consultation. A lot of policy consultations and conversations take place without transmitting meaningful information. Transparency requires that relevant interests be fully informed about the nature of a policy problem, and how particular proposals might be expected to address them. In other words, it requires that people understand what is going on in the minds of policy makers, so that they are in a position of being able to tell government whether that accords with their own experience and how they are likely to be affected by particular measures.

When done openly and thoroughly, consultation can have great informational and political value, as exemplified by the Productivity Commission's 2005 inquiry into the *Impact of Competition Policy Reforms on Rural and Regional Australia*. Private or poorly conducted consultations, on the other hand, can result in bad policy decisions because they are vulnerable to capture by the organised or the "impassioned", whose interests rarely coincide with those of the wider community.

To the extent that there is anything akin to revealed truth in public policy, it depends more on iteration than revelation. In public inquiries the key conduits for this are the public availability of submissions and, importantly, the exposure of preliminary findings and recommendations.

There are few inquiries that would not benefit from feedback on draft findings. The convention that no recommendations from the Productivity Commission go to government without first having been circulated in a draft report has been crucial to the Commission's effectiveness. In many cases, as a result of feedback, the final recommendations have differed significantly from those in its draft reports.

Yet there are still many instances of public inquiries where submissions are released late, or kept secret, or where recommendations are not tested in advance. The lack of a draft report might have been a factor in undoing the proposals on mining taxation in the Henry Tax Review and in reinforcing suspicions that the McCallum *Fair Work Act Review Panel* was merely about endorsing the status quo and closing down debate.

Handling the report well

Even the best inquiry may come to nought if its report is mishandled. The key point is that a public inquiry is only one input into policy decision-making. Ultimately, decisions will be made in the political realm, where the views and skills of leaders – including how they read the politics and their capacity to influence opinion – play a decisive role.

Government may find a report's key recommendations unpalatable on ideological or political grounds (assuming it is technically sound) and simply reject them out of hand. Vintage examples of reports meeting this fate include former Prime Minister John Howard's rejection of the Productivity Commission's draft recommendation to remove subsidies for Bass Strait shipping the night before the report was released, and the pre-emptive rejection of "student centred funding" (vouchers) following the West Review. A more contemporary case is the Productivity Commission's inquiry into "default" superannuation provisions in industrial awards where, prior to the finalisation of the report, the minister publicly indicated a policy position on the union funds' role that was contrary to the Commission's draft recommendation.

The rejection or setting aside of key recommendations need not negate an inquiry's longer-term value. Many inquiries have had their recommendations spurned initially, only to have them revisited and implemented at a later date, following a change of government or in a different political climate. Taxation is a classic example. Recommendations of the Asprey *Taxation Review Committee*, commissioned by the McMahon Coalition Government in 1972, languished for over a decade before being revived under the Hawke Labor Government, with a further decade passing before one of the recommendations, for a consumption tax, was finally implemented. The report of the Henry Tax Review similarly contains many recommendations of enduring relevance, despite the short shrift they received. Tariff reform provides another illustration, with the Industry Assistance Commission's advocacy of top-down general reductions taking several years to be reflected in policy, again under the Hawke Government. And developments in higher education financing and regulation have seen many of the West Review's proposals gradually adopted over time. It can take quite a while for novel policy ideas to be properly understood and to gain acceptance.

Even where a government is broadly supportive of an inquiry's findings from the outset, a number of factors influence eventual implementation. How and when government chooses to release the inquiry report, relative to its own response, is crucial. There is no rule book here; it is a matter for political judgment. There are two main options, either to release a report ahead of a full response, or to release the report and announce the response at the same time. Both options have been exercised often, but not always to good effect.

Early release of a report enables additional lobbying to occur. At this point, the lobbying will be politically directed and take place behind closed doors, negating the transparency value of the public inquiry. This can be particularly difficult with a minority government, where advocacy groups can target those individual parliamentarians who find themselves fortuitously in a position of great influence, but who may lack the knowledge or incentive to distinguish the national interest from their own electoral or personal interests. The unsatisfactory outcomes for gambling regulation and carbon policy for the Gillard Government were in large part due to the leverage that pressure groups were able to apply through one or two independent parliamentarians. Early release is therefore best reserved for reports where complexity and implementation detail warrant additional testing, or where for some reason there has been no opportunity to adequately test a report's findings in advance.

Simultaneous release is most valuable where an issue is politically contentious, where due process has been upheld, and of course where government is confident that the recommended course of action is in the best interests of the public.

The worst strategy is to keep a report under wraps for too long, or not to respond to it at all. This can only serve to diminish the standing and the value of a public review. The first tactic has recently been adopted by some state governments for their commission of audit reports. An ironic instance of non-response is the Commonwealth's failure to respond to a review it commissioned in 2009 from the Australian Law Reform Commission into the efficiency and effectiveness of public inquiries (see chapter 1: Croucher). A good feature of the Productivity Commission legislation is a requirement that all inquiry reports be tabled in the Commonwealth Parliament within 25 sitting days.

Irrespective of timing, the outcomes of an inquiry will depend on how skilfully any negotiations are conducted. This is not just about clinching a deal (any deal) for the sake of early agreement and a triumphant press conference, as the Rudd Government's decision on a minerals resource rent tax (RSPT) shows. The policy which emerged from quick and exclusive negotiations might best be characterised as throwing the revenue baby out with the RSPT bathwater. Another, less extreme, example was the Coalition government's deal with the Australian Democrats a decade earlier to get the Goods and Services Tax (GST) over the line. To succeed in introducing a consumption-based tax, even an imperfect one, was preferable to failing for a third time, but the exemptions and design inflexibility that formed the *quid pro quo* have left an increasingly costly legacy.

Political negotiation can be rendered more tractable where an inquiry has helped educate the public about what is at stake. The negotiations leading to the introduction of the National Disability Insurance Scheme and the Opposition's support for the policy were assisted by the broadening of the public's own understanding as a result of the Productivity Commission's inquiry. The inquiry report was frequently invoked in the public debate.

The same could not be said of gambling reform, where sound evidence, broad community support and even signs of political will ultimately failed to prevail over vested interests. The gambling story shows how political deals can weaken the integrity of a policy package. Removing a measure that is complementary to others, or changing the sequencing of a carefully devised program rollout may end up strengthening the hand of those opposing reform. In the gambling case, the perceived need for speed to satisfy a key independent member of parliament, contrary to the more cautious, incremental approach advised by the Productivity Commission, meant the undoing of real reform.

Conclusion

A long-term observer of the Australian scene might easily conclude that the quality of public policy in this country is inversely related to its quantity, and that this holds true most strongly in times of plenty.

The accumulated deadweight cost of poor policy is substantial. But, as Adam Smith reportedly replied to a young Hanrahan of his time, "Be assured, my young friend, there is a great deal of ruin in a nation." Smith himself, however, campaigned consistently and eloquently against policies (such as protectionism) that he saw as potentially the most ruinous. There are certain areas of policy where bad decisions inflict a particularly heavy price. Unfortunately, these tend to be the policy areas with a greater predisposition to poor decision-making, areas where complexity and ignorance can be exploited to benefit special interests rather than the public interest.

Well-targeted and properly conducted public inquiries provide a useful mechanism for penetrating complexity, and countering asymmetric political pressures on government. There is more reason to employ such arrangements today than ever before. Loss of policy analytic capability within the public service, compounded by erosion of procedural protections, have in some areas made policy "co-production" with special commissions and taskforces more of a necessity than a luxury.

Experience tells us that governments do not always resort to public inquiries with noble intent. Yet when they do, there are pitfalls to avoid if their goal is to be realised. For one thing, it is crucial that the right topics be addressed in the right timeframes, and not too many at any one time; for another, the reviews need to be conducted by the right people, who are acting under the right governance arrangements. Even when all these boxes have been ticked, a successful outcome is still not assured. How well the commissioning government handles the inquiry's report will often be a deciding factor.

All that being said, policy experience in sensitive areas suggests that even a poorly structured public inquiry may sometimes be better than the alternative.

Public inquiries mentioned in chapter

(in chronological order by year of appointment, with name of chair)

Taxation Review Committee (Asprey: 1972)

Committee of Inquiry into the Australian Financial System (Campbell: 1979)

Independent Committee of Inquiry into National Competition Policy (Hilmer:1993)

Review of Higher Education Policy (West: 1997)

Review of Pricing Arrangements in Residential Aged Care (Hogan: 2004)

Taskforce on Reducing the Regulatory Burden on Business (Banks: 2005)

International Comparison of Australian Tax Comparison Review (Warburton and Hendy: 2006)

Prime Ministerial Task Force Group on Emissions Trading Scheme (Shergold: 2006)

Climate Change Review (Garnaut: 2007)

Australian Future Tax System Review Panel (Henry: 2008)

Pension Review (Harmer: 2008)

Inquiry into the Automotive Industry (Bracks: 2008)

Fair Work Act Review Panel (McCallum: 2010)

Building the Education Revolution Implementation Taskforce (Orgill: 2010)

Independent Inquiry into the Media and Media Regulation (Finkelstein: 2011)

References

Banks, G., 2010, *An Economy-wide View: Speeches on Structural Reform*, Canberra: Productivity Commission

Banks, G., 2012, *Advancing the Reform Agenda: Selected Speeches*, Canberra: Productivity Commission

Prasser, S., 2006, *Royal Commissions and Public Inquiries in Australia*, Sydney: LexisNexis Butterworths

Endnotes

1 This chapter is adapted from the *Inaugural Peter Karmel Lecture in Public Policy*, hosted by the Academy of the Social Sciences in Australia in conjunction with the Australian New Zealand School of Government and delivered at the Shine Dome, Canberra on 3 July 2013.

Section 3

What inquiries do and how they do it

Scott Prasser and Helen Tracey

Governments have various reasons for their persistence in creating new independent external inquiries, but the major impetus comes from a desire to be seen as rational decision makers, relying on the best available evidence to make decisions that serve the public interest. For the appearance of rational policymaking in the public interest, a public inquiry is an instrument without peer.

In modern government, the stakes for rational guidance for policy decisions are high. Governments risk losing trust and legitimacy if their decisions appear to be purely political, serving narrow or partisan interests at the expense of other groups in society. The best public inquiries gather evidence, conduct research, garner expert advice, establish facts, provide analysis, test ideas, assess options and propose a solution, appropriate action or a way forward. The report of an independent public inquiry ideally is a key instrument for legitimation of government action, an assurance that national rather than sectional interests are being served.

With seemingly limitless demands on the public purse, the need to justify policy decisions in terms of the best available evidence is paramount. A government which rolls out untested or heavily contested programs requiring large-scale public investment or takes legislative action without a strong rationale is acting irresponsibly, failing the first principles of good governance. Evidence is clearly not everything – politics as well as policy have a large part to play in government decision-making; the two need to find a proper balance. But evidence is critically important to good public policy and sound political decisions. The political negotiation involved in most government decision-making can be rendered more tractable where an inquiry has already aired the issues, educated the public about what is at stake and provided reasoned arguments for alternative courses of action. Policies that are poorly conceived, not informed by evidence, may miss the mark entirely, need to be adapted and altered soon after introduction, be costly, represent a lost opportunity or actually do harm. While there can never be certainty that a particular policy will work, the probability of failure is increased if policies are determined without evidence or analysis. Such policies more easily fall prey to the law of unintended consequences and can lead to costly and damaging mistakes. As a former Finance Minister in the first Rudd Government, Lindsay Tanner, observed when lamenting the decline in the quality of public policymaking, every government dollar wasted on a poor program is a dollar lost to the poor, and to the government to spend on its policy priorities.

With such a premium on good policy advice, it is small wonder that governments frequently choose an independent expert inquiry as a way of investigating complex, significant or contentious issues and ultimately creating confidence in their policy decisions. Inquiries enable governments to learn more about difficult policy problems and how to handle them.

As they involve a significant investment of public resources, public inquiries are expected to follow good process. It is an adage in policymaking that good process is integral to good policy. Good processes may be no guarantee of good policy, but poor processes inevitably lead to poor policy. The processes of public inquiries are a major source of their strength. They generally involve commissioned research, consultation, public submission and often both draft and final reports. A good process will be genuinely consultative, transparent as far as that is appropriate to the issue at hand, informed by evidence from a wide range of sources, and educational. It will involve gathering information effectively and objectively, digesting the evidence, establishing the facts, considering alternatives and testing possible solutions with an engaged public before making recommendations. Through these processes, the best public inquiries promote greater understanding of a complex issue and inform political decision-making.

The various inquiries considered in this section exemplify both the achievement and non-achievement of these benefits of public inquiries and demonstrate the many factors that influence the operation and impact of an inquiry.

Father Frank Brennan, Professor of Law at the Australian Catholic University, chaired the *National Human Rights Consultation*, an independent inquiry (by yet another name) appointed by the Rudd Labor Government in December 2008. The main purpose of the Consultation was to seek the views of the Australian community on the need for protection of human rights. It was also expected to raise awareness about human rights, seek out diverse views, identify key issues for government, and report "on the issues raised and the options identified for the Rudd Government to consider to enhance the protection and promotion of human rights". The Consultation was asked to consider the advantages and disadvantages of each of the options it presented, with the proviso that "the options identified should preserve the sovereignty of the Parliament and not include a constitutionally entrenched bill of rights".

Brennan's account of the processes adopted by his inquiry for gathering and analysing evidence could be a template for any policy process relying on the collection and analysis of public views in order to bring new evidence forward to underpin policy action. In chapter 8, he outlines the different approaches his committee used to collect public opinion and describes the detailed analysis undertaken. The chapter well illustrates the highly educative role a public inquiry can play. A well designed and well managed public consultation has the potential to educate and inform as well as to listen. On the basis of the information gathered, the Brennan committee recommended that Australia enact a comprehensive Human Rights Act and a range of other measures to protect human rights in Australia, including strengthening the Australian Human Rights Commission, enhancing human rights education, improving parliamentary scrutiny of human rights, improving access to justice and addressing Indigenous disadvantage and exclusion. In response, on 21 April 2010 the Attorney-General announced a new 'Human Rights Framework' for Australia, which accepted many of the committee's recommendations but did not commit to a Human Rights Act. For all that its main recommendation was not accepted, the Consultation report stands as a guide to the views of the Australian community on human rights and an analysis of the pros and cons of different policy directions. It signals the great informational and political value of a public consultation when it is done openly and thoroughly and when the findings are soundly analysed.

Another government inquiry whose main recommendations failed to become law, for reasons more to do with the political context than the intrinsic merit of the inquiry process, was the 2011 Finkelstein *Independent Inquiry into the Media and Media Regulation.* In chapter 9, Rodney Tiffen, a Professor of Government who worked on the inquiry, explains how factors such as the political motivation for the inquiry, tight timelines, constrained terms of reference, and the political context in which the report was delivered, militated against acceptance of the inquiry's recommendations. Half the battle for an effective public inquiry is fought at the outset, in the way the problem is presented, the objectives set and the questions framed. If policy problems, especially controversial ones, are poorly framed or tilted in a particular direction, the result is likely to be distorted. The Finkelstein Inquiry was set up in the wake of phone hacking scandals by the media in the UK, which led to the appointment there of the Leveson *Inquiry into the Culture, Practice and Ethics of the Press.* Leveson's attention was mainly focused on the activities of the Murdoch-owned *News of the World.* At home, the Gillard Labor Government was feeling aggrieved at their coverage in the Murdoch press, and it was this grievance that lay behind the inquiry's task to examine media codes of ethics, their effectiveness and enforcement. This aspect of the inquiry coloured the reaction to the Finkelstein proposals by the media, which was quick to interpret them as an attack on the freedom of the press.

Despite the pressure on the Finkelstein Inquiry to report in a constricted timeframe, a pressure the Inquiry met, the government's response was delayed and then mishandled politically, in both style and content. The media – not an uninterested party in this case – had a field day, presenting many different interpretations of the content of the report, only some of which accorded with reality. The inquiry therefore failed in its public education function as well as in terms of policy impact. After a fierce and antagonistic reaction from the press, the government's reform proposals were abandoned and the inquiry itself, unfairly according to Tiffen, was judged a failure.

One criticism sometimes levelled at public inquiries is that they slow down the business of government. Sometimes, it is said, they are deliberately set up to do just that. Not so Philip Flood's *Inquiry into Australian Intelligence Agencies*, which commenced on 4 March 2004, was completed on 20 July 2004 and was accepted by government two days later. In chapter 10, Flood, a former Commonwealth agency head and senior diplomat, recounts the approach he took to achieving his well-nigh impossible deadline, and the factors that led to the inquiry's recommendations being fully accepted at such speed. Perhaps in other areas of public policy, the high level cooperation the inquiry attracted would not be forthcoming and the streamlined processes it adopted would not be appropriate. But where national security is at issue, the stakes are high and the inquiry instrument, more renowned for being slow and cumbersome than lean and lithe, met the need.

As Flood reveals, his inquiry's effectiveness owed much to the high calibre of the people involved – both experts and secretariat support - and the timeliness of its report as well as the fit-for-purpose processes followed and the intelligent non-partisan response from both politicians and the commentariat. These are all critical factors in a successful inquiry. Lack of respect for the membership of an independent review and poor processes will quickly undermine its legitimacy. The quality of the people involved and the operational arrangements of an inquiry are interconnected and are largely within the control of the inquiry chair. The political environment however is not.

It was the political environment which influenced the impact of two inquiries into drought policy almost twenty years apart, in 1990 and 2008, analysed in chapter 11 by Professor Linda Botterill, a rural policy expert at the University of Canberra. Botterill shows how similar inquiries can have very different impacts on policy. She finds that the secret of an inquiry's success, measured in terms of influence on policy, lies more in questions of timing, political motivation and a government's policy 'readiness' than in factors intrinsic to the inquiries themselves. The more comprehensive, open inquiry of 2008 had less impact on the directions of drought policy than the more limited 1990 *Drought Policy Review Task Force*. The 1990 inquiry brought about a major shift, with drought policy thereafter being based on principles of risk management and self-reliance rather than being dealt with as a disaster response. This success was the result of the inquiry having a clear mandate for change, at a time when government was embarked on an extensive program of economic and agricultural policy reform. The later inquiry, by contrast, was more reactive to specific problems and lacked the sense of being a genuine, open policy review within a clear political narrative.

This stands in stark contrast to the political motivation behind the *Royal Commission on Australian Government Administration* (Coombs Commission) appointed by the Whitlam Labor Government in 1974 in order to find ways to harness the public service more effectively to the government's purposes. In chapter 12, Paddy Gourley, a former senior Commonwealth public servant, explores the nature of this iconic review and the reasons for its enduring impact on Australian public administration. The seeds of its success lie in the quality of its personnel, the broad scope of the inquiry and the thoroughness and openness of its processes. The Coombs Commission's recommendations, made in 1976 to the new Fraser Coalition Government in a five-volume, 2000 plus page report, have had a long lasting influence on Australian public life, standing well above partisan politics. As Gourley explains, this positive impact is founded on the quality of the inquiry itself, the extensive evidence it collected and the cogent arguments it put forward for action, in addition to the considered approach to implementation, initially by the Fraser Government which had a particular interest in some aspects of the reforms proposed, and subsequently by the Hawke Labor Government which came to power in 1983 with a commitment to more comprehensive "quality of government" reform. In this case, only an independent expert inquiry could have achieved such major change.

The example of the Coombs Commission shows, however, that the success of any inquiry depends not only on how well it goes about its task, but also on the design of the task in the first place and a raft of accidental factors to do with timing, people and political events.

8

The National Human Rights Consultation

Fr Frank Brennan SJ AO

Introduction – the committee of inquiry

I was privileged to chair the *National Human Rights Consultation* established in 2008 (henceforth, the Consultation) with a committee – Mary Kostakidis, Mick Palmer and Tammy Williams, assisted by Philip Flood – who had diverse views about how best to protect human rights in Australia. The Murdoch press was fond of portraying us as a group of like-minded "lefties". The diversity of our views, however, ensured the transparency and integrity of our processes, especially given that we did not reach agreement on our recommendations about a Human Rights Act until five minutes to midnight.

As chair, I was on the record favouring a modest statutory human rights act. But our individual opinions were irrelevant to the task at hand, which was to conduct a public consultation on three questions posed in our terms of reference:

1. Which human rights (including corresponding responsibilities) should be protected and promoted?
2. Are these human rights currently sufficiently protected and promoted?
3. How could Australia better protect and promote human rights?

We were asked to identify options that would preserve the sovereignty of parliament and not include a constitutionally entrenched bill of rights.

The consultation process

In seeking the views of the Australian public on these questions, we made use of new technologies, conducted community consultations, and received tens of thousands of submissions. I ran a Facebook page. We hosted a blog and commissioned academics on opposite sides of the argument to steer the blog debate. We held three days of hearings, which were broadcast on the new Australian Public Affairs Channel. During the course of our consultation, various groups ran campaigns for and against a Human Rights Act in the wake of Australia's ongoing exceptionalism, Australia being the only remaining country in the British common law tradition without some form of Human Rights Act. Groups like GetUp! and Amnesty International ran strong campaigns in favour of a Human Rights Act, accounting for 25,000 of the 35,000 submissions we received. My committee did not see itself as having the competence or authority to distinguish campaign-generated submissions from other submissions. We simply decided to publish the figures and let people make their own assessments.

We engaged a social research firm, Colmar Brunton, to run focus groups and administer a detailed random telephone poll of 1200 persons. The poll highlighted the issues of greatest concern to the Australian community.

Figure 1. Relative Importance of Social Issues

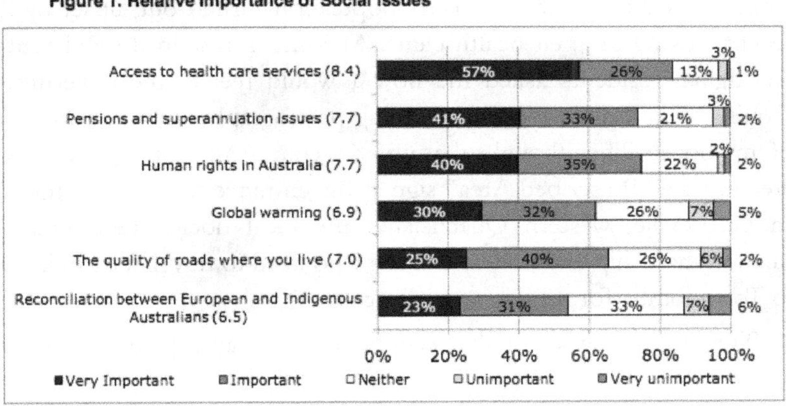

At community roundtables, participants were asked what prompted them to attend. Some civic-minded individuals simply wanted the opportunity to attend a genuine exercise in participative democracy; they wanted information just as much as they wanted to share their views. Many participants were people with grievances about government service delivery or particular government policies. Some had suffered at the hands of a government department or at least knew someone who had been adversely affected – a homeless person, an aged relative in care, a close family member with mental illness, or a neighbour with disabilities. Others were responding to invitations to involve themselves in campaigns that had been instigated when the Consultation was launched. Against the backdrop of these campaigns, the committee heard from many people who claimed no legal or political expertise in relation to the desirability or otherwise of any particular law; they simply wanted to know that Australia would continue to play its role as a valued contributor to the international community while pragmatically dealing with problems at home.

Outside the capital cities and large urban centres, the community roundtables tended to focus on local concerns, and there was limited use of "human rights" language. People were more comfortable talking about the fair go, wanting to know what constitutes fair service delivery for small populations in far-flung places. At Mintabie in outback South Australia, a quarter of the town's population turned out, upset by the recent closure of their health clinic. At Santa Teresa in the red centre, Aboriginal residents asked me how I would feel if the government required that I place a notice banning pornography on the front door of my house. They thought that was the equivalent of the government erecting the "Prescribed Area" sign at the entrance to their community. In Charleville, western Queensland, the local doctor described the financial hardship endured by citizens who need to travel 600 km by bus to Toowoomba for routine specialist care.

The committee learnt that economic, social and cultural rights are important to the Australian community, and the way they are protected and promoted has a big impact on the lives of many. The most basic economic and social rights – the rights to the highest attainable standard of health, to housing and to education – matter most to Australians, and they matter most because they are the rights at greatest risk, especially for vulnerable groups in the community.

Which rights to protect?

The community roundtables bore out the finding of Colmar Brunton Social Research's 15 focus groups that the community regards the following rights as unconditional and not to be limited:

- basic amenities – water, food, clothing and shelter;
- essential health care;
- equitable access to justice;
- freedom of speech;
- freedom of religious expression;
- freedom from discrimination;
- personal safety;
- education.

Many of the more detailed submissions presented to the committee argued that all the rights detailed in the primary international instruments Australia has ratified without reservation should be protected and promoted. Most often mentioned were the *International Covenant on Civil and Political Rights 1966* and the *International Covenant on Economic, Social and Cultural Rights 1966*, which, along with the *Universal Declaration of Human Rights 1948*, constitute the "International Bill of Rights".

Some submissions also included the *International Convention on the Elimination of All Forms of Racial Discrimination 1965*, the *Convention on the Elimination of All Forms of Discrimination against Women 1979*, the *Convention against Torture and Other Cruel, Inhuman and Degrading Treatment or Punishment 1984*, the *Convention on the Rights of the Child 1989*, and the *Convention on the Rights of Persons with Disabilities 2006.*

Having ratified these seven important human rights treaties, Australia has voluntarily undertaken to protect and promote the rights listed in them. This was a tension for us in answering the first question. Many roundtable participants and submission makers spoke from their own experience, highlighting those rights most under threat for them, or for those in their circle. Others provided us with a more theoretical approach, arguing that all Australia's international human rights obligations should be complied with.

True to what we heard from the grassroots, we singled out three key economic and social rights for immediate enhanced attention by the Australian Human Rights Commission – the rights to health, education, and housing. We thought that government departments should be attentive to the progressive realisation of these rights, within the constraints of what is economically deliverable. However, in light of advice received from the Solicitor-General, we did not think the courts could have a role to play in the progressive realisation of these rights.

We recommended that the federal government operate on the assumption that, unless it has entered a formal reservation in relation to a particular right, any right listed in the seven international human rights treaties should be protected and promoted.

Is there sufficient protection now?

Colmar Brunton Social Research found that only 10 per cent of people reported that they had ever had their rights infringed in any way, while another 10 per cent reported that someone close to them had had their rights infringed. Ten per cent is a good figure, but only the most naïvely patriotic would invoke it as a plea for the complacent status quo. The consultants reported that the bulk of participants in focus groups had very limited knowledge of human rights. Of the survey respondents, 64 per cent agreed that human rights in Australia are adequately protected; only 7 per cent disagreed; the remaining 29 per cent were uncommitted.

Figure E5. Perceptions of adequate protection and sufficient education

Human rights in Australia are adequately protected
20% 44% 29% 4% 3%

People in Australia are sufficiently educated about their rights
12% 33% 42% 10% 3%

0% 20% 40% 60% 80% 100%

■Strongly agree ■Agree □Neither □Disagree ■Strongly disagree

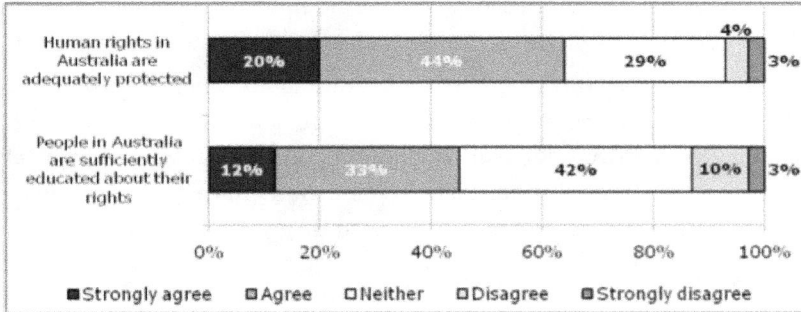

Q3. Using a scale of 0-10, where 0 means 'totally disagree' and 10 means 'totally agree', how much do you disagree or agree with the following statements?

Base = Total Sample (Weighted to national distribution by gender and jurisdiction ; N=1188-1212)

A total of 8671 submissions expressed a view on the adequacy or inadequacy of the present system. Of these, 2551 thought human rights were adequately protected, whereas 6120 (70 per cent) thought they were not.

Figure 7: Preferences for balancing community good and individual rights

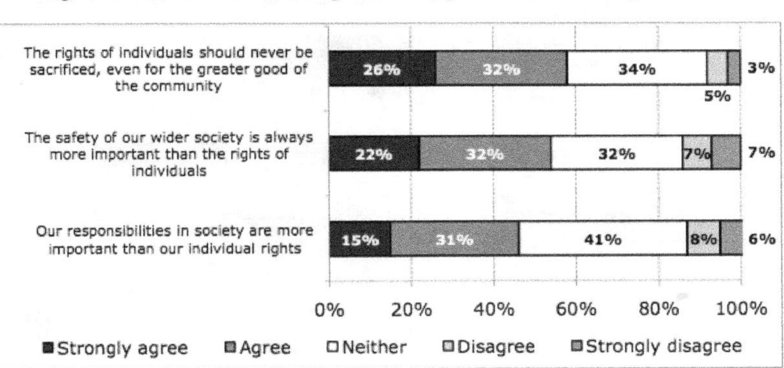

One of the challenges in conducting a public consultation is that respondents with limited education in law and jurisprudence might express internally inconsistent views. We found this to be the case when asking people how best to balance individual rights and the public interest. A majority espoused both that the rights of individuals should always prevail and that public safety and security should always prevail.

There is enormous diversity in the community when it comes to an understanding of rights protection. Though two-thirds of those who participated in the random survey thought human rights were adequately protected in Australia, more than 70 per cent identified three groups in the community whose rights were in need of greater protection.

Figure E8. Amount of Protection Required By Groups

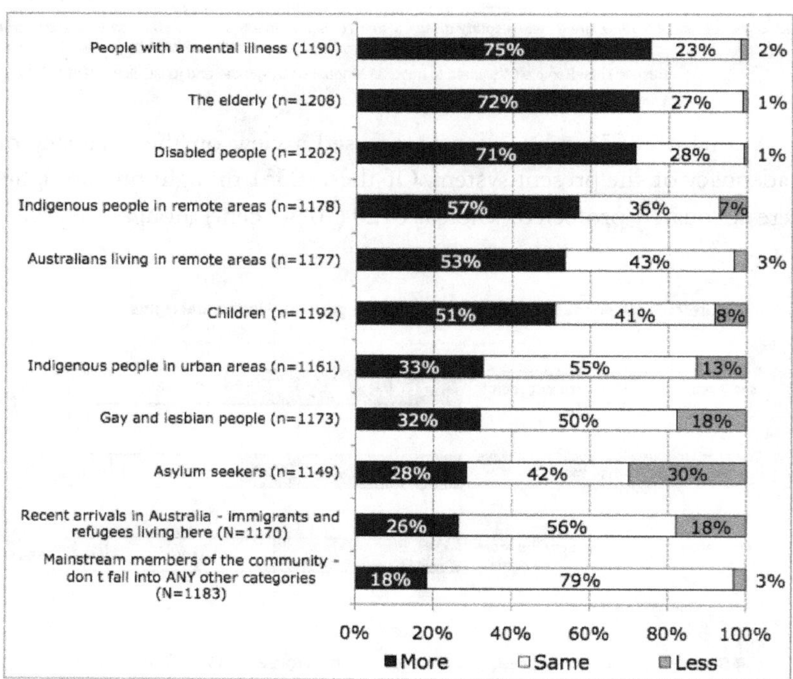

The majority of those surveyed also saw a need for better protection of the human rights of those living in remote rural areas. The near division of the survey groups when it comes to the treatment of asylum seekers highlights why this issue recurs at Australian elections.

How can protection and promotion of human rights be improved?

The committee commissioned the Allen Consulting Group to conduct cost-benefit analyses of a selection of options proposed during the Consultation for the better protection and promotion of human rights in Australia. The consultants developed a set of three criteria against which the potential effects of various options were assessed – benefits to stakeholders, implementation costs and timeliness, and risks. The options evaluated were a Human Rights Act, human rights education, a parliamentary scrutiny committee for human rights, an augmented role for the Australian Human Rights Commission, review and consolidation of anti-discrimination laws, a new National Action Plan for human rights, and maintaining the status quo.

This cost-benefit exercise was our most problematic task. Given the 2013 decision of the then Gillard Government to drop a proposed consolidation of anti-discrimination laws, it is salutary to revisit the consultancy report's finding:

> The introduction of consolidated anti-discrimination legislation may pose a risk in terms of future resourcing and the potential for an increase in litigation. However, new legislation does not pose a risk to parliamentary sovereignty and is likely to be strongly supported by the community.

We put forward three tranches of measures to be considered for further protecting and enhancing human rights. I will deal with them in ascending order of controversy and in descending order of broad community endorsement. The Gillard Government ultimately implemented those measures winning the broadest community endorsement while deciding not to enact a Human Rights Act which, though supported by the majority of people consulted, was supported less strongly than other options.

Table E10. Most preferred protection option

Option	Most preferred
Parliament to pay attention to human rights when making laws	29%
More human rights education	23%
More Government attention to human rights when developing laws and policies	18%
A statement of principles available to everyone	11%
Legislation by Federal Parliament	10%
None of these	*8%*

Education and culture

At many community roundtables, participants said they did not know what their rights were and did not even know where to find them. When reference was made to the affirmation made by new citizens pledging loyalty to Australia and its people, "whose rights and liberties I respect", many participants confessed they would be unable to tell the inquiring new citizen what those rights and liberties were and would not even be able to tell them where to look to find out. In the report, we noted the observation of historian John Hirst "that human rights are not enough, that if rights are to be protected there must be a community in which people care about each other's rights". It is necessary to educate the culturally diverse Australian community about the rights all Australians are entitled to enjoy. Some 81 per cent of people surveyed by Colmar Brunton said they would support increased human rights education for children and adults as a way of better protecting human rights in Australia.

At community roundtables there were consistent calls for better education. Of the 3914 submissions that considered specific reform options, 1197 dealt with the need for human rights education and the creation of a better human rights culture. This was the most frequent reform option raised. While 45 per cent of respondents in the opinion survey agreed that "people in Australia are sufficiently educated about their rights", Colmar Brunton concluded:

> There is strong support for more education and the better promotion of human rights in Australia. It was apparent that few people have any specific understanding of what rights they do have, underlining a real need as well as a perceived need for further education.

The committee's recommendation that a readily comprehensible list of Australian rights and responsibilities be published and translated into various community languages follows from Colmar Brunton's finding that there was "generally more support for a document outlining rights than for a formal piece of legislation per se". There was wide support for this idea in the focus groups, and 72 per cent of those surveyed thought it was important to have access to a document defining their rights. More significantly, Colmar Brunton found:

> In the devolved consultation phase with vulnerable and marginalised groups there was a very consistent desire to have rights explicitly defined so that they and others would be very clearly aware of what rights they were entitled to receive.

Some 61 per cent of people surveyed supported "a non-legally binding statement of human rights principles issued by the Federal Parliament and available to all people and organisations in Australia". We recommended a readily comprehensible list of Australian rights and responsibilities.

During the course of our public consultation, the Murdoch press (News Corp) made a strong claim that existing protections for human rights were adequate and that the occasional shortfall could be rectified by the investigative journalism of credible broadsheets such as their masthead *The Australian.* The public did not share this view.

Figure E9. Support Levels for Various Protection Options

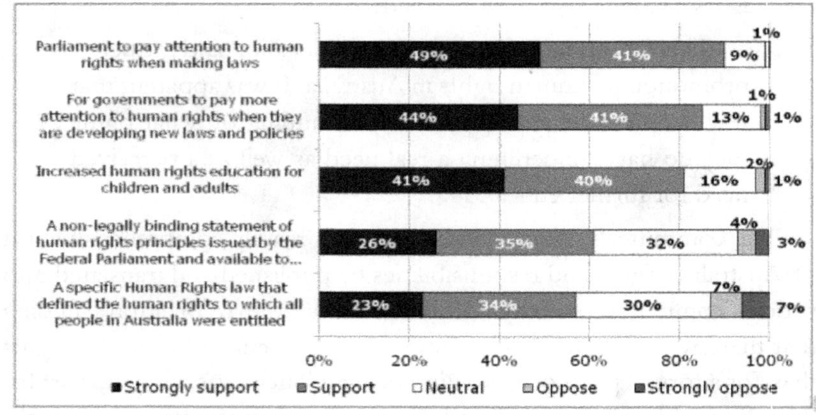

Figure E7. Perceived Levels of Responsibility for Rights Protection

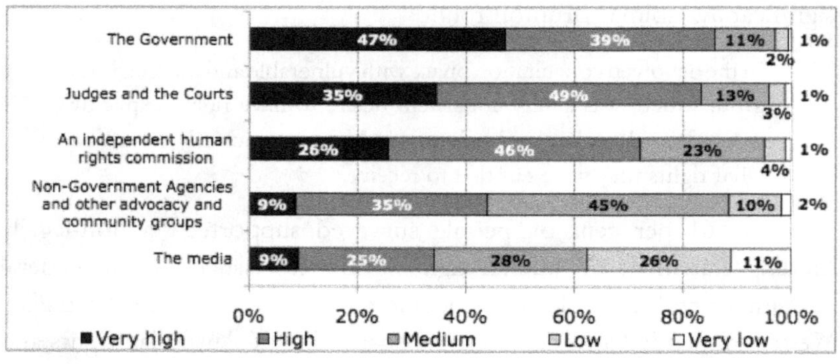

More government attention

The second tranche of proposals for enhancing human rights protection included recommendations for ensuring that Commonwealth public authorities could be more attentive to human rights when delivering services and for guaranteeing compliance of Commonwealth laws with Australia's voluntarily assumed human rights obligations. We recommended that the Human Rights Commission have much the same role in hearing complaints of human rights violations by Commonwealth agencies as it presently has in relation to complaints of unlawful discrimination.

We also recommended an audit of all past Commonwealth laws so that government might consider introducing amendments in parliament to ensure human rights compliance, that all future Commonwealth bills be accompanied by a statement of human rights compatibility, and that there be a parliamentary committee which routinely reviews bills for such compliance. These measures are fully respectful of parliamentary sovereignty, yet are stronger than other models where parliament is able to receive the parliamentary committee report on human rights violations long after the legislation has been passed. We saw no point in window dressing procedures that close the gate only once the horse has bolted.

A Human Rights Act?

The third tranche of our recommendations related to a Human Rights Act. Many Australians would like to see national government take more notice of human rights as they draft laws and make policies. The majority of those attending community roundtables favoured a Human Rights Act, and 87 per cent of those who presented submissions to the committee and expressed a view on the question supported such an Act. In the national telephone survey, 57 per cent expressed support for a Human Rights Act, 30 per cent were neutral, and only 14 per cent were opposed.

Our committee did recommend a Human Rights Act, which would grant judges the power to interpret Commonwealth laws consistent with human rights, provided that interpretation was always consistent with the purpose of the legislation being interpreted. This power would be more restrictive than the power granted to judges in the United Kingdom where parliament has been happy to give judges a stronger power of interpretation because a failed litigant there can always seek relief in Strasbourg before the European Court of Human Rights. Understandably, the English would prefer to have their own judges reach ultimate decisions on these matters, rather than leaving them to European judges. We have no such regional arrangement in Australia.

An Act would give a person claiming that a Commonwealth agency had breached their human rights the right to bring an action in court. For example, a citizen disaffected with Centrelink might claim that their right to privacy has been infringed. The court would be required to interpret the relevant Centrelink legislation in accordance with the Human Rights Act. The court might find that Centrelink was acting beyond its power, infringing the right to privacy or alternatively, that Centrelink was acting lawfully but that the interference with the right to privacy was not justified in a free and democratic society. It would then be a matter for the parliamentary committee on human rights to decide whether to review the law and recommend some amendment. Ultimately, it would be a decision for the responsible minister and the government as to whether the law should be amended. The sovereignty of parliament would be assured.

Consistent with international human rights law, we acknowledge that economic and social rights such as the rights to health, education and housing are to be progressively realised. Nothing in our recommendations would allow a citizen or non-citizen to go to court claiming a right to health, education or housing. The progressive realisation of these rights would be a matter for government and the Human Rights Commission in dialogue. We recommended that some civil and political rights such as the right to life, precluding the death penalty, protection from slavery, torture and cruel and degrading treatment be non-derogable and absolute, that is they cannot be suspended or limited, even in times of emergency.

Some will argue that there is no prospect of these rights being infringed in Australia, so why bother to legislate for them? The facts that any infringement of these rights would be indefensible and that most Australians hold such rights as sacrosanct create a strong case, in the opinion of the committee, for these rights being guaranteed by Commonwealth law.

Most civil and political rights can be limited in the public interest, or for the common good, or to accommodate the conflicting rights of others. Nowadays the limit on such rights is usually determined by inquiring what is demonstrably justified in a free and democratic society. Under the dialogue model we proposed, courts could express a contrary view. But, ultimately, it would always be parliament's call. This makes it a very different situation from the United States where, under a constitutional model, judges have the final say.

Some politicians have said that they or their colleagues would be too timid to express a view contrary to the judges and thus the judges, in effect, would have the last word on what limits on rights are demonstrably justified in a free and democratic society. Such timidity is not my experience of Australian politicians. After all, if the contest is about what is justified in a free and democratic society, who is better placed than an elected politician to claim that they know the country's democratic pulse on the legitimate limit of any right?

One of the complex legal questions my committee had to face was whether declarations of incompatibility by a court would be constitutional. We did have an opinion from the Solicitor-General advising that they would be constitutional, but that was not the end of the matter. After considering all the complications, our recommendation on "declarations of incompatibility" read:

> The Committee recommends that any federal Human Rights Act extend only to the High Court the power to make a declaration of incompatibility. (Should this recommendation prove impractical, the Committee recommends alternatively that any federal Human Rights Act not extend to courts the formal power to make a declaration of incompatibility).

In the alternative to court declarations we proposed that:

> [T]he parties to the proceedings, and perhaps the Australian Human Rights Commission, could be given the power to notify the Joint (Parliamentary) Committee on Human Rights of the outcome of litigation and the court's reasoning indicating non-compliance of a Commonwealth law with the Human Rights Act. It would then be a matter for members of parliament themselves to trigger the processes of the Joint Committee, which could seek the Attorney-General's response.

The government's response

Our elected leaders were able to adopt many of the recommendations in our report without deciding to grant judges any additional power to scrutinise the actions of public servants, or to interpret laws in a manner consistent with human rights. In future, they could decide to take the extra step, engaging the courts as a guarantee that politicians and the public service will be kept accountable in respecting, protecting, and promoting the human rights of all Australians. Our report sets out how this could best be done – faithful to what we heard, respectful of the sovereignty of parliament, and true to the Australian ideals of dignity and a fair go for all.

In the section of our report dealing with a Human Rights Act, we set out previous attempts to legislate for an Act in Australia and analysed why those attempts failed. We also gave an overview of the statutory models in New Zealand, the United Kingdom, Victoria and the Australian Capital Territory (ACT). We followed this with a dispassionate statement of the case both for and against an Act. Finally, we outlined the range of "bells and whistles" that could be included in any Human Rights Act. This part of our report stands alone as a useful resource for anyone undecided about the usefulness or desirability of a Human Rights Act. The intended reader is the person who is agnostic about this question, not altogether convinced of the social worth of lawyers, wanting "bang for the buck" with social inclusion and protection of the vulnerable in society.

Government decided to put a Human Rights Act on the "long finger". But they did legislate to provide for statements of compatibility and for a parliamentary committee on Human Rights, in the *Human Rights (Parliamentary Scrutiny) Act 2011*, which came into effect in early 2012. Parliament appointed a 10-member Parliamentary Committee on Human Rights, which is required to examine bills and legislative instruments "for compatibility with human rights". The Committee may also examine existing Acts and inquire into any matter relating to human rights referred to it by the Attorney-General. "Human rights" are defined to mean "the rights and freedoms recognised or declared" by the seven, key international human rights instruments on civil and political rights, economic, social and cultural rights, racial discrimination, torture and other cruel inhuman or degrading treatment, including the conventions on women, children and persons with disabilities. Anyone introducing a bill or legislative instrument to Parliament is required to provide "a statement of compatibility" that must include an assessment of whether the bill (or instrument) is compatible with human rights.

So at a national level, neither the executive nor the legislature can escape the dialogue about legislation's compliance with UN human rights standards. Neither can the courts, because of the provisions of the *Acts Interpretation Act* that make reports of the Parliamentary Committee on Human Rights and statements of compatibility relevant in court proceedings, determining the meaning of new Commonwealth statutes which impinge on internationally recognised human rights and freedoms.

Ultimately, Australia will require a Human Rights Act to set workable limits on how far ajar the door of human rights protection should be opened by the judges in dialogue with the politicians. We will now have a few years of the door flapping in the Canberra breeze as public servants decide how much content to put in the statements of compatibility, as parliamentarians decide how much public access and transparency to accord the new committee processes, and as judges feel their way in interpreting the laws. There is no turning back from the federal dialogue model of human rights protection.

Conclusion

Four years on from our report and two years into the operation of the new federal human rights framework, the *National Human Rights Consultation* is still perceived as a failed attempt to enact a federal Human Rights Act. It was nothing of the sort. The Consultation was faithful to its public trust in providing government and parliament with accurate information about community perceptions on the protection of human rights. The government responded by adopting the three most popular remedies for enhancing human rights protection: human rights education; statements of compatibility from the executive; and a parliamentary committee for human rights. There is every indication that most Australians are content with this Australian exceptionalism. It remains to be seen if the new measures are sufficiently robust.

References

Colmar Brunton Social Research, 2009, *Final Report, National Human Rights Consultation – Community Research Phase*, Canberra: Attorney General's Department

National Human Rights Consultation (Brennan [Chair]), 2009, *Report*, Canberra: Attorney General's Department

9

Finkelstein Inquiry into the media

Rodney Tiffen

Introduction

Professor Gary Banks, Dean of the Australia and New Zealand School of Government and former Chairman of the Productivity Commission, when reviewing the value of public inquiries, singled out the *Independent Inquiry into the Media and Media Regulation* (henceforth the Finkelstein Inquiry) as one that failed on "all counts", being "neither being taken forward by government nor likely to benefit the community in the long term" (Banks 2012: 7). If this is the measure of success, there is no doubt the Finkelstein Inquiry was a failure, although in my view that failure stems not from the intrinsic merits of its report so much as the environment into which it was delivered.

Setting up the inquiry

The Minister for Broadband, Communications and the Digital Economy, Senator Stephen Conroy of the Gillard Labor Government, commissioned the Finkelstein Inquiry on 14 September 2011. The commission was given to former Federal Court Judge Ray Finkelstein, to be assisted by Matthew Ricketson, Professor of Journalism at the University of Canberra. The Finkelstein Inquiry was required to report by the end of February 2012. This tight time line was because the Gillard Government had also commissioned the *Convergence Review*, which was to report by the end of March 2011, after which legislation could proceed arising from the two reports taken together.

The short period placed severe constraints on the Finkelstein Inquiry. It made it impossible for the Inquiry to undertake or commission major independent research of its own. In addition, the Inquiry was expressly directed not to examine issues to do with concentration of ownership.

The Finkelstein Inquiry arose from an unpromising mix of motives. Once it was underway, these motives had no impact on how it was conducted, but they were probably pertinent to the lack of effective follow-through afterwards.

The immediate impetus for the Inquiry was the phone hacking scandal in the United Kingdom (UK), the biggest scandal to affect English-speaking democratic media in living memory. The scale of the criminality and its institutionalised nature, plus the immoral and cynical disregard for those whose privacy was being invaded were shocking to many, and, of course, the fact that the organisation that committed the offences was one owned by the biggest proprietor in Australia, Rupert Murdoch's News Corp, all fed into a sense of urgency about investigating the conduct of the media in this country. Most observers (including myself) thought it was unlikely that such abuses were occurring in Australia, at least not in the institutionalised, systematic way they had in Britain.

The UK scandal fed into two longer standing senses of grievance with the behaviour of the Australian press, and how it was having a detrimental rather than beneficial effect on Australian democracy. The Greens leader, Senator Bob Brown, after years of what he believed was unfair and damaging coverage, had labelled the Murdoch press the "hate media" (Flew and Swift 2013: 187). Similarly, there was a strong feeling among parts of the Gillard Government that they were being unfairly treated, summed up by Senator Conroy's claim that *The Daily Telegraph* was intent on regime change. In July, at an address at the National Press Club, Prime Minister Julia Gillard had called on the media to "stop writing crap" about the government (AustralianPolitics.com 2011).

Judgements will differ on the validity of such criticisms – in my view there was considerable justice in the claims. But the key point is that these are not grievances that could be solved by public policy, or their validity settled by a public inquiry.

From these cross-pressures, an inquiry with four (overlapping) terms of reference was announced. These formed three main concerns, and the first two can be dealt with briefly.

The future of the press

One concern was the future viability of newspapers because of the impact of the internet. The Finkelstein Inquiry brought together a considerable amount of data and recommended the Productivity Commission should conduct a further study within the next two years. It did not recommend any direct government support or intervention because all the major companies opposed it, and there were still many uncertainties about how the situation was evolving. Moreover, even if everyone were agreed on the desirability of action, there are many policy dilemmas about how to intervene – dilemmas not only about competing principles, but about effectiveness, and about how to intervene while maintaining commercial neutrality and promoting media diversity. So under very tight time constraints, the Finkelstein Inquiry decided it should not rush in.

A second concern was about media convergence, and how technological change was impacting on traditionally separate regulatory domains. The Finkelstein Inquiry in its report recommended that the Australian Press Council (or a successor body) should include websites. More problematically it recommended that a News Media Council should eventually take over some functions from the Australian Communications and Media Authority (ACMA). Handling viewer complaints about news and informational programming is only one of many responsibilities that ACMA has, and not necessarily one where it is most expert. Moreover, its procedures are intrinsically slow – a complaint first to the station and then only much later to ACMA itself, which then often took a considerable time to give its finding.

Media codes of ethics

The third set of issues – the one where the Finkelstein Inquiry made its strongest recommendations and which created the greatest controversy – related to media codes of ethics and their effectiveness and enforcement. In particular, it involved the effectiveness of the Australian Press Council in offering redress to those who felt wronged by media coverage.

The Australian Press Council had been formed in 1976. Several proprietors had disliked the idea, or been harsh critics of its effectiveness. In 1972, for example, Rupert Murdoch was opposed to the idea of a Press Council: "The Press Council was invented as a fig leaf by a frightened British press establishment at a time of genuine concern. Surely we do not need such hypocrisy in Australia" (Finkelstein 2012: 224). Sir Warwick Fairfax haughtily dismissed the idea because of the "high standard of responsibility to the public [our papers] have shown for 144 years". "We do not think it would have any appreciable effect on newspapers which aimed at different standards. It is not our function to sit in judgement on other newspapers and we would strongly resent their sitting in judgement on us" (quoted in Mayer 1994: 9). Kerry Packer, appearing before the House of Representative Committee into the Print Media in 1991, said the Australian Press Council was "a complete and absolute piece of window-dressing" (Muller 2012). However, by the time of the Finkelstein Inquiry all the companies were vocal advocates for the desirability and effectiveness of the Australian Press Council.

As an institution for offering redress and a means of accountability of the press, the Australian Press Council had five major failings, and several of these were intrinsic to its structure and needed institutional change to be rectified.

The first was that publishers could opt out whenever they wished.

In the past, they sometimes had – for example after the Press Council criticised the coverage by the *Adelaide News* of the South Australian election in 1979, News Limited simply withdrew and stayed out until its takeover of the *Herald and Weekly Times* in 1987. As if to underline the validity of the report's criticism on this point, West Australian Newspapers withdrew from the Press Council soon after the report was published, and set up its own in-house procedures for handling complaints.

The second was that there was no consistency in where and how, or even whether, Council adjudications were published. The Press Council kept a record of all its decisions, but had no data on how these decisions were published in the relevant newspapers. Impressionistically, there seemed a pattern whereby adjudications favourable to the newspaper were published more prominently than critical ones. There was variation between papers, but in some at least it seemed that adverse findings were published much further back in the paper with non-descript headlines and reported more briefly. There were at least some times when critical adjudications were simply not published.

Third, the Press Council suffered from inadequate and insecure funding. Several former chairs of the Council told the inquiry that their greatest problem was that the Council did not have the funding base needed to undertake its roles. The present chair, Professor Julian Disney, said the budget needed to be doubled for the Council to meet the goals it had proclaimed for itself. Moreover, publishers could arbitrarily change their funding as they wished. When the Council undertook a research project on the State of the News Print Media, News Limited disapproved, and cut its funding by $100,000.

Fourth, the Press Council had a low public profile. Many people either knew nothing about it, or they saw it as an ineffectual forum for pursuing complaints. Sam North, a journalist for 35 years, including four on the Press Council, said that now he was working with business in public relations, he had been surprised by three things: "the general acceptance that the media will get it wrong; the fear that the media will exact retribution should anyone complain; and the almost total lack of awareness of the Press Council" (North 2012).

Finally, especially on difficult and contentious cases, there were sometimes long delays. In some cases, at least, justice delayed was justice denied. The Greens complained about a *Herald Sun* story before the 2004 election. The Council eventually found in their favour, but not until a long time after the election.

Finkelstein's solutions to these problems were:

- first, and most contentiously, to prevent publishers from opting out by giving the work of the Council statutory underpinning;
- second, to have agreed formulas for how and where adjudications would be published;
- third, to guarantee secure funding by having government finance the Council, indexed at twice the current level.

It should be stressed that there was no proposed change in standards. Rather these would continue to be the current ones, ones which the industry says that it already embraces. There was to be no change in the composition of the Council – it would remain as half industry and half public representatives. Finally, the sole punishment was publication of the adjudication, and in some cases offering a right of reply.

The Finkelstein Inquiry's main aim was to offer a forum for redress that was a) as conciliatory as possible; b) carried no financial or legal risk for either party; c) procedurally was simple, quick and cheap; and d) would enlarge rather than restrict the flow and exchange of information and views.

Apart from the Press Council, the other main avenue available to those who wanted redress against a newspaper unwilling to admit its error was to sue for defamation. This carried large financial risks for both sides, long delays and strong inhibitions on further coverage while the case was in train. Moreover, of course, only a small number of errors in newspapers are defamatory. Anyone wanting to proceed with a complaint to the Council would have to waive any rights to other legal action.

The thrust of the proposals was "about making the news media more accountable to those covered in the news, and to the public generally" (Finkelstein 2012: 9). Although the report recommended secure government funding and a statutory basis to underpin the Council's authority, it would not give the government of the day any extra power to influence news coverage than it already possesses. The report explicitly set out procedures to ensure its independence. The proposal was one of compulsory self-regulation, with standards, procedures and outcomes closely following the current practices of the Press Council.

The inquiry was proposing minimal reforms. They would have little impact on the practice of journalism. They would not affect at all issues of newsworthiness or story selection. The complaints that the Greens and Labor held about the Murdoch press, for example about double standards in news judgement, would not be touched at all. But it would give better procedures for testing and resolving issues of misrepresentation.

After the report was published, its public reception was almost entirely hostile. The major lines of criticism are considered later. But Banks noted that, "I cannot think of any inquiry by the Productivity Commission during my years there that didn't benefit from feedback on a draft report" (Banks 2012: 14). The short time frame made this impossible in the Finkelstein Inquiry, but there were a few errors and ambiguities that would have been easily resolved by such a preliminary airing, which are considered here.

Reaction to the Inquiry

The first, and the most trivial, was that the report had decided that very small websites, for example newsletters, should not be subject to the

News Media Council. While this principle is probably sound, it was not clear how to draw the line. The report arbitrarily recommended that only websites which attracted more than 15,000 hits a year should be included. This was setting the bar far too low, and many commentators seized on the error with some relish as showing the Inquiry's naïveté about the internet.

There were a couple of typos that found their way into the 468-page report, one of which had consequences. In the Executive Summary, it said that if conciliation could not be achieved, then complaints should be adjudicated within weeks rather than months. Unfortunately, on page 297, where a paragraph begins by reiterating the same time frame, the later part scrambled the timing of conciliation and adjudication, and suggests that complaints should be resolved within days. Jonathan Holmes repeated this on the ABC's *Media Watch* program as evidence of the report's lack of realism. Several other journalists – apparently relying on Holmes rather than the report – repeated the criticism of the report's unrealistic time frame.

Two unanticipated lines of criticism could have been easily solved. One was the claim that there was no appeal against the Council's findings. The report was silent on this, thinking that appeal processes would not be different from the current practice of the Press Council. However, it did not mean that the Council's ruling had to be the last word. The report at several points talks of resolving disputes in ways that promote rather than restrict the exchange of views. It was entirely consistent with the report that, once an adjudication or reply had been published in the agreed place and format, a paper could express its dissent, although the inquiry would probably also have stipulated that the complainant be given equal space and prominence. The promotion of dialogue and the search for conciliation were central to the inquiry's intentions.

The other unanticipated line of attack stemmed from the fact that the publication of adjudications was to be compulsory rather than optional. Logically therefore a refusal to publish was – like failing to pay a traffic fine – a contempt of court. That was all that was said in the report. It had received only passing attention by the Inquiry because no one considered it likely that newspapers would refuse to publish. It should be noted that contempt of court proceedings would apply not to the journalists involved in the original story, but to whomever was held responsible for refusing to publish the adjudication. As Bruce Guthrie commented, raising the spectre of contempt of court, "raised the prospect of editors going to jail for failing to publish an apology. That one clause in an otherwise persuasive 468-page report was a gift to those who wanted to paint him as an enemy of a free press" (Guthrie 2013).

The overwhelming majority of contempt of court cases result in a fine, but a small number can result in imprisonment. Because the report did not specify the sanction as a fine, critics were able to conjure fears that were never intended. An alternative might have been, for example, a fine sufficient to pay for the adjudication to be published as an advertisement in competing outlets. It should be stressed again that the only sanction the News Media Council would impose is publication of the adjudication or affording someone a right of reply. This further sanction would only come into play if an editor was determined to withhold from a paper's readers that it had been criticised by a group of the public and its industry peers.

Freedom of the press was constantly invoked over this issue. But it should be stressed that what is at issue here is the power to suppress, the right of an editor to withhold from a paper's readers the knowledge that an independent body had criticised it.

Government action

The Finkelstein Inquiry was obliged to finish by the end of February 2012, and did so. The deadline was said to be fixed so that there would be clear air for the publication of the Convergence Report a month later. There was then the expectation that Senator Conroy and the Gillard Government would publicly respond in the following weeks.

Instead there was silence for the following year. Then, without warning, in March 2013, Senator Conroy announced a series of measures. There were several bills, all about media, but otherwise unrelated. For example, one measure made permanent the 50 per cent licence fee rebate that the government had granted for commercial TV broadcasters, subject to their meeting new Australian content obligations, particularly on their digital multi-channels. Another would allow TV networks to extend their ownership to reach all TV markets around the country, abolishing the 75 per cent limit that now exists.

Conroy's central purpose, however, was to respond to the Finkelstein and Convergence inquiries. Conroy proposed to introduce a public interest test for future media takeovers and mergers, over and above the rules of the normal regulator, the ACCC, to be ruled on by a Public Interest Media Advocate. Press and Opposition reaction immediately seized on the vagueness of the criteria for weighing the public interest and interpreted the anti-monopoly move as designed at curbing the biggest media company, News Corp.

The second role for the Public Interest Media Advocate would be to oversee the functioning of press councils. If a news organisation did not agree to participate in a press council it would lose its exemption from the *Privacy Act 1988*. So there was not strictly compulsion, but a mix of carrot and stick. The Australian Press Council would have been able to continue functioning as is, as would West Australian Newspapers' own complaints handling body. Some saw this as less interventionist than the Finkelstein proposal of a compulsory body. However, it would have given the government slightly more control than in the Finkelstein recommendations, where the government would have had no role in the appointment of the Council.

There was a ferocious reaction in the press and by the Opposition to Conroy's proposals. Most infamously, Murdoch's *Daily Telegraph* led the way with a front-page series of photos of dictators such as Mao and Stalin, and including Conroy, as another who believed in controlling the press. Inside they photoshopped Conroy dressed as Stalin (Jones 2013a, b). The next day, it published a mock apology to Stalin. Moving around in Russian history, *The Australian* headline instead had "Press tsar to regulate standards" (Crowe 2013). Later in the week three tabloids all had freedom prominently on their front pages – *Herald Sun* "Fight for Freedom"; *West Australian* "Freedom fight"; and *Daily Telegraph* simply "Freedom" (*Crikey* 2013).

Amid the outpouring of outrage, there was one notable misrepresentation. ABC journalist and presenter Michael Rowland described how 32 of the nation's best-known male TV presenters were gathered for a photo-shoot about TV presenters in general. But the occasion was hijacked by the *Sunday Telegraph*, which falsely claimed they were there opposing Labor's media reforms. Only eight of the 32 were quoted, all opposing the reforms, but others with different views were not (Rowland 2013).

Just as important as the content of the proposals was the style of their introduction. Senator Conroy introduced them at the beginning of one week, and said that they had to be passed by the end of the next week or they would be withdrawn. He also issued a take-it-or-leave-it ultimatum: that the whole package must be accepted without any amendments. When he made these public announcements, MPs had not yet seen the intended legislation. Whatever his motives, and whatever the cross-pressures he was under, this process was a travesty, one that the Independents holding the balance of power would find insulting, and one that was almost guaranteed to fail. Fail, it did. The Gillard Government withdrew the legislation the following week. As Peter Hartcher observed, "the government had antagonised the media, [and also failed] in the parliament. It was a major loss for no gain" (Hartcher 2013).

Conroy's actions were puzzling and clearly counter-productive. It seems likely he had been subject to a stalemate within the government over how to respond. A government already internally divided between the Gillard and Rudd forces, hopelessly behind in the polls, and lacking a majority in either house of parliament, was not in a strong position to proceed. Moreover, as always, there was a large "pragmatic" faction arguing that you can't take on the press. One Labor MP told a journalist "Why don't we piss off the biggest interest group, the media, a few months before the election … not a great idea" (Holgate 2013).

The debate

The lines of criticism greeting the Conroy proposals had already been pre-figured in the responses to the Finkelstein *Report*. Much of that antagonism was directed towards a report that did not exist.

One frustration was that everyone invented their own Finkelstein *Report*. This was particularly true of those commentators whose outpourings of rhetoric were rarely disciplined by any empirical reality. Visiting literary celebrity Naomi Wolf called it "step one to fascism" (Buchanan and Han 2012). The former head of News Limited, John Hartigan, said the government used the inquiry, "as a sort of jihad against News … I think it is a total outrage" (White and Chessell 2012). The head of West Australian Newspapers, Bob Cronin, described it as "the most outrageous assault on our democracy in the history of the media," and compared it with Stalin and North Korea. The economist Henry Ergas (2012) wrote in *The Australian* that "Finkelstein's proposals would empower state-appointed officials to silence dissent". Columnist Andrew Bolt (2012) thought that such "thought police could only stifle debate".

Others saw even grander and more sinister designs. The *Sydney Morning Herald* (2012) editorial saw the Finkelstein *Report* as wanting to impose "reason" on society, but, "That experiment was tried in the last century and, in 1989 it collapsed amid rejoicing with the Berlin Wall. But the spirit of that disastrous experiment [ie presumably communism] clearly lives on in reports such as this." The Executive Director of the Institute for Public Affairs, John Roskam thought it was "intellectual arrogance at its most breathtaking ... the totalitarian fallacy: don't let the people decide (because the people are too stupid), let judges and academics decide for them. The Finkelstein Report overturns two centuries of Western political philosophy". Roskam did make a single reference to what was in the report. He claimed that paragraph 4.10 argued that a "Council should control speech in Australia because more people are too dumb or ignorant to decide for themselves." That paragraph simply says readers are not always in a position to establish the accuracy of facts behind a story. It is clearly a statement about their access to evidence, not their capacities.

Opposition leader Tony Abbott was squarely in the critics' camp. He thought the Finkelstein Inquiry looked like "an attempt to warn off News Limited from pursuing anti-government stories" (Ireland 2012). "It's easy to imagine the fate of Andrew Bolt or Alan Jones, for instance, at the hands of such thought police," he argued (Abbott 2012).

The Shadow Attorney-General, Senator George Brandis, made his longest contribution after the Conroy bills had disappeared, but his rhetorical denunciations perhaps surpassed all earlier efforts. For Brandis, in interview with Emma Alberici (ABC *Lateline*), Conroy's proposal was "the most invasive interference with press freedom in Australian history since before the Commonwealth of Australia began, in 1825". It was, he thought, "the first measure, at least in peace time, that had been undertaken in this country which could have had the consequence of a government official telling newspapers and media outlets what they were at liberty to say in their media". The introduction of a public interest media advocate "could, in certain circumstances, have resulted in the Government or officials sitting around Lake Burley Griffin making decisions about what ordinary citizens were allowed to listen to on their radio or to read in their newspapers". It all stemmed from "an instinct on the part of this Government to diminish the centrality of belief [in] freedom of speech" (ABC *Lateline* 2013).

These inventions had almost nothing to do with the content of either the Finkelstein *Report* or the Conroy legislation. Two misrepresentations should be addressed more explicitly. The *Australian Financial Review* greeted the report with the front-page headline "Labor Plan to Control the Media" (Tingle and White 2012). The headline was inaccurate first because the report did not represent any sort of Labor plan. No member of the inquiry had communicated its conclusions and recommendations to Conroy or any other government member before the report was given to him a couple of days before publication. His response to it – let alone the response of other government members, who were perhaps now seeing it for the first time – was unknown. Finkelstein had protected fiercely the independence of his independent inquiry, but that did not stop external critics attributing without any basis all sorts of motives to him and the report. Second, the headline was fundamentally inaccurate in that the report offered no formula for controlling the media. It simply proposed a stronger form of redress for those who felt they had been misrepresented.

Hartigan's replacement as head of News Limited, Kim Williams, was equally extravagant in his misrepresentations: the Finkelstein recommendations "taken as a whole amount to a grave threat to press freedom". Further, he stated that:

> Under Finkelstein's recommendations, journalists can be fined and even jailed, with no appeal rights to bodies such as the Administrative Appeals Tribunal. The super-regulator does not have to publish reasons for its decisions ... It overthrows important principles of due process and natural justice … It junks natural justice in favour of fast processes and absolute authority – it is nothing more than a star chamber. (Williams 2012a, b)

As noted above, no journalist could ever go to jail under the Finkelstein recommendations. Williams has invented the phrase "super-regulator". It is true in the sense that the News Media Council would apply to more than one medium, but it is false in the far more important sense that the Council would have only a very focused role and circumscribed powers. Williams said that the super-regulator does not have to publish reasons for its decision, but its main outcomes would be the publication of its adjudication, which, like the Press Council's findings, would mainly consist of publishing its reasons. Finally Williams called it a "star chamber" – it was to be a "star chamber" consisting of a paper's industry peers and public representatives, whose sole sanction would be the publication of the adjudication or a right of reply.

There were many criticisms that were more factually based and reasonably argued than the ones cited above. Most journalists and media scholars share a binary discourse where the state is equated with despotism and the media with freedom. So any compulsion of the press by the government is seen as an infringement on democracy. Even if, as in this case, that involvement is to enlarge rather than restrict the exchange of information, to strengthen rights of redress and hence responsiveness, it still becomes labelled as "draconian", for example by the ABC's former *Media Watch* presenter Jonathan Holmes (ABC *Media Report* 2013).

The key feature of the debate is that it is more theological than empirical. It overlooks the extent to which the press is already subject to laws. Thomas Jefferson – one of the few philosophers to be quoted on the front page of the *Daily Telegraph* – is often cited: the freedom of the press cannot be limited without being lost. In fact, probably every stable advanced democracy has laws regarding defamation, contempt of court, obscenity, privacy, national security, commercial confidentiality, official secrecy, racial vilification, and/or copyright protection. The lines of how such laws are drawn and how they are enforced are often contested. But the essential point is that every society limits the freedom of the press but that does not mean it is lost.

When talking about the press, any government involvement is seen as leading to state control. This overlooks that commercial television is licensed and regulated far more than the press, and yet there is little sign that its news coverage is beholden to the government of the day. Most dramatically, the public service broadcaster, the ABC, wins any competition for the most trusted and credible news outlet in the country.

Conclusion

The failure of the Conroy proposals confirmed that in terms of immediate policy impact the Finkelstein Inquiry was a failure. In terms of public education and promoting informed debate, it was also, at least in the short-term, a failure, because the capacity to promote public discussion was largely in the hands of those it was inquiring into. And through a mixture of tribal loyalty and vested interests, of wilful misrepresentation and sheer incompetence, the press performed more like propaganda vehicles than democratic news media. The publicity at times resembled what I am tempted to call "Murdoch's Law": the crudity of the propaganda was in inverse proportion to the strength of the argument.

While the press has succeeded in all its short-term aims, it is not clear that it has acted in its own enlightened long-term self-interest. There was constant invocation of the public by the newspapers, but in fact the outstanding feature of public opinion is what low regard the press is held in, as the Finkelstein Report so amply documented. Newspapers are a medium in sharp decline, and a system of compulsory self-regulation in which their accountability is transparent to their readers might have helped to boost their declining credibility.

Acknowledgements

I would like to thank Ray Finkelstein, Matthew Ricketson, Franco Papandrea, Denis Muller, Kristen Walker, Chris Young, Graeme Hill and Brian Kelleher for the privilege of working with them on the Finkelstein Inquiry.

Public inquiries mentioned in chapter

(in chronological order by year of appointment, with name of chair)

Convergence Review (Boreham: 2011)

Independent Inquiry into the Media and Media Regulation (Finkelstein: 2012)

References

Abbott, Tony, MP, 2012, "News media council could muzzle debate," *The Australian* 17 March

ABC *Lateline*, 2013, Emma Alberici interview with Senator George Brandis, 7 May

ABC *Media Report* Radio National, 2013, Richard Adey interview with Jonathan Holmes, 16 May

AustralianPolitics.com, 2011, "Julia Gillard's Carbon Tax Speech at The National Press Club," 14 July

Banks, G., 2013 "Public Inquiries, Public Policy and the Public Interest," *The Inaugural Peter Karmel Lecture in Public Policy*, Academy of the Social Sciences in Australia, 3 July

Bolt, A., 2012, "Thought police can only stifle debate," *Daily Telegraph*, 5 March

Buchanan, M., and Han, E., 2012, "Finding out if you're free," *Sydney Morning Herald*, 6 March

Conroy, S., Senator The Hon, 2013, "Government response to Convergence Review and Finkelstein Inquiry," *Media Release*, 12 March

Crikey, 2013, "Media Wrap: Papers unite against press reforms," 13 March

Crowe, D., 2013, "Press Tsar to regulate standards," *The Australian*, 13 March

Ergas, H., 2012, "Watchdog can muzzle government's critics," *The Australian*, 12 March

Finkelstein, R., 2012, *Independent Inquiry into the Media and Media Regulation Report*, Canberra: Department of Broadband, Communications and the Digital Economy

Flew, T., and Adam S., 2013, "Regulating journalists? The Finkelstein Review, the Convergence Review and News Media Regulation in Australia," *Journal of Applied Journalism and Media Studies,* 2(1), 181-200

Guthrie, B., 2013, "Rupert still riding high," *The Age,* 24 March

Hartcher, P., 2013, "Conroy runs distraction for PM," *Sydney Morning Herald*, 16 March

Holgate, B., 2013, "Stokes leads media rebellion," *Australian Financial Review*, 14 March

Ireland, J., 2012, "Government 'howls down' down its critics: Abbott," *Sydney Morning Herald*, 16 August

Jolly, R., 2012, "Media reviews: all sound and fury?" Canberra: Commonwealth Parliamentary Library, Background Note, 5 October 2012

Jones, G., 2013, "Gillard's henchman attacks freedom of press," *Daily Telegraph*, 13 March

Jones, G., "These despots believe in controlling the press – Conroy joins them," *Daily Telegraph*, 13 March

Mayer, H., 1994, *Mayer on the Media: Issues and Arguments*, Sydney: Allen and Unwin

Muller, D., 2012, "Time to jolt thick-skinned media into action," *Sydney Morning Herald*, 11 March

North, S., 2012 "Finkelstein's 'monster' not so big and scary," *Sydney Morning Herald*, 13 March

Roskam, J., "A failure to defend liberty," *Australian Financial Review*, 9 March

Rowland, M., 2013, "The men of TV and a media regulation stitch-up," ABC *The Drum*, 18 March

Sydney Morning Herald, 2012, 'Editorial: Not a media blueprint," 6 March

Tingle, L., and White, A., 2012, "Labor plan to control the media," *Australian Financial Review*, 3 March

White, A., and Chessell, J., 2012, "Politicians 'running a jihad' against news," *Australian Financial Review*, 5 March

Williams, K., 2012, Address to the South Australian Press Club, 13 July

Williams, K., 2012, "Media futures – observations through a rather frosty crystal ball," *A.N. Smith Lecture in Journalism*, University of Melbourne, 4 October

10

Inquiry into Australian Intelligence Agencies

Philip Flood

Introduction

The *Inquiry into Australian Intelligence Agencies* arose from parliamentary and public concern about Australia's involvement in the 2003 Iraq War. This public inquiry was unique in that the terms of reference were set by Commonwealth Parliament which also specified the kind of person who should conduct the inquiry. Another unusual aspect was that all recommendations in the inquiry report were accepted by Howard Coalition Government, welcomed by the Opposition and then implemented promptly.

Appointment

The Inquiry commenced on 4 March 2004 and the Inquiry report and the government's acceptance of the recommendations were announced 4½ months later, on 20 July. Such speedy government action was a reflection not only of the acute public interest in the stated reasons for the Iraq War, but also the reservations many Australians held about the commitment of Australian forces to a conflict in the Middle East, public scepticism about the quality of intelligence available to the government before the commitment of Australian forces, and doubts in some quarters as to whether the government was being truthful about the intelligence it had received on the issue of Iraq's possession of weapons of mass destruction (WMD). In the event, there was a high degree of public and media endorsement for the report's conclusions.

At the end of February 2004, a parliamentary committee with the complex acronym PJCAAD, the Parliamentary Joint Committee into the Australian Security Intelligence Organisation (ASIO), Australian Secret Intelligence Service (ASIS) and Defence Signals Division (DSD), produced a report into intelligence on Iraq's weapons of mass destruction. The Parliamentary Joint Committee (2004: Recommendation 3, xii) recommended that:

> [T]here should be an independent assessment of the performance of the intelligence agencies, conducted by an experienced former intelligence expert with full access to all material, which will report to the National Security Committee of Cabinet and which, in the light of the matters raised by the consideration of the pre-war intelligence on Iraq, will recommend any changes that need to take place for the better functioning of the agencies.

The media correctly speculated that if government were to follow this advice, there were only four or five people who satisfied the stated criterion (and they might have added who had, or could quickly obtain, the necessary high-level security clearance to conduct the inquiry expeditiously).

I was approached first by the Minister for Foreign Affairs, to ascertain my availability, and shortly afterwards, on 3 March, I was phoned by Prime Minister John Howard to see whether I would agree to conduct the inquiry on the basis recommended by the parliamentary committee. The Prime Minister knew I had conducted a previous inquiry for his government (on immigration detention centres) and also previous internal inquiries for the Hawke Government, and, of course, he knew also of my work as Secretary of the Department of Foreign Affairs and Trade (DFAT) and as an ambassador abroad. He readily agreed to accommodate some personal travel I had committed to and to two requests: first, that I have a free hand to select the inquiry secretariat; and second, that I would be indemnified against any legal action arising from the inquiry. The Prime Minister indicated that he wanted a report by 30 June but if this timing proved too tight, he could agree on request to an extension to end July or end August. He also sought my immediate reaction to the draft terms of reference for the inquiry, before they were released publicly.

In a hand-delivered letter dated 4 March, I was formally requested to undertake the inquiry, with terms of reference specified by the parliamentary committee. I was asked, "without seeking to limit your examination", to provide advice on the effectiveness of the intelligence community's current oversight and accountability mechanisms, the suitability of the current division of labour among the intelligence agencies, the maintenance of contestability in the provision to government of intelligence assessments, and the adequacy of current resourcing of intelligence agencies, and, in particular, the Office of National Assessments (ONA). The Prime Minister's letter made clear that the inquiry should focus primarily on the five agencies concerned with foreign intelligence – ONA, Defence Intelligence Organisation (DIO), ASIS, DSD, and the Defence Imagery and Geospatial Organisation (DIGO) – and that it could consider linkages to other organisations including ASIO. Both a classified and an unclassified version of the report were requested. The terms of reference were broader than I expected and I particularly welcomed the latitude to interpret them liberally.

Once I had assented to the terms of reference, on the same day, 4 March, the Prime Minister released his letter publicly and also mentioned the inquiry to parliament, noting that I had worked for both sides of politics and had been appointed to head ONA by his predecessor, Paul Keating.

At the outset, following a maximum of two minutes conversation with the Prime Minister about formal aspects of the inquiry (and, quite properly, no discussion whatsoever about the Iraq War), I had clear terms of reference, no restriction on widening the inquiry, no directions of any kind about methodology or *modus operandi*, a free hand to select a secretariat, and a prime ministerial direction to all relevant departments and agencies to cooperate fully.

Inquiry processes

The first task was to assemble a secretariat. A small compact group had clear advantages. Given the complex subject matter and tight timetable, all had to be of the highest quality. I also felt it would be best to exclude people currently working in any intelligence agency. Ideally, the secretariat should comprise experienced officers from major departments with a sound knowledge of the use of foreign intelligence but no current intelligence agency role, so that the parliament and public would feel no agency had privileged access to the inquiry. With the ready cooperation of the departmental heads, I was quickly able to secure the services of an exceptional team of people drawn from the departments of Prime Minister and Cabinet, Foreign Affairs and Trade, and Defence. A senior serving officer with recent military intelligence experience in the Middle East was also released to join the secretariat, making a high-quality secretariat of six.

Within a week of the Prime Minister's announcement, the team met to discuss modalities and allocate tasks. Our approach was to invite public submissions through notices in leading Australian newspapers (on 13 March); to hold confidential but not open public hearings; to require comprehensive submissions from all relevant departments and agencies; to ask agencies to have all relevant records identified, including all reports and advice to the Prime Minister and relevant Commonwealth ministers, for inspection by the team; and to hold confidential hearings and interviews with all relevant staff and ministers, key members of the Opposition and senior military officers. Prime Minister Howard had already mentioned publicly that he and his ministers expected to be called to give evidence. I resolved also to interview his three immediate predecessors, Keating, Hawke and Fraser, in addition to a range of former senior intelligence and military leaders as well as academic authorities known to be knowledgeable about intelligence. I met also with all persons who asked to be interviewed by the Inquiry. In addition, the Inquiry had a message conveyed to all staff of the Australian intelligence community inviting any individual who wished to do so to contact or make comment to the Inquiry. A number did so. At the initiative of the British High Commissioner, I met Lord Hutton who had recently completed a relevant inquiry in the United Kingdom and was visiting Australia. Two members of the secretariat visited London and Washington to secure additional information. Arrangements were also made to examine reports of all previous major Australian inquiries on intelligence matters (those by Hope, Hollway, Richardson, Samuels and Codd).

A matter requiring particular attention was whether to have verbatim transcripts of oral evidence taken by the Inquiry. It was decided that nothing would be gained and much lost by verbatim transcripts, whether in writing or recording. Rigour and integrity of analysis has nothing to do with whether transcripts are verbatim. I kept notes of the key points made by witnesses in the confidential hearings as did the relevant secretariat member present at such interviews. After each interview I would discuss with the secretariat the key points that had emerged and the action required. Indeed before important meetings I would discuss with the secretariat the matters to be probed. The interviews went hand in hand with exhaustive examination of agency records. Provision of verbatim transcripts would have added no substance and may well have hindered frank discussion. They would certainly have necessitated a much larger secretariat and would have delayed the Inquiry and added significantly to its cost. Finally, I resolved to have no contact with the media during the course of the Inquiry and to let the Inquiry report be the means for media advice.

Inquiry focus

The Inquiry focused particularly on the systemic issues identified in the terms of reference and on ways to improve the future operation of the intelligence agencies.

For the most part, the Australian media and public were interested in only one issue, the claims about Iraq's possession of weapons of mass destruction. I felt I would learn more about the performance of the agencies and provide better advice to government and parliament if I conducted three detailed case studies: first, an examination of the pre-war intelligence on Iraq, in order to establish the full basis and nature of the intelligence assessment provided to government in the lead-up to the launch of military action on 19 March 2003; second, the intelligence provided to government concerning Jemaah Islamiyah (JI) prior to the Bali bombings on 12 October 2002; and third, the intelligence provided in advance of the despatch of Australian military personnel and police to the Solomon Islands in July 2003. This would involve examining the equivalent of many thousands of pages of highly classified intelligence.

The Inquiry needed to be clear about the nature and uses of intelligence. Intelligence is covertly obtained information. While it may take a number of forms, the key characteristic of intelligence information is that it is obtained without the authority of the government or group who "owns" the information. For all its value, intelligence is only one of a range of factors that influences the policy decisions of governments and is rarely the decisive factor. Commentators can sometimes ascribe an importance to intelligence as a factor in decision-making that fails to recognise the range of broader considerations, such as strategic issues, political and economic objectives, long-standing alliance relationships, legal considerations or other interests that might determine policy. Also the failure to detect plans for the World Trade Centre attack in 2001, Iraq's intention to invade Kuwait in 1990, the imminent collapse of the Berlin Wall in 1989 or, much earlier, the failure to anticipate the strength of Turkish forces in the Dardanelles in 1915, or Japanese plans for Pearl Harbour provides a cautionary lesson for anyone who believes intelligence is always accurate or can provide guarantees.

Iraq's weapons of mass destruction – causes of the intelligence gap

The Inquiry concluded that Australia shared in the allied intelligence failure on the key question of Iraq WMD stockpiles. Intelligence was thin, ambiguous and incomplete. Australian intelligence agencies failed to judge accurately the extent and nature of Iraq's WMD programs.

The report noted that the large body of United Nations Special Commission (UNSCOM) material, together with Iraq's history of use of WMD, deceit and obfuscation, contributed heavily to the failed intelligence assessments. Saddam Hussein's behaviour in the months before March 2003 and his ultimate miscalculation, which saw his regime fall, his sons killed and his own capture, further complicated the assessment challenge. By any measure, his was a miscalculation of massive proportions. The fact that Saddam chose to resist inspections to the bitter end suggested strongly that he had WMD to protect (and perhaps that he hoped to avoid defeat by using them). With hindsight it was clear that Saddam placed great value on avoiding capitulation on the WMD issue. But the difficulty in assessing that at the time was underlined by the fact that Saddam's own calculation of the situation was proven clearly wrong. He ended up without power and his standing destroyed, clearly not the outcome that he wished to achieve by his continued resistance to intrusive inspections in the face of war. Prior to 19 March 2003, the only government in the world that claimed that Iraq was not working on, and did not have, biological and chemical weapons or prohibited missile systems was the government of Saddam Hussein.

Despite the key failure of intelligence judgments on WMD stockpiles, the assessments produced by ONA and DIO up to the commencement of combat operations reflected reasonably the available information and used intelligence sources with appropriate caution. They drew the most likely conclusions from the available information. The obverse conclusion – that Iraq did not have WMD aspirations and capability – would have been a much more difficult conclusion to substantiate. Both agencies had formulated assessments independent of those of the US and UK, in several notable cases choosing not to endorse allied judgments. The Inquiry found no evidence to suggest political or policy influence on assessments of Iraq WMD.

The Inquiry set out at length where and why DIO and ONA had failed rigorously to challenge preconceptions or assumptions about the Iraq regime's intentions and made recommendations to address these deficiencies.

The report also noted it was regrettable that ONA did not coordinate a formal national assessment on Iraq. The material provided to government "did not take a holistic approach to Iraq, its strategic environment and imperatives, the broader regional and domestic context in which its WMD decisions were made, its likely strategic objectives and the likely capacity of its WMD." Reports by ONA and DIO did not cover "the likely strategic cost implications for Australia of contributing to military action against Iraq, the likely strategic costs and issues involved in post-Saddam Iraq and the impact of military action on the safety of Australia and Australians".

The report recognised the existence of four key factors in the backdrop to the Iraq conflict which influenced Australian involvement. Saddam Hussein's egregious breaches of United Nations Security Council Resolutions relating to WMD, his history of use of those weapons, the brutal nature of his regime, and his support for Palestinian and anti-Iranian terrorism were perceived as forming a potent threat to the Iraqi people, the Middle East region and the international community.

Jemaah Islamiyah

While they began slowly, and with ONA better than DIO, Australian agencies developed a good understanding of Jemaah Islamiyah, its development of terrorist capabilities and its intentions towards western targets. There was nothing to suggest that any Australian agency had any specific intelligence warning of the attack in Bali in 2002.

Solomon Islands

Here Australian intelligence became accurate and useful and significantly ahead of government policy.

Assessment of the Australian intelligence community

The Inquiry found that the Australian intelligence agencies were performing well overall and represented a potent capability for government but they could do better to meet the demands of the new security environment. The main recommendations are summarised briefly below:

- arrangements to support oversight of the intelligence community by the National Security Committee of Cabinet needed to be improved;
- the Parliamentary Joint Committee on ASIO, ASIS and DSD should be extended to cover all six intelligence agencies in a Parliamentary Joint Committee on Intelligence and Security and the powers of the Inspector-General of Intelligence and Security to initiate inquiries should be enhanced;
- ONA's role as the peak foreign intelligence agency should be asserted through a stronger mandate and its resources doubled;
- a Foreign Intelligence Coordination Committee should be established, under the chairmanship of the Director-General of ONA;
- there should be rationalisation of the overlap between ONA and DIO, emphasising ONA's role as the provider of all-source national assessments and DIO's focus on defence assessment in support of Defence planning and operational needs;

- there should be a revised mandate for DIO and new guidelines for the Joint Operations Intelligence Centre;
- the key foreign language capabilities of ASIS should be bolstered;
- guidelines should to be developed to manage the public presentation of intelligence;
- the intelligence community should be subject to periodic external review every five to seven years.

Reaction to report

As already noted, the Howard Government accepted the Inquiry's conclusions and recommendations. They were also accepted by the Opposition. Senator Robert Ray, the main Opposition speaker in the parliamentary debate that followed the report, told parliament on 3 August:

> We want ministers who are entrusted with these agencies to get in there and drive them, and I hope the Flood Report stimulates them to do so … governments should not use intelligence to publicly justify their political decision making ... I think the Flood Report will advance the cause in this area … I am pleased the government has said they will accept all recommendations … (Senate Hansard, 3 August 2004, 25369)

There was a high degree of public and media endorsement. The media described the report as "comprehensive and hard hitting" (*Australian Financial Review*), "dynamite" (*The Courier-Mail*), "valuable (and) may just make this country a bit more secure" (*The Age*), and "a tight, down to earth, realistic appraisal of our intelligence" (*The Australian*), and noted that it "will make it that much harder for any future government to excuse itself by saying it built its case on intelligence" (*Sydney Morning Herald*).

There were of course broader concerns, well summarised by Paul Kelly in *The Weekend Australian* on 24 July 2004:

> [T]he intelligence debate about Iraq – driven by the absence of WMDs is of importance but of secondary importance. The Howard Government decided in principle, probably at an early stage in 2002, that it would fight in Iraq with Bush and that was before most of these intelligence assessments were done … But what of the bigger question – the advice from the policy departments, Prime Minister's, Foreign Affairs and Defence? That was not Flood's brief ... Historians may have to wait 30 years for the cabinet papers but the extraordinary feature of our role in Iraq won't be the intelligence or the WMD debate that rages today but the early nature of the decision and the lack of contestable policy debate on the strategic issues.

At the same time, Hugh White wrote in *The Age* (2004):

> Thanks to the Flood report … we now find that intelligence, usually regarded as the most opaque and secretive element of the machinery of government, is more open, contested, and reviewed than the policy processes that lead more directly to the key decisions … key beliefs about Iraq's WMD were not the prime factor in the Government's decision to go to war. The key reason was a desire to support the US Administration in what Washington viewed as a key element of the war on terrorism.

Apart from the important issues of substance, a range of factors contributed to the success of the Inquiry. These included the high degree of expertise about intelligence among the key opposition members of parliament (notably Beazley and Ray), and among the relevant government ministers (Howard, Downer, Costello and Hill); the high quality of the Inquiry's secretariat; the latitude given to the Inquiry, particularly the fact the Prime Minister's written instruction stated he did not seek to limit examination; timing, which meant that relevant material was readily available and the period of the Inquiry did not overlap with a federal election; the fact that key public commentators outside government who were influential in shaping the public debate such as Paul Kelly, Hugh

White, Michelle Grattan and others had a sophisticated understanding of the role of intelligence and of the primacy of strategic and other factors in influencing policy decisions by government; and the fact that the intelligence agencies had for some time had a proven record of not being involved in partisan politics. None of these factors diminishes the finding that the intelligence agencies failed seriously in their assessment of intelligence and the Inquiry report set out explicitly where and how these failures occurred.

Implications

The *Inquiry into Australian Intelligence Agencies* well demonstrates the potential of public inquiries to achieve improved policies and hence secure better outcomes for the community. Inquiries are a means of marshalling additional expertise and experience across different disciplines, drawing contributions from varied sections of the community and also for letting members of the community express their views on public policy and have them taken into account. Particularly when the community questions the integrity of government actions, or where a matter is so complex that established bureaucratic structures are unable to give a minister the information and policy options needed, an independent expert inquiry is an appropriate response.

Inquiries raise community expectations however and governments have to be careful what they are seeking and how an inquiry is constituted. The option of adopting the more formal approach of an inquiry headed by a judge needs to be carefully considered. Commissions and inquiries headed by distinguished judges may be indispensable for investigating matters where there has been significant loss of life or suspected criminal behaviour, or where key witnesses need to be compelled to appear, but I would take issue with the recommendations of the Australian Law Reform Commission in its 2009 report *Making Inquiries: A New Statutory Framework*, which would tip the balance more towards judicial inquiries (see chapter 1: Croucher). Australian judges have a proud record of conducting thorough inquiries of this kind, but my experience across six inquiries (Customs Administration, Schools Commission, Immigration Detention, Intelligence Agencies, Plasma Fractionation and Human Rights) has been that, even for matters of the highest public importance, less formal inquiries are often more effective, more efficient and certainly less costly than formal inquiries headed by judges. They avoid the sometimes cumbersome legalistic framework of a judge-headed inquiry, they leave it open for a wider range of people to conduct an inquiry, and they give individual ministers more flexibility in deciding the most effective form of inquiry.

Of the reviews mentioned above, the *Plasma Fractionation Review of Australia's Arrangements* (2006) demonstrated the particular value of embracing diverse expertise in persons appointed to conduct an inquiry, in this case a distinguished business leader, an eminent dean of a medical school, a respected professor of pathology, and a retired, experienced public administrator. This form of independent inquiry was essential in this instance because a foreign government (the United States) had reservations, in the event unfounded, about the integrity of procedures of the Australian Department of Health and a community organisation.

The *Inquiry into Australian Intelligence Agencies* benefited greatly from an outstanding secretariat of high competence, imagination, credibility and integrity, demonstrating that a quality secretariat can enhance the speed, efficiency, rigour and depth of a public inquiry. While appreciating the difficulties departments face in releasing staff from their mainstream responsibilities, a high-quality secretariat is an essential ingredient for inquiry effectiveness.

Having decided to take the route of a public inquiry, my experience suggests that government is best advised to act on it quickly, and to release the report promptly for public scrutiny. The timing of an inquiry, and the period allocated for its deliberations, are not matters governments should take lightly.

Public inquiries mentioned in chapter

(in chronological order by year of appointment, with name of chair)

Australia:

Royal Commission on Intelligence and Security (Hope: 1974)

Royal Commission on Australia's Security and Intelligence Agencies (Hope: 1983)

Commission of Inquiry into the Australian Secret Intelligence Service (Samuels and Codd: 1994)

Inquiry into Immigration Detention Centre Procedures (Flood: 2000)

Review of Australia's Plasma Fractionation Arrangements (Flood: 2006)

National Human Rights Consultation (Brennan: 2008)

United Kingdom:

Inquiry into the Circumstances Surrounding the Death of Dr Kelly (Hutton: 2003)

References

Flood, P., 2004, *Inquiry into Australian Intelligence Agencies Report*, Canberra: Commonwealth Government

Parliamentary Joint Committee on ASIO, ASIS and DSD, *Intelligence on Iraq's Weapons of Mass Destruction*, Canberra: Commonwealth Parliament

White, H., 2004, "Let's not confuse intelligence failures with policy failures," *The Age*, 27 July

11

Making drought policy through public inquiries – managing risk or coping with disaster?

Linda Courtenay Botterill

Introduction

Australia is generally considered to have the most developed drought policy in the world. The National Drought Policy, which commenced in January 1993, was developed through the Federal Council of Agriculture Ministers (the forum for Commonwealth and state ministers for agriculture and primary industry) following a report from a public inquiry, the *Drought Policy Review Task Force* (DPRTF), reporting in May 1990. It is based on the principle that drought is a normal part of the Australian climate and, as such, is not a natural disaster, but a risk to be managed. Apart from some incremental shifts over the past two decades, the policy has remained basically unchanged in terms of its objectives and underlying principles. Another major external review of the policy took place in 2008 and was notable in that it comprised reports from three separate inquiries.

This chapter examines these two processes for reviewing drought policy, which were quite different in terms of purpose, process and influence, and assesses their impact. It illustrates the incremental nature of policymaking. No one public inquiry will provide the answers for all time, no matter how sound and comprehensive the inquiry process. It also shows that a ground-breaking public inquiry like the DPRTF, which provided a platform for major reform, is a hard act to follow, and points to the importance of government-wide policy coherence if individual policy objectives are to be achievable.

Drought policy in Australia and the 1990 review

Until 1989, drought was treated by Australian governments as a natural disaster and the policy response was, accordingly, the same as for events such as cyclones, bushfires and earthquakes. Constitutionally, natural disasters are a state government responsibility. Until 1939, when it provided £1000 to the Tasmanian Government to assist its response to severe bushfires, the Commonwealth had no involvement in disaster response. From then on, it became involved in other disasters on an ad hoc basis, providing financial assistance to state governments and, over time, this evolved into a formula for Commonwealth funding that was formalised in 1971 into the natural disaster relief arrangements.

In 1989, the Commonwealth government decided that drought was to be removed from these disaster relief arrangements. There were several reasons for this decision. First, expenditure on drought relief was dominating outlays under the program. Second, there were reports that the Queensland Government was rorting the scheme, using it as "a sort of National Party slush fund to be distributed to National Party toadies" (Walsh 1989: 189). Third, scientific understanding of the determinants of Australia's climate had improved and it was clear that droughts were a normal feature of the Australian environment.

Following the decision to remove drought from disaster relief, the Minister for Primary Industries and Energy, John Kerin, (Hawke Labor Government) announced in 1990 the establishment of a *Drought Policy Review Task Force* chaired by Dr Peter McInnes, with a balanced and expert membership that assured "buy-in" to the inquiry's findings by key interest groups. Representatives of the National Farmers Federation (NFF), the Australian Conservation Foundation (ACF), Commonwealth Scientific and Industrial Research Organisation (CSIRO), the New South Wales

Soil Conservation Service, the Rural Adjustment Finance Corporation of Western Australia, and the Commonwealth departments of Finance and Primary Industries and Energy, along with a wheat grower and a cattle producer, made up the Task Force.

The Task Force was set three main objectives to:

1. identify policy options that encourage primary producers and other segments of rural Australia to adopt self-reliant approaches to the management of drought;
2. consider the integration of drought policy with other relevant policy issues; and
3. advise on priorities for Commonwealth government action in minimising the effects of drought in the rural sector.

The terms of reference suggest that the DPRTF was expected to support and add substance to a change in policy direction that had already been decided by government, acting as a device "to enable governments to do what they want to do anyway … clothing it in the legitimacy provided by research" (Bulmer 1983: 436) and consultation. Certainly the language of "self-reliance" was quickly adopted, not only by the DPRTF in its report but by a later Senate inquiry into the government's response to the DPRTF recommendations. This was clever framing of the issue as not only was it consistent with the overall economic policy direction of the Hawke-Keating governments of deregulation and market liberalism, but at the same time it appealed to the individualism popularly attributed to farmers. Although these values sets are often incompatible, particularly with respect to the delivery of farm welfare policy, the framing of drought policy in terms of self-reliance ensured broad support for the approach across the political spectrum.

In terms of substance, the DPRTF's recommendations provided the Commonwealth with concrete suggestions for the way forward in its negotiations with state governments over changes to drought policy.

The DPRTF recommended the implementation of a national drought policy "as a matter of urgency" and called on government to review other areas of rural policy to support the new approach. Concurrently with finalisation of the drought policy, the Commonwealth initiated reviews of two of its key agricultural programs – the Rural Adjustment Scheme and the income smoothing mechanism, the Income Equalisation Deposits Scheme.

The DPRTF's success was signalled by the agreement of the Council of Agriculture Ministers in July 1992 to a National Drought Policy based on the principles of risk management and self-reliance. The new policy contained several key components. A revised Rural Adjustment Scheme was introduced to facilitate structural adjustment in the farm sector. The scheme included "exceptional circumstances" provisions, which, when triggered, increased the level of support available to eligible producers. The second major component was a loans-based Farm Household Support Scheme designed to meet the welfare needs of marginal farmers while they decided whether to exit agriculture. The rationale for offering this support as a loan was to avoid the welfare payment becoming a *de facto* subsidy to otherwise unviable farm businesses, and thereby slowing the rate of structural adjustment in agriculture. The third component was a revised Income Equalisation Deposits Scheme, which was an income-smoothing measure offered through the tax system. In addition to the revised income equalisation scheme, the government introduced a new Farm Management Bond (later renamed the Farm Management Deposit) specifically designed to encourage farmers to put aside financial surpluses in high income years to be drawn down during drought.

The Commonwealth government promoted these schemes as a cohesive policy package. When introducing the legislation for the revised Rural Adjustment Scheme into Parliament, the then Minister for Primary Industries and Energy, Simon Crean stated:

> We will ensure that the Government's rural policies and programs, such as the National Drought Policy, the Income Equalisation

> Deposits Scheme and the Rural Adjustment Scheme, function in an integrated way and encourage good management practices. (Crean 1992: 2412)

Although the National Drought Policy was consistent with the overall recommendations of the DPRTF, the inclusion of the "exceptional circumstances" provisions in the revised Rural Adjustment Scheme became a problem for policymakers. The Senate inquiry had called for the national drought policy to make provision for additional assistance during severe drought, and agriculture ministers had agreed to this. The difficulty arose in implementation. Criteria for distinguishing between "normal" and "severe" drought were not developed prior to the policy's introduction and the relevant legislation was silent on what constituted an "exceptional circumstance". Over time, criteria were developed and amended – all based on the identification of geographical regions that were eligible for assistance. The use of both drought definitions and "lines on maps" to determine eligibility for support was contrary to the spirit and the letter of the DPRTF report, which had been explicit about the impossibility of arriving at a definition of drought:

> [I]t is not possible to identify independent or objective physical criteria that specify when drought conditions exist. Indeed, we believe the search for an objective, scientific definition of drought has distracted attention from a proper understanding of the issues involved.

However, successful implementation required the development of appropriate criteria and indicators.

In addition to consideration of "exceptional circumstances" declarations, the National Drought Policy has been subject to a series of incremental changes, the most important of which was the introduction of a welfare payment. It became clear by 1994 that the loans-based Farm Household Support Scheme was not meeting the needs of many farm families in drought-affected areas. A new welfare payment was announced in September 1994 to meet this need. It was available to all eligible farmers in areas declared to be experiencing exceptional circumstances. The availability of the relief payment made "exceptional circumstances" declarations considerably more attractive and put further pressure on the governments to develop a workable definition.

The incoming Howard Coalition Government in 1996 initiated a review of the Rural Adjustment Scheme, which saw the scheme wound up and replaced with alternative farm support measures. The "exceptional circumstances" measures were retained in a stand-alone program comprising both interest rate subsidies and a relief payment. In 1999, Commonwealth and state governments agreed to refocus the program on the welfare component, and, in 2005, the means test for the relief payment was relaxed, making it much more generous than other comparable welfare payments. In spite of these incremental changes, the broad approach, and certainly the rhetoric of policymakers, remained consistent with the recommendations of the 1990 DPRTF report emphasising self-reliance, risk management and acceptance that drought is a normal part of the Australian climate.

It is clear that the DPRTF met many of the criteria of success for a public inquiry. It addressed a clear policy question, the review panel was nonpartisan and the timing was right. Although the immediate timing was influenced by the politics around the alleged misuse of the natural disaster relief arrangements in Queensland, it coincided with a policy reform agenda across government that had been underway throughout the 1980s. The Commonwealth government came under some criticism from the 1992 Senate inquiry for its slow response to the DPRTF report; however, given the amount of reform that accompanied the policy and the need to negotiate the new approach with state governments, just over two years is not excessive. By contrast, the response to the 2008 review process took nearly five years to emerge.

The 2008 reviews

In 2008, the newly elected Rudd Labor Government announced a review of the National Drought Policy, the primary rationale for which was the severity and length of drought in the first decade of the 21st century. Links were also made to the impact of climate change on rainfall variability.

In announcing the review in parliament, the then Minister for Agriculture, Fisheries and Forestry, Tony Burke, acknowledged the problems with the "lines on maps" approach to exceptional circumstances declarations, noting that, "With the benefit of time and experience, both sides of the House would probably now agree that creating distinct geographical regions within which a drought event is declared has its own challenges and difficulties" (Burke 2008: 4750).

These problems had been gradually building up over the two decades of the implementation of the National Drought Policy so the time was right for a review. The priority given by the first Rudd Government to climate change provided additional context for the revisiting of the policy.

This review had three components, and in this case, they were addressed separately including the:

1. likely impact of climate change on the frequency and severity of droughts in Australia;
2. social impacts of drought; and
3. effectiveness and efficiency of existing drought response measures.

The climate review was completed first in order to inform the other two inquiries.

The Climate Review

The Bureau of Meteorology and the CSIRO were requested to assess the likely impact of climate change on future drought events, and were asked specifically in the terms of reference to "comment on the appropriateness of the current one-in-20-to-25-year Exceptional Circumstances event trigger based on the historic record". This agency review concluded that Australia is facing a hotter and drier future, and that, therefore, the frequency and severity of drought is likely to increase. Accordingly the established exceptional circumstances event trigger was found to be "not appropriate under a changing climate".

The Expert Social Panel Report

An Expert Social Panel (Kenny Review) was established to analyse the social dimensions of the impacts of drought and the range of government and non-government social support services available to farm families and rural communities. The Panel had a diverse membership, although arguably it did not cover as wide a range of interests as the 1990 Task Force. It was chaired by a former president of the Queensland rural lobby group AgForce, Peter Kenny, and comprised a former President of the New South Wales Farmers' Association, two academics (a rural sociologist and an expert in remote health practice), two former politicians and a representative of the Country Women's Association. The review process was comprehensive, including literature reviews and the commissioning of independent research and surveys, 25 public consultation forums which attracted more than 1000 participants, meetings with government and non-government agencies and organisations and receipt of more than 230 written submissions.

The findings of the Kenny Review covered issues as diverse as taxation policy; access to education, including flexible training delivery for adult learning; mental health services; and trade and professional skills shortages. The 37 recommendations varied in the degree of specificity from an overarching call for government to make a "high-level statement of commitment to a strong, healthy, vibrant and sustainable rural Australia" to a recommendation for state government assistance for students faced with school closures.

In common with the trend in drought policy statements since 1992, the

Kenny Review emphasised the "normal" nature of drought in Australia and called for a "new national approach to living with dryness ... rather than dealing with drought" (Kenny 2008: 1). Nevertheless, the final report was replete with agrarian language about the contribution of rural Australia and the characteristics of its people. The report appears to have been playing to more than one audience, containing very sympathetic language towards drought-affected families and communities while seeking to meet the terms of reference set by government. As a result, it lacks coherence in its focus and recommendations. The Productivity Commission which conducted the review of the effectiveness and efficiency of existing drought response measures neatly summarised the findings of the Kenny Review as follows:

- there is widespread distress in drought-affected rural communities and too many farm decisions are made under stress;
- while it is hard to separate the social impacts of drought from long-term trends contributing to decline in some rural populations, drought adversely impinges on the wellbeing of farm families and communities;
- policy needs to address the social needs of farm families, rural businesses and communities in ways that do not inhibit the efficiency of agricultural industries; and
- the connection between the farm as a place of work, residence and family tradition has important implications for the effectiveness of institutional support. (Productivity Commission 2009: xxvi)

The Productivity Commission review

The Productivity Commission's 2009 report *Government Drought Support* was something of a capstone in the tripartite process. The Productivity Commission was asked to assess drought support provided to farmers, farm businesses and farm-dependent, rural, small businesses, to examine the "appropriateness, effectiveness and efficiency" of government drought response measures, and recommend the best way to build self-reliance and drought preparedness among farmers, associated businesses and their communities.

The Productivity Commission conducted 82 meetings, attended 24 roundtables, visited rural cities in all states and received 107 written submissions. Following the release of its draft report, it received a further 81 submissions and held an additional seven public hearings and five roundtables. The Productivity Commission (2009) recommended that the key mechanism for supporting drought-affected farm businesses under the National Drought Policy – the "exceptional circumstances" interest rate subsidy – be terminated, and called for an end to "exceptional circumstances" drought declarations.

There was some evidence of the influence of the Kenny Review on the Productivity Commission's thinking, in recommendations for "a Farming Family Income support scheme designed for farming circumstances" and also for "significant funding" to be directed to "a continuous learning program" encompassing "advice and training for managing climate variability and for farm business management" (Productivity Commission 2009: LII).

The Productivity Commission also called for an intergovernmental agreement to underpin drought policy commitments.

Government responses to the 2008 Review

As an initial response, in 2010 a Drought Policy Pilot Program was initiated in Western Australia, supported by government, to test a package of new measures developed out of the 2008 reviews. Initially planned to roll out over 12 months, the pilot was extended to run for two years. A review of the pilot undertaken in the second year was overwhelmingly positive about the reform measures, noting that they had been implemented as intended, and noting also "the strong demand for many of the pilot programs" (Keogh *et al* 2011: 2).

Very little has happened between this review of the pilot in 2011 and the announcement late in 2012 of a "new package" of drought response measures to be implemented from 1 July 2014. The package included a farm household support payment; farm management deposits and taxation measures; a national approach to farm business training; a coordinated, collaborative approach to the provision of social support services, and tools and technologies to inform farmer decision-making.

Consistent with the Productivity Commission's recommendation, an intergovernmental agreement on National Drought Program Reform was signed in May 2013. At the time of writing, the policy lacked detail about the content and funding arrangements for all of the various components, except for a commitment of $99.4 million for farm household support. Also consistent with the Productivity Commission's recommendations, governments agreed to abolish the "exceptional circumstances" program although without indicating what type of support will be offered in its place. The intergovernmental agreement simply states: "Future programs providing temporary in-drought support will be consistent with the principles and processes agreed." These principles are vague and leave open the possibility of a wide range of policy responses.

The outcome and impact of the two drought policy reviews

The 1990 DPRTF had a profound effect on drought policy. Its recommendations were adopted almost in their entirety and the language of self-reliance and risk management became entrenched in drought policy discourse. Even in instances where policy developments have appeared to move back in the direction of a disaster response, ministers have been careful to continue to acknowledge drought as a normal part of Australia's climate and a risk to be managed.

By contrast, the 2008 review appears to have had limited impact on policy. The 2013 intergovernmental agreement differed little in its wording from the original 1992 announcement establishing the National Drought Policy. Where the 1990 report marked something of a paradigm shift in policy thinking, the 2008 reviews constituted further steps in an incremental process of policy development.

While the 2013 policy has more explicitly addressed the welfare dimension of drought, with its emphasis on "farm families" and welfare support, this shift had been occurring since the introduction of the drought relief payment in 1994 so it is not clear how much of the welfare emphasis is attributable to the Kenny Review's report. The 1992 policy was more focused on farming as an industry, with the welfare support that was offered structured as a loan to avoid providing de facto support to otherwise unviable farm businesses. This difference reflects the different emphasis of the two reviews and the different political contexts within which they were set up. The 1990 DPRTF review reported at the end of a decade of ongoing policy reform across the Australian economy in general and the rural sector in particular. The 2008 review appears more reactive to problems, both experienced and predicted, in the implementation of the existing policy.

Conclusion

The original drought review of 1990 by the DPRTF was clearly influential. Its recommended move away from a disaster response to one based on self-reliance and risk management, reflected in the 1992 National Drought Policy, has echoed through drought policy discourse for more than 20 years. The National Drought Policy was a significant development. It had the agreement of state governments and sought to integrate a range of Commonwealth rural programs to ensure that they were all working towards the objective of "a farm sector which is able to thrive in a highly variable economic and natural resource environment, without relying on government assistance for survival and growth" (Crean 1992: 2412). In spite of shortcomings in implementation, the underpinning principles outlined by the DPRTF continue to be influential as the policy has evolved incrementally over time.

By contrast, the 2008 review, which was far more extensive and detailed, appears to have had little real impact on policy directions. The new intergovernmental agreement lacks detail and the policy rhetoric closely resembles the language of the past two decades. The Productivity Commission's recommendation for the end of the exceptional circumstances provisions and "lines on maps" merely formalised the response to complaints that had swirled around this program for some time. The influence of the Kenny Review is possibly evident in the increased emphasis in the current policy on the welfare of farm families and the need for social support, but, again, the trend was already in this direction. The climate report drew attention to the links between drought frequency and severity and climate change and was useful in highlighting for policymakers the problem with the existing definition of exceptional circumstances. However, it is unlikely to have received much traction in the farming community. Notably, the intergovernmental agreement refers not to "climate change" but to "increased climate variability".

The hand of government is clearer in the 1990 review. The scene was set for the Task Force in the opening sentence of its terms of reference: "Drought is a recurring natural condition and in most circumstances, is a normal risk that should be included in the management of an Australian rural enterprise." By contrast, the government's announcement of the 2008 review lacked a sense of a real policy rethink, focusing instead on problems with implementing the existing policy. There was no sense of an overarching policy intent in the establishment of the tripartite process. The rather limp response that has emerged to the 2008 reviews reinforces the view that they did not create the same level of policy momentum as the earlier inquiry.

The experience of the DPRTF shows that a public inquiry can serve both government and national interest when it has strong government policy leadership and a clearly nonpartisan committee with scope to make real recommendations. Clear terms of reference, which set the policy context for the review but also left scope for independent advice, resulted in a report that has had enduring impact. The 2008 reports, although apparently more comprehensive in nature, lacked a sense of policy direction, beyond concern that climate change would render the existing policy unworkable. It was not apparent what the government was seeking from the review and the tripartite nature of the process did not lend itself to a coherent approach.

A key difference between the 1990 and 2008 processes was the conception of the former as a true "policy review", whereas the 2008 inquiries were set up to collect evidence to feed into policy consideration. The 1990 DPRTF operated at a more abstract level in terms of how drought should be conceptualised in Australia, and the types of programs that would comprise an appropriate response. The 2008 Expert Social Panel to a large extent accepted that conceptualisation and focused more on the detail of drought response programs. It is therefore unlikely to have the ongoing impact of the 1990 inquiry.

Public inquiries mentioned in chapter

(in chronological order by year of appointment, with name of chair)

Drought Policy Review Task Force (McInnes: 1990)

Drought Policy Review Expert Social Panel (Kenny: 2008)

References

Bulmer, M., 1983, "Increasing the Effectiveness of Royal Commissions: A Comment," *Public Adminstration* (London), 61, Winter, 436-443

Burke, T., MP, 2008, "Ministerial Statement: Drought," *Commonwealth Parliamentary Debates,* House of Representatives, 24 June, 5749-5752

Crean, S., MP, 1992, "Rural Adjustment Bill 1992: Second Reading Speech," *Commonwealth Parliamentary Debates*, House of Representatives, 3 November, 2412

Hennessy, K., Fawcett, R., Kirono, D., Mpelasoka, F., Jones, D., Bathols, J., Whetton, P., Stafford Smith, M., Howden, M., Mitchell C., and Plummer N., 2008, *An Assessment of the Impact of Climate Change on the Nature and Frequency of Exceptional Climatic Events*, Canberra: Commonwealth Government, Bureau of Meteorology and CSIRO, http://www.daff.gov.au/__data/assets/pdf_file/0007/721285/csiro-bom-report-future-droughts.pdf

Kenny, P., 2008, *Drought Policy Review Expert Social Panel: It's About People: Changing Perspective on Dryness*, Canberra: Commonwealth Government

Keogh, M., Granger, R., and Middleton, S., 2011, *Drought Pilot Review Panel: A Review of the Pilot of Drought Reform Measures in Western Australia*, Canberra: Commonwealth Government

McInness, P., 1990, *Drought Policy Review Task Force, National Drought Policy Report*, Canberra: Australian Government Publishing Service

Productivity Commission, 2009, *Government Drought Support*, Report No 46, Canberra: Productivity Commission

Senate Standing Committee on Rural and Regional Affairs, 1992, *A National Drought Policy – Appropriate Government Responses to the Recommendations of the Drought Policy Review Task Force: Final Report*, Canberra: Commonwealth Parliament

Walsh, P., Senator The Hon, 1989, "Question Without Notice: Natural Disaster Relief Arrangement", *Commonwealth Parliamentary Debates*, The Senate, 1 March, 189

12

Inquiring into government administration

Paddy Gourley

Introduction

In the history of Australian public administration there has been nothing like the 1970s *Royal Commission on Australian Government Administration* (RCAGA, henceforth the Coombs Commission*)*. The two wide-ranging royal commissions into the Commonwealth's administration and public expenditure in the aftermath of the World War I and those in some state governments cannot compare in scope, depth and openness with the Coombs Commission. Beside it the Commonwealth government's 2010 *Ahead of the Game – Blueprint for the Reform of Australian Government Administration,* chaired by the then Secretary of the Department Prime Minister and Cabinet Terry Moran is a pale shadow, a document mired in jargon, lacking an analytical base and largely disowned by the government that spawned it.

It took more than ten years to deal adequately with the Coombs Commission's report and its hundreds of recommendations. On some matters the Coombs Commission did not get its way and on others the tide of events ran against it. For example, instead of the more unified administration it wanted, the Commonwealth now has a more fragmented one. Nevertheless, most of the Coombs Commission's main recommendations and many of its lesser ones were implemented. Its effects have been pervasive.

This chapter briefly outlines the history of the Coombs Commission and a few myths created around it and seeks to draw some lessons from the experience.

Background – appointment and members

The Coombs Commission was established by the Whitlam Labor Government in 1974, but with its loss of office in December 1975, it reported to the incoming Fraser Coalition Government in 1976.

The commission was headed by Dr H.C. Coombs, a former long-serving senior public servant and Reserve Bank Governor. Its other members were Peter Bailey, a Deputy Secretary in the Department of the Prime Minister and Cabinet; Professor Enid Campbell from the Law Faculty at Monash University; J.E. Isaac, a Deputy President of the then Conciliation and Arbitration Commission; and Paul Munro, the Secretary of the Council of Commonwealth Public Service Organisations.

The history of the Coombs Commission has been described at length in academic and other literature. However, as the memories of it have dimmed it is necessary to recap the reasons for it, its operational methods, the nature of its report, and its implementation that stretched out for more than 10 years.

Reasons for appointment

There were mixed reasons for the appointment of the Coombs Commission. It had been more than 50 years since the previous wide-ranging examination of the Commonwealth Public Service and administration. In that time, its size and the nature of its functions had changed markedly, particularly as a consequence of the Commonwealth becoming solely responsible for income taxing during World War II.

In 1973, the Whitlam Government had established a royal commission (Vernon Commission) into the Postmaster-General's Department (PMG). Decisions based on the Vernon Commission's recommendations abolished the PMG and established its functions in two statutory authorities not staffed under the *Public Service Act*. At a stroke, the size of the Commonwealth Public Service was reduced by 120,000 staff and its character was changed from one dominated for its entire history by the PMG to one without it.

The decade before the Coombs Commission had been a season for major public inquiries into public services in Canada (Glassco Royal Commission, 1960), New Zealand (McCarthy Royal Commission, 1962), Ireland (Devlin Review, 1966), the United Kingdom (Fulton Committee, 1966), and the United States (Ash Advisory Committee, 1969). At the time of the Whitlam Government coming to office, there had also been public inquiries into state administrations in South Australia (Corbett Inquiry, 1973), and Victoria (Bland Review, 1973). These inquiries were watched in influential quarters and they, along with the changing nature of Commonwealth public administration and a vague sense that the time had come for another major review, helped to create a favourable climate for appointing a public inquiry. Of themselves, however, these factors would have been insufficient to bring forth anything like the Coombs Commission.

Rather, it was the changing political scene with the election of the Whitlam Government in December 1972 that gave rise to the appointment of the Coombs Commission. Prior to the election there had been apprehensions within the Labor Party about the capacity and willingness of the Commonwealth Public Service – since 1973 known as the Australian Public Service (APS) – to get properly and effectively behind a new Labor government. As Labor had been out of office for 23 years and the APS had become used to working under non-Labor administrations, there were concerns about its ability to work effectively with a new government. In addition, because Labor had developed what Whitlam called a "program" that would more deeply involve the Commonwealth in health, education, social welfare, urban and regional development, and the environment, among other areas, there was a question of whether the APS had the capacity to respond to these new demands.

Consequently, after Labor gained office, the Whitlam Government almost immediately set about establishing new organisations and importantly appointed a host of public inquiries to assist in further policy review, development and advice across a wide array of areas (see Prasser 2006: 287-307 for a full list of the Whitlam Government's public inquiries).

This was partly a vote of no confidence in the ability of existing institutions in general and the APS, and its senior ranks in particular. Notwithstanding the considerable professional goodwill towards the new Labor Government within the APS, elements within the Labor Party feared that its senior levels may have been, even if inadvertently, captured by the Coalition or that its old ways might die hard. As Whitlam (1973) said in his Garran Oration given to the Royal Institute of Public Administration, he saw the appointment of more than 70 public inquiries plus 13 royal commissions as the "most effective way of producing a high quality report in a short time which combines the skills and insights of prominent citizens with the background and experience of the actual working of government". Whitlam (1976: 223) later reflected that on coming to office there was a need for public inquiries because:

> The Labor Government found that the scarcest commodity after 23 years of conservative rule was information. In whole areas of public policy, schools, health, the environment, industrial conditions, the National Estate, social welfare, local government – no body of facts or evidence existed … There was no core of information on which federal or state governments could take decisions.

As Lloyd and Reid (1974: 254) commented at the time, not only was the appointment of so many external public inquiries perceived as a vote of no confidence in the APS, they also represented a "considerable threat to the traditional supremacy of the Public Service".

Further, it did not take long for relations between parts of the APS and several of the new Labor ministers to sour to the point where some ministerial staff thought "senior public servants ... should be regarded as hostile until they proved themselves otherwise" (Edwards 2006: 219). Even before the so-called "Loans Affair"[1] rolled around at the end of 1974 there was strong support within the Whitlam Government for a public inquiry that would help to find ways in which the APS could be more effectively harnessed to the government's purposes. This was the critical reason for the establishment of the Coombs Commission. Hawker, Smith and Weller (1979: 249) write that the Coombs Commission "was not an inquiry fuelled by particular political purposes". In some senses that is exactly what it was.

So in this political context, support for an independent, external review of the APS quickly grew. Consequently, early in the life of the Whitlam Government a caucus committee formulated terms of reference for a public service inquiry. While these included a reference to "ministerial control of departments and the role of permanent heads of departments", the terms were narrow and were largely confined to the role of the Public Service Board and personnel matters.

Nature of the inquiry, its terms of reference, processes and report

The Coombs Commission's terms of reference were broad. With the exception of the PMG, which, as noted had already been subject to its own royal commission review, no part of Commonwealth civilian administration was exempt except for the question of superannuation for Commonwealth employees.

The Commission employed a large research staff, arranged reports from academics and expert consultants, called for submissions from government agencies, their staff and the general public and conducted extensive public hearings. More than 750 submissions were received; 356 witnesses appeared at 55 days of public hearings giving rise to more than 3000 pages of transcript evidence. In its scope and methods the Coombs Commission far exceeded most of the major overseas inquiries that immediately preceded it, few of which had public hearings or called for submissions.

Of government agencies, the Public Service Board was forthcoming. It had been at the forefront of management improvement in the 1960s and it had a track record on which it was prepared to advance. It provided eight volumes of background information, two large submissions, and 26 detailed memoranda with many proposals for change.

The Department of the Treasury, which had not been prominent on internal public service management innovation, was defensive, and its stance may have been affected by the strained relations that had developed between the Treasury Secretary, Sir Frederick Wheeler and the Commission's Chairman Dr Coombs. Treasury's submission confined itself largely to a description of the portfolio and its operating methods, contained no significant proposals for change, and emphasised what it saw as the importance of retaining its responsibilities for macroeconomic policy and financial and budgetary control within the Treasury. Many other Commonwealth departments and agencies provided thoughtful submissions and some were enthusiastic about the prospect of greater devolution of powers from central agencies.

In general, the Coombs Commission's operating methods wrapped participants into its proceedings and reflected their views in its report, thus creating a constituency within the administration for the changes it advocated.

The final report was a massive document – five volumes (a covering report with 337 recommendations and four volumes of appendices), more than 2000 pages in all and tipping the scales at 3.5 kilograms. It was cogently expressed and drew conscientiously on submissions, evidence gathered at public hearings, and the wealth of detailed, sophisticated research it commissioned, much of which was published in the report's appendices.

Prominent academics were divided on the Coombs Commission.

In support, R.S. Parker, Professor of Political Science at the Australian National University believed the report was "an unprecedented achievement in the genre" and that "it will have so much value for so long for so many people, if they pay attention to it" (Parker 1977: 58-59). However, R.N. Spann, Professor of Government and Public Administration of the University of Sydney, pointed out tensions in what he saw as the main themes of closer working relations between ministers and officials, greater accountability of officials and the devolution of responsibilities to more junior staff so that they could be more flexibly responsive in providing services (Spann 1977). Spann and the Commission recognised that these "slippery" themes co-exist uneasily; trying to reconcile them was not only difficult for the Commission, but also for those who had to deal with its recommendations.

Implementation

The Coombs Commission's final report provided to the new Fraser Coalition Government in July 1976 was, of course, seen by those in the incoming government as a product of the old regime and it was delivered at a time of considerable tension between the major parties following the circumstances that had caused the Whitlam Government to lose office. The rhetoric of the Fraser Government made much of the alleged extravagance of its predecessor, attacked the use of public inquiries and it had soon commissioned Sir Henry Bland, a former departmental secretary not short of views about public service profligacy, and who had chaired the review of the Victorian Public Service for a Liberal government in 1973, to head a committee to advise on how best to cut back.

In part the Coombs Commission did not help itself. It asked the Fraser Government "to approve in principle the main recommendations of the report … and direct that action be taken to give effect to the principles that underlie them …" (Coombs 1976: 412). No recommendation of the Commission was more unrealistic. A Whitlam Government could not have been expected to accept it; the Fraser Government could have been excused for thinking it arrogant.

If offence was taken, it did not show, although Fraser's first impulse was to wind up the Coombs Commission early until he was told that that could only be done by the Governor-General who had formally established it. Nevertheless, the Fraser Government made elaborate arrangements for the consideration of the Coombs Report, including an interdepartmental committee chaired by the Department of the Prime Minister and Cabinet that worked to a group of senior departmental secretaries reporting to the Machinery of Government Committee of Cabinet. The early operation of these arrangements has been detailed by a participant (see Matthews 1978).

In December 1976, some five months after the Coombs Commission had reported, Fraser announced decisions on a number of significant recommendations. Work continued on others and the results are summed up in an answer to a parliamentary question on notice in 1980 (see Senate Hansard, 23 May 1980, 2863-71).

The Fraser Government did not accept one of the major recommendations of the Coombs Commission, which was for a new Department of Industries and the Economy to provide "intelligence, particularly as it relates to structural developments within industry" (Coombs 1976: 303). Journalist Peter Samuel (1977: 150) described this recommendation as "pure socialism". However that may be, the recommendation was inopportune as the seemingly intractable problems of high inflation and high unemployment ("stagflation" as it was tagged) raised greater doubts about the ability of governments to affect the workings of the economy.

On the other hand, the Fraser Government did what Treasury had feared and which the Coombs Commission had not recommended. It removed the financial and accounting control functions from Treasury and established them in a new Department of Finance to be headed by a notable former Treasury official, Sir William Cole. Under a succession of imaginative secretaries, this new Department of Finance was to play an important role in the development of better financial management within the Commonwealth, much of which was consistent with the views of the Coombs Commission.

Governments and ministers are usually as keen about the grind of administrative change as their electors. When, towards the end of its time in office, the Fraser Government became plagued by various administrative failings, it could not see answers in the Coombs report. It set up a new inquiry – the *Review of Commonwealth Administration* headed by a businessman, J.B. Reid. Reid's report was finalised in the very last days of the Fraser Government and it then fell into the lap of the incoming Hawke Labor Government in March 1983.

The Hawke Government came to office with a detailed election platform for administrative change set out in a document titled *Labor and Quality of Government.* Members of this government and some of its advisers saw that the Fraser government had:

- dragged the chain on the development of forward estimates, in particular their publication;
- rejected the Coombs Commission's suggestion for a new Department of Industries and the Economy;
- not pursued the idea of a "unified Public Service", a concept developed by the Public Service Board and which has now receded into oblivion;
- adopted a different and flawed approach to the role, appointment and tenure of departmental secretaries from that recommended by the RCAGA;
- not accepted the Coombs Commission's recommendations on ministerial staff; and
- in the view of some, not pressed firmly enough on equal employment opportunity.

So with the memories of the politically consequential administrative failings of the Whitlam era, the Hawke Government had a plan for the public service.

Little happened in the first months of the Hawke Government, however, when the Finance Minister John Dawkins also became the Minister Assisting the Prime Minister for the Public Service, the moment had arrived. Dawkins was an intelligent and restlessly energetic minister who liked change. Significantly his Senior Private Secretary, Michael Delaney, had been the main advocate in Prime Minister Whitlam's office for the inquiry that became the Coombs Commission, and he had an almost proprietary interest in seeing the neglected parts of Coombs' recommendations addressed. Dawkins had the backing of Prime Minister Hawke and a number of senior ministers as well as the ready cooperation of key officials in the departments of the Prime Minister and Cabinet and Finance and the Public Service Board some of whom had been directly involved with the Coombs Commission.

In this environment Dawkins, aided by Delaney's advice, established the means to produce a series of policy discussion papers that, among other things, mopped up the worthwhile outstanding recommendations of the Coombs Report. These papers[2] attracted bipartisan political agreement, the support of trade unions and widespread acceptance within the APS with the exception of Treasury under its then Secretary John Stone. The Treasury's coordination comments in Dawkins' Cabinet submissions sneeringly referred to "Public Service reform (sic)": not so much frank and fearless advice as a case of bureaucratic insolence that confirmed to the Hawke Government the good sense of what was being proposed.

When the last paper in the series, *Policy Guidelines for Commonwealth Statutory Authorities and Government Business Enterprises*, was released by Dawkins' successor at Finance, Senator Peter Walsh, in 1987, it could be said that, 11 years after it had reported, the Fraser and

Hawke governments had between them given the Coombs report the consideration it deserved.

Myths around the Coombs Commission

In a National Press Club address shortly after the publication of his final report, Coombs alleged that the Commonwealth bureaucracy reflected "already privileged sections" of society and that it thus leaned "heavily towards the preservation of the *status quo*". While younger public servants, he said, were "impressive" and the "best of the top levels … are men of capacity and vigour", the rest were not much to write home about. For more senior staff in Canberra Coombs observed that, "years of involvement in routine and ritualistic processes, and inability to see the outcome of work done, a sense of isolation from those with whose affairs government administration is concerned and a prevailing flatness in the quality of life, official and unofficial, generally has destroyed much of the vitality and concern", they no doubt had when they were first recruited. But for the person in what Coombs called "the non-Canberra part of the bureaucracy", things were worse. Here the "shades of the prison house no doubt close in around him even more quickly … unless he reacts by treating his hours of work as purely instrumental to the purposes to which he devotes his leisure time" (see Coombs 1977: 49–52 for above).

Coombs might have been better to keep these stereotypical impressions, refracted presumably through his extravagantly cultured life, to himself. They were not supported by material published by his Commission nor were they reflected in its recommendations except to the extent that some sought to improve general employment arrangements and enhance opportunities for all. It would have been possible at the time to find staff matching Coombs' cavalier caricatures, but were they a fair and reasonable portrayal of the work and private lives of the mass of engineers, nurses, policy advisers, technicians, diplomats, motor drivers, examiners of patents, research scientists, meat inspectors, trades and clerical staff and many others in the APS? Almost certainly they were not.

The unfairness of this casual denigration by Coombs is neither here nor there. The point is that in indicating that these flaky impressions had been important in guiding his thinking, Coombs may well have affected the credibility of his Commission's recommendations and the attitude of those within the APS who would need to help give effect to them. Who could blame those labouring in the "shades of the prison house" or burdened with "a prevailing flatness in [their] quality of life" for not caring all that much? Offence was taken and it was not helpful.

A second myth is that the Fraser Government did little or nothing about the Coombs report. Dr Peter Wilenski was a prominent exponent of this view. He was in Whitlam's private office when the Coombs Commission was born and was, for a brief period, its Special Adviser. Wilenski (1986: 184) wrote that "despite the great flurry of activity it [Coombs Commission] engendered in the bureaucracy, it is a text book case of non-implementation of administrative reform".

It is true that the interest of the Fraser Government in the Coombs Commission was not great, but Fraser did as well by Coombs Report as most other governments do by the general run of reports of other inquiries. Certainly, it did more than the Rudd and Gillard governments did with the *Ahead of the Game* blueprint for which they were responsible, and on which ministers made no significant statements other than to announce the withdrawal of most of the funding for the things it envisioned.

Wilenski's claims would have been more reasonable if he had said that what had been done with the Coombs Report under Fraser was a textbook case of the non-implementation of the kind of administrative reform for which he had hoped. At least Wilenski had the consolation of playing a part in the changes brought about by Dawkins and the Hawke Government.

Lessons

It is probably too much to expect telling lessons to be drawn from a sample of a single, atypical public inquiry now of some vintage. Nevertheless, it might be worth looking at what seemed to work and not work for the Coombs Commission and to speculate as to whether that experience might contain any pointers, no matter how vague for the future appointment and use of public inquiries.

For much of its life improvements in the Commonwealth Public Service and other parts of the Commonwealth administration have come from within its agencies, particularly those responsible for its central management.

In the 1960s the Public Service Board directed major micro-economic reforms within almost all of Commonwealth civilian employment through union–agency enterprise bargaining. It was the kind of thing Prime Minister Paul Keating pretended to have introduced into Australia in the early 1990s. These changes, largely unacknowledged in academic and other commentary, made the decade of the 1960s the most important period of reform the Commonwealth administration has experienced, and it happened without significant ministerial involvement. That is to say, the APS had proved to be amenable to a kind of large scale change that left the Coombs Commission free to concentrate on matters other than pay and conditions fixing, and classification structures. The section in the Coombs Report on the "organisation of work" runs to 7½ pages and contains no recommendations of significance.

However, by 1974 the interests of the Whitlam Government in public administration were unlikely to be served by gradual change produced from within the APS. It wanted public agencies to be more responsive to ministers, that is to say, it wanted to rebalance the relative powers of ministers and officials. Dr Coombs is right to observe that "It is a characteristic of power that it tends to be self-aggregating" (Coombs 1977: 51). Thus, to ask those responsible for internal management within the APS to provide advice on how their powers might be changed or modified would be to put the question into the wrong forum.

So the first lesson from the Coombs Report may be that if governments wish to seek an alteration in powers within their agencies, especially where that includes the relative powers of ministers and officials, advice might best be sought from a disinterested external inquiry whose results should not be left primarily to officials to play with – these should be matters fundamentally for ministers.

As has been observed, the Coombs Commission was a fully open inquiry. For instance: it called for submissions; held public hearings; provided opportunities for participants to comment on the submissions and the views of others; distributed and sought comments on major papers prepared by its staff or others; and provided an immense report in which it explained, often eloquently, the reasons for its recommendations and showed how it had weighed the evidence before it. While these methods may have allowed some to plan resistance, it is also the case that they helped to build a constituency for change. Many who had made submissions could see their views being played back to them, including in agencies like the Public Service Board. In other cases, the strength of the Coombs Commission's arguments eventually convinced some agencies of the merit of a range of proposals, for example, the Department of Finance on forward estimates and program budgeting.

While the Fraser Government could have been more attentive, it did more with it than it did with the review it commissioned from Sir Henry Bland, which sank without leaving a ripple (Wettenhall and Gourley 2009). The Bland Review was conducted almost entirely behind closed doors. It held no public hearings, it made half-hearted requests for submissions, and its reports were never made public. Bland may have thought the sheer force of his will and strong personality would be sufficient to get the Fraser government to do what he suggested without going to all the trouble of the Coombs Commission's methods. There is little evidence his recommendations survived in either the short or the long term.

Thus, the experience of the Coombs Commission might suggest that, other things being equal, the more open the inquiry and the more it is prepared to articulate a public rationale for its propositions, the greater the chance it has of getting its views accepted, if in some cases over the longer haul.

The Coombs Commission experience supports another proverbial observation: accidents of timing and other events can affect the fate of public inquiries. If the Coombs Commission had reported to a Labor government it is likely that some of its recommendations would have been acted upon earlier. And as the Fraser Government in its last years became bogged down in thickets of administrative failings and allegations of corruption and maladministration, some of which came to light as a consequence of the Costigan *Royal Commission on the Activities of the Federated Ship Painters and Dockers Union* that had been established in 1980, the Coombs Report slipped into the background.

Then, in a number of ways, the election of the Hawke Government made for propitious circumstances in which to deal with hitherto neglected aspects of the Coombs Report. The reformist instincts of the Hawke Government were accentuated by double digit inflation, unemployment and interest rates and it changed traditional Labor Party economic policy to address these problems by embracing financial deregulation, and floating the exchange rate. As it was prosecuting these significant changes for the rest of the community, it was natural enough for it to practise what it preached in its backyard. And it was fortuitous that that task fell to an activist minister in Dawkins, whose Senior Private Secretary Michael Delaney had been, as noted, when in Whitlam's office, one of the main godparents of the Coombs Commission.

The fate of the Coombs Report might suggest, therefore, that individual governments should try to get first crack at reports they instigate. Of course that will not always be feasible and it might be hoped that the inherent merits of the proposals of most inquiries would be sufficient to carry the day. After all, the Reid Review commissioned by the Fraser Government in 1982 and bequeathed to Hawke was promptly dealt with and many of its main recommendations were accepted. However, if the apparent bitterness between the major political parties in the Commonwealth now means that new governments will have less regard for the products of those they replace, it might be better for each one to get the reports of those they set up in sufficient time to deal with them.

Even so, if the Coombs Commission is anything to go by, it might be expected that large reports, containing numerous and often inter-related recommendations with a good number couched in general terms requiring further development before implementation, may take many years for their proposals to be realised. It took more than a decade for the Coombs Commission Report to be properly considered. The experience has been similar with other public inquiries. For example, inquiries on taxation and the financial system and many of the reports of the former Industries Assistance Commission (IAC), especially when headed by Alf Rattigan, all took time to be of consequence for a range of reasons, including the need to obtain adequate political support. The significance and consequences of many large-scale reports is often not confined to their recommendations, but extends to the information they publish and the further research and discussion they foster. This was certainly so with the Coombs Commission.

Finally, the experience of the Coombs Commission shows the importance of ministerial will. For the most part, these exercises are initiated by governments and ministers or at least they require their approval. They are their babies. But too often when it comes to the grisly business of fixing up their administrative machines, ministers falter or flick pass responsibility to officials. It is as if they have been willing to be persuaded by those false prophets who tell them that they are "customers" of their departments and that management business should be left to those in them. For example, in many recent inquiries dealing with Defence (see chapter 15: Ergas) and Immigration departments, ministers, aided and abetted by incompetent and ignorant reviewers, have been able to stand aside and leave the follow up to their officials. This is high-order ministerial irresponsibility. As the Coombs Report emphasised, ministers are the leaders of their departments (in modern parlance, their chief executive officers) and they should accept the associated management burden. If they do not, the point of external inquiries on the functioning of their agencies is largely lost.

Another royal commission into the Australian public service?

Major inquiries into government administrations were popular in Australia and a number of other countries in the 1960s and 70s. That popularity has waned and there seems to be little appetite for a further round of them. No one is suggesting a repeat of the Coombs and perhaps there is no need.

There was nothing like it in the first 100 years of Commonwealth and, short of some major failing, maybe another could be left until its 100th anniversary comes around in 2074.

In general, gradualist change inspired from within agencies and with occasional peaks of ministerial interest has kept the Commonwealth public administration in reasonable order and the need for another wide-ranging investigation is not obvious.

Moreover, during the last 50 years there has been a major devolution of powers to agencies within the Commonwealth and this was accelerated by the Coombs Commission. In some respects this has gone too far, for example, the present arrangements for fixing pay and conditions for APS staff, but the devolved functions, no matter how distasteful and costly to perform, appear to be close to the hearts of line agencies. That is to say, the prospect of a general inquiry into Commonwealth administration that would inevitably bring with it the prospect of having some of these powers reduced would be resisted.

Now, the Coombs Report sits on the shelf, probably largely

undisturbed by modern managers or others seeking inspiration about what best to do in public administration. It is an artefact from another age and maybe there is not a lot to regret about its being pensioned off. Yet, for all its imperfections and age the Coombs Commission might still be capable of some part-time work through its report, or some of the material in its appendices. It is unlikely to be consulted, however, as many now are only too happy to tell one another tall stories about the unprecedented newness, difficulty and complexity of contemporary public policy problems that might be thought to be well beyond the Coombs Report to illuminate. The vanity of the present has rarely been such a burden.

Public inquiries mentioned in chapter

(in chronological order, by year of appointment with name of chair)

Australia

Commonwealth:

Royal Commission on Public Service Administration, Commonwealth of Australia (McLachlan: 1918)

Royal Commission on Public Expenditure of the Commonwealth of Australia (Gibson: 1918)

Australian Post Office Commission of Inquiry (Vernon: 1973)

Royal Commission into Australian Government Administration (Coombs: 1974)

Royal Commission on the Activities of the Federated Ship Painters and Dockers Union (Costigan: 1980)

Review of Commonwealth Administration (Reid: 1982)

State:

South Australia

Committee of Inquiry into the Public Service in South Australia (Corbett: 1973)

Victoria

Board of Inquiry into the Victorian Public Service (Bland: 1973)

Other inquiries mentioned in chapter:

Administrative Review Committee (Bland: 1975)

Overseas public inquiries:

Royal Commission to Inquire and Report Upon the State Services of New Zealand (McCarthy: 1962)

Royal Commission on Government Organization (Glassco: 1960) – Canada

Committee of Inquiry into the Civil Service (Fulton: 1966) – United Kingdom

Public Services Organization Review Group (Devlin: 1966) – Eire

Advisory Council on Executive Organization (Ash: 1969) – USA

References

Advisory Group on Reform of Australian Government Administration, *Ahead of the Game – Blueprint for the Reform of Australian Government Administration*, Canberra: Commonwealth Government (Moran Review)

Coombs, H.C., 1976, *Royal Commission into Australian Government Administration Report*, Canberra: Australian Government Publishing Service

Coombs, H.C., 1977, "The Commission Report," in Hazlehurst, C., and Nethercote, J.R., (eds), *Reforming Australian Government: The Coombs Report and Beyond*, Canberra: Royal Institute of Public Administration (ACT), with Australian National University Press, 49-52

Edwards, P., 2006, *Sir Arthur Tange: Last of the Mandarins*, Sydney: Allen and Unwin

Hawker, G., Smith, R.F.I. and Weller, P., 1979, *Politics and Policy in Australia*, St Lucia: University of Queensland Press

Hazlehurst, C. and Nethercote, J.R., (eds), 1977, *Reforming Australian Government: The Coombs Report and Beyond*, Canberra: Royal Institute of Public Administration (ACT), with Australian National University Press

Lloyd, C.J., and Reid, G.S., 1974, *Out of the Wilderness: The Return of Labor*, Melbourne: Cassell

Matthews, T., 1978, "Implementing the Coombs Report: The First Eight Months," in Smith, R.F.I., and Weller, P., (eds), *Public Service Inquiries*, St Lucia: University of Queensland Press, 256-301

Parker, R.S., 1977, "What Can Be Said for the Coombs Commission?," in Hazlehurst and Nethercote, 58-64

Prasser, S., 2006, *Royal Commissions and Public Inquiries in Australia,* Sydney: LexisNexis Butterworths

Reid, J.B., 1982, *Review of Commonwealth Administration Report, Canberra: Australian Government Publishing Service*

Samuel, P., 1977, "The Treasury and the Treasury Line," in Hazlehurst, C. and Nethercote, J.R., 150-3

Smith, R.F.I., and Weller, P., (eds), 1978, *Public Service Inquiries in Australia*, St Lucia: University of Queensland Press

Spann, R.N., 1977, "The Coombs Doctrine," in Hazlehurst and Nethercote, 78-86

Wettenhall, R., and Gourley, P., 2009, "Sir Henry Bland and the Fraser Government's Administrative Review Committee: Another Chapter in the Statutory Authority Wars?," *Australian Journal of Public Administration*, 68(3), September, 351-69

Wilenski, P., 1986, *Public Power and Public Administration*, Sydney: Hale and Iremonger

Whitlam, E.G., 1973, "Australian Public Administration Under a Labor Government," *The Sir Robert Garran Memorial Oration*, 12 November

Whitlam, E.G., 1976, *Commonwealth Parliamentary Debates*, House of Representatives, 24 February, 223

Endnotes

1 The "Loans Affair" refers to attempts by ministers in the Whitlam Government to seek loans from what Treasury regarded as "unorthodox" sources. It resulted in the then Opposition delaying the passing of the Budget Bills in the Senate and eventually in the Governor-General sacking the Whitlam Government.

2 Papers outlining public service reform during the Hawke-Keating governments included: *Reforming the Australian Public Service – A Statement of the Government's Intentions*, Canberra: AGPS, 1983; *Budget Reform: A Statement of the Government's Achievements and Intentions in Reforming Australian Government Financial Administration*, Canberra: AGPS, 1984; *Policy Discussion Paper Concerning the Efficiency and Accountability of Statutory Authorities and Government Business Enterprises*, Canberra: AGPS, 1986; *Policy Guidelines for Commonwealth Statutory Authorities and Government Business Enterprises*, Canberra: AGPS, 1987.

Section 4

What is there to show for it? Assessing inquiry effectiveness

Scott Prasser and Helen Tracey

The conventional test of a successful public inquiry is the fate of its findings and recommendations. A failure to implement the findings of an independent review that government has invested in heavily diminishes the credibility of the inquiry and can rebound unhappily on government. By the time an inquiry reports, its work is ended. Public inquiries are temporary bodies, disbanding after they report. They have no continuing powers to enforce or even advocate for the implementation of their proposals, although occasionally members of an inquiry panel choose not to play by these rules. The lasting power of an inquiry, and the real measure of its effectiveness, lies in the persuasiveness of its arguments and the quality of its report.

The failure of governments to implement inquiry recommendations has long been a great source of dissatisfaction with the appointment of inquiries. Governments are free to ignore inquiry recommendations, but non-implementation brings its own risks. A failure to implement fuels the popular cynical view of inquiries as a device to delay decision-making, to obfuscate rather than clarify, to pretend to act but in reality to defer action, to show concern, to defuse political heat and to feed the illusion that something is being done about a problem. To the cynic, in the absence of government action, inquiries are a wilful waste of private time and public money.

This widespread concern about the lack of accountability for the public investment in inquiries led the Australian Law Reform

Commission, in its 2009 review of the statutory framework for making inquiries, to recommend that governments be required to report on the implementation of the inquiry recommendations they accept. As Croucher explains (chapter 1), this would require governments to place on public record which inquiry recommendations they accepted, and to publish an update on progress within 12 months of the release of the inquiry report. This reporting, to cover only those recommendations accepted by government, would allow implementation to be monitored without intruding on government decision-making powers and would vastly improve accountability for the considerable investment in inquiries and increase public confidence in their value.

The immediate acceptance of an inquiry's recommendations however is a fairly blunt measure of inquiry effectiveness. In the first place, implementation is not easily defined. Whatever it is, it is more than an announcement of aspiration and intent, the headline "announceable" delivered when government chooses to make an inquiry report public, which may be some time after the report is submitted and will not necessarily be after full consideration of all recommendations. There is often a long lag between the announcement of acceptance of an inquiry's report and the details of an implementation plan. Government action can take many forms. Depending on the nature of the inquiry, action may range from minor incremental or technical change to major systemic reform. It may encompass new policy directions, new legislation, a new program, new funds, the establishment of a new institution or the restructuring of existing institutions.

Nor does the rejection or setting aside of an inquiry's key recommendations necessarily negate its long-term value. Many inquiries have had their recommendations spurned or ignored initially, only to see them revisited and implemented at a later date, in a different political or budgetary climate. Paddy Gourley's analysis of the Coombs *Royal Commission on Australian Government Administration* (chapter 12) provides an excellent example of a considered, long drawn out implementation process, founded on a high quality report.

Therein lies the danger inherent in measuring the impact of an inquiry by the extent of immediate implementation of its recommendations. By this measure, a poor inquiry will be judged a success if political expediency dictates quick and wholesale acceptance of its recommendations, even if those recommendations are questionable in terms of their public policy outcomes.

A more appropriate measure of the impact of a public inquiry is a judgement about the value of the policy changes it recommends, assessed in terms of the public interest or common good. This may entail, as it did with Coombs and other "successful" reviews, revisiting the inquiry's findings through interdepartmental committees or other bureaucratic devices to assess their feasibility and practicality.

Once the first question about an inquiry's impact – what, if anything, has changed as a result – is answered, a second, more meaningful question needs to be asked - is the outcome of the inquiry better public policy? To be judged "successful" from a public interest perspective, an inquiry needs to do more than lead to change; it needs to support change that can ultimately be seen as bringing about better outcomes for the nation as a whole. The objective of public policymaking is to produce sustainable, efficient, effective and legitimate responses to real problems in society and the economy. The soundness of an inquiry's findings rather than their actual implementation is therefore what should be measured.

A judgement of success is ultimately a judgement about the quality of the inquiry. As Gary Banks has observed in chapter 7, the quality of public inquiries and their contribution to public policy in Australia appear to have diminished in recent years. Public inquiries seem to have lost some of their ability to foster good policy. The experience of recent years stands in contrast to the experience of the economic reform era of the 1980s and 1990s, when major and effective public inquiries preceded most significant public policy reforms and can be seen to have yielded enduring benefits to the community.

The chapters that follow take this bigger picture approach to assessing the impact of inquiries and explore the many factors that affect the quality of an inquiry. Some of these factors are in the control of the appointing government – how an inquiry is framed, the timing of its appointment, the time and resources allocated to the task, the selection of personnel, how many inquiries it has on the go at any one time, how the inquiry's report is handled. Others are the responsibility of the inquiry itself – the independence and expertise it brings to bear on the issue, the processes it chooses to follow, and the feasibility of its recommendations, including whether or not they have been tested.

Yet other factors, such as the prevailing political climate, are outside the control of either the appointing government or the appointed inquiry.

Among all the factors controllable by government, how the inquiry is framed is paramount. The potential contribution of an inquiry depends on what it is expressly required to report on. In the end, it is government that decides how broad or narrow an inquiry will be, through its control of the terms of reference. It will always be important to the commissioning government that an inquiry be directed and that it not be left to roam freely around an issue. However, if it is directed to do unproductive things as part of its brief, or is excluded from doing things that, from a public interest perspective, should be examined, then the inquiry is predestined for failure, or at least to making a lesser contribution than desirable.

In chapter 13, Stephen Bartos, Executive Director of ACIL Allen Consulting, shows how narrow terms of reference limited the potential impact of the Cole *Inquiry into Certain Australian Companies in Relation to the UN Oil-for-Food Programme* and how government therefore missed an opportunity to make institutional reform that might mean similar scandals can be avoided in the future. The Cole Inquiry was set up in 2005 by the Howard Coalition Government which took it on rather unwillingly, under considerable political pressure to investigate claims made in a report to the United Nations about the involvement of an Australian company, AWB Ltd, in illegal practices in the sale of wheat to Iraq.

The concern was that AWB (formerly the government-owned statutory body, the Australian Wheat Board) had paid kickbacks to the Saddam Hussein regime in Iraq during the period of UN sanctions prohibiting such payments. The inquiry's terms of reference limited the investigation to the actions of AWB and did not stretch to systemic problems, structural issues or the involvement of other players, including government officials. Bartos describes how these limited terms of reference were strictly adhered to, despite considerable pressure for the inquiry to adopt a broader remit.

Judged purely in terms of follow-up action on recommendations, the Cole Inquiry might be considered a success. Many legal cases ensued and civil prosecutions were brought against directors and officers of the company. Judged however on its potential to improve public administration or public policy settings, it fell short. Unlike other royal commissions, the Cole Inquiry did not have a lasting impact on the conduct of government business.

Limited terms of reference were also a factor in restricting the impact of the *Building the Education Revolution Implementation Taskforce* (Orgill Taskforce), set up by the Rudd Government in 2010 to review the economic stimulus spending program on new school buildings introduced by the government in response to the global financial crisis in 2008. In chapter 14, economics academic Professor Tony Makin and Visiting Lecturer John Humphreys from Griffith University decry the constrained terms of reference given to the Orgill Taskforce and the limited approach taken by the inquiry. By asking the Taskforce to focus only on complaints that many of the school building projects did not represent value for money, government missed an opportunity for careful analysis of the quality of stimulus spending, in relation to either the school building program itself or economic activity on a broader scale. Like the Cole Inquiry, the Orgill Taskforce had the potential to inform public administration and public policymaking, but failed to look beyond its narrow remit and undertake serious economic analysis.

Its findings that the stimulus program, designed to create employment in the building and construction industry, had succeeded in completing the welcome construction of school halls, libraries and classrooms in all Australian schools, leading to a high degree of popular satisfaction with the program, ignored the broader questions of whether this kind of spending on public infrastructure is effective in its overall purpose of stimulating the economy more broadly, and whether the spending itself was efficient and effective or had unintended consequences. That is, it ignored the broader public interest questions which could inform future economic policymaking.

Both the Cole and Orgill inquiries exemplify once-off reviews, responding to a specific matter of concern – the actions of an Australian company, and the implementation of a once-off government investment program respectively. While both inquiries resolved the immediate issue they were set up to address, and therefore met their political imperative, giving government the ammunition needed to rebut outside criticism, they each failed to deliver on their real potential to inform and improve public policymaking in the long term.

Unlike such one-off inquiries, some areas of public policy – education, security and particular industries such as sugar and coal, to name a few – have been subject to frequent review. Questions are inevitably raised about the value of a review process that fails to resolve a policy problem once and for all, where subsequent inquiries need to be appointed to traverse similar territory. Policymaking, however, is an iterative process, with policies needing to continually adapt to changing circumstances, unexpected developments and different political, social and economic contexts. Repeat inquiries are not necessarily a signal of ineffectiveness.

The number of public inquiries into defence since federation is commensurate with its significance as an important public good and a major area of government expenditure. In chapter 15, economist Henry Ergas and senior analyst Mark Thomson appraise a succession of external defence reviews since the 1970s aimed at securing efficiency in defence spending and greater organisational strength, culminating in an astonishing 22 defence-related reviews in 2011-2012. Ergas and Thomson reflect on the mixed and often disappointing results of past reviews and discusses various factors that made some of those reviews effective and others of little value.

They find that knowledge and understanding of the past, including an awareness of the careful and considered findings from previous reviews and why they succeeded or did not, is critical to achieving desired reform. While none of the numerous defence reviews was without impact, they have mostly been ineffective in bringing about anything other than incremental improvement in defined areas. Systemic problems have eluded solution and will continue to do so until the reviews address underlying problems affecting efficiency which, in the author's view, lie in the strength of the central headquarters function relative to other defence operations. Without that deeper investigation, we probably face a continuing stream of reviews over the next few decades which deal with particular problems but leave the central questions of defence efficiency and effectiveness unaddressed.

The following chapter by journalist Christian Kerr gives a media perspective on what makes a successful inquiry. From this vantage point, impact is measured by the extent to which an inquiry makes a good story. Inquiries, especially in their "Rolls Royce" form, a royal commission set up to deal with impropriety, a disaster, incompetence or corruption, are intrinsically newsworthy. The lure of inquiries of this kind for the media can be interpreted, as Kerr explains, either as pandering to the public taste for scandal and personality-driven politics, or as serving the public interest. The role of the press in fostering open and transparent government is a legitimate base for intense media interest in what a royal commission or investigative public inquiry might uncover. That the kind of salacious reporting that mostly attends public inquiries helps to sell newspapers is only a welcome side effect.

Kerr highlights a number of Australian inquiries since the 1970s that have been particularly successful in feeding the hungry beast of media attention, from their initiation in a public scandal through plot twists and turns to often sensational conclusions. The Cole *Royal Commission into the Building and Construction Industry* (2001) has a special place in the annals of long-running good inquiry stories.

As the Costigan Commission showed, when interest in the substance of an inquiry subsides, the press can turn its attention and analytical eye to processes, personalities and costs, thereby bringing the full force of public scrutiny to the public inquiry instrument. There is an argument to be made that, as a much-used instrument of public policymaking, public inquiries merit more of this *post hoc* qualitative analysis and assessment, and not by the media alone.

13

Sweeping the wheat under the carpet – how much have we learnt from the AWB oil for food kickbacks scandal?

Stephen Bartos

"Those who cannot remember the past are condemned to repeat it," George Santayana, 1905, *Reason and Common Sense*, Harvard.

Introduction

The *Inquiry into Certain Australian Companies in Relation to the UN Oil-For-Food Programme*, a royal commission chaired by the Hon Terence Cole (henceforth the Cole Inquiry) was appointed in November 2005 and presented its report in November 2006. It was a detailed and exhaustive inquiry report, in five volumes, completed at a cost to taxpayers of $10.5 million. Although prevented by its terms of reference from investigating any involvement by government in the affair, it canvassed almost every other aspect of the wrongdoing by the Australian Wheat Board (AWB) Ltd in paying kickbacks to the Saddam Hussein regime in Iraq during the period of United Nations (UN) sanctions prohibiting such payments.

In the report's prologue, Commissioner Cole was scathing about the conduct of AWB. He noted that "it is not my function to make findings of breach of the law; my function is to indicate circumstances where it might be appropriate for authorities to consider whether criminal or civil proceedings should be commenced"; however, he did say that he had "found such circumstances to exist" and that "AWB has cast a shadow over Australia's reputation in international trade" (Cole 2006: Vol 1, xi).

The legal cases arising from the AWB scandal continued for many years after. However, there were not the criminal prosecutions that most observers at the time of the Cole Inquiry, including the counsel assisting, had expected. Instead, we saw the criminal investigations quietly wound up and in the end the only prosecutions were civil ones, brought by the Australian Securities and Investments Commission (ASIC) against former directors and officers of the company AWB Ltd for breach of duties. These were important in terms of establishing the duties of directors and officers, and had financial consequences for some of those involved, but there were no criminal proceedings. If there had been then the extent of government involvement in the AWB affair might have become public, because those accused would have faced potentially severe sentences. Their defending counsel would therefore have been expected to call for a great deal of government information as part of the discovery process in order to determine what, if any, licence had been given either directly, or indirectly, to AWB to pay the kickbacks. Any endorsement by government of AWB's actions (an unlikely prospect) or a more subtle indication that AWB would be left to its own devices (more likely) would have been uncovered. As it is, whether or not ministers or officials were involved in aiding or abetting AWB remains a mystery. It never arose during the Cole Inquiry because it was excluded from the terms of reference, was not raised in the civil cases that followed the Inquiry, and was not pursued by the incoming Rudd Labor Government.

It seems unlikely, as outlined by Bartos (2006), that there was ever any explicit, written endorsement by government of the payment kickbacks. There is, however, ample evidence that there was knowledge within government circles of the strong possibility that AWB was doing something untoward. Whether that constituted tacit endorsement, wilful blindness, or simply a failure of systems and processes is difficult to tell in the absence of information held only inside government. As time passes all of those who were involved will move on either to different positions or into retirement.[1] The relevant records will be archived. This increases the risk that, were a similar circumstance to arise in future, Australia will repeat history rather than learning from the affair.

The Cole Inquiry and its findings

The AWB affair involved a deliberate act by a government-owned statutory body to subvert a government-endorsed UN sanctions regime, while keeping the relevant minister in the dark; an inadequate due diligence process that occurred when AWB was privatised, which meant that the problem was not uncovered and kickbacks continued; and a failure of government to take action to investigate AWB, even when alerted to the possibility that it was paying illegal kickbacks.

The kickbacks started while the AWB was in government hands, but continued after it was privatised in 1999. As the Australian Wheat Board, the forerunner to AWB, it was a statutory marketing authority owned by the government that had a monopoly over Australian wheat exports, the so-called single-desk policy. After privatisation, it was no longer the Wheat Board, but kept the acronym and was listed on the Australian Stock Exchange as AWB Limited. This was as much as anything for marketing purposes, to create the impression among both growers and government-controlled wheat purchasers in other countries that it still had a link to government. As AWB, it was notionally grower-controlled, but continued to work within the parameters of the legislation governing the single-desk arrangement. Its subsidiary, AWB (International) Limited, exercised monopoly powers in relation to Australian wheat exports.

The AWB affair had its genesis in the sanctions regime instituted after the Iraqi invasion of Kuwait in August 1993. The UN condemned the invasion (Security Council resolution 6604) and instituted a regime of economic sanctions via Security Council resolution 661, which provides:

> [A]ll States shall not make available to the Government of Iraq, or to any commercial, industrial or public utility undertaking in Iraq or Kuwait, any funds or any other financial or economic resources and shall prevent their nationals and any persons within their territories from removing from their territories or otherwise making available to that Government or to any such undertaking any such funds or resources and from remitting any other funds to persons or bodies within Iraq or Kuwait, except payments exclusively for strictly medical or humanitarian purposes and, in humanitarian circumstances, foodstuffs.

The problem for Iraq was that its only source of funds to buy food and medicines was oil exports, forbidden under the sanctions. As a result, the civilian population suffered enormously. When this became public, opinion began to turn against sanctions. Researchers with a Food and Agricultural Organization (FAO) study in Iraq wrote to *The Lancet*, the journal of the British Medical Society, asserting that sanctions were responsible for the deaths of 567,000 Iraqi children. *The New York Times* picked up the story and declared "Iraq Sanctions Kill Children". CBS Television followed up with a report on their *60 Minutes* program (Cortright 2001).

In light of this, UN Security Council resolution 986 of 14 April 2005 authorised the "Oil-for-Food" (OFF) program that allowed the Iraqi government to use funds from the sale of oil to purchase food, medical supplies and other humanitarian goods approved by the UN. From 1999, the AWB won a series of lucrative wheat contracts under OFF. Wheat, classed as food, was an acceptable Iraqi import under OFF. It was the way the contracts were won that was a problem. They were revealed by the UN's *Independent Inquiry Committee into the Iraq Oil-for-Food Programme* (IIC), chaired by Paul Volcker, and the subsequent Cole Inquiry to have been won through illicit payments designed to circumvent the sanctions regime and put funds into the hands of the Saddam Hussein regime for expenditure on other purposes.

The Cole Inquiry was only allowed to examine the actions of the Australian companies mentioned in the UN report about the OFF program[2] (Volcker 2005). Among the issues not covered in the terms of reference were: the extent to which government policy encouraged or discouraged kickbacks, whether ministers ought to have inquired further once they received warnings, and how the government managed its relationship with AWB.

As a result, the terms of reference for the Cole Inquiry were attacked vigorously by the then Opposition. Kevin Rudd, as Shadow Minister for Foreign Affairs, issued numerous media releases on the topic.[3] The Howard Government refused to expand the terms of reference, arguing that the Inquiry had adequate powers and that if it wanted more powers it only had to ask for them (Howard 2006).

The Cole Inquiry did investigate some aspects of government involvement insofar as they related to the companies concerned. It heard testimony from an Australian diplomat, Ms Bronte Moules, stationed at the UN at the time of the kickbacks, that she had sent a cable to Canberra in January 2000 advising of concerns raised about AWB. The interesting aspect of this, from the perspective of public policy, is that although ministers were alerted to a possible problem, they did not inquire further. It never seemed plausible to them that AWB could do any wrong. John Agius SC, counsel to the Cole Inquiry, asked the then Prime Minister John Howard, "did you ever have any suspicion that any Australian company, including AWB, one of the largest exporters to Iraq, might have been involved in that rorting?" Howard answered, "No, I didn't," and after further questioning said "… I'd never been presented with any hard evidence. I was, I guess, conscious only of AWB because of the predominant role of AWB in the wheat trade, and I had always believed the best of that company, as had most people in the government … it hadn't crossed my mind that it would have behaved corruptly" (testimony to Cole Inquiry, 13 April 2006).

The comment by the Prime Minister that he had never been presented with evidence of rorting does raise the question as to why the Department of Foreign Affairs and Trade (DFAT) itself had not gathered more of such evidence to put before the Prime Minister. In addition to the cables from Ms Moules, it is evident from the Cole Inquiry that the Australian intelligence community was aware that the Iraqi company used to channel the kickback payments, Alia, was involved in circumventing sanctions. Cole found that DFAT "took no steps to independently investigate". It had accepted AWB's assurances that it had done nothing wrong, taking those at face value, and so had no "actual knowledge" (the term the report uses) of kickbacks (Cole 2006: Vol 4, 81-4). Remember that the Cole Inquiry was established to determine whether the listed companies might have broken the law. It had no mandate to assess whether or not DFAT had been overly trusting, or whether its processes were adequate. It appears from the evidence put to the Inquiry that the senior levels of the department in Canberra were prepared to believe glib assurances from AWB rather than undertake vigorous investigations for themselves.

There is an important public policy question that arises from this experience: whether government departments should take assertions by large and respected companies simply on trust. There is a parallel to be drawn with other processes in government that take a very different approach. At the opposite end of the social spectrum, no government official would take assertions made by an applicant for a *Newstart* or similar allowance about their eligibility for benefit at face value without evidence, especially if they had already received a tipoff that the person concerned was falsely claiming the benefit. One of the key lessons from past corporate government scandals both in Australia and internationally is that being large and well respected is no guarantee of honesty (Eichenwald 2004). An enduring lesson from the AWB affair is that a government department should be as sceptical about large corporations as they are about small individuals.

This was however not a conclusion that the Cole Inquiry was ever likely to reach. The Commissioner had been chosen carefully: Cole was known as a black-letter lawyer and expected to adhere to his terms of reference. His focus was thus on conduct that might constitute a breach of the law, and he did not explore questions of public administration. Although public servants did appear before the Cole Inquiry, it was only to answer questions put to them (volunteering additional information to an inquiry is known among senior public servants as a "career limiting move").

The Cole Inquiry released its final report in November 2006. It found that AWB might have breached various sections of the *Crimes Act 1914*, the Criminal Code, the *Victorian Crimes Act* and ss 5 of the Banking (Foreign Exchange) regulations. It found that 10 officers of AWB might have been accessories, and that they and one other might have breached sections of the *Corporations Act 2001*. The Inquiry report recommended these be referred to a task force of Victorian and Commonwealth police, directors of public prosecutions, and the Australian Securities and Investments Commission to consider possible prosecutions. Note that the use of the word "might" was in no way an indication of doubt about the matters: the wording in the report and its findings conveys great certainty. It was simply a reflection of the words from the terms of reference

Cole also recommended that "an appropriate body" be given power to obtain evidence about suspected breaches of sanctions (Recommendation 3) and that there be a review of the powers, functions, and responsibilities of the body charged with controlling Australian monopoly wheat exports (Recommendation 5). Other than this there were no recommendations in relation to public service advice or processes. The then Howard Government had no reason to air the broader questions of public administration involved. Through its careful construction of the terms of reference for Cole, and its management of the release of the Inquiry report, it had effectively shifted blame and avoided being implicated despite this being a "policy fiasco" (McConnell *et al* 2008). It emerged out of the whole process with no blame attached.

More surprising was that the new Rudd Labor Government elected in November 2007, a year after the release of the Cole Report, showed no inclination to investigate or document whether there had been involvement of the public service or ministers in the AWB affair. The consequences of this for policy learning are discussed next.

The aftermath of the Cole Report

The Board of AWB resigned in the aftermath of the findings of the Cole Inquiry, as did the previous managing director. AWB Ltd lost half its shareholder value, and, with the subsequent deregulation of the wheat market, also lost most of its market share of wheat exports. However, it remained a viable company rather than collapsing. Bankruptcy or closure is the more usual fate of companies caught up in large public scandals (Enron in the United States being a prime example). AWB's survival was largely due to a new CEO, Gordon Davis, who had no association with the scandal and saw one of his key tasks as rebuilding the organisation from the massive loss of reputation and value that it had suffered. It involved, in part, greater transparency and honesty, as opposed to the "cover up" approach that had only exacerbated the crisis under the previous management (Grebe 2013).

Within a few years the diminished AWB was taken over by Canadian agribusiness firm Agrium in 2010, and subsequently sold to US agrifoods giant Cargills. It still trades in Australia as AWB. Its website describes the company as "Cargill Australia's grain origination business, with a network [of] 40 grain marketers in 26 locations located throughout the Australian grain belt".

One of the positive legislative changes arising out of Cole's recommendations was an amendment to the criminal code to make it clear that a breach of UN sanctions, which Australia has agreed to, is a criminal offence. Prior to the Cole Inquiry there had been some doubt on this matter; there no longer is.

The export wheat monopoly was also abolished. The *Wheat Marketing Act 1989* that had conferred the monopoly export powers was repealed with effect from July 2008. The government maintained some light-touch regulation of the industry under the *Wheat Export Marketing Act 2008*, which established a statutory authority, Wheat Exports Australia (WEA) to oversee the market. The industry was further deregulated over the subsequent five years and – following government acceptance of recommendations from the Productivity Commission – WEA ceased operations in December 2012.

The end of the export monopoly was not a direct result of the Cole Inquiry. There had been a rising tide of dissatisfaction with the arrangement. From the 1980s onwards, influential agricultural economists (Longworth and Knopke 1982) had described the loss of national welfare as a result of the single desk. A national competition policy review in 2000 found there was no justification for the monopoly. The regulation of domestic wheat marketing from 1989 had been a success, and other compulsory rural marketing schemes in Australia at both Commonwealth and state level had progressively been abandoned. Although there was still support for the single desk on the east coast of Australia, representing the bulk of wheat growers by number, growers in Western Australia – the majority in terms of export volumes – were far more convinced of the merits of deregulation. Representative bodies such as the Western Australia Pastoralists and Graziers Association advocated the benefits of an open market.

In the face of these pressures, the single desk was inevitably due for abolition. It is possible that the OFF scandal may have brought forward the timetable by a year or two. It made the inevitable perhaps a little quicker, but was not the fundamental reason for the change.

It is worth noting however that Cole was very cognisant of the dangers of misbehaviour associated with a monopoly:

> A government grant, by legislation, of a monopoly power confers on the recipient a great privilege. It carries with it a commensurate

> obligation. That obligation is to conduct itself in accordance with high ethical standards. The reason such an obligation is imposed is because, by law, persons are denied choice with whom they may deal. (Cole 2006: Vol 1, xii)

If AWB had been operating in a more open market it may still have engaged in kickbacks. Some other private companies did, as shown by the UN Volcker Inquiry (Volcker 2005). But without monopoly powers the organisation would have been far less likely to have developed what Cole described as its "closed culture of superiority" (Cole 2006: Vol 1, xii).

The long term interests of Australia as a whole, and wheat growers, have improved as a result. Far from precipitating a decline, deregulation has been associated with record wheat exports (ABS 2012). The share of exports to Asia is growing dramatically (from about 30 per cent to 70 per cent during the past five years) as new wheat exporters have exploited opportunities outside the traditional Australian markets in the Middle East that were favoured under the single desk.

But what of the officials who were responsible for the kickbacks? Cole came as close as his terms of reference allowed to recommending that criminal charges be laid. They never were. In June 2012 the ABC's *7.30 Report* broadcast claims that the Australian Federal Police (AFP) had not adequately resourced the task force that investigated AWB and had prematurely shut it down. The senior investigator involved, Ross Fusca, told the ABC "he was offered a promotion if he'd shut the inquiry down" (ABC 2012). Both the ABC and *The Age* newspaper (Baker 2012) applied under freedom of information legislation for the advice on which the AFP had claimed prosecutions were unlikely to be successful. However, the AFP refused to release the advice. ASIC had been considering criminal charges but in mid-2010 decided instead to pursue only civil claims (Wood 2010). Thus, despite expectations raised during the *Cole Inquiry*, there have been no criminal charges brought against any of the people responsible for the illicit circumvention of the sanctions regime.

A class action by shareholders against AWB was settled in April 2010 for $39.5 million. The case had gone to trial for only three days before it was settled, and revealed no new information beyond what had already been well documented through the Cole Inquiry and other sources. The corporate regulator ASIC has pursued civil penalties against former directors and officers. Former chief executive Andrew Lindberg was fined $100,000 and disqualified from directorship for two years (*ASIC v Lindberg* [2012] VSC 332). ASIC also reached a settlement with former chief financial officer Paul Ingleby to pay a $40,000 fine: this was reduced by the first trial judge to a modest $10,000 (*ASIC v Ingleby* [2012] VSC 339), but on appeal (*ASIC v Ingleby* [2013] VSCA 49) the $40,000 penalty was restored. The Ingleby case has implications for negotiated settlements in general (Hargovan 2013) but can hardly be regarded as representing a sense of closure on the OFF scandal.

The financial penalties imposed or reached through settlement are small in light of the fact that this was by any measure Australia's largest international kickbacks or bribery case. This very likely reflects the practicalities of conducting legal action in a highly complicated matter involving massive amounts of detailed documentation. Thus, the decision to settle the shareholder class action was taken against the likelihood of appeal, "regardless of the initial decision, resulting in significant additional legal costs and delays in recovering compensation for shareholders" (Geisker 2010: 405-406).

The absence of criminal cases and the narrow focus of the civil cases on losses incurred and appropriate penalties means that none of the lessons for future conduct of Australian policy were given an airing via legal processes.

There might have been an opportunity to document some of these lessons had the incoming government in 2007 commissioned some sort of inquiry from parliament or an external review body to investigate the matters that Kevin Rudd while in Opposition had vigorously argued were excluded from the Cole Inquiry terms of reference. It remains a mystery why the incoming Rudd Labor government did not do so. Letting bygones be bygones might be the sentimental favourite, but is not a good basis for policy.

The lack of action may have been because the political motivation for pursuing the case had disappeared. John Howard and his government had been defeated in the 2007 election. An inquiry aimed at pinning blame on former ministers would have seemed merely vindictive. It would also hold risks, given the low likelihood of any hard documentary evidence of ministerial endorsement of kickbacks. But that would have been beside the point. All the indications from the limited amount of evidence presented at the Cole Inquiry is that this was not a matter of personal failings or corruption by officials – that is, they were unlikely to be guilty of aiding or abetting AWB – but more a systemic failure to conduct diligent investigations to establish the truth or otherwise of rumours about corporate misconduct. Clearly government and its departments are not resourced to track down every rumour, but, given the strength of advice and sensitivity of Australia's involvement in the Iraq War, this was clearly both in hindsight, and, in the view of some officers of DFAT at the time, one that was worth investigating.

There may be other reasons for the lack of action, ranging from the mundane (the new Rudd Government had other things on its mind) to the sinister (senior serving officials were implicated and persuaded the government to have the affair swept quietly under the carpet). Whatever the reason, the risk that a systemic failure of the sort might happen again is now higher.

A further lesson to be drawn is that a scandal such as this is more likely to happen in the absence of an obvious deterrent. Unlike all of the Australian states, the Commonwealth has no independent corruption investigation body. Had there been one in place at the time of the OFF kickbacks, they might have come to its attention. The presence of an independent body to which information about misconduct in government can be provided is a very useful mechanism for control of corruption.

There is no guarantee, given the lengths to which AWB went to disguise its payments (Bartos 2006), that they would have been uncovered. Even so, the mere existence of such an independent oversight body acts as a deterrent, increasing the likelihood that illicit or corrupt behaviour will be found out. As it was, AWB officials knew that there was no such body in place.

Conclusion

If we see the AWB scandal as an isolated incident involving a few rogue traders, we misunderstand the implications for the future. It was clearly a failure not only of corporate culture but of corporate governance, and of government oversight of a body to which it had granted monopoly powers.

It would be a mistake to think of this as only a private sector scandal. It involved a failure of the relationship between a major company that had been granted a legislated monopoly and the ministers who were meant to hold it to account. The saving grace for the conduct of Australian policy into the future is that this monopoly has been repealed, and there will be great reluctance on the part of legislators to grant bodies similar monopolies in future.

There have been numerous royal commissions and inquiries in Australia (Prasser 2006). Some have a lasting impact on how the nation conducts its affairs. The Cole Inquiry was not one of these. From the perspective of the then Howard Government, it could probably be called a resounding success, shielding ministers and officials from blame. From the perspective of drawing up lessons for public administration, it was less successful. There were some small positive outcomes as a result, desirable of themselves but hard to justify at a royal commission price tag. Why further and more tangible action was not taken remains a mystery. It means a far greater risk of a similar scandal once the immediate players with a personal memory of this affair are no longer on the scene.

References

Australian Broadcasting Corporation (ABC), 2012, *7.30 Report*, "Former investigator claims AWB kickbacks case mishandled," 7 June

Australian Bureau of Statistics (ABS), 2012, *Wheat Stocks and Exports, Australia* (Cat No 7307.0)

Australian Wheat Board, *Annual Reports*, 1999-2004

Baker, M., 2012, "AFP keeps legal advice on AWB secret," *The Age*, June 8

Bartos, S., 2006, *Against the Grain: The AWB Scandal and Why it Happened*, Sydney: UNSW Press

Botterill, L., 2005, "Policy Change and Network Termination: The Role of Farm Groups in Agricultural Policy Making in Australia," *Australian Journal of Political Science*, 40(2), June, 207-19

Cole, T.R.H., 2006, *Inquiry into Certain Australian Companies in Relation to the UN Oil-For-Food Programme Report, Volumes 1 to 5*, Canberra: Commonwealth Government

Cortright, D., 2001, "A hard look at Iraq sanctions," *The Nation*, 3 December

Eichenwald, K., 2004, *A Conspiracy of Fools: A True Story*, New York: Broadway Books

Geisker, J., 2010, "The AWB shareholder class action – lessons in continuous disclosure," *Keeping Good Companies*, 62 (7), August, 402-6

Grebe, S.K., 2013, "Things can get worse: how mismanagement of a crisis response strategy can cause a secondary or double crisis: the example of the AWB corporate scandal," *Corporate Communications: An International Journal*, 18(1), 70-86

Hargovan, A., 2013, "Negotiated settlement and penalties in AWB scandal – lessons from appeal court in ASIC v Ingleby," *Keeping Good Companies*, 65(5), June, 88-291

Howard, J.W., MP, The Hon, 2006, Press Conference, 13 April

Kurtz, J., 2006, "A look beyond the Cole Inquiry: AWB Ltd, bribery and Australia's obligations under international law," Discussion Paper 18/06 Democratic Audit of Australia, Canberra: Australian National University

Longworth, J., and Knopke, P., 1982, "Australian Wheat Policy 1948-79: A Welfare Evaluation," *American Journal of Agricultural Economics*, 64(4), 642-654

McConnell, A., Gauja, A., and Botterill, L., 2008, "Policy Fiascos, Blame

Management and AWB Limited: The Howard Government's Escape from the Iraq Wheat Scandal," *Australian Journal of Political Science*, 43(4), December, 599-616

Prasser, S., 2006, *Royal Commissions and Public Inquiries in Australia*, Sydney: LexisNexis Butterworths

United States Government Accountability Office (GAO), 2005, *Testimony Before the Permanent Subcommittee on Investigations, Committee on Homeland Security and Governmental Affairs*, US Senate, 15 February, (GAO-05-346T), Washington DC

Volcker, P.A., 2005, *Report on Programme Manipulation: Independent Inquiry Committee (IIC) into the United Nations Oil-for-Food Programme*, New York: United Nations

Weller, P., 2002, *Don't Tell the Prime Minister*, Melbourne: Scribe

Wheat Export Authority, 2004, *Annual Report 2003-2004*, www.wea.gov.au

Wood, L., 2010, "Six former AWB chiefs escape criminal charges over kickbacks," *Sydney Morning Herald*, 4 June

Endnotes

1 The Secretary of the Department of Foreign Affairs and Trade at the time of the kickbacks, Dr Ashton Calvert, died on 16 November 2007.

2 There were some other minor players among Australian companies, but by far the largest offender was the AWB.

3 For example, saying that it should cover "investigation of the Government's own involvement in the facilitation of contracts between AWB and the Iraq Grain Board, as well as the Australian Government's adherence or otherwise to Security Council Resolution 661. To exclude either of these critical areas will render the inquiry a complete whitewash" (Media Release, 31 October 2005).

14

Reviewing the review of a fiscal "stimulus" program

Tony Makin and John Humphreys

Introduction

The Building the Education Revolution (BER) program was a key, yet highly controversial, element of the Rudd Labor Government's fiscal stimulus response to the 2007-08 global financial crisis. This fiscal stimulus involved a mix of new public expenditure on school buildings, social housing, home insulation, limited tax breaks for business, and income transfers to select groups. The fiscal response epitomised the notion, following Keynes (1936), that government induced spending during economic downturns is substitutable for depressed private spending, an idea that has appealed to governments since the Great Depression of the 1930s.

The BER program was the most expensive of the then federal government's suite of fiscal stimulus measures, which have often been credited with saving Australia from a technical recession, defined narrowly as two subsequent quarters of negative real GDP growth. However, other macroeconomic factors, such as a drastically weakened exchange rate, lower interest rates, a flexible labour market, and strong foreign demand for mining exports, especially from China, were more important in saving the economy from a narrowly defined recession at the critical time – the March quarter of 2009 (Makin: 2010a; 2010b). All the while, Australia's banks remained relatively sound, in part due to federal government intervention to underwrite deposits and other borrowing, compared to those in stricken North Atlantic economies, whose systemic banking problems precipitated the global financial crisis.

Aimed primarily at creating employment in the building and construction industry, the BER program was administered by the Department of Education, Employment and Workplace Relations and entailed direct public spending of $16.2 billion. The bulk of this spending was on new and refurbished school halls, libraries and classrooms ($14 billion), with the remainder on new and refurbished science and language learning centres and outdoor learning areas.

This program attracted considerable media attention and criticism, particularly in the Murdoch press (News Corp), with the ensuing public debate focused mainly on cases where the spending on school infrastructure was considered either unnecessary, too costly, or both. In response, in April 2010 the first Rudd Government commissioned a public inquiry, the *Building the Education Revolution Implementation Taskforce* (henceforth the Orgill Taskforce) chaired by Brad Orgill, former Chairman and Chief Executive of UBS Australasia, and two deputy chairs with construction and quantity surveying expertise, to examine the complaints about the program. This inquiry was established by the Rudd Government as an instrument for independently assessing the many criticisms made, primarily by school communities, about the BER program and, as such, was intended to raise the issue above the ongoing political fray over it at the time.

A series of reports culminating in a final report provided detailed accounts of investigations into complaints about the program, including a thorough state-by-state assessment of whether there was value for money in the construction that was undertaken. The final report of the Orgill Taskforce, was delivered to the then Minister for Tertiary Education, Skills, Jobs and Workplace Relations, Senator Chris Evans in July 2011. It concluded that the majority of BER projects had been successfully completed, with complaints made by only about 3 per cent of schools covered by the program, mostly from New South Wales.

However, to assess adequately the efficiency and effectiveness of the BER program it is necessary to consider two key questions:

- How effective was the BER program in stimulating the economy?
- Was the BER spending efficient (low cost) and effective (spent well)?

Both of these questions are economic, one macroeconomic and one microeconomic, yet the Orgill Report is devoid of serious economic analysis. Specifically, the report failed to address the wider, albeit unseen, economic implications of the BER spending. While it could be argued that the terms of reference for the Orgill Taskforce did not stipulate economic issues, this did not prevent it conveying that the BER program was an economic success. At a minimum, if the Taskforce was not supposed to consider the economics of the BER program, it should have remained silent about its economic effectiveness. Ideally, the terms of references should have outlined all relevant economic issues, clearly identifying which questions were (and were not) to be answered in the report. It is misleading to commission a report that ignores important issues, but draws broad conclusions.

In crafting the fiscal response to the North Atlantic banking crisis the Treasury assumed that fiscal expansion, primarily focused on spending, was an effective means of countering an economic slowdown, despite the lack of compelling empirical evidence from the international academic literature. As the International Monetary Fund (IMF) concluded in a survey of the effectiveness of fiscal stimulus, the evidence was ambiguous, with estimates of the effects of fiscal policy on national output differing "... not merely in degree but in sign" (IMF 2008: 164).

Unseen economic problems with the BER program

The construction that resulted from the $16.2 billion BER spending is highly visible and its usefulness may seem obvious to many. However, when all economic benefits and costs (seen and unseen) are taken into account, the contribution of this spending to the economy becomes highly dubious. By not considering macroeconomic issues, the Orgill Taskforce implicitly assumed there were no unseen negative consequences of stimulus spending of this magnitude. This is inconsistent with mainstream theory and available evidence, and is dangerously misleading.

Fiscal activism of the kind embodied in the BER program had been largely discredited by Monetarist and New Classical economists on numerous grounds in preceding decades. Although pump priming seemingly offers policymakers a ready economic solution for countering economic downturns and rising unemployment, this narrow Keynesian perspective ignores that expanding public spending has negative economic side effects that worsen employment conditions elsewhere in the economy. To evaluate the impact of a stimulus program, it is necessary to count both the benefits (often direct and highly visible) as well as the costs (often indirect and less visible).

The effectiveness of stimulus spending has been challenged previously on numerous theoretical and practical grounds. The classic textbook on the macroeconomic model (Mundell 1963; Fleming 1962), for example, concludes that even during recessions fiscal policy is ineffective in raising aggregate demand in an open economy with a floating exchange rate because it "crowds out" net exports. In an alternative, extended version of this approach, which explicitly models the role that asset prices and exchange rates play during a foreign financial crisis, Makin (2010c) shows that extra government spending in response to an asset price collapse tends to push up interest rates attracting foreign capital inflow. This strengthens the exchange rate, worsens industry competitiveness, and causes job losses elsewhere in industries such as manufacturing and tourism, as indeed has happened. If many economies are implementing fiscal stimulus simultaneously, the *relative* size of the stimulus matters in this context. In Australia's case, the degree of fiscal stimulus exceeded that of many significantly worse affected economies.

Alternatively, imagine the economy produces two broad classes of goods and services: tradeables (actual and potential internationally traded goods and services), and non-tradeables (including housing and construction, public sector services, utilities, and local transport services). The prices of these non-tradeables are set by domestic demand and supply factors, whereas the prices of internationally tradeable goods and services are mainly influenced by world prices and the prevailing exchange rate.

Increased government spending on school related construction raises total spending in the non-tradeable sector of the economy. This increases the prices paid for non-tradeables relative to the prices paid for tradeables, where the ratio is a measure of the economy's overall competitiveness. Reserve Bank data can be used to show this ratio rose because non-tradeables inflation persistently exceeded above the official 3 per cent inflation ceiling. By increasing imports and attracting resources away from tradeable sector production, worsened competitiveness also contributed to the current account deficit, consistent with a model outlined more formally in Makin (2013a).

The net result is that government spending of the BER type becomes economically ineffective as a macroeconomic stimulus instrument because the benefit to the non-tradable sector is offset by losses in the tradeable sector of the economy. The Orgill Report remained entirely silent about these costs.

A more robust report into BER-type government spending would have considered the following unintended consequences:

- government borrowing, mostly from abroad, puts upward pressure on interest rates and the exchange rate which hurts trade-exposed sectors, decreases net exports, and potentially crowds out some local investment;
- the public debt incurred has to be repaid, requiring higher taxes or spending cuts in the future;

- some households save more in light of the prospect of higher future taxes, resulting in less private spending elsewhere in the economy (the so-called "Ricardian effect"[1]). This implies that over the long term private saving will rise significantly to offset a fall in public saving, evidence of which for Australia is provided by Makin and Narayan (2011);
- higher public debt not matched by income yielding public assets has to be serviced, and when owed to foreigners, acts as a drain on the economy.

Did BER spending help stabilise the economy?

Basic Keynesian economics simplistically proposes that additional government spending can raise aggregate spending in the economy by a multiplied amount. If extra fiscally induced domestic spending raises national output, multipliers are positive, and fiscal stimulus is effective, as presumed by Treasury (Australian Treasury 2009). However, if multipliers are negative due to crowding out effects, "fiscal stimulus" becomes a misleading term since expansionary fiscal policy contracts economic activity elsewhere by more than the visible stimulus benefit.

Fiscal multipliers associated with government programs like the BER have been estimated for different countries and for different fiscal instruments using general equilibrium models and econometric approaches (see Cogan *et al* 2010; Forni *et al* 2009; Ramey 2011; and Born *et al* 2013). These estimates vary considerably, prompting Auerbach *et al* (2010) in a recent survey of multiplier estimates to comment that the range is "almost embarrassingly large". Many multiplier estimates are positive because they consider short term effects only and are based on Keynesian assumptions without regard to longer-run, public-debt-related implications.

On the contrary, and with reference to Australia's experience, Guest and Makin (2011; 2013) and Humphreys (2012) have estimated negative long-run multipliers for the federal government's stimulus spending. The multiplier turns negative in the longer term due to subsequent unseen effects that were neglected by the Orgill Taskforce, such as changes in interest rates, the tax rate, and the real exchange rate.

Another economic flaw with the BER program not acknowledged in the Orgill Report was that, due to administrative and operational delays, the spending continued well after the worst of any business cycle downturn had passed. Previous empirical studies have, for instance, concluded that public infrastructure spending has arrived, on average, about a year after a major downturn began. This means, contrary to intent, in practice fiscal stimulus of this kind is usually either weakly countercyclical, or pro-cyclical in advanced economies.

A more specific claim is that Australia's fiscal stimulus response saved 200,000 jobs. Yet, this assertion is based on spurious Treasury modelling of the long-run relationship between GDP and employment, without factoring in the flexible labour market that existed at the time of the financial crisis. As Vito Tanzi (2012), former IMF Fiscal Affairs Director and fiscal stimulus critic, has argued, workers in advanced economies now have more specialised skills than ever. Hence, in practice, any jobs that fiscal stimulus measures may create are rarely likely to match those that are lost, especially in the financial sector during a crisis (Makin 2013b).

Federal Treasury predicted in the 2009-10 Budget papers that, reflecting the stimulus spending, the economy would be growing at an incredible 4.5 per cent by the basic GDP measure in 2012-13. In reality, GDP growth was under 3 per cent this financial year. In short, the fiscal stimulus measures, most notably the BER program, failed to deliver as originally expected.

This is not to say that public spending on infrastructure cannot positively influence national income in the same way as foreign-financed private investment does. However, additional public investment should be verified via rigorous project-by-project cost-benefit analysis, and be as productive for the economy as the private investment it crowds out (see Makin 2009 for elaboration).

Was BER spending efficient?

The above sections have considered the macroeconomics of the BER spending, but there are also microeconomic issues at play. Macroeconomic analysis tends to assume that government spending (such as the BER spending) is just as good as any other spending. In reality, this is often not the case. Nobel Laureate Milton Friedman astutely noted that when people spend their own money for their own purposes they tend to be careful about quality and price, but if they spend other people's money they are less careful about price, and if they spend on other people they are less careful about quality. Government spending gives us the worst of both worlds and government stimulus spending also suffers from being rushed and often politically motivated.

It was concern about the efficiency of BER spending that originally inspired the Orgill Review. One of the main points of evidence highlighted in the report was that only 3.5 per cent of BER projects undertaken were the subject of complaint, implying there was a high level of satisfaction with the scheme. Yet, this should not have been interpreted as a measure of the success of the program, since provision of new facilities at no direct cost to its beneficiaries who therefore effectively deem them "free" is likely to evoke minimal dissent. In other words, school communities were naturally reluctant to look their gift halls in the rafters.

The Orgill Review provided an excellent opportunity for some careful analysis of the quality of stimulus spending. Unfortunately, the analysis was either lacking or deficient. The main methodology was to provide a scorecard, awarding each school project a quality mark out of six, a timeliness mark out of four, and a cost mark out of 10. The total score is out of 20, and if the project gets above 11 then in the Orgill Report it is considered "value for money". This is not economics.

The first problem with this approach is that it reports too many false positives. If a project is legal and considered useful, is started and finished four weeks late, and costs 20 per cent more than estimated value, then that project would score 12/20 and be considered value for money. Suffice to say, in the real world delays and cost blowouts are not normally considered value for money.

Using some actual examples, in The Oaks Public School (New South Wales) the market appraisal for a new classroom was $1.8 million but the cost came in at $2.1 million and the project was completed five months late. At Mill Park Heights Primary School (Victoria) a hall was valued at $900,000, but was built for $1 million. At Canning Vale Primary School (Western Australia) new classrooms were valued at $1.6 million but cost $1.7 million and were built more than three months late. The North Ainslie Primary School (Australian Capital Territory) got a $2.2 million library for the price of $2.4 million, which was delivered two months late.

All of these examples were considered "value for money" in the Orgill Report with no further consideration of any efficiency loss. Amazingly, even using the Orgill metric (where failure is counted as success) the report still finds that only 66 out of 137 projects were "successful". The remaining 71 projects evaluated were even worse than the above examples, often considerably.

It seems clear from these numbers that there is a serious efficiency loss due to the BER spending. Unfortunately, the Orgill Report does not attempt to measure the size of this cost. The correct metric of efficiency is not "how many projects are over-cost" (or "how many projects score 11/20 in an arbitrary and meaningless scale"), but rather "on average, how much are projects over cost?" The report did not record this statistic, although there were hints at the average size of the cost blow-out. Half of the projects considered ended up costing more than 10 per cent over the estimated value and over a quarter of projects ended up costing more than 20 per cent over the estimated value. It should be noted here that the estimated value was already inflated by a premium to compensate for "allowable" government waste.

Elsewhere in the report, the building costs at government schools are compared with the building costs for Catholic and Independent schools. For NSW, government school building costs were over 60 per cent more than Independent school building costs. The government costs were 54 per cent higher in Victoria; 57 per cent higher in Queensland; 36 per cent higher in South Australia; 11 per cent higher in Tasmania; and marginally cheaper in Western Australia. The Orgill Report does not provide an estimate for average waste, although based on the above information it could have conceivably been anywhere from 10 per cent to 30 per cent of spending, or more, implying an efficiency loss of $1.6 to $4.9 billion. In other words, up to $5 billion of the $16 billion BER project was pure waste, but this wasn't included in the report.

Was BER spending of value?

Measuring efficiency is only one part of measuring economic success. The other relevant issue is whether the money was spent in the best possible way. Even in the cases where school projects came in on or under budget (20 per cent of the projects considered) it is not clear that these produced full value for money, since the money might have been better spent elsewhere.

The Orgill Report did consider whether the BER projects were well built and complied with all laws (what they called "quality"), but that is a very shallow concept of consumer welfare. In a proper economic analysis it would be necessary to consider what benefit people get from the BER spending and compare that to what benefit people would have received from alternative projects.

The Orgill Taskforce implicitly, yet dubiously, assumed that if a hall was built, then by definition that was the best way of spending that money. It is difficult to measure the consumption value received from government spending, and making an estimate is beyond the scope of this chapter. By way of anecdote, the Public Schools Principals Forum survey found that more than one-third of NSW public school principals reported that their BER building was not in their top four preferences, so there is good reason for thinking that the money was spent in the wrong place.[2] It is also possible that the same money could have been spent elsewhere in the economy (perhaps in health, transport infrastructure, or university research) with more benefit. The cost from building the wrong projects could easily run into many billions of dollars, further eroding any benefit from the BER stimulus, though this was not covered in the Orgill Report.

Conclusion

This chapter has critically assessed the way the Orgill Taskforce evaluated the BER program. This review was commissioned by the first Rudd Government as an instrument for providing an independent assessment of claims that the BER program was poorly administered, too costly and wasteful of resources. The main theme of this critique is that there was inadequate economic focus in the Orgill Taskforce, reflecting its mis-specified terms of reference. Given that it was intended to review wastage in a major government spending program, it is ironic that the Orgill Taskforce's $14 million price tag added to that spending, delivering little of lasting economic value.

The BER program it evaluated was, first and foremost, an economic program designed to stimulate broader economic activity. As such, whether stimulus spending of this kind and on this scale was economically effective should have been examined, especially in light of the precedent it set and its unseen economic side effects. The neglect of these side effects brings to mind the comment of Frederic Bastiat, the French classical economist:

> There is only one difference between a bad economist and a good one: the bad economist confines himself to the visible effect; the good economist takes into account both the effect that can be seen and those effects that must be foreseen. (Bastiat 1848: 1)

Former Federal Treasurer Wayne Swan frequently asserted that this fiscal stimulus, with the BER spend at its heart, saved Australia from recession following the financial crisis and was the most notable economic achievement of the Rudd-Gillard governments. While often repeated by the government and media, there is no evidence for this claim (Creighton 2013). Fiscal stimulus of the kind that was implemented, especially unproductive government spending instead of income and company tax cuts, was arguably a net cost to the economy.

In sum, the Orgill Report implicitly endorsed the federal government's rationale for Australia's seriously flawed fiscal stimulus program, of which the BER program was a major part. However, the Australian government's fiscal response to the transatlantic crisis subsequently weakened the economy by contributing to the dollar's strength, and by creating pervasive policy uncertainty about how the large budget deficit it created was to be reversed.

References

Auerbach, A., Gale, W., and Harris, B., 2010, "Activist Fiscal Policy," *Journal of Economic Perspectives*, 24(4), 141-64

Australian National Audit Office, (ANAO), 2010, *Building the Education Revolution: Primary Schools for the 21st Century*, Canberra: Australian National Audit Office

Australian Treasury, 2009, *Briefing Paper to Senate Inquiry into the Government's Economic Stimulus Initiatives*, Canberra: Commonwealth of Australia, November, http://www.aph.gov.au/senate/committee/economics

Barro, R., 1989, "The Ricardian Approach to Budget Deficits," *Journal of Economic Perspectives*, 3, 37-54

Bastiat, F., 1848, "What is seen and what is not seen," http://www.econlib.org/library/Bastiat/basEss1.html

Born, B., Juessen, F., and Muller, G., 2013, "Exchange Rate Regimes and Fiscal Multipliers," *Journal of Economic Dynamics and Control*, 37, 446-65

Cogan, J., Cwik T., Taylor J., and Wieland, V., 2010, "New Keynesian versus Old Keynesian Multipliers," *Journal of Economic Dynamics and Control*, 34(3), 281-95

Creighton, A., 2013, "Damning verdict on stimulus," *The Australian*, 13 July

Department of Education, Employment and Workplace Relations, 2009, *Building the Education Revolution*, Canberra: available at http://deewr.gov.au/building-education-revolution

Fleming, J., 1962, "Domestic Financial Policies Under Fixed and Under Floating Exchange Rates," *IMF Staff Papers*, 12, 369-80

Forni, L., Monteforte, L., and Sessa, L., 2009, "The General Equilibrium Effects of Fiscal Policy: Estimates for the Euro Area," *Journal of Public Economics*, 93(3), 559-85

Guest, R., and Makin, A., 2011, "In the Long Run, the Multiplier is Dead: Lessons from a Simulation," *Agenda*, 18(1), 13-21; Humphreys, J., 2012, "The Treasury's Non-modelling of the Stimulus," *Agenda*, 19(2), 39-51

Guest, R., and Makin, A., 2013, "The Dynamic Effects of Fiscal Stimulus in a Two Sector Open Economy," *Review of Development Economics* 17(3), 609-626

International Monetary Fund, (IMF), 2008, *World Economic Outlook*, Washington DC: International Monetary Fund, September

Keynes, J.M., 1936, *The General Theory of Employment, Interest and Money* Basingstoke: Macmilllan

Klan, A., 2011, "BER waste tops $1.5 billion," *The Australian*, 8 July

Makin, A., 2009, "Fiscal 'Stimulus: A Loanable Funds Critique," *Agenda*, 16(4), 25-31

Makin, A., 2010a, "Did Fiscal Stimulus Counter Recession? Evidence from the National Accounts," *Agenda*, 17(2), 5-16

Makin, A., 2010b, "Saddled with the legacy of fiscal extravagance," *The Australian*, 30 August

Makin, A., 2010c, "How Should Macroeconomic Policy Respond to Foreign Financial Crises?," *Economic Papers*, 29(2), 1-10

Makin, A., 2013a, "The Policy (In)effectiveness of Government Spending in a Dependent Economy," *Journal of Economic Policy Reform*, DOI: 10.1080/17487870.2013.812937

Makin, A., 2013b, "Stimulus was anything but a success story," *The Australian*, 15 April

Makin, A., and Narayan, P., 2011, "How Potent is Fiscal Policy in Australia?," *Economic Papers*, 30(3), 377-385

Mundell, R., 1963, "Capital Mobility and Stabilization Policy Under Fixed and Flexible Exchange Rates," *Canadian Journal of Economics and Political Science*, 29, 475-85

Ramey, V., 2011, "Identifying Government Spending Shocks: It's All in the Timing," *Quarterly Journal of Economics*, 126(1), 1-50

Ricciutti, R., 2003, "Assessing Ricardian Equivalence," *Journal of Economic Surveys*, 17(1), 55-78

Tanzi, V., 2012, *Realistic Recovery: Why Keynesian Solutions Will Not Work*, London: Politeia

Endnotes

1 This effect is named after classical economist, David Ricardo. See Barro (1989) and Ricciutti (2003) for elaboration.

2 http://www.theaustralian.com.au/news/features/busting-the-many-ber-myths/story-e6frg6z6-1226007190063

15

Inquiries into defence – why no difference?

Henry Ergas and Mark Thomson

Introduction

Few areas of public administration have been subjected to as frequent review as defence. That is perhaps unsurprising – after all, there is much at stake. The Department of Defence (Defence) currently spends around 1.7 per cent of GDP and directly or indirectly employs close to 1 per cent of the Australian labour force. The goal of this massive diversion of human and financial resources is to be able to defend Australia from attack.

Given the high cost and potentially grave consequences of failure, there are strong incentives to make our defence effort as efficient as possible. Quite apart from the substantial opportunity cost, greater efficiency allows stronger defence within a given budget. Yet identifying, let alone securing, efficiency in defence spending poses formidable analytical and practical problems. External reviews have been an important element in the never-ending quest to tackle those problems.

This chapter reviews some of those efforts. First, the chapter surveys some economics of defence. Second, the chapter recounts past attempts to improve efficiency. Last the chapter examines the most recent round of reviews. The chapter concludes with reflections on the effectiveness of Defence reviews.

Economics of Defence

Defence is a public good. Once provided, individuals can consume it without diminishing the amount available to others and, in practice, no individual can be excluded from its benefits. As such, defence is manifestly non-marketable and it therefore falls to national governments to deliver. Consequently, the usual market dynamic which ensures that products are produced at minimum cost (production efficiency) and in the quantities and type desired relative to alternatives (efficiency in the product mix) is lacking. Instead, what is produced and how is determined by one group of people – the government and the military – spending other people's money.

Reflecting this fact, defence efficiency is hampered by widespread principal–agent problems. Those problems arise when one party (the agent) undertakes a task on behalf of another (the principal) and two conditions are met: first, the principal and the agent have different preferences (or more generally, differing valuations of outcomes) and, second, the principal cannot "costlessly" monitor the agent's characteristics or performance.

Principal–agent problems expose the principal to the risks of "adverse selection" and "moral hazard". Adverse selection arises when the principal cannot confidently select the most productive agent nor pay them accordingly. Moral hazard occurs when incomplete monitoring allows agents to pursue their own outcomes at the expense of the principal. As these problems will be anticipated by the parties, or at least encountered by them in the course of their interaction, they give rise to ways of structuring and implementing relationships that cannot fully secure the potential gains from trade.

While principal–agent problems are not unique to defence, they are especially acute because defence performance is hard to define, let alone monitor. Not only does defence entail highly specialised knowledge, but – in peacetime at least – it lacks the sort of tangible public feedback available in areas such as health and education. To makes matters worse, to the extent that performance can be and is measured, the results are all too often withheld from the parliament and public (and sometimes even the government). Even more critically, defence capability is frustratingly hard to measure; it only has utility relative to that of potential adversaries, and then only in the context of dimly foreseeable contingencies with difficult-to-estimate likelihoods, consequences and outcomes.

The inherent difficulty of monitoring defence performance creates the potential for principal-agent problems at many levels, including between the community and its government, the government and its defence organisation, and the defence organisation and its external suppliers.

Indeed, even within a defence organisation, the competing agendas of its constituent parts (not least the individual services) mean there is little alignment of interests and incentives. Even when this multiplicity of agents does give rise to competition, that competition may well be inefficient, for instance, as each unit imposes unnecessary costs on others. And no less often, it may instead give rise to collusion at the expense of the principal.

The result is that production efficiency – minimising the cost of outputs – is eroded in several ways. Governments themselves often pursue inefficient options to satisfy political imperatives – especially regarding the location of facilities, where regional politics can take precedence over efficiency, and the sourcing of defence materiel, exemplified in particular by the local production of military uniforms and ballistic munitions. Naval shipbuilding, for example, has been and still is being undertaken in Australia even when doing so involves effective rates of assistance well in excess of 100 per cent, which hardly seems consistent with the public interest.

Moreover, with absent effective oversight of performance, defence organisations have few reasons to strive for higher productivity (at least in peacetime). Instead, they face many temptations to do the opposite. There are few incentives for defence managers to take risks with cost-reducing innovation and process improvement, and they rarely do.

The standard remedy for public sector inefficiency has been to outsource activities with the goal of achieving private sector productivity levels through competition and high-powered incentives for cost minimisation. Of course, success then depends (among other things) on the acumen with which contracts are struck and managed, all the more so as the high-powered incentives create risks that added profits will be sought from inflating charges to taxpayers. Ultimately, outsourcing exchanges one set of problems for another, and the problems associated with contracting for the supply and support of defence materiel can be acute.

Australian defence

Defence has been shaped by the efforts of successive governments to improve efficiency, beginning with the amalgamation of the single service departments into a unitary department in the early 1970s under the reforms issued following the Tange Review of Defence organisation. While not explicitly aimed at improving efficiency, the amalgamation sought to "strengthen central control of military operations and of resources allocated to defence activities" (Ergas and Thomson 2011). And in tacit recognition of the principal–agent problem, the first objective of the reforms was "an organisation that will place control in the hands of responsible government" (Ergas and Thomson 2011). This was in contrast to a structure that was viewed as primarily driven by the interests of the individual services, with insufficient coordination between them and little effective oversight of overall effectiveness.

So as to address these issues, the Tange reforms created a federated structure with centralised policy development, materiel acquisition, and financial management. As a result, the services retained control over most of their day-to-day activities, but lost formal responsibility for force development (the evolution of the force structure through the acquisition and disposal of military equipment). In principle at least, the size and shape of the defence force would, henceforth, be planned centrally rather than emerge from the separate plans of the navy, army and air force.

Subsequent reviews and reforms in the 1970s and 1980s tinkered with the model (Andrew 2001), including hiving off materiel production to form the Department of Supply before reattaching it to Defence proper. But it was not until close to the end of the 1980s that the search for efficiency gained real momentum. Figure 1 shows the key milestones thereafter.

First came the 1986 Cooksey Report, which led to the corporatisation and subsequent privatisation of the government's notoriously inefficient shipyards, aircraft factories and munitions plans. Through the 1990s, this saw about 20,000 workers taken off the public payroll. Next came the 1990 Wrigley Report, which led to the *Commercial Support Program* report by the Australian National Audit Office (ANAO 1998) leading to the market testing of more than 16,000 uniformed and civilian positions, of which around 66 per cent were transferred to the private sector. Activities transferred ranged from equipment maintenance to catering and cleaning.

But the most far-reaching reforms of Defence followed McIntosh's 1997 *Defence Efficiency Review*, which saw the accelerated out-sourcing of support activities and the sale of surplus property under the subsequent Defence Reform Program (DRP). More critically, Defence was restructured to remove duplication between the three Services and to create a central delivery model for a range of support activities.

For a variety of reasons, it is questionable whether the DRP achieved the savings that had been promised. Of the $941 million in planned savings, only $644 million was ever reported as achieved, and most of this was used to reverse planned military personnel reductions for no visible increase in military capability (ANAO 2001; Thomson 2003). Nonetheless, it significantly changed the way Defence operates. Most directly, by moving to a shared services model it stripped the services of control of many of the resources necessary to deliver their capability outputs, including garrison support, information technology, personnel services, and equipment repair and maintenance. The result was matrix management on a grand scale run from the centre. This arrangement

Figure 1: Defence Reforms 1985 to 2010

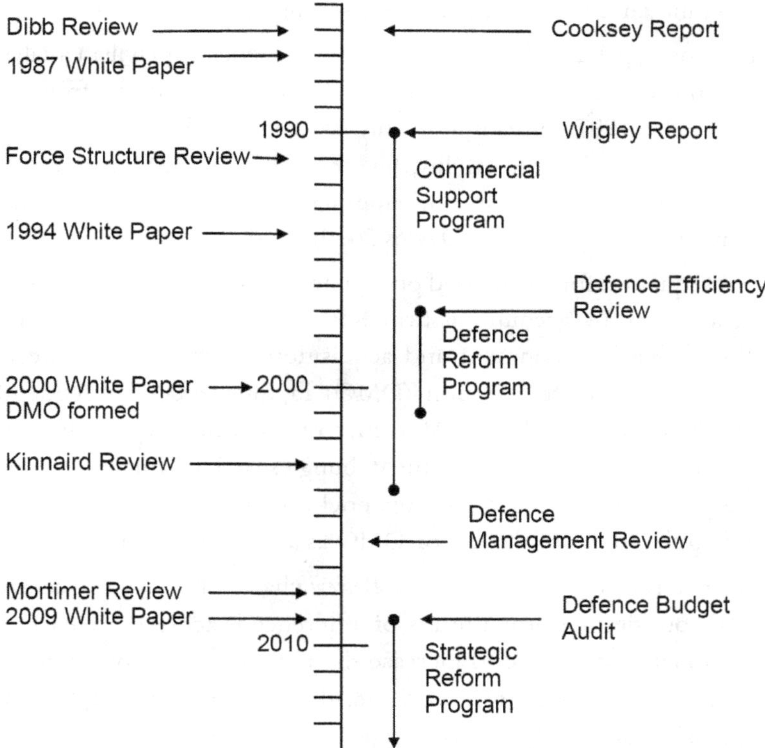

Source: Defence Annual Reports 1984 to 2010

replaced vertical principal-agent relationships within the services with tripartite arrangements between central planners and supplier and consumers across the breadth of the organisation.

Less visible was the amalgamation of previously duplicate civilian and military policy development functions, such as personnel policy and force development. While the removal of duplication reduced overheads temporarily, it removed the civilian oversight that was intrinsic to the arrangements established by the Tange reforms a quarter century earlier. The unstated purpose of civilian oversight was to constrain the moral hazard inherent in having the military setting its own agenda.

Moreover, prior to 1997 it was standard practice for civilian analysts to scrutinise, and contest force development proposals from the military. The 1997 reforms not only weakened (where they did not eliminate) internal contestability, but the DRP saw responsibility for advising government on force development proposals pass from senior civilians to military officers (Davies 2010).

Subsequent reforms focused on equipment acquisition and support. First, a review by accounting firm KPMG led to the amalgamation of the materiel sustainment and acquisition functions to create the Defence Materiel Organisation (DMO) in June 2000. Subsequently, the 2003 Kinnaird and 2008 Mortimer reviews, initiated in the wake of successive defence procurement bungles, led to further reforms to the planning and delivery of materiel acquisition and sustainment, including the re-establishment of DMO as a quasi-independent agency.

An external *Defence Management Review* chaired by Proust occurred in 2007, but despite broad terms of reference it achieved remarkably little, though it did serve to increase the number of senior executives and officers. Between 2000 and 2008, there was a series of "savings programs" as part of the annual budget process (Thomson 2008). These various programs are claimed to have delivered around $600 million in recurrent annual savings – though this is highly implausible given the absence of substantive changes to business practice and continued strong growth in the budget and workforce (Thomson 2008).

In the first decade of the 2000s, Australian defence funding increased more quickly than it had at any time since the end of the Vietnam conflict: an effective annual rate of 4.4 per cent above inflation exclusive of operational supplementation. As the *Defence Management Review* observed in 2007, the "current comparative wealth of Defence means that there is now less concern about efficiency than in the past" (Proust 2007: 4). Consistent with this, administrative overheads grew rapidly during that time as measured by the proliferation of senior executives, middle managers and non-combatant civilians (see Table 1).

Highlighting the risks, funding was so generous that on a number of occasions Defence was literally unable to spend its annual budget by a substantial margin. This was indicative not just of the rapid growth in funding but also of Defence's incomplete understanding of its costs – neither of which boded well for efficiency.

The seeming generosity of that funding notwithstanding, as the end of the last decade grew near, the clear view emerged that the government's long-term goals for the defence force could not be afforded within planned funding. To begin with, costs continued to rise rapidly. And these pressures would be greatly accentuated by the scheduled entry into service of a wide range of costly-to-operate new platforms, such as the Air Warfare Destroyers. The outlays associated with those platforms had not been fully taken into account in previous spending estimates, with the result that Defence was under-funded relative to the commitments it had made. Moreover, embarrassing crises continued to occur in the availability of crucial materiel and in the timeliness and cost-effectiveness of procurement. The result was another round of reviews, to which we now turn.

Table 1: Workforce Growth 2000 to 2009*

	2000–01	2009–10	Growth
Top executives			
Civilian	11	16	45%
Military	5	7	40%
Senior executives			
Civilian	103	164	59%
Military	120	173	44%
Middle managers			
Civilian	3317	5534	67%
Military	1415	1937	37%
Other staff			
Civilian	12,872	14,360	12%
Military	48,820	55,587	14%

* Top executives are three-star military officers and above, and civilian deputy secretary and equivalent and above. Senior executives are star-ranked military officers and civilian Senior Executive Service employees. Middle managers are military colonel and lieutenant-colonel equivalent and civilian executive level 1 and 2 employees.

The 2010–12 reviews

With earlier attempts at reform yielding such mixed, often disappointing, results, the years since 2009 have seen a series of reviews aimed at improving performance, culminating in 22 defence-related reviews in 2011-12 alone.

Of those, eight deal primarily with the fallout from the so-called Skype incident at the Australian Defence Force Academy (ADFA), in which an ADFA cadet allegedly broadcast images of himself and a female cadet engaged in sex. While those reviews are of considerable interest and potentially significant consequence, they will not be discussed here; rather, the focus is on the reviews that go directly to the efficiency with which Defence uses resources.

Of those, the most far-ranging are the *Audit of the Defence Budget*, undertaken by George Pappas with support from McKinsey and

Company in 2009, and the *Review of the Defence Accountability Framework* by Rufus Black in 2011. Others, such as the *Collins Class Submarine Sustainment Reviews* by Coles in 2011 and 2012, and the Rizzo *Plan to Reform Support Ship Repair and Management* in 2011, are more narrowly focused. There are nonetheless, some common themes.

Central to these are persistent deficiencies in Defence's management systems. Simply put, there are many plans, but no plan, and myriad accountabilities, but no accountability. The result is a structure in which decisions are poorly integrated and in which individuals, while they know what they are intended to do, are not responsible for it being done. Moreover, while the structure generates torrents of data, the sheer scale and diffusion of information, and the lack of tight connection between decisions on the one hand and what is measured on the other, further undermine accountability.

Adding to the lack of accountability is the reluctance of senior management, and of the leadership in the services, to use what powers they have to hold individuals to account for poor performance. The unsurprising consequence is a chronic failure to exploit opportunities for improvement, accompanied by periodic instances of acute breakdown.

Nothing better illustrates the chronic problems than the saga of the Collins Class submarines, now in its 25th year. Astutely analysed by Schank (Schank *et al* 2011), this was a project in which, from the start, almost everything that could be done wrong was done wrong. As Coles (2011: 7) put it, "the problems originate from the very beginning of the program when, perhaps without fully appreciating the potential consequences, the Commonwealth embarked on the acquisition of a submarine which, for good reason, is quite unlike any other in the world". Many years later, Coles (2011: 9) found "despite the fact that virtually all senior people we spoke to were clear that the Collins Class capability is 'strategic' for Australia, there is no clear or shared public understanding of why this is a strategic capability nor of the implications this has for sustainability".

Acute breakdowns have also been in abundant supply beyond

the problems with the Collins class, with the most recent visible in September 2010 when the Chief of Navy imposed an operational pause on the seaworthiness of *HMAS Manoora*, causing a collapse in Australia's amphibious ship capability. That collapse, which would have made it impossible for the Australian Defence Forces (ADF) to respond promptly to a major disturbance in our archipelagic region, is thoroughly diagnosed in the Rizzo Review. The causes, Rizzo finds, include:

> [P]oor whole-of-life asset management, organisational complexity and blurred accountabilities, inadequate risk management, poor compliance and assurance, a "hollowed out" Navy engineering function, resource shortages in the System Program Office in DMO (the Defence Materiel Organisation), and a culture that places the short-term operational mission above the need for technical integrity. (Rizzo 2011: 7)

Even more disturbingly, Rizzo notes that these problems were "long-standing, well known to Defence and DMO, and the subject of many prior reports" (Rizzo 2011: 7). And there are indeed close parallels between the conclusions of the Rizzo review and those of the 2007 Board of Inquiry into the Sea King accident at Nias Island, which concluded that the tragedy causing the death of nine ADF members during the response to the Indian Ocean tsunami was not an "isolated random event", but was the result of "a complex interaction of individual and systemic failings across the ADF and parts of the Defence Organisation" (Defence 2007: exec-7).

It is against the backdrop of those grim assessments that the reviews' recommendations must be seen. Some of those recommendations have been somewhat overtaken by events. This is especially so for the cost-reduction recommendations of the Pappas review, which formed the basis of a major search for savings known as the Strategic Reform Program (SRP). As Thomson (2012) shows, some of the savings targets were more credible than others. Moreover, while some of the targets (notably for sustainment spending) were achieved, others (notably for personnel costs) were not, statements by Defence to the contrary notwithstanding. Be that as it may, systematic reporting of outcomes against SRP targets was effectively abandoned following the 2012 Budget, although some efforts at implementing the efficiency improvements identified by Pappas have continued.

As well as savings initiatives, the Pappas Review also recommended changes to Defence's planning and control framework, including a streamlined planning process and especially, a tighter integration of strategic planning on the one hand and capability decisions on the other. Achieving such tighter integration between the identification of future military challenges and the selection of major weapons systems has been a central goal of Australian defence reformers since the Tange reforms.

Tange was determined to introduce into Defence's weapons acquisition process the techniques of systems analysis and program budgeting pioneered by Robert McNamara during his tenure as US Secretary of Defense (1961-1968). Those techniques were, in Tange's view, crucial to moving away from a "requirements" approach, in which the services specified the weapons systems they intended to purchase with little or no regard to cost. Rather, Tange insisted, a "disciplined" framework needed to be applied, which balanced system capabilities with costs and took full account of substitution possibilities between alternative ways of achieving a military objective. While some progress in this direction was made in the Tange years and in the subsequent decade, by the late 1990s those gains had been lost, and capabilities selection had returned to being largely based on "wish lists" and logrolling between the services.

Finally, the Pappas Report also highlights the problems that still arise in the actual acquisition of capabilities, including cost overruns and serious delays. The formation of the DMO in 2000, and the reviews that followed, brought new disciplines to the acquisition process, including a two-stage governmental review process before major programs proceed. Nonetheless, Pappas shows that cost overruns and delays persist, with the greatest problems being in projects that involve systems especially built for, or extensively customised to, Australian conditions. In the light of those problems, Pappas, echoing an earlier recommendation by Mortimer, recommends that all "customised" solutions be subjected to rigorous cost-benefit testing compared to a military off-the-shelf alternative.

The Black Review takes Pappas's emphasis on improved planning and control and pushes it considerably further. At the heart of the Black Review is a sensible attempt to deal with three principal-agent problems that are of central importance to defence efficiency. These are the relations between the government as the principal and Defence as its agent; between the Department as the principal and its staff as the agent; and between each of the military services as the principal and the support services of the Department and DMO as their agent. In each of these, Black proposes ways to clarify expectations, improve the measurement of performance and enhance incentives for success.

Specifically, Black noted that while Defence had myriad plans, and a complex, multi-tier planning process, it lacked a corporate plan. Rather, it had a Defence Management and Finance Plan, which, in practice, was an amalgam of a range of stand-alone plans often prepared by individual fiefdoms within Defence, with targets for the current year and projections four to ten years ahead. As a remedy, Black proposed an over-arching annual corporate plan that would succinctly set out the guidance for the Department, including the targets it would achieve. This, he argued, would allow both better monitoring of Defence by the government and parliament, and improved communications of priorities within Defence itself.

Such a plan, Black suggested, would be naturally linked to the objectives set for individual units within Defence, and hence would inform a cascading series of targets and associated performance indicators, reaching down to individuals. It would, in this way, help address principal-agent issues within Defence. The first Defence corporate plan arising from Black's recommendations was published in 2012.

Black noted three additional prerequisites for enhanced accountability, which remain works in progress. First, the current structure of management by committee, which diffuses responsibility and excuses poor performance, must be replaced by a system in which major decisions are associated with a clearly identified individual decision-maker. Second, the practice of frequent rotation, which results in uniformed personnel shifting jobs every two years or so, needs to be replaced by an arrangement that provides sufficient stability for performance to be assessed, accompanied by opportunities to develop and exploit specialist skills in areas such as project costing and delivery. Last but not least, there must be real rewards and penalties associated with individual performance, though Black emphasises (and possibly somewhat exaggerates) the constraints imposed by the *Public Service Act 1999* and by the regulations made under the *Defence Act 1903* (which apply to members of the ADF).

Finally, with respect to issues between the three services and the procurement and support arms of the Department, Black proposes substantial reforms to the existing system of performance agreements. While these generally include targets and associated metrics, Black finds that the metrics rarely allow timely and effective monitoring of outcomes. Additionally, Black notes that the agreements neither include unit cost information nor allow for trade-offs between unit cost and capability. Black recommends that the agreements be structured in a way that both informs and permits such trade-offs, presumably along with some mechanism for sharing of gains. This would help move these agreements closer to customer-contractor relationships in the commercial world.

There is much to commend in these recommendations. But there are also inherent limitations. Black, for example, greatly overestimates the power of "contract like" mechanisms within what remains a centrally planned economy, with no scope for contestability, few tools for price discovery, and far weaker incentives to seek gains than to avoid losses. Moreover, long experience shows developing the kinds of contracts

Black recommends is as costly and time-consuming as it is technically challenging. It is therefore an open question whether the gains exceed the added transaction costs, which Black assumes but certainly does not demonstrate.

The greatest weakness, however, lies in the failure of the reviews to address the question of how it is that the difficulties have proven so persistent in the face of determined reform efforts. There is, in these reviews, a startling absence of historical perspective: each does a good job of addressing its remit; but none asks why previous, no less competent, reviews did not succeed or succeeded to such a limited extent. If there are systemic sources of failure – and we believe there are – they have remained largely unaddressed.

Conclusions

It is unlikely the defence reforms implemented from Tange to the present could have occurred without systematic external reviews. Nor is it easy to identify any review that has been entirely without consequences – and some have been far-reaching in their effects, the McIntosh and Kinnaird reviews being cases in point.

Yet it would be fair to say the most recent reviews have been more effective in bringing about incremental improvements – concerted efforts to address well-defined problems – than in addressing root causes. Rizzo's Review, for example, should lead to better maintenance practices in the Navy; Coles has contributed to action on submarine fleet availability and should inform future acquisition processes; and even though Defence no longer reports against the SRP savings targets, Pappas has spurred continued efforts to address the efficiency of sustainment practices and to better manage shared resource functions within Defence.

But the underlying problems remain. The organisational recommendations coming out of Pappas and Black have not altered Defence management processes, which have struggled to keep up with the greater scale on which Defence operates today, the greater complexity and cost of the platforms it operates, and the greater demands of accountability being placed on government departments, generally. Overall, Defence's corporate centre has not been strong enough to control its greatly scaled up parts, leading to a complete mismatch between promises and achievements.

And that is the nub of the problem. Lasting reform is impossible unless it greatly strengthens Defence's corporate centre, in terms of its ability to challenge the services, for instance on capability decisions, develop meaningful plans and monitor and enforce outcomes. That was always a problem with the Department: unlike McNamara, who had greatly strengthened the Office of the Secretary of Defense (OSD), Tange managed through sheer intelligence and force of personality. The result was that while OSD was able to force the services to substantially lift their game, its Australian counterpart was far too weak to do so.

As a result, even by the 1980s, it was apparent that the corporate headquarters function in Defence was unable to achieve Tange's goal of ensuring "a disciplined relationship between strategy and force structure within the constraints of what is financially feasible". And here, too, DRP, in its quest to avoid duplication, made matters worse, by removing that element of review and criticism of the services' capability wish lists that civilian analysts had previously provided.

But none of the proposals advanced in the recent reviews tackle head-on the need to significantly strengthen Defence's corporate centre, nor has the government shown any appreciation of its importance. It is therefore difficult to see how the sensible outcomes of these reviews could be successfully implemented in their substance, rather merely being adhered to in their form (as has happened to so many reform proposals in the past).

There are obvious risks that the proposals advanced in these reviews will ultimately go that way. That would be a pity, for they reflect a mass of careful, considered work. But then again, so did their predecessors.

Public inquiries mentioned in chapter

(in chronological order by year of appointment, with name of chair)

Review of Australia's Defence Exports and Defence Industry (Cooksey: 1986)

Review of the Defence Force and the Community (Wrigley: 1990)

Defence Efficiency Review (McIntosh: 1996)

Review of Defence Governance, Acquisition and Support (KPMG: 1999)

Defence Procurement Review (Kinnaird: 2003)

Defence Management Review (Proust: 2007)

Defence Procurement and Sustainment Review (Mortimer: 2008)

Audit of the Defence Budget (Pappas with McKinsey and Company: 2009)

Plan to Reform Support Ship Repair and Management Practices (Rizzo: 2011)

Review of the Defence Accountability Framework (Black: 2011)

Review of the Sustainment of Australia's Collins Class submarines (Phase 1) (Coles: 2011)

Study into the Business of Sustaining Australia's Strategic Collins Class Submarine Capability (Coles: 2012)

References

Andrew, E., 2001, *The Department of Defence,* The Australian Centenary History of Defence, V, Oxford: Oxford University Press

Australian National Audit Office (ANAO), 1998, *Commercial Support Program,* Audit Report No 2 1998-99, Canberra: Commonwealth Government

Australian National Audit Office (ANAO), 2001, *Defence Reform Program – Management and Outcomes,* Audit Report No 16, 2001-02, Canberra: Commonwealth Government

Black, R., 2011, *Review of the Defence Accountability Framework*, Canberra: Department of Defence

Coles, J., 2011, *Collins Class Sustainment Review Phase 1 Report*, Canberra: Department of Defence

Coles, J., 2012, *Study into the Business of Sustaining Australia's Strategic Collins Class Submarine Capability*, Canberra: Department of Defence

Cooksey, R., 1986, *Review of Australia's Defence Exports and Defence Industry*, Canberra: Australian Government Publishing Service

Davies, A., 2010, *Let's Test That Idea – Contestability of Advice in the Department of Defence*, Canberra: Australian Strategic Policy Institute

Department of Defence, 1997, *Future Directions for the Management of Australia's Defence*, Report of the Defence Efficiency Review, Canberra: Commonwealth Government

Department of Defence, 2004, *Defence Annual Report 2003-04*, Canberra: Commonwealth Government

Department of Defence, 2009, *Defending Australia in the Asia Pacific Century: Force 2030*, Defence White Paper, Canberra: Commonwealth Government

Department of Defence, 2012, *2012-17 Defence Corporate Plan,* Canberra: Commonwealth Government

Ergas, H., and Thomson, M., 2011, "More Guns Without Less Butter: Improving Australian Defence Efficiency," *Agenda,* 18(3), 31-52

James, N., 2000, *Reform of the Defence Management Paradigm: A Fresh View*, Working Paper, Canberra: Australian Defence Studies Centre

Kinnaird, M., 2003, *Report of the Defence Procurement Review*, Canberra: Department of Defence

Mortimer, D., 2008, *Going to the Next Level: The Report of the Defence Procurement and Sustainment Review*, Defence Materiel Organisation, Canberra: Commonwealth Government

Pappas, G., with McKinsey and Company, 2009, *2008 Audit of the Defence Budget*, Department of Defence, Canberra: Commonwealth Government

Proust, E., 2007, *Report of the Defence Management Review*, Canberra: Department of Defence

Rizzo, P.J., 2011, *Plan to Reform Support Ship Repair and Management Practices*, Canberra: Department of Defence

Royal Australian Navy, 2007, *Nias Island Sea King Accident: Board of Inquiry Report*, Canberra: Commonwealth Government

Schank, J.F., Ip, C., Kamarck, K.N., Murphy, R.E., Arena, M.V., Lacroix, F.W., and Lee, G.T., 2011, *Learning from Experience Vol IV: Lessons from Australia's Collins Submarine Program*, Santa Monica, CA: RAND Corporation (Prepared for Australia's Department of Defence)

Tange, A., 1973, *Australian Defence; Report on the Reorganisation of the Defence Group of Departments*, Department of Defence, Canberra: Australian Government

Publishing Service

Tange, A., 2008, *Defence Policy-Making: A Close-Up View, 1950-1980*, Canberra: ANU E Press

Thomson, M., 2003, *Sinews of War: The Defence Budget in 2003 and How We Got There*, Canberra: Australian Strategic Policy Institute

Thomson, M., 2008, *The Cost of Defence 2008-09*, Canberra: Australian Strategic Policy Institute, 101-123

Thomson, M., 2012, *The Cost of Defence: ASPI Defence Budget Brief 2012-2013*, Canberra: Australian Strategic Policy Institute

Wrigley, A., 1990, *The Defence Force and the Community*, Canberra: Australian Government Publishing Service

16

Royal commissions and the press – seagulls at the lawyers' picnic

Christian Kerr

Introduction

In an age when the media is changing at an almost impossible pace and faces daunting challenges, some things stay the same. A good story remains a good story.

And while some old journalistic saws have long been left behind, others, like "if it bleeds, it leads", linger on. There will always be a market for sensation: gory accidents; shocking crimes; sexual peccadillos, especially, here in Australia, among sportspeople and show business types. Scandal. Incompetence. Mismanagement. Negligence. And corruption.

Those final five are particularly pertinent to this chapter as their scope and scale can lead our politicians to throw up their hands and promptly dump the problem into that legalistic too-hard basket, a royal commission. And the media do love a royal commission. There's really nothing quite like it. A good royal commission can easily be turned into an "if it bleeds, it leads" story. And even better for journalist sensitivities, an "if it bleeds, it leads" story that, rather than pandering to prurience and voyeurism, serves the public interest, at least "allegedly" – to use a word that journalists pepper their copy with on these sorts of things.

The hottest ticket in Sydney for the first few months of 2013 was not for the Sydney Theatre Company's adaptation of Kate Grenville's novel *The Secret River*, much-lauded as it was. It was for the Independent Commission Against Corruption (ICAC) investigation into the dealings of the former Labor Minister for Primary Industry and Mineral Resources, Ian McDonald, and his allegedly corrupt dealings with his former parliamentary colleague and party powerbroker, Eddie Obeid and with Obeid's family, over the granting of lucrative coal licences in 2008.

The *Secret River* featured legends of the Australian stage, such as Bruce Spence and Jeremy Simms, but the ICAC inquiry starred more senior Labor powerbrokers than the number of "Redgraves" who have ever taken to the stage: McDonald, Obeid and his wider family (along with their financial and legal advisers), former New South Wales Premier Nathan Rees, his ministerial colleague and one-time lord mayor of Sydney Frank Sartor, and former federal minister and ACTU boss Greg Combet, along with a platoon of ministerial advisers and bureaucrats past and present, and a coal train full of mining executives.

It dominated headlines and led news bulletins for days. Curious members of the public queued down Elizabeth Street in the hope of a peep into the hearings and a ticket for the public galleries. Its report, released on 31 July 2013, as anticipated among the political and media classes as any Harry Potter book ever was by J.K. Rowling fans, did not disappoint, making a number of corrupt conduct findings and recommending the referral of various offences to the Director of Public Prosecutions.

Yet this is only an ICAC inquiry, the same instrument that might investigate an apparent case of one lunch too many between a planning clerk at a suburban council and a small-scale property developer wanting to put up a dozen units. With royal commissions, we are dealing with a very different beast indeed.

The "royal" in public inquiries

It is fascinating to note that the 2009 Australian Law Reform Commission's (ALRC) Report on the *Royal Commissions Act 1902* (Cth) considered the relevance of the very term "royal commission" before concluding the nomenclature should stay for the highest statutory form of public inquiry (see chapter 1: Croucher).

While no doubt most of the media and even fewer of the general public were even aware of the ALRC's deliberations, their decision was of the greatest importance. For while "royal commission" may appear to be a traditionalist and conservative title, it was seen to convey the degree of prestige, solemnity and gravitas warranted by this "Rolls-Royce" version of a public inquiry.

In our modern Australian lexicon, few bodies or institutions have the "royal" epithet attached. We have the Royal District Nursing Association and Royal Lifesaving Associations. We have a small handful of royal automobile associations, and centres such as the Royal Children's Hospital in Melbourne and the Royal Prince Alfred in Sydney, but that is really it. And the title "royal" makes Victoria's peak drivers' body, the Royal Automobile Club of Victoria (RACV), no different from its NSW cousin, the National Roads and Motorists' Association (NRMA), just as the Royal Adelaide Hospital serves exactly the same purposes as its southern suburban cousin, the Flinders Medical Centre.

But the "royal" in royal commission is hugely significant. Even if only subliminally, it elevates a public inquiry and awards it an entirely different degree of status in the eyes of both the media and the general public. It guarantees that the commission will be seen as more than just another committee or taskforce or whatever.

The public, and much of the media, have little or no idea of the role of the Crown in the judicial and political life of Australia. Few would realise that a royal commission is just that, an inquiry based on Letters Patent issued by the Governor-General or a state governor exercising their obscure but unique and potent powers (see chapter 2: Aroney).

Yet, despite not knowing the detail behind a royal commission, Australians understand that it is not just another inquiry. The term "royal" conjures up a certain degree of pomp. Perhaps, at the back of their minds, some of us think of a bewigged and berobed Lord Chancellor or a parade of strange and exotic creatures like Iolanthe's peers.

The word "royal" also imposes solemnity. And solemnity bestows importance and authority, the need for respect, a sense of occasion. In turn, that occasion guarantees newsworthiness.

It is why governments far prefer to talk about and hold "judicial inquiries". They simply sound legalistic and dull. It is why oppositions and those who claim to be wronged clamour for royal commissions. They suggest scandal. And where there is scandal, one finds the media out scouting for a story and an angle of their own.

Part of this, of course, is a rod governments have made for their own back. It is a long time since 1974 when Prime Minister Gough Whitlam established the far-reaching Coombs *Royal Commission on Australian Government Administration* (see chapter 12: Gourley), let alone that even more "Whitlamesque" of inquiries, the 1974 Evatt *Royal Commission into Human Relationships.*

Increasingly, our royal commissions are only reactive to public scandals or what has been described as "political wrongdoing" of some type (see chapter 4: Ransley). They are mopping up exercises. Post mortems. Investigations into what has been and gone. A close, detailed and lengthy examination of the stable door after the horse has bolted, designed above all to smother, strangle and drown an issue, to give an illusion that something is being done about a problem.

Such royal commissions either obfuscate or, like the *Royal Commission into Institutional Responses to Child Sexual Abuse* announced in November 2012, they are asked to address problems too big and too complicated to be tackled by any of the other tools that governments have at their disposal. The sheer size and scope of royal commissions of this kind may lead to difficulties down the track for the commission itself and its commissioning parties in terms of absorbing and implementing their recommendations.

All of this complexity and confusion is a delight to the media. A list of the key Commonwealth public inquiries badged as royal commissions since Elizabeth Evatt was charged with examining human relations in 1974 shows the weighty and sensitive matters they deal with, and their variety:

- *Royal Commission on Intelligence and Security* (Hope:1974-1977)
- *Royal Commission into Alleged Payments to Australian Maritime Unions* (Sweeney:1974-1976)
- *Royal Commission to Inquire into and Report upon Certain Incidents in which Aborigines were Involved in the Laverton Area* (Clarkson:1975-1976)
- *Royal Commission on Norfolk Island* (Nimmo:1975-1976)
- *Royal Commission of Inquiry into Drugs* (Williams:1977-1980)
- *Royal Commission of Inquiry into Matters relating to Electoral Redistribution Queensland, 1977* (McGregor:1978-1978)
- *Royal Commission of Inquiry into the Viability of the Christmas Island Phosphate Industry* (Sweetland:1979-1980)
- *Royal Commission on the Activities of the Federated Ship Painters and Dockers Union* (Costigan:1980-1984)
- *Royal Commission of Inquiry into Drug Trafficking* (Stewart:1981-1983)
- *Royal Commission into the Activities of the Australian Building Construction Employees' and Builders Labourers' Federation* (Winneke:1981-1982)
- *Royal Commission into the Australian Meat Industry* (Woodward:1981-1982)
- *Royal Commission of Inquiry into the Activities of the Nugan Hand Group* (Stewart:1983-1985)
- *Royal Commission on the Use and Effects of Chemical Agents on Australian Personnel in Vietnam* (Evatt:1983-1985)
- *Royal Commission on Australia's Security and Intelligence Agencies* (Hope:1983-1985)
- *Royal Commission into British Nuclear Tests in Australia* (McClelland:1984-1985)
- *Royal Commission of Inquiry into Alleged Telephone Interceptions* (Stewart:1985-1986)

- *Royal Commission of Inquiry into Chamberlain Convictions* (Morling:1986-1987)
- *Royal Commission into Grain Storage, Handling and Transport* (McColl:1986-1988)
- *Royal Commission to Inquire into Aboriginal Deaths in Custody* (Muirhead, then Johnston:1987-1991)
- *Royal Commission of Inquiry into the Leasing by the Commonwealth of Accommodation in Centenary House* (Morling:1994)
- *Royal Commission of Inquiry into HIH Insurance* (Owen:2001-2003)
- *Royal Commission of Inquiry into the Building and Construction Industry* (Cole:2001-2003)
- *Inquiry into the Centenary House Lease* (Hunt:2004-2004)

This list omits several important Commonwealth commissions of inquiry not formally badged as royal commissions despite enjoying almost the same powers, such as the *Equine Influenza Inquiry* established by the Howard Government in 2007 under the *Quarantine Amendment (Commission of Inquiry) Act 2007* (Cth). There are also other inquiries without the "royal" in their formal title that were appointed under the *Royal Commissions Act 1902* (Cth) and were thus royal commissions. Examples include: the *Commission of Inquiry into the Efficiency and Administration of Hospitals* (1979); the *Commission of Inquiry into Compensation Arising from Social Security Conspiracy Prosecutions* (1984); and, more recently, the 2005 *Inquiry into Certain Australian Companies in Relation to the UN Oil-for-Food Programme*. Why this is so is never clear to journalists, nor, it seems, to experts in the field.

Generally, though, having the "royal" in a commission of inquiry is guaranteed to pique the interest of both the media and the public alike.

Effectiveness of royal commissions

Sir Humphrey Appleby of *Yes Minister* fame, in one of his most memorable declarations, decreed, "Railway trains are impartial unless you lay down guidelines." It is, of course, a constant complaint that the governments that establish royal commissions with extensive powers to inquire and investigate immediately hobble their effectiveness with restrictive and selective terms of reference.

Despite restrictions on their scope, hope springs eternal in the journalistic breast that royal commissions will defy Sir Humphrey's maxim, jump the track and go crashing away in some other direction, in the style of the Costigan *Royal Commission on the Activities of the Federated Ship Painters and Dockers Union.*

Indeed, the Costigan Royal Commission is surely the source of the modern media obsession with royal commissions and the way they are reported. Its plotline was full of twists and turns. It plunged into a dark underworld where trade union communists, criminals and captains of industry conspired together. It was a quintessentially Australian story of sleaze, but far more dramatic that anything author Peter Corris has sent his hard-boiled fictional private eye Cliff Hardy out to pursue.

The Costigan Commission was established in 1980 by the Fraser Coalition Government in conjunction with the Victorian Government, to investigate criminal activities, including violence and standover tactics, associated with the Painters and Dockers Union. As the Costigan Commission probed the Union's criminal misdeeds, it emerged that the Union had assisted with the asset-stripping of companies to avoid tax liabilities and then sent these "to the bottom of the harbour". Such asset-stripping often involved the destruction of company records. And the Australian Taxation Office, like any other unsecured creditor of an insolvent company, ended up with next to nothing.

This, ultimately, led the Costigan Commission to investigate some of Australia's wealthiest people. Few now recall that, in a spectacular irony, it was one of these wealthy individuals who helped spark the inquiry. It was journalist David Richards' reporting on the Union in Kerry Packer's *Bulletin* magazine that prompted Fraser to establish the royal commission.

The final lurid conclusions in the 1984 Costigan Report made thrilling reading. For instance, the Costigan Commission found that "[t]he Union has attracted to its ranks in large numbers men who have been convicted of, and who continue to commit, serious crimes," and "[v]iolence is the means by which they control the members of their group. They do not hesitate to kill" (Costigan 1984: 119-120).

Included in the crimes of union members were "taxation fraud, social security fraud, ghosting, compensation fraud, theft on a grand scale, extortion, the handling of massive importations of drugs, the shipments of armaments, all manner of violence and murder" (Costigan: 119-120). And despite the Painters and Dockers Union's members being "careless of their reputation, glorying in its infamy", that very reputation attracted "employment by wealthy people outside their ranks who stoop to use their criminal prowess to achieve their own questionable ends" (Costigan: 119-120). That, of course, was the introduction to the other sensational part of the Costigan Commission's findings, namely, the Union's link to the rich, the powerful and the criminal, and their tax evasion schemes.

What the Costigan Commission had uncovered was already dramatic enough before anyone had even heard of "the Goanna", but when a leaked and gently tweaked section of the report raising allegations that an influential and fearsome figure in the business community was linked to drug trafficking, pornography, money-laundering, and possibly murder appeared in September 1984 in not just any newspaper, but in a newspaper that challenged authority and the commercial and political establishment, Fairfax's radical *National Times*, the legend of Costigan and journalistic expectations of just what could come from royal commissions were cemented.

The "Goanna", it emerged, was Kerry Packer, the man whose magazine's investigations, as noted, had led to the establishment of the Costigan Commission in the first place.

Packer had been interviewed by the Costigan Commission, which was particularly interested in a supposed loan of $225,000 he had received from a near-bankrupt Queensland businessman. When asked why he had requested a cash payment, Packer had replied "I like cash. I have a squirrel-like mentality." The Commission codenamed Packer "the Squirrel". The *National Times* editor, Brian Toohey, afraid of publicly identifying Packer, canvassed a new name with his staff as the publication deadline loomed. His deputy suggested "the Goanna".

Packer immediately responded, despite not being named. He came out all guns blazing, denying the allegations and describing them as "grotesque, ludicrous and malicious." He sued Fairfax for damages in a high-profile case and won. The extent of tax evasion and the string of prosecutions that followed kept the Costigan Commission in the news, along with suspicions over Packer's tax arrangements. And it was news yet again when in March 1987 Attorney-General Lionel Bowen told the House of Representatives that Packer, in the eyes of the Commonwealth, had no charges to answer. "He is entitled," Bowen said "to be regarded by his fellow citizens as unsullied by the allegations and insinuations which have been made against him" (Bowen 1987: 3575).

Packer escaped prosecution, but in the aftermath of the Costigan Royal Commission, the Tax Office was reinvigorated, there was a new determination to end rorts, and tax promoters and their clients were jailed. As one lengthy newspaper obituary observed when Costigan died in 2009: "In shifting the mood of the nation and putting some backbone into the fight to preserve the revenue, Frank Costigan had an indispensable and honoured role" (Marr: 2009).

Then again, industry had every reason to be grateful. The Costigan Commission had given the media world almost three decades of sensational stories, stories told time and time again.

All the "Goanna" stories were repeated at the time of Costigan's death, just as they had been after Packer himself died earlier at the end of 2005. Indeed, at his state funeral the next year, Packer's son James, stated that the Packer family had never forgiven Frank Costigan for what they saw as a smear on his father's name.

Costigan himself had publicly responded that as royal commissioner, he simply investigated, but did not make allegations or prosecute. His response explained another reason for media fascination with royal commissions. Notwithstanding their length, their expense and their complexity, they are often just a warm-up act. They are often the first step in an even more lengthy, costly and complex set of processes in the courts.

As Costigan stated, royal commissions investigate. Courts, tribunals and various regulatory bodies then take up their findings. The initial concerns are repeated – the media rehash their old stories, hopeful that a dash of previously unknown detail will emerge to make a more piquant product. But this time, the findings are also tested.

After two runs with the royal commission material, the media then makes the commission process itself the subject of its scrutiny. This can be accompanied by a whole new set of stories. Were the terms of reference rigged? Was the commissioner up to it? Was he or she nobbled? Was the inquiry worthwhile? Was it timely? Did it go on too long? Did taxpayers get value for money? Who deserves blame? Who is worthy of praise?

It is more than two decades since the *Royal Commission to Inquire into Aboriginal Deaths in Custody* reported in 1991, for example, but its findings are constantly cited because of the continued prevalence of the problem it sought to solve.

Media, politicians and the public should all fear that the *Royal Commission into Institutional Responses to Child Sexual Abuse*, hastily announced in November 2012 by Prime Minister Julia Gillard (formal appointment by the Governor-General did not occur till January 2013), then under considerable political pressure on a variety of fronts, will become Australia's equivalent of the Saville Inquiry, the British inquiry into the shootings in Derry, Northern Ireland, on "Bloody Sunday", 30 January 1972 that claimed 13 civilian lives.

The Saville Inquiry, established by Tony Blair in 1998, took 12 years to complete its investigations and release its report. Unsurprisingly, close to half a millennia of sectarian strife proved to be a complex area for the Inquiry to explore. Moreover, it was a very costly exercise. Four years after the Inquiry's creation, journalist Peter Oborne reported that it was likely to cost the astounding sum of £200 million (Oborne 2002). Four years later a hapless Labour minister, Tessa Jowell, let slip that the cost had doubled (reported in *The Daily Telegraph*, 5 July 2006). The true final cost remains unknown. The estimated costs of the aforementioned *Royal Commission into Institutional Responses to Child Sexual Abuse* is expected to exceed $400 million according to estimates in the 2013-14 Commonwealth Budget.

Royal commissions, while investigating scandals, can themselves become scandals for the media, politicians, and public. Costs, length, their ultimate findings, and the success or otherwise of the response to their recommendations are all issues.

These are legitimate areas for media scrutiny and community concern, as are the motives of the politicians who may establish a royal commission as a means of deflecting or postponing responsibility.

Even while appointing them, governments dismiss royal commissions as lawyers' picnics, but the media are excited by them in the same way as seagulls are excited by fish and chips at the beach. The media will always be there, circling, swooping and shrieking, for as the Costigan Commission taught us, who knows what morsels we might find. Indeed, the modern media might be even nosier and more persistent than the most stubborn seagull.

Just before the tale of "the Goanna" broke in 1984, the nation was rocked by another scandal, a series of telephone intercepts made by the Australian Federal Police and their New South Wales counterparts. The transcripts revealed alleged conversations between controversial former Whitlam Labor Government Attorney-General and High Court Judge Lionel Murphy and NSW Chief Magistrate Clarence Briese, which appeared to indicate that Murphy had attempted to influence a court case against Sydney lawyer Morgan Ryan, whom Murphy had allegedly referred to as "my little mate".

The material was obtained by Melbourne's *The Age* newspaper, then enjoying a golden era under the command of editor Creighton Burns. He published the material in 1984 as a three-part series entitled "Network of Influence". What become known as "The Age Tapes" created a national sensation and led, in March 1985, to the appointment of a joint Commonwealth-New South Wales royal commission (*Royal Commission of Inquiry into Alleged Telephone Interceptions,* under Mr Justice Stewart) and consequently to new phone tapping legislation and the conviction of Murphy on a charge of attempting to pervert the course of justice, which, while later overturned, effectively destroyed his career.

Among the constraints of the modern media world, any editor would love to have a scandal to call their own and a royal commission they could point to, saying "I did that". For the media regard royal commissions with the utmost respect for their importance.

The British Indian writer Salman Rushdie, in one of his rare moments of levity, wrote about "PTCTBEs" (in *Haroun and the Sea of Stories*, 1990), a magical realist bureaucratic acronym for "Processes Too Complicated To Be Explained".

Our systems of law and government and regulation are full of complex processes, yet sometimes they fail. Unlike in Rushdie's imagined world, the cause and nature of these failures need to be examined and understood if good governance is to prevail.

Instead of PTCTBEs, there are failures of process that are too complicated for government and bureaucrats to examine, or are so concerning or of such impact that they demand independent examination. That independence is essential to accountability.

Conclusions

The media considers itself a vital tool of accountability. It recognises the significance and weight – the gravitas – of royal commissions. It knows that even the creation of a royal commission is a significant story, let alone any evidence it receives, or findings it might make.

The media may criticise the detail – the choice of commissioners, their terms of reference, their processes and even their findings – but in the foreseeable future the media will continue to have the utmost respect for royal commissions. They will always be considered a vital instrument for discovering the truth, for good governance, for improving accountability – almost a handmaiden to the media itself.

Public inquiries mentioned in chapter

(in chronological order by year of appointment, with name of chair, not including royal commissions separately listed in chapter)

Australia:

Royal Commission into Human Relationships (Evatt: 1974)

Royal Commission on Australian Government Administration (Coombs: 1974)

Commission of Inquiry into the Efficiency and Administration of Hospitals (Jamison: 1979)

Commission of Inquiry into Compensation Arising from Social Security Conspiracy Prosecutions (Mitchell: 1984)

Equine Influenza Inquiry (Callinan: 2007)

Inquiry into Certain Australian Companies in Relation to the UN Oil-for-Food Programme (Cole: 2005)

Royal Commission into Institutional Responses to Child Sexual Abuse (McClellan: 2013)

Overseas (United Kingdom):

The Bloody Sunday Inquiry (Saville: 1998)

References

Australian Law Reform Commission (ALRC), 2009, *Making Inquiries: A New Statutory Framework*, Report 111, Canberra: Commonwealth Government

Bowen, L., MP, 1987, *Commonwealth Parliamentary Debates*, House of Representatives, 28 May, 3575

Costigan, F., 1984, *Royal Commission on the Activities of the Federated Ship Painters and Dockers Union Final Report, Volume 3*, Canberra: Australian Government Publishing Service

Marr, D., 2009, "Crime fighter's taxing war on big shots," *Sydney Morning Herald*, 15 April

Oborne, P., 2002, "The politics of bloody murder," *The Spectator*, 12 January

Section 5

Other countries' inquiries

Scott Prasser and Helen Tracey

In the Westminster systems of government in the United Kingdom, Australia, Canada and New Zealand, public inquiries are appointed at the discretion of executive government. Hence their establishment is seemingly ad hoc and unpredictable – governments decide whether it is in their political interests to seek independent, expert advice. The decision is not without risk. If the advice is truly independent, it is outside of political control and will not necessarily accord with the governing party's ideological and policy leanings. The Westminster approach contrasts with other political systems where the investigative and policy advisory functions of the independent public inquiry are more likely to be carried out by agencies or committees within the machinery of government, including the legislature.

In Australia, New Zealand and Canada, public inquiries are a legacy of the colonial era, drawing on their established use for over a thousand years within the British system of government. In the early days of Australian settlement, royal commissions and public inquiries were appointed by the states to inquire into a wide range of matters, from coal mining accidents to industry development to the establishment of universities. Most states have maintained their own legislation for royal commissions while the *Royal Commissions Act 1902* (Cth) continues as the statutory foundation for royal commissions at the national level.

In New Zealand, the enactment of the enabling legislation for commissions of inquiry occurred in 1908, about the same time as the Australian Act, while in Canada, legislation to enable the executive to appoint inquiries and to empower those inquiries was enacted as early as

1846. All these statutes in the colonies came into force well before the United Kingdom standardised its own processes for public inquiries with the enactment of the *Tribunals of Inquiry (Evidence) Act* 1921 (UK).

In Westminster systems, governments have the choice of investigating or seeking advice from inside or outside the machinery of government. Increasingly, they lean towards the former, although Australian governments, at both state and federal level, have been more inclined than the UK, Canada and New Zealand to persist in the use of public inquiries. In the UK the tendency now is to appoint departmental committees rather than royal commissions and independent inquiries to examine urgent and complex policy problems. Royal commissions have become increasingly rare with each decade since the 1970s. In Canada, the use of the inquiry instrument at the national level has been in decline, although it remains popular with some provincial governments. In New Zealand, the use of the public inquiry mechanism is markedly down from its highpoint in the 1970s.

The chapters in this Section describe the background and current use of the inquiry instrument in the UK, New Zealand, Canada and the USA. In chapter 17, political and policy analyst Graeme Starr tracks the use of royal commissions in the UK from their origin in the *Domesday Book* of William 1 in 1085 and flags their seminal role in important areas of public policy such as poverty and transport. Now, however, both the investigation and policymaking functions that were commonly conducted by specially appointed commissions of inquiry are generally carried out within government. Some of the territory formerly occupied by independent inquiries has been ceded to new mechanisms including committees of Privy Councillors, parliamentary inquiries and external bodies such as policy institutes and think tanks, although in recent years, there have still been several noteworthy independent inquiries which have kept questions of inquiry effectiveness in the public mind.

In the UK context, Graeme Starr explores some of the universal themes in the use of public inquiries, including the motivation for their establishment, expertise of personnel, fairness of process and reasonableness of costs. Some of these issues were taken up in a new legislative framework for public inquiries introduced in 2005 which embeds the inquiry instrument squarely in the executive and provides a statutory base for controlling costs and processes which, while not without critics, is judged to have been successful in making the independent inquiry instrument more effective.

The history of the use of the public inquiry instrument in New Zealand runs very much parallel to Australia's, as University of Waikato academic Alan Simpson reveals in chapter 18. The origins are the same, part of the political and administrative inheritance from United Kingdom; the distinction between royal commissions and other inquiries holds true in both countries; and the instrument has developed in much the same way over the years. Just before the Australian Law Reform Commission embarked on its review of inquiries in 2009, the New Zealand counterpart undertook a parallel review, examining the continuing role of inquiries and the relevance of the underpinning legislation. Neither country has proceeded to implement the resulting proposals for a refreshed statutory base.

As in Australia, many alternative mechanisms now exist within the machinery of government in New Zealand to investigate issues that were once the province of independent ad hoc inquiries. Governments therefore have even more discretion in the extent to which the inquiry instrument is used. A predilection for appointing inquiries appears to come down to a question of style – governments which come to office with a strong reform agenda and clear objectives, on both sides of politics, prefer to engage directly with policy change rather than take the risk of relying on external advice.

Both countries share the same frustrations and concerns with public inquiries, ranging from scepticism about the government's motivation in appointing them to questions about their costs and value to the public. Simpson's conclusion for New Zealand, that for all their flaws, independent public inquiries are likely to continue to prove a valuable device for governments seeking solutions for complex policy problems or needing to address accidents and disasters, such as the Pike River coal mine tragedy in 2010 and the Christchurch earthquakes in 2011, is equally apt for Australia.

In chapter 19, lawyer and academic Grant Hoole reveals the enduring use of commissions of inquiry in Canada and their significant influence on Canadian political life. As in other jurisdictions, over time Canadian inquiries have addressed issues as diverse as national security and intelligence and industry policy; they have reviewed criminal cases; and they have investigated corruption, impropriety and disasters. A spike in the number of inquiries has tended to coincide with moments of heightened social or political controversy or with changes in social, political and economic attitudes. In recent decades, governments have been more reluctant to use the inquiry instrument other than to investigate specific high profile controversies. This may be understood as the result of fiscal restraint, or may be, as has been the case in New Zealand, an indication of a leader's political style and personal preference. A uniquely Canadian explanation for the declining use of inquiries lies in the impact of the *Charter of Rights and Freedoms.* This legislation, in force since 1982, has had the effect of shaping social policy change in a way that inquiries have done in the past. It also places constraints on the operation of commissions of inquiry and their use of powers.

Hoole observes the mixed legacy of public inquiries in Canada in securing policy change. As elsewhere, at times they have been instrumental in achieving significant reform which can be seen to have brought long-term benefits to the nation. At other times, their recommendations have been ignored. An understanding of inquiries however shows a need for caution in evaluating their impact by whether or not their recommendations are immediately adopted. Hoole underlines the importance of taking time to assess an inquiry impact, pointing out that some of the most significant effects will only be seen over a long period of time. The capacity of inquiries to influence social attitudes and understanding of an issue is perhaps their most significant contribution to public life. The Canadian experience shows that an inquiry's great strength, compared with other policy instruments, is its capacity to add to knowledge and understanding and transform the way issues are approached and discussed.

While Australia, New Zealand and Canada inherited the public inquiry instrument from the United Kingdom, in the USA the operation of public inquiries is framed by the dispersion of powers written into the US Constitution. As in the Westminster systems, there is a plethora of investigative and advisory mechanisms within the executive, legislature and judiciary for government to call on when the need arises to address issues of national significance. In chapter 20, Professor Kenneth Kitts from the University of North Carolina at Pembroke explains how, within the wide variety of types of public inquiry in the US (where they are rarely referred to as "public inquiries"), one type, the presidential commission, has had a key role in investigating high profile events. However, whether or not a commission is appointed and its scope and constitution depend not on the significance of the event but on politics and presidential preference. Tensions inherent in the separation of powers between the executive and legislative arms of government play out in the process of determining the nature of an inquiry and its powers.

Major milestones in modern US history can be tracked by following a succession of presidential commission investigations, from the 1941 Japanese attack on Pearl Harbour, the 1963 assassination of President Kennedy, the 1979 Three Mile Island Nuclear Accident and the 1986 and 2003 space shuttle explosions to the 2001 9/11 terrorist attacks. Instructive also is the list of events of national significance which did not lead to a presidential commission, including the 1929 stock market crash and the 2007 financial crisis.

In the US as in other jurisdictions, an understanding of the interplay of history and politics is necessary for a full appreciation of the practice and potential of public inquiries. In all polities, however, the judgement is that they will continue to play a valuable role in public policy and public administration.

17

Public inquiries in the United Kingdom

Graeme Starr

Introduction

Public inquiries, in their various forms, have long been a feature of the policymaking, legislative, administrative and investigative processes of the British system of government as it has evolved over nearly 1000 years. They perform vital functions in enabling government to obtain information, advice and opinion from outside the civil service. More importantly, in a political culture where tradition has had an enduring role, public inquiries have a flexibility that invites people and interest groups to engage in consultation, and to inject expertise and new ideas into public policy.

With various adaptations, the British public inquiries practice has been followed by countries like Australia, Canada, New Zealand and others that have embraced the Westminster model in their constitutional arrangements. This chapter summarises the development and use of these public inquiries in the United Kingdom and some of the problems experienced by them.

The origins of royal commissions and committees of inquiry

Royal commissions

The royal commission is the form of public inquiry that is most widely known and popularly held to be more prestigious than other arrangements. While the use of royal commissions has declined in Britain over recent years, it is an ancient institution usually said to have originated in England in the process adopted under William I with features resembling those of a royal commission to establish the basis for the *Domesday Book*. In 1085, not 20 years after the Norman Conquest, William met with his key advisers in what would today be regarded as a serious cabinet planning session and sent panels of commissioners throughout England and parts of Wales to record the amount and value of land, hides and stock held by every landholder. The records of the surveys conducted in their appointed counties by the groups of commissioners were collected in extraordinary detail in 1086, and subsequently compiled as the *Domesday Book*.

In the context of royal commissions, the *Domesday Book* was significant for a number of reasons, but notably because it was a commission from the Crown and for the prescribed inquiry process, its detailed and careful administrative arrangements, the objective of clarifying the facts for the definition and execution of important law, and the production and publication of an extensive report of the commissioners' findings. Of course, *Domesday* also differed somewhat from royal commissions as they have since developed in that its findings became the law from which there was no appeal (its title was analogous to "the day of the last judgment") and as such its decisions were final.

The principles of the royal commission system evolved over the centuries, during which their popularity surged and ebbed. They were used most frequently in the 19th century, with some 388 commissions, or more than an average of five a year, established between the *Reform Act* of 1832 and 1900 (Riddell and Barlow 2013). Their use declined in the 20th century, although there were some good cases to demonstrate the role and potential of the royal commission in the public policy process. The *Royal Commission on the Poor Law 1906-09*, for example, through its minority report by Beatrice Webb, anticipated many of the features of the British welfare system that emerged decades later (Bulmer 1981: 79). Similarly, the *Royal Commission on Transport* in 1931 confronted issues relating to national and local government policy, along with complex and conflicting differences among a wide range of competing and influential interest groups. These included some 15 transport associations, motoring associations, trade unions, major chambers of commerce, and manufacturers, among others. The royal commission negotiated a level of agreement that enabled the government to introduce important and controversial road and rail traffic legislation in an important area of policy that was undergoing significant and unprecedented change.

Some 30 royal commissions, or an average of only one a year, were appointed between 1945 and 1975. In the subsequent years to 2000, however, only seven were appointed, and three of these appointments were in 1976 – on gambling, the National Health Service, and legal services – and one in 1977 on criminal procedure. No royal commission was appointed under Prime Minister Margaret Thatcher and only one by her successor Prime Minister John Major, the *Royal Commission on Criminal Justice,* in 1991. The last two to be appointed dealt with the long-term care of the elderly, reporting in 1999, and with the reform of the House of Lords, reporting in January 2000. Most royal commissions have been concerned with such matters of broad policy rather than with specific issues or problems requiring prompt consideration, early reporting and expeditious action.

Committees of inquiry

Issues and problems requiring urgent investigation and report now tend to be dealt with by departmental committees of inquiry, the use of which has increased significantly in recent decades as the appointment of royal commissions has declined. Royal commissions and committees of inquiry carry out their investigations in a similar manner (Bradley and Ewing 2003: 305). Unlike Australian royal commissions, bodies established by government initiative in both forms in the UK were non-statutory and lacked powers to compel the attendance of witnesses or the production of documents (Gay and Sear 2012: 16). Committees of inquiry still lack the formality and the prestige of royal commissions, but this may well be changing.

A number of significant inquiries with features similar to those characteristic of modern committees of inquiry were held as early as the 17th century (Salmon 1967: 313). Notable examples include the controversial inquiry into the inadequate state of education in Wales and its report published in three volumes as the *Blue Books* in 1847, and the 1880 report of the court of inquiry into the causes and circumstances of the Tay Bridge disaster with great loss of life in 1879. Later, the Haldane Committee inquiring into the UK executive government proved notable and, in its 1918 landmark report, called for the better use of committees of inquiry, among its other recommendations for the reform of the machinery of government. Haldane subsequently became a model for royal commissions and other inquiries on government and administration.

Committees of inquiry really came to be widely used in the period after World War II, with more than 600 inquiries of various levels of importance being established between 1945 and 1970 (Cartwright 1975: 42-4). The trend then slowed. As in the case of royal commissions, there was a lapse in the appointment of inquiries during the years of the Thatcher and Major Conservative governments from 1979 to 1997, and the subsequent Blair and Brown Labour governments displayed considerably less enthusiasm for public inquiries than was shown by earlier Labour prime ministers. Nevertheless, there were some very noteworthy non-statutory ad hoc committees of inquiry appointed during this period, including the 1992 Scott Inquiry into the export of defence equipment to Iraq, and the 2004 Hutton Inquiry into the circumstances surrounding the suicide of weapons of mass destruction expert David Kelly.

Committees of Privy Councillors

A variation on the non-statutory ad hoc form of inquiry was introduced in 1982 when Prime Minister Thatcher announced her decision to appoint a Committee of Privy Councillors with access to the most sensitive material to review the actions of the government in the period leading up to the invasion of the Falkland Islands. This approach has subsequently been used in the Butler *Inquiry into Intelligence on Weapons of Mass Destruction* in 2004, and the *Iraq Inquiry* which was announced by Prime Minister Gordon Brown in 2009, but which is still to report on the lessons to be learnt from the Iraq conflict. These might be considered as "public" inquiries in only the broadest sense, but the statement by the chairman, Sir John Chilcot, at the launch of his *Iraq Inquiry* is instructive:

> Our terms of reference are very broad, but the essential points, as set out by the Prime Minister and agreed by the House of Commons, are that this is an Inquiry by a committee of Privy Counsellors. It will consider the period from the summer of 2001 to the end of July 2009, embracing the run-up to the conflict in Iraq, the military action and its aftermath. We will therefore be considering the UK's involvement in Iraq, including the way decisions were made and actions taken, to establish, as accurately as possible, what happened and to identify the lessons that can be learned. Those lessons will help ensure that, if we face similar situations in future, the government of the day is best equipped to respond to those situations in the most effective manner in the best interests of the country. (Chilcot 2009)

Parliamentary inquiries

The other form of inquiry that has gained some popularity in the United Kingdom and elsewhere over recent decades is the parliamentary inquiry, relying on committees of parliament. Parliamentary inquiries appear to have taken on a greater importance in the second half of the 20th century with the increased use of green papers, white papers and draft bills, all of which provide better opportunities for public consultation on issues and proposed legislation. Similarly, the emergence of bodies like think-tanks and policy institutes, and the extension of departmental consultative arrangements have enhanced the scope for public scrutiny and input to policy without the need for public inquiries.

While the committee system works well enough in the American legislatures, it has some significant weaknesses and is not always an appropriate means for obtaining the sorts of results that can be obtained by a royal commission or other forms of public inquiry. On controversial questions, particularly those on which the political parties have taken a policy stand, members of a parliamentary committee can usually be expected to toe their party line, with the result that committee meetings can come to resemble debates rather than investigations, and reports can lack coherence and be saddled with extensive minority reports.

In contrast with extra-parliamentary public inquiries, which can be prolonged to delay their report until the relevant problems and issues have been fully explored, a parliamentary inquiry is restricted by its inability to continue its work beyond the session in which it is appointed. Further, membership of parliamentary committees is limited essentially to members of parliament, who are sometimes (or perhaps often in the case of government backbenchers) appointed to keep them busy by giving them something seemingly useful to do. A royal commission or committee of inquiry enables government to appoint appropriate eminent experts in order to ensure that issues are examined objectively or at least to give an impression of impartiality. With these reservations, however, there have been many very effective parliamentary inquiries in Britain, and it is not uncommon to have several new inquiries commence during any sitting week. In the week from 25 July to 2 August 2013, for example, new parliamentary committee inquiries were announced on the following subjects: the EU's contribution to food waste prevention, the future Justice and Home Affairs Programme 2015-19, women and sport, the transatlantic trade and investment partnership, and the scrutiny of arms exports. Any one of these might otherwise have been the subject of a public inquiry.

Issues that arise with public inquiries

Public inquiries have clearly played a very important and valuable role in the public policy process in the United Kingdom, but they have also provoked some very serious questions and issues. Perhaps the most obvious problem relates to the motives for setting up a public inquiry. Former Deputy Prime Minister Lord Geoffrey Howe suggested six motives: to establish the facts; to learn from events; to provide catharsis for "stakeholders"; to reassure the public; to make people and organisations accountable; and to serve the political interests of government (Howe 1999: 294). Harvard political scientist Carl Friedrich could see four real motives for royal commissions, and presumably for all public inquiries: to prepare the way for a predetermined policy; to ascertain the most feasible solution to a problem; to have a non-parliamentary body resolve a major controversy in order to forestall criticism and public pressure; and to gain time (Friedrich 1968: 360).

Others have been less generous, such as Lord Kennett (1937) who explained the motives for royal commissions in terms of "tribal dances", "medicine huts", and "dogfights". Whatever set of motives is accepted, it is clear that the basic reason for a public inquiry is invariably, to a greater or lesser degree, political, and this, of course, explains the truism that any British government will always be very reluctant to launch an inquiry if it does not know what the inquiry will report.

The issue of appointment of people to conduct a public inquiry has also received much attention, and there is no real consensus among the answers. On the question of numbers, for example, on some issues a one-person "panel" might be quite appropriate, while on other matters a ten-member panel might not be sufficient. Similarly, there is little agreement on what sort of person should chair an inquiry. Given their independence and experience in hearing evidence, there is often a preference for judges to lead inquiries, but this can also prolong hearings and not always lead to clear conclusions (Riddell 2013). The controversial Saville and Scott inquiries (see below) do not appear to have been helped to great success by the judges in the chair. Bulmer (1983: 17) argues that the skills required in a good chair are more likely to be found among "senior professionals" than among "members of the judiciary". This view has been taken in many important inquiry appointments, especially when some particular expertise is required, such as the recent Chilcot Inquiry into Iraq. Bulmer also suggests that "the chairman should be sufficiently young to be active throughout the life of the commission and preferably under 60 years of age" (Bulmer 1983: 17-18) – an age considered by this writer to be alarmingly young and one that would exclude many Australian inquiry chairs.

Equally serious problems arise about an inquiry's consultations and participatory processes. Clearly, consultation is of the utmost importance to a public inquiry. Public consultation, after all, is part of the common practice in British government of seeking to obtain advice from informed and interested individuals and groups from outside the civil service. But can there be too much consultation? Again, the Saville Inquiry, set up in 1998 in response to pressure from the families of 14 people killed on "Bloody Sunday" in Londonderry in 1972, is instructive with regard to consultation, having received what must have been an all but unmanageable 2500 witness statements and compiled some 160 volumes of evidence, 13 volumes of photographs, 121 audiotapes and 110 videotapes. Similarly, the Scott Inquiry report was based on 200,000 pages of evidence and 430 hours of public hearings.

The burden of consultation, moreover, can reflect on the timing of the inquiry's report, along with the report's quality and the number of its recommendations. Just as there can be too much consultation, an inquiry report can contain too many recommendations. An over-long report, such as the Scott report, which ran to 1806 pages in five volumes, or one with too many recommendations, like the Francis Inquiry into conditions at Mid Staffordshire hospital released in February 2013, which contained 290 recommendations, might be thorough but might also be incapable of being properly implemented. Decisions about implementation rest with the government, of course, not with the inquiry, but that is another matter.

Along with these machinery problems of public inquiries, a central issue has been the question of costs. This became an important consideration, especially with the Saville Inquiry, which was expected to cost £11 million but expenses quickly mounted and, after 12 years, it totalled more than £192 million. Time was clearly a factor, with most inquiries lasting one to two years from trigger to report, and rarely lasting more than four years. It has been noted that the problems with Saville were caused by the open-ended nature of the inquiry and by the use of very senior and expensive lawyers to support the inquiry or to represent witnesses, with one law firm said to have been paid £13 million to provide 32 lawyers and support staff, and leading QCs being paid upwards of £4 million each to work on aspects of the inquiry (Gay and Sear 2012: 5).

Other inquiries established around the same time did not have such extravagant costs, but some were still quite expensive. The Scott Inquiry into illegal arms export, for example, was set up in 1992 and reported in 1996 with a five-volume report which, at a total cost of £7 million, resulted in little more than an unsuccessful confidence motion calling for the resignation of two ministers in the Major government. It was the Saville Inquiry, however, that raised concern about the value of public inquiries and resulted in calls in Parliament for reform, including cost-control measures.

Twenty-first century reform

The processes for public inquiries did not become standardised until 1921 when the *Tribunals of Inquiry (Evidence) Act 1921* gave Parliament a formal role in establishing inquiries. The main provisions of the 1921 Act allowed for a tribunal to inquire into a matter of urgent public importance, required a resolution of both Houses of Parliament to set up such an inquiry, gave tribunals the powers of the High Court to call for witnesses and evidence, defined the obligations, immunities and privileges of witnesses, and specified that proceedings would be public unless the tribunal judged that to do so would not be in the public interest. The "tribunals of inquiry" set up under the Act were statutory bodies (and thus somewhat equivalent to Australian royal commissions) and proved a reasonably effective means of investigating allegations of misconduct, police corruption and brutality, and serious crimes and accidents.

The 1921 Act met considerable criticism, however, and was itself subjected in 1966 to examination by a royal commission – the Salmon *Royal Commission on Tribunals of Inquiry* – which was set up in response to misgivings about the Act. It was in the report of this inquiry that its chairman, Lord Justice Salmon, set out his six "Salmon Principles" on procedural justice that subsequently became influential in thinking about public inquiries in many jurisdictions (Salmon 1967: 329-30; Prasser 2013: 256), although the question that concerned Salmon, which was how to protect individual citizens who may become involved in an inquiry against injustice and unnecessary hardship, remains a problem.

Only 20 inquiries were held under the 1921 Act in its first 57 years to 1978, followed nearly two decades later by the last four tribunals: the *Public Inquiry into the Shooting at Dunblane Primary School* (1996); the *Child Abuse in North Wales Inquiry* (1996); the *Bloody Sunday Tribunal of Inquiry* (1998); and the *Harold Shipman Tribunal of Inquiry* (2001). The experience with these inquiries resulted in the adoption of a number of reform measures concerning public inquiries in 2005.

The *Tribunals of Inquiry (Evidence) Act 1921*, along with more than 30 other provisions relating to inquiries established under various other Acts such as the *Police Act 1996* (Prasser 2013: 242), was replaced by the *Inquiries Act 2005*. The new Act consolidates and updates relevant existing legislation and among its many provisions, enables ministers to set up formal independent inquiries, set the terms of reference, appoints a chairman and panel members, and informs Parliament of these decisions. It also enables the establishing minister or the chairman, or both, to place restrictions on public access to the inquiry where appropriate.

Such provisions inevitably attracted some criticism. It was argued, for example, that, where the 1921 Act had given Parliament a formal role in establishing inquiries, the new Act represented a strengthening of ministerial control over statutory inquiries and that it "bundled up too much power in ministers, including the power to suspend or wind up an inquiry; to prevent disclosure or publication of any evidence or documents given; and to bar the attendance of witnesses" (Harlow 2013). The Act has been criticised on human rights grounds, specifically with regard to the power of a minister to bring an inquiry to a conclusion before publication of the report, to restrict attendance and the disclosure or publication of evidence, intrusive probing of witnesses, and other threats to procedural fairness principles. The UN Human Rights Committee noted in its 2008 report on the United Kingdom that the *Inquiries Act 2005* allows a minister who establishes an inquiry too much power to control important aspects of that inquiry. In response to such criticisms, the Ministry of Justice noted some concerns about the way in which the inquiry rules were working, but concluded that:

> Having assessed the operation of the Inquiries Act 2005 by reference to all thirteen inquiries either set up under the Act or converted into 2005 Act inquiries, we believe that overall the Act has been successful in meeting its objectives of enabling inquiries to conduct thorough and wide ranging investigations, as well as making satisfactory recommendations. We do, however, take the view that the Act can only enable effective inquiries if the inquiry is conducted by a chairman with the appropriate skill set and who is supported by an appropriately experienced inquiry team. We have no evidence of any serious suggestion that the Act should be repealed in any substantive way. The overwhelming evidence, however, is that the Inquiries Rules as currently drafted are unduly restrictive and do not always enable the most effective operation of the Act. (*Memorandum to the Justice Select Committee: Post-legislative assessment of the Inquiries Act 2005*, Ministry of Justice, October 2010, cited in Gay 2012: 4)

The reforms included the introduction of "pragmatic control measures in the 2005 Act" (*Memorandum to the Justice Select Committee,* cited in Gay and Sear 2012) and the commitment that "the factors that the Government will be taking into account include consideration of the potential duration and cost of an inquiry" (HL Deb 15 June 2011 c198WA, cited in Gay 2012). These controls appear to have had some effect, with the costs of major recent inquiries still being considerable, but also being somewhat contained at reasonable levels. The overdue Chilcot *Iraq Inquiry,* for example, is expected to cost close to £7.5 million, and the Leveson *Inquiry into the Culture, Practice and Ethics of the Press* came in at just under £5.5 million.

Some other recent inquiries, however, are less encouraging. The Wright Inquiry, reporting in 2010 on the death of Billy Wright in Maze Prison in 1997, cost £30.6 million, and the *Inquiry into the Death of Rosemary Nelson,* under the *Police (Northern Ireland) Act 1998,* reported in 2011 with a final cost of £46.5 million. The subjects of these inquiries are certainly important for the people involved, of course, and for the most part they deal with important principles, but the costs indicate that, when appointing an inquiry, careful consideration must be given to the question raised by Lord Rothschild about one of his own inquiries: "Was the sweat worthwhile?" (cited in Bulmer 1981: 76). Is the cost always worthwhile? The House of Commons Northern Ireland Affairs Committee hinted at an answer to this question: "The cost of inquiring into the past is an issue that, at some point, will have to be faced. Such inquiries cannot become a permanent feature … " (Northern Ireland Affairs Committee, 2007-08: Paragraph 11). Clearly, however, public inquiries are already a long-established feature of British public policy, and probably a permanent one.

Conclusion

Many problems still arise with respect to public inquiries and, like all government institutions, they have passed through some dark patches in British history over nearly 1000 years. But they have also made very significant contributions to public policy, and have brought useful social, economic and political benefits and reforms. As Carl Friedrich (1968: 361) observed:

> When it is considered desirable for interested groups to have access to policy making in a society yet strongly elitist in its governmental tradition, but challenged by powerful public opinion, an instrumentality like the royal commission seems favoured and suitable as a procedural device.

The royal commission seems to have given way to other forms, but the future role of the public inquiry in Britain is assured as the complexities of public policymaking continue to increase.

United Kingdom public inquiries mentioned in chapter

(in chronological order by year of appointment, with name of chair)

Inquiry into the State of Education in Wales (Lingen: 1847)

Tay Bridge Disaster Inquiry (Rothery: 1880)

Royal Commission on the Poor Law and Relief of Distress (Hamilton: 1905)

Machinery of Government Inquiry (Haldane: 1918)

Royal Commission on Transport (Griffith-Boscawen: 1928)

Royal Commission on Tribunals of Inquiry (Salmon: 1966)

Inquiry into the Export of Defence Equipment and Dual-Use Goods to Iraq (Scott: 1992)

Royal Commission on Criminal Justice (Runciman: 1993)

Public Inquiry into the Shooting at Dunblane Primary School (Cullen: 1996)

Child Abuse in North Wales Inquiry (Waterhouse: 1996)

Royal Commission on Care of the Elderly (Sutherland: 1997)

Bloody Sunday Tribunal of Inquiry (Saville: 1998)

Royal Commission on the House of Lords (Wakeham: 1999)

Harold Shipman Tribunal of Inquiry (Smith: 2001)

Inquiry into the Circumstances Surrounding the Death of Dr Kelly (Hutton: 2003)

Inquiry into Intelligence on Weapons of Mass Destruction (Butler: 2004)

Inquiry into the Death of Billy Wright (MacLean: 2004)

Inquiry into the Death of Rosemary Nelson (Morland: 2005)

Iraq Inquiry (Chilcot: 2009)

Mid Staffordshire NHS Foundation Trust Inquiry (Francis: 2009)

Inquiry into the Culture, Practice and Ethics of the Press (Leveson: 2011)

References

Bradley, A.W., and Ewing, K.D., 2003, 13th ed, *Constitutional and Administrative Law*, London: Longman

Bulmer, M., 1981, "Applied Social Research? The Use and Non-Use of Empirical Social Inquiry by British and American Governmental Commissions," *Policy Study Review Annual,* 57-82

Bulmer, M., 1983, *Royal Commissions and Departmental Committees of Inquiry*, London: Royal Institute of Public Administration

Cartwright, T.J., 1975, *Royal Commissions and Departmental Committees in Britain,* London: Hodder and Staunton

Chapman, R.A., (ed), 1973, *The Royal Commission in Policy-Making,* London: Allen and Unwin

Chilcot, J., 2009, *Inquiry into Iraq*, *Reports*, (still investigating), viewed 17 August 2013, www.iraqinquiry.org.uk

Friedrich, C.J., 1968, *Constitutional Government and Democracy*, Waltham: Blaisdell Publishing

Gay, O., 2012, *The Inquiries Act 2005,* House of Commons Library, SN/PC/06410

Gay, O., and Sear, C., 2012, *Investigatory Inquiries and the Tribunals of Inquiry (Evidence) Act 1921*, House of Commons Library, SN/PC/02599

Gilligan, G., 2002, "Royal Commissions of Inquiry," *The Australian and New Zealand Journal of Criminology,* 35(3), 289-307

Gilligan, G., 2008, "Royal Commissions," *International Encyclopaedia of the Social Sciences*, viewed 17 August 2013, Encyclopedia.com: http://www.encyclopedia.com/doc/1G2-3045302313.html

Harlow, C., 2013, "What Price Inquiries?" *UK Const. L. Blog* (28th February 2013), viewed 15 August 2013, http://ukconstitutionallaw.org

Howe, G., 1999, "The Management of Public Inquiries," *Political Quarterly*, 70(3), 294-304

Kennett, Lord, 1937, "On the Value of Royal Commissions in Sociological Research," *Journal of the Royal Statistical Society*, 100, 396-414

Northern Ireland Affairs Committee, Third Report of Session 2007-08, *Policing and Criminal Justice in Northern Ireland: The Cost of Policing the Past*, London: HC, 333

Prasser, S., 2006, *Royal Commissions and Public Inquiries in Australia*, Sydney: Lexis Nexis Butterworths

Prasser, S., 2013, "Australian Royal Commissions and Public Inquiries: Their Use and Abuse and Proposals for Reform," in Jacob, L., and Baglay, S., (eds), *The Nature of Inquisitorial Processes in Administrative Regimes: Global Perspectives*, Farnham: Ashgate, 243-270

Riddell, P., 2013, "Public Inquiries – Be Careful What You Wish For," Institute for Government, 3 April

Riddell, P., and Barlow, P., 2013, "The Lost World of Royal Commissions," Institute for Government, 19 June

Salmon, C., 1967, "Tribunals of Inquiry," *Israel Law Review*, 2(3), 313-331

Smith, B., 2013, *Chilcot Inquiry: An Update,* House of Commons Library, SNIA/6215

Sulitzeanu-Kenan, R., 2006, "If They Get It Right: An Experimental Test of the Effects of the Appointment and Reports of UK Public Inquiries," *Public Administration*, 84(3), 625-653

18

Commissions of inquiry – the New Zealand way

Alan Simpson

Introduction

This chapter analyses the way governments in New Zealand over time have used the public inquiry instrument to investigate matters of importance and to provide advice on public policy issues. It discusses trends in the appointment of inquiries and concerns that are held about their use, as background to examining proposals for reform presented by the New Zealand Law Commission (NZLC) in 2008 and assessing the value of inquiries. The chapter concludes that, with or without the recommended reforms, the public inquiry instrument will continue to be a valuable instrument in the New Zealand government's public policymaking toolkit.

The nature of public inquiries in New Zealand

The public inquiry instrument in New Zealand was part of the cargo of political and administrative organisation that early settlers brought with them from the United Kingdom, and has been a feature of New Zealand's governmental processes from the earliest days. The first commission of inquiry was appointed in 1864.

While a number of public inquiries in the form of royal commissions and commissions of inquiry were appointed over the next 45 years, only those appointed from 1909, after the passage of the *Commissions of Inquiry Act 1908*, are considered here. In recent years, the NZLC (NZLC:

2007 and 2008) has reviewed the *Commissions of Inquiry Act* and made recommendations for amendments, as discussed below.

The inquiry instrument has taken various forms over the years including ad hoc temporary statutory commissions of inquiry, non-statutory ministerial inquiries, standing ongoing statutory bodies, and parliamentary committees. This chapter focuses on ad hoc, temporary public inquiries established by executive government with members drawn from outside of government, the public service and parliament.

The statutory royal commission and the commission of inquiry are established by the Governor-General by Order-in-Council and sit "at the apex of the inquiry pyramid" (NZLC 2008:4). Further down the pyramid are committees of inquiry appointed by the minister of the relevant portfolio (ministerial inquiries), and boards of inquiry and tribunals appointed under separate legislative provisions by appropriate authorities.

An inquiry appointed under the *Commissions of Inquiry Act 1908* has significant powers, including the ability to compel the production of information and witnesses, order the commission's procedures in the way it determines is best, and decide who will be recognised before the commission. A commission of inquiry is not a court of law, although lawyers are invariably involved in one capacity or another, with the consequent reliance on formality and due process. It is part of the chair's role to ensure that the commission remains a commission of inquiry and does not become a battleground for the assembled heavyweight legal battalions. In eliciting the information needed by the commission, a good chair relies not on formality and adversarial procedures but on creating the conditions under which the necessary information can be obtained. There have been some occasions when counsel, present at a commission to support one or more parties, have challenged the ruling of the chair through the high court, only to have the court uphold the capacity of the chair to determine the conduct and procedures of the commission.

Commissions of inquiry have far greater scope than a court of law in providing an environment in which parties gain a greater understanding of the issues and are assisted to resolve their conflict. Being able to pursue an issue without being tied to the legal conventions and interpretations of the law courts is one of the many strengths of the inquiry process.

The chair therefore has a key role in ensuring an ordered and thorough inquiry, and the New Zealand practice has been to resort to the judiciary for the great majority of its appointments of chairs of inquiries. By default, it is simpler for a government to appoint a judge to chair an inquiry. Suitable persons from other walks of life are not as readily available, and the judiciary offers a pool of well-qualified people.

Commissions of inquiry enjoy a constitutional status not shared by other similar bodies. Commissions of inquiry also enjoy support from independent administrative and legal staff in order to carry out their functions effectively and fully and to ensure their independence.

In New Zealand, royal commissions and commissions of inquiry both enjoy the same powers. Both are appointed under the same *Commissions of Inquiry Act 1908* and, to all intents and purposes, there are no differences in their purposes, functions, procedures and effects. The only distinction between them is the warrant issued in the name of the Sovereign for a royal commission, as a result of which royal commissions are commonly seen as having greater prestige and standing.

Government may use the title "royal" to give weight to an inquiry, or as a means of encouraging prospective commission members to participate in it. It has been claimed that a royal commission considers matters of greater importance, leaving less significant matters to a commission of inquiry. However, the record shows that the two kinds of commission cannot be distinguished on the basis of the significance of the issues they address. Both royal commissions and commissions of inquiry have investigated a wide range of issues, including accidents and disasters, defence, the economy, Maori land, local government, public service, maladministration, and more. They have also dealt with major and minor public policy issues, including housing, broadcasting and telecommunications, drug trafficking, taxation and police conduct, although more often committees of inquiry, or ministerial inquiries, appointed by ministers are used for substantive policy issues.

Trends in inquiry appointments

Between 1909 and 2013, a total of 222 commissions of inquiry were appointed under the *Commission of Inquiries Act 1908*, 69 (31 per cent) of them were royal commissions and 153 (69 per cent) were commissions of inquiry. An average of four inquiries a year was appointed from 1909 to 1929, compared with an average of 0.4 appointed from 1990 to 2013.

In the early decades, the number of commissions appointed varied quite considerably – from 48 in the 1910s and 39 in the 1920s, to only 15 in the 1930s. Recent years have seen a marked reduction in those numbers, down to 12 in the 1980s, two in the 1990s and five since 2000. The five commissions appointed since 2000 – on genetic modification (2000), police conduct (2007), Auckland governance (2007), the Pike River Coal Mine tragedy (2010) and building failures caused by the Canterbury earthquakes (2011) – illustrate five very different uses of the commission of inquiry, each focusing on an issue falling outside the scope of normal parliamentary and governmental provisions, requiring open processes of investigation and reporting and full public participation.

Many of the issues that in earlier years were the subject of public inquiry are no longer to be found on the lists, as the capacity of government has developed with the creation of new government agencies and instrumentalities. There is now an extensive alternative array of devices other than the formal commission of inquiry process available to a government wishing or needing to embark on an inquiry. What was once the standard fare of public inquiries in previous decades is now dealt with within existing structures and provisions.

For example, local government, which has been a popular subject for public inquiry over the years, has all but disappeared from the listings following the local government reforms of the 1980s. These reforms, which came about as part of the expansive economic and social reforms of the Lange Labour Government, gave local government the capacity to address the issues of their communities rather than await the report of a commission of inquiry.

Education, rivers and railways also no longer occupy the public inquiry agenda, as they are now the responsibility of specific government agencies, and Maori land issues, once a subject of public inquiry almost as popular as local government, are now dealt with by the Waitangi Tribunal. When it was established in 1975, the Waitangi Tribunal became the authoritative body for addressing a wide range of issues affecting Maori people. When the Tribunal's powers were extended in 1985 to investigate any Crown breaches of the Treaty, the Tribunal was able to consider cases since 1840. The Tribunal now enjoys considerable constitutional importance, and its recommendations are invariably implemented. Related to the Tribunal's increasing sphere of competence and authority has been the greater willingness of successive governments to negotiate with the Maori people about land and about reparation for actions contrary to the Treaty. There has been a change in the political culture, as seen in the ways successive governments have looked to the Waitangi Tribunal for consideration and recommendations in many matters, particularly, but not exclusively, involving Maori people.

It is now mainly when an issue falls outside existing government administrative arrangements that it is referred to a commission of inquiry, or when a sudden event occurs requiring a government response. Accidents and disasters, which account for a significant number of inquiries in New Zealand, are in this category.

The appointment of inquiries to provide advice on policy issues is more discretionary than establishing an investigative inquiry following an accident or disaster. Different governments have taken different approaches to the establishment of policy inquiries. Some have used them extensively, while others have preferred to engage directly with major economic or social reform rather than rely on an independent commission to come up with proposals.

These contrasting approaches are reflected in the record of National Party Prime Minister Robert Muldoon (1975-1984), who appointed 25 inquiries during his term of office – including royal commissions on contraception, sterilisation and abortion (1975), nuclear power (1976), the courts (1976), Maori land courts (1978), a murder conviction (1980), the crash on Mount Erebus, Antarctica (1980), and drug trafficking (1982) – and Labour Prime Minister Helen Clark (1999-2008), who used the public inquiry instrument more sparingly, although on some significant issues such as genetic modification

While the two prime ministers represent both sides of politics in New Zealand, a predilection for inquiries is more a matter of personal style than a party preference. When Labour came to power under David Lange in 1984, defeating the Muldoon Government, it was focused on major legislative, economic and machinery of government changes and had little interest in commissions of inquiry. Two main royal commissions were appointed in Lange's first term, one on the electoral system in 1985 and one on social policy in 1986. Prime Minister Lange had not intended to establish a royal commission on the electoral system, but found it necessary after promises were inadvertently made in public to set one up after the 1984 election.

Over time, however, there is little to distinguish between the main parties in their use of the public inquiry instrument. The introduction of the mixed-member proportional electoral system in 1996, as a result of the 1985 royal commission, has seen greater reliance on negotiating policy issues with coalition and affected parties before embarking on a commission of inquiry to remove a troublesome area from a government's agenda.

Concerns with public inquiries in New Zealand

As in other Westminster systems, public inquiries in New Zealand are not without their detractors and disparagers.

First, although the demand for a review or investigation of an issue, allegation or event may be long and loud, there is nevertheless some cynicism about the motives of governments in their appointment of public inquiries. Some have seen the appointment of a public inquiry as an excuse for government to do nothing. This was the perception of the 1932 *Commission of Inquiry on National Expenditure*, appointed at a time when the then government did not know how to address the realities of the Great Depression and was looking for direction, which, it was hoped, would enjoy wide public support.

Others think that governments do not pay much attention to commissions anyway, that they are appointed to delay action, or to recommend to government what it already wants to do. Examples of inquiries that came up with recommendations that appeared to just buy time, or simply deliver what the government wanted, include the 1966 *Commission of Inquiry into Security Service and University Attendance*, established in response to public reaction to security service operations on Auckland University Campus at the time of the Vietnam War, and the 1971 *Commission of Inquiry into Equal Pay*, which reflected the government's desire to meet growing pressures that equal pay be implemented.

Second, there can be frustration with the non-implementation of an inquiry's recommendations. The 1986 *Royal Commission on Social Policy*, for instance, after 18 months of inquiry produced a five-volume report and many recommendations, which were so extensive and wide-ranging that they could serve only as a limited policy guide. Some comments referred to the Commission's report as serving best as a door stop. While inquiries are only advisory bodies and governments are not bound to follow their advice, disregarding a commission's report risks voter displeasure as well as public distrust. For that reason, governments generally do take the recommendations of a commission of inquiry seriously and implement them in whole or in part.

Rarely has a public inquiry in New Zealand, in whatever form, been closed down before completing its report. Only one royal commission since 1908 was abandoned in this way, when the incoming Labour Government in 1972 decided not to proceed with the *Royal Commission into Hospitals and Related Services* because the newly elected government had its own well-known policy on the issue, and was intent on pursuing it. Otherwise, public inquiries have generally run their course.

Some inquiries have not been able to submit their reports within the time set when they were appointed and have consequently applied for, and usually received, extensions for their final reporting date. The 1979 *Commission of Inquiry into the Abbotsford Landslip Disaster* received four extensions.

A few inquiries have had their terms of reference broadened, such as the 1972 *Royal Commission on Salary and Wage Fixing Procedures in the State Services*, which needed to test assumptions about public or private sector wage increases and the pressure they put on state service salaries and wages.

A third concern with public inquiries is the nature of their recommendations. Although they are independent bodies, most are constrained by their specific terms of reference and do not seek to present recommendations that are radical or out of step with government thinking. An inquiry's terms of reference frequently allow it to consider other matters that may appear relevant, but few follow up the implied invitation to look beyond the defined terms of reference.

Some inquiries with a wide brief have gone on to make radical recommendations to government. For example, the 1966 *Royal Commission on Workers' Compensation*, chaired by the Hon Justice Woodhouse, recommended the introduction of a publicly funded and independent Accident Compensation Commission to deal with accidents that, invariably, were taken to court in the search for redress for losses suffered. This new publicly funded and independent body would replace the expensive and time consuming court-based process where the determination of "fault" was the main issue and was seen as a major new direction in this important policy area.

Another royal commission to make radical recommendations was the 1985 *Royal Commission on the Electoral System*, chaired by the Hon John Wallace, which recommended the introduction of the mixed-member proportional system (MMP). This was a major departure from the existing "first past the post" (FFP), two-party dominant electoral system. Eventually, in 1993, and after considerable public debate, a national referendum voted to adopt the Wallace Commission's proposals for the MMP system. In this case, the royal commission informed debate, influenced public opinion, and contributed to major policy change (see Easton 1994: 236).

In the main, the recommendations of major investigative inquiries have been adopted and implemented, although there are instances where inquiry reports and recommendations have unsettled government and have had unwelcome and unexpected repercussions. A prime example of this was the Erebus Royal Commission. It was appointed in 1980 with the Hon Justice Mahon, a High Court Judge, as sole commissioner to investigate why in 1979 an Air New Zealand airliner crashed into Mount Erebus in the Antarctica with a loss of 257 lives. Mahon's report in 1981 was not what either the then Prime Minister or Air New Zealand wanted to hear. The report contradicted an earlier report by the Chief Inspector of Air Accidents that the accident had been caused by "pilot error". Mahon exonerated the pilots from this assessment and concluded that the accident had been caused by the changed setting of the navigation coordinates that had not been communicated to the flight crew. What aroused considerable reaction in Mahon's report was his comment that there had been a "pre-determined plan of deception" and "an orchestrated litany of lies" by Air New Zealand (Mahon 1981: 150, para 377). Air New Zealand took grave exception to this assessment and consequently gained a review of the report in the New Zealand Court of Appeal. The Court's verdict was that Justice Mahon should have given warning to Air New Zealand that they were not going to be believed. Mahon appealed to the Privy Council in the United Kingdom, which, while concluding that Mahon had exceeded his brief in claiming he had had to listen to "an orchestrated litany of lies", found that he had been correct in setting aside the Chief Inspector of Air Accidents' attribution of the accident to pilot error.

The Erebus Royal Commission Report has been the most contentious of any New Zealand public inquiry, with arguments still being traversed on the accident and on the Commission's findings. The great majority of royal commission inquiry reports are accepted and, to a greater or lesser extent implemented by a government only too glad to have a difficult issue, if not resolved, then at least moved from the immediate political agenda. The legal action taken following the Erebus Royal Commission Report is without precedent in New Zealand.

The value of inquiries

Generally, commissions of inquiry are seen in a positive light. They allow major interests to take part in the inquiry process and thus help secure acceptance of the outcome. They allow relatively novel proposals to be made in a form which government, depending on public reactions, can decide to accept or reject. They help educate public and group opinion through the dialogue that takes place while the inquiry proceeds and through their reports. Only rarely are they a substitute for action. Inquiries provide for incremental and controlled change when that is called for, and recommend necessary action where failings and shortcomings have been uncovered.

Commissions of inquiry are a remarkably flexible mechanism, adaptable for a wide range of situations. They provide a unique channel for interested parties to participate directly in making policy or reviewing events, such as an accident or natural disaster, and bring together a large volume of information from a wide variety of sources, which is eventually made public.

Review and reform

After years of increasing discussion about the adequacy of the legislation relating to commissions of inquiry, the NZLC embarked, with government approval, on a review of the legislation and role of public inquiries, seeking a better understanding of their purpose, processes, powers and end product, in order to assess whether the *Commissions of Inquiry Act 1908* was appropriate and relevant to current demands. The Act had been amended many times, not always resulting in greater clarity.

In its review, the NZLC (2008) identified three broad problems with the existing framework. First, the *Commissions of Inquiry Act 1908* was found to be antiquated, needing an overhaul if it was to be suitable for contemporary use. A second concern was the cost of commissions of inquiry and their reliance on legalistic procedures, which tended to act as a constraint on their use. The third problem was the increasing use of ministerial inquiries, which lacked the statutory framework of the commission of inquiry and yet needed the advantages of the commission of inquiry provisions.

To address these problems, the NZLC proposed a new Inquiries Act, to maximise flexibility and enable inquiries to operate without the "procedural constraints and traditions that have dogged commissions." Like the similar 2009 review by the Australian Law Reform Commission (see chapter 1: Croucher), the NZLC proposed two forms of inquiry – public inquiries and government inquiries. The former would cover the ground previously inhabited by royal commissions and commissions of inquiry, while the latter would, in effect, be the simpler and quicker ministerial inquiries. The benefit was seen as providing both forms of inquiry with the same legal powers and protections. The distinction made between public and government inquiries was an acknowledgement of the lack of legal powers and protections for non-statutory ministerial inquiries under the present arrangements.

A number of other significant changes were also proposed by the NZLC, including removal of the adversarial concepts of "parties" and "persons entitled to be heard", together with the attendant provisions for contempt and the differing powers of the status of individual inquirers. It was also proposed that a commission of inquiry be given greater powers to control behaviour surrounding inquiries and their conduct. The NZLC review wanted to get away from the adversarial practices included in the *Commissions of Inquiry Act 1908*. It recommended that commissions have the freedom to decide on the holding of oral hearings, whether cross examination is permitted, if witnesses would be called, and whether to receive oral evidence and submissions. There was an emphasis on the requirements of natural justice, and an aim for legislation not to force formal procedures on inquiries.

In effect, the NZLC review sought a culture change in the use of commissions of inquiry. The main outcome it envisaged was more effective and efficient inquiries that were also more accessible and usable, with more flexibility in their procedures and less reliance on formality. A greater use of ministerial inquiries in the future was expected as a result.

The NZLC report on *A New Inquiries Act*, released in May 2008, is still, several years later, with the government, which, it is safe to say, does not regard the matter as a high priority. Since then, the New Zealand Government has appointed two royal commissions, both after an unforeseen event: one an accident (the 2010 *Royal Commission on the Pike River Coal Mine Tragedy*), and the other a natural disaster (the 2011 *Royal Commission of Inquiry into Building Failure caused by the Canterbury Earthquakes*). The proposed changes to legislation would have made no difference to the appointment, processes and outcomes of these inquiries.

The future of public inquiries in New Zealand

Public inquiries are a most valuable mechanism in the New Zealand government's arsenal of public, independent, structured bodies to use at the appropriate time. They are political devices used by governments as and when appropriate, and governments will continue to appoint them.

From the record of the last 20 or more years, the continuing steady appointment of commissions of inquiry should be expected, and if the statute changes, perhaps many more ministerial inquiries. As other countries have found, even with expanded machinery of government, there is no shortage of complex policy issues that would benefit from independent examination by experts in a public inquiry process, or of new developments that lie outside any particular area of government and that would be best advanced through public consultation and inquiry.

It is certain that accidents and disasters will continue to occur and errors will be made that need thorough and expert investigation. The commission of inquiry will continue to be an invaluable part of a government's toolkit for review, investigation and advice.

New Zealand public inquiries mentioned in chapter

(in chronological order by year of appointment, with name of chair)

Royal Commission on Local Authority Finance (Stanton: 1957)

Royal Commission on State Services in New Zealand (McCarthy: 1961)

Royal Commission on Workers' Compensation (Woodhouse: 1966)

Commission of Inquiry into Security Service and University Attendance (Hutchison: 1966)

Royal Commission on Social Security (McCarthy: 1969)

Commission of Inquiry into Housing (Cooke: 1970)

Commission of Inquiry into Equal Pay (McGrath: 1971)

Royal Commission to Inquire into and Report Upon Hospitals and Related Services (Hutchison: 1972)

Royal Commission on Salary and Wage Fixing Procedures in the State Services (McCarthy: 1972)

Commission of Inquiry into Certain Allegations (Davison: 1974)

Royal Commission on Contraception, Sterilisation and Abortion (McMullin: 1975)

Royal Commission on Nuclear Power Generation (McCarthy: 1976)

Royal Commission on the Courts (Beattie: 1976)

Royal Commission on the Maori Land Courts (McCarthy: 1978)

Commission of Inquiry into the Abbotsford Landslip Disaster (Gallen: 1979)

Royal Commission to Inquire into and report Upon the Crash on Mount Erebus, Antarctica, of a DC-10 Aircraft Operated by Air New Zealand Ltd (Mahon: 1980)

Royal Commission to Inquire into the Circumstances of the Convictions of Arthur Allan Thomas for the Murders of David Harvey Crewe and Jeanette Lenore Crewe (Taylor: 1980)

Royal Commission to Inquire into and Report Upon Certain Matters Related to Drug Trafficking (Stewart: 1982)

Royal Commission on Broadcasting and Related Telecommunications (Chapman: 1985)

Royal Commission on the Electoral System (Wallace: 1985)

Royal Commission on Social Policy (Richardson: 1986)

Commission of Inquiry into Certain Matters Relating to Taxation (Davison 1994)

Royal Commission on Genetic Modification (Eichelbaum: 2000)

Commission of Inquiry into Police Conduct (Robertson: 2004)

Royal Commission on Auckland Governance (Salmon: 2007)

Royal Commission on the Pike River Coal Mine Tragedy (Pankhurst: 2010)

Royal Commission of Inquiry into Building Failure caused by the Canterbury Earthquakes (Cooper: 2011)

References

Australian Law Reform Commission (ALRC), 2009, *Making Inquiries – A New Statutory Framework*, Report 111, Canberra: Commonwealth Government

Department of Internal Affairs, 2001, *Setting Up and Running Commissions of Inquiry*, Wellington: New Zealand Government Printer

Easton, B., 1994, "Royal Commissions as Policy Creators: The New Zealand Experience," in Weller, P., (ed), *Royal Commissions and the Making of Public Policy*, Melbourne: Macmillan, 230-243

Holmes, P., 2011, *Daughters of Erebus*, Wellington: Hodder Moa

Mahon, P., 1981, *Royal Commission to Inquire into and Report Upon the Crash on Mount Erebus, Antarctica, of a DC-10 Aircraft Operated by Air New Zealand Ltd Report*, Wellington: New Zealand Government Printer

New Zealand Law Commission (NZLC), 2007, Issues Paper 1, *The Role of Public Enquiries*, Issues Paper 1, Wellington: New Zealand Government Printer

New Zealand Law Commission (NZLC), 2008, Report 102, *A New Inquiries Act*, Wellington: New Zealand Government Printer

19

Commissions of inquiry in Canada

Grant R. Hoole

Introduction

Commissions of inquiry are a ubiquitous feature of Canada's legal and political landscape. The past decade has seen inquiries tender reports on subjects as diverse as the conduct of Canada's security and intelligence officials; police investigation of the disappearance of vulnerable women from Vancouver's downtown eastside; the use of conducted energy weapons by police; the decline of sockeye salmon in British Columbia's Fraser River; and the response of justice officials to allegations of widespread sexual abuse in an Ontario municipality. The Charbonneau Commission, a particularly high-profile inquiry underway in Quebec at the time of writing, has generated almost daily headlines as it investigates allegations of collusion between public officials and members of the province's construction industry. While the commission will not report until 2015, the atmosphere of scandal surrounding its work has already precipitated the resignation of high ranking officials, including the former mayor of Montreal.

This chapter is intended to provide an introduction to Canadian commissions of inquiry. Part 1 provides an overview of their legal characteristics and outlines key trends in their usage. Part 2 considers significant proposals for the reform of commissions of inquiry, and describes how the conduct of inquiries has been impacted by Canada's *Charter of Rights and Freedoms* and by important developments in administrative law. Finally, Part 3 addresses the question of how commissions of inquiry are to be evaluated. It is argued that the success of commissions of inquiry should not be measured solely by the adoption of their recommendations in public policy. Focusing on the immediate policy impact of an inquiry may divert attention from other important features and contributions. It also neglects the crucial variable of time, overlooking the fact that some of the most significant impacts of inquiries do not occur immediately, but over a long term, as societal attitudes and understandings of a given issue change. A more nuanced assessment of inquiries must account for the value of process as much as outcome, recognising that in addition to their status as instruments of public policy, commissions of inquiry represent a distinct form of "social influence" (Le Dain 1972: 85) mediating the perspectives and interests of diverse groups.

Overview of commissions of inquiry in Canada

Certain basic features of commissions of inquiry will be familiar to observers of Canadian law or politics. Inquiries are ad hoc institutions, commissioned by the executive branch of government, but functionally independent, mandated to investigate and report on a given issue or matter of concern. Given that inquiries frequently overlap with processes of civil or criminal litigation, an important and oft-repeated institutional characteristic is that they report factual conclusions and recommendations, but do not reach legally enforceable findings.[1] Both federally, and in each of Canada's ten provinces and three territories, legislation exists to authorise the appointment of commissions of inquiry by order-in-council (see Ruel 2010: 1-2 and 183-285). These statutes afford broad discretion to the executive in determining when to appoint a commission of inquiry, and in stipulating terms of reference. Once appointed, inquiries are governed by a framework of basic powers and procedures set out in their respective statutes, subject to limitation by their individual orders-in-council, and supplemented by external legal constraints. These include the administrative law principle of fairness, and the constitutional dictates of Canadian federalism and of the *Charter of Rights and Freedoms*.[2]

Very often the individuals appointed to lead commissions of inquiry are either active or retired judges. This might be explained by the association of judicial office with independence and impartiality; the relevance of the judicial skill-set to scrutinising testimony and evidence; and the likelihood that inquiries will confront interlocutory legal issues concerning the rights of witnesses or questions of jurisdiction (Ruel 2010: 13-14). The propriety of judicial involvement in an institution that serves as an ad hoc extension of the executive branch of government has received relatively sparse attention in Canada. Unlike Australia, Canada does not have a strict constitutional separation of powers, and, accordingly, lacks a developed legal doctrine of *persona designata* or a doctrine of incompatibility to govern the appointment of judges to extra-judicial tasks. For this reason, the service of active judges as inquiry commissioners is likely more common in Canada than in Australia. There is some recognition among Canadian authorities, however, that service on commissions of inquiry may place public confidence in the judiciary in jeopardy should it cast judges in politicised roles or lack adequate safeguards for independence (Campbell 2003: 392; Manson and Mullan 2003: 5-6; Ratushny 2009: 154-55). The Canadian Judicial Council (CJC), which regulates Canada's federally appointed judiciary, has issued a protocol aimed at addressing these concerns. Among other things, it requires that judicial acceptance of an inquiry commission be approved by the Chief Justice of the relevant jurisdiction (CJC 2010:2).

Of those powers conferred on commissions of inquiry by statute, the most consequential is the ability to compel the attendance and testimony of witnesses. Other coercive powers include the ability to compel document production, or to enter and inspect premises, the latter typically requiring prior authorisation by a court. Inquiries are not bound by strict rules of evidence (with the exception of most classes of privilege), meaning they have broad discretion to admit evidence based on general determinations of relevance (Ruel 2010: 73). Because of the dangers that inquiry powers pose to individual rights, corresponding protections lie at common law and under the *Charter*. These may also be formally codified in the relevant inquiries statutes. At a minimum, those subject to findings of misconduct by a commission of inquiry are entitled to prior notice and a meaningful opportunity of reply (Ruel 2010: 141). Additional protections may arise in the specific context of an inquiry. Consequent to the administrative law principle of fairness, these protections will increase in proportion to the adversity faced by individual witnesses and participants.

Technically, the power to appoint a commission of inquiry also exists as a matter of royal prerogative, independent of statutory authorisation (Ratushny 2009: 24; Macdonald 1980: 368). This means that the executive may appoint an inquiry at will, but without the coercive powers conferred by statute. Although prerogative appointments are rare, it is not uncommon for governments to appoint statutory inquiries that do not make use of coercive powers. A distinction is sometimes made in Canada (as in Australia) between inquiries that "advise" and those that "investigate". Advisory inquiries, such as the 1991-96 *Royal Commission on Aboriginal Peoples*, focus on broad questions of public policy, serving as vehicles for public consultation and the development of independent opinion. They have no need to compel witnesses or evidence, and thus do not exercise these powers. By contrast, investigative inquiries typically focus on explaining the causes of a more definite event or controversy, and will exercise coercive powers as part of their efforts to discern key facts and information. One area in which such inquiries have had particular impact is in investigating instances of wrongful criminal conviction, where they have been instrumental in motivating institutional reforms to safeguard against racial profiling, the misuse of forensic evidence, prosecutorial bias, and other systemic errors contributing to miscarriages of justice (Ratushny 2009: 67-85). It is nevertheless important to note that most inquiries cannot be neatly categorised as either "advisory" or "investigative", rather, they sit somewhere on a continuum, blending advisory and investigative functions (Salter 2003: 186; ALRI 1992: 198).

Despite having inherited the inquiry instrument from Britain, Canada preceded its colonial forebear by 76 years in enacting legislation to confer broad discretion on the executive to appoint inquiries, and to empower those inquiries with the ability to compel witnesses. The first such statute – an *Act to Empower Commissioners for Inquiring into Matters Connected with the Public Business, to Take Evidence on Oath* – was enacted by the Province of Canada in 1846.[3] Its flexible and inclusive language, enabling the appointment of inquiries "into and concerning any matter connected with the good government of Canada, or the conduct of any part of the public business thereof", is retained in the modern-day federal *Inquiries Act*.[4]

To estimate the total number of commissions of inquiry that have occurred at either the federal or provincial level is fraught with difficulty, as no consistent databases or record-keeping practices have been maintained. Canada's Privy Council Office recently began to compile a public database of records of federal commissions of inquiry. While the database presents only a partial picture, it is nevertheless the most comprehensive resource available. The inquiries listed at the end of the chapter are derived from the database. The list is limited to inquiries appointed between 1945 and the time of writing and includes 84 inquiries. A brief review of the list proves the observation that "much of the history of Canada can be interpreted through the work of commissions of inquiry" (LRCC 1977: 11).

Inquiries associated with notable historic events and public controversies include the Kellock-Taschereau Commission, appointed in 1946 to investigate the infiltration of Canada's government by a Soviet spy ring, and foreshadowing the impending Cold War; the Dubin Commission, appointed in 1988 to investigate the use of drugs and other banned substances by athletes, following the stripping of Canadian sprinter Ben Johnson's gold medal at the Seoul Olympics; the Krever Commission, appointed in 1993 to investigate the regulation of medical blood services in Canada, following the accidental infection of thousands of individuals with HIV and hepatitis C through "tainted" blood and blood products; the Somalia Inquiry, appointed in 1995 to investigate the commission of atrocities by Canadian forces in Somalia, and controversially terminated in 1997 before completing its investigation; the Gomery Inquiry, appointed in 2004 to investigate allegations of corruption and mismanagement in a federal program designed to promote federalism in Quebec, and notoriously contributing to the downfall of the Martin Liberal Government in 2006; the Air India Inquiry, appointed in 2006 to review the investigation of the bombing of Air India Flight 182 in 1985, Canada's worst incident of domestic terrorism; and the Arar Inquiry, appointed in 2004 to investigate the conduct of police, security and intelligence officials surrounding the rendition of a Canadian citizen to Syria, where he faced torture, due to the suspicion of American authorities that he was affiliated with a terrorist organisation.

Several commissions also serve as historic markers for broad social, political, and economic change. These include inquiries appointed during the late 1950s and early 1960s that focused on industrial subjects – energy, transportation, the automotive industry – reflecting Canada's economic modernisation, and on matters of governance – taxation, unemployment insurance, and government organisation – reflecting the growth of the administrative state. The late 1960s saw the appointment of commissions on the non-medical use of drugs and on the status of women, reflecting the liberalisation of social attitudes on these subjects. In 1963, Prime Minister Lester Pearson appointed the *Royal Commission on Bilingualism and Biculturalism*, leading ultimately to the adoption of the *Official Languages Act* in 1969,[5] which affirmed both French and English as Canada's official languages. The 1982-85 *Royal Commission on the Economic Union and Development Prospects for Canada* recommended, among other things, that Canada pursue greater trade openness and economic exchange with the United States. This recommendation played a significant role in building political support for the *North American Free Trade Agreement*, completed in 1992.

It is intriguing to note an apparent reduction in the rate of federal commissions of inquiry since the early 1990s. Each of Canada's prime ministers to govern for periods greater than one year between 1957 and 1990 appointed commissions of inquiry at a rate averaging between one and two commissions a year. However, under the tenure of Liberal Prime Minister Jean Chrétien (1993 to 2003), only three commissions of inquiry were appointed. Canada's current Conservative Prime Minister, Stephen Harper, has appointed slightly more – four commissions of inquiry in seven years – but still not at the rate of the majority of his predecessors. Also noteworthy is a shift in the type of inquiry appointed. Of those inquiries appointed since 1993, only one – the *Commission on the Future of Healthcare in Canada* – was focused on broad, "advisory" questions of public policy. The remainder were primarily investigative inquiries, prompted by highly specific controversies.

Several hypotheses can be offered to explain these changes. For one, the federal politics of the past two decades have emphasised fiscal restraint. A signature achievement of the Chrétien Government was to eliminate Canada's budget deficit, largely through cuts to departmental spending and to fiscal transfers to the provinces. Despite stimulus spending and the accumulation of a deficit following the 2008 financial crisis, Canada's current Harper Conservative Government is ideologically and rhetorically attuned to fiscal conservatism. It is perhaps foreseeable that governments with these political orientations might avoid an institution sometimes criticised for its heavy consumption of time and public resources.

More simply, variation in the appointment of public inquiries might be explained by the leadership styles of recent prime ministers. Reticence to use inquiries may indicate reticence to cede control over the public perception of an issue. This hypothesis receives some support from the decision of the Jean Chrétien Liberal Government to terminate the Somalia Inquiry. Ostensibly, the inquiry was terminated when the federal government refused to grant a further extension to its already prolonged deadline. Critics suggest that the initial deadlines set for the inquiry were never feasible, and that refusing a final extension provided the government a convenient escape from daily "bad news" about the conduct of Canada's military and defence officials (Ratushny 2009: 46-50, 275-6; Witelson 2003: 317-8).

Finally, a range of factors quite apart from the idiosyncrasies of governments may have contributed to the recent decline in the federal usage of inquiries. It is trite to point out that the past two decades have seen the proliferation of digital media and communication. New resources consequently at the disposal of government and non-governmental actors to sample public opinion, market ideas, and shape dialogue may in some circumstances have supplanted the utility of commissions of inquiry. The rise of the *Charter* may also have had an impact. The *Charter* serves as a rallying point for individuals and groups historically marginalised from mainstream electoral politics. Some critics allege that the *Charter* has given rise to a "Court Party": a set of organised interest groups using constitutional litigation to further their agendas and subvert the will of elected governments (Morton and Knopff 2000). Defenders contend that the *Charter* enriches Canadian democracy by lending voice to a more diverse and inclusive range of participants without diminishing the scope of legislative innovation (Roach 2001; Hogg and Bushell 1997). Neither deny that the legal regulation of many complex and controversial issues – prostitution, polygamy, assisted suicide, safe injection sites, to name but a few – is presently being shaped by *Charter* litigation in Canada's courts. The participants in these disputes include not just those immediately affected (the individual claimants and government respondents), but a variety of intervener groups presenting distinct knowledge, perspectives, and goals. Constitutional litigation may thus provide a focal point for social action that has been previously fulfilled by commissions of inquiry. It is also possible that legal constraints placed by the *Charter* on the work of commissions of inquiry, and the possibility of *Charter* challenges to their work with consequent costs and delay, have made them less attractive to recent federal governments.[6]

Reform and review of commissions of inquiry

Few attempts have been made to propose comprehensive reforms to commissions of inquiry. Perhaps the most prominent exceptions are three reports prepared by the independent law reform commissions of Canada, Ontario, and Alberta. The Law Reform Commission of Canada (LRCC 1979) prepared a report on commissions of inquiry in 1979, recommending most notably that a formal distinction between advisory and investigative commissions be enacted in law, with separate powers and procedures codified for each. The Ontario Law Reform Commission (OLRC) and Alberta Law Reform Institute (ALRI) both completed reports on commissions of inquiry in 1992.

The timing of the three reports is significant. The LRCC prepared its report before the enactment of the *Charter* in 1982, and before the embrace of a broad, flexible approach to the enforcement of procedural fairness in Canadian administrative law. The OLRC and ALRI reports both post-dated the *Charter*; however, little opportunity had yet arisen in case law to test the application of the *Charter* to commissions of inquiry. These factors lend important context to the attention devoted by each report to clarifying, and statutorily codifying, the rights of inquiry witnesses. The reports exhibit a common concern for ensuring that the legitimate ends of inquiries not lead to unjust means in the treatment of individuals, particularly compelled witnesses. The OLRC went furthest in this respect, arguing that inquiry witnesses should be entitled to refuse testimony on the basis of self-incrimination. Both the ALRI and OLRC reports recommended that individuals against whom criminal proceedings have commenced should not be compellable to testify concerning common subject matter at an inquiry. The ALRI and OLRC also recommended codifying an absolute prohibition against commissions of inquiry making findings of civil or criminal fault. All three reports recommended that commissions of inquiry be able to place restrictions on the publicity of their proceedings, either through *in camera* hearings or publication bans, in order to safeguard the fair trial interests of criminally accused witnesses.

None of the law commission studies succeeded in motivating statutory amendments, yet several of the concerns they identified have since been given stronger treatment by Canada's courts. In 1997, the Supreme Court released its decision in *Canada (AG) v Canada (Commission of Inquiry on the Blood System in Canada)* (Krever),[7] a case concerning the rights of inquiry witnesses facing potential findings of misconduct. While it has long been accepted that the findings of commissions of inquiry are not legally enforceable, there has nevertheless been confusion as to whether their findings can include statements of civil or criminal wrong. Previous case law had held that inquiries could not issue such findings, yet the basis and scope of this restriction remained unclear. *Krever* indicated for the first time the Supreme Court's broad endorsement of the restriction, on the basis that inquiry witnesses do not benefit from the same evidentiary and procedural protections as participants in civil or criminal trials. Without evoking a specific *Charter* provision, the Court's decision nevertheless reinforces important protections underlying Canada's justice system, such as the right to security of the person, the presumption of innocence, and the right not to be compelled as a witness against oneself. In effect, the decision indicates that where these rights are not protected in a manner equivalent to a formal trial, equivalent statements of legal fault cannot be made. This restriction chiefly concerns the appropriate use of *language* in an inquiry report: commissioners are prohibited from stating conclusions of civil or criminal fault as such. They may still report misconduct, however, from which inferences of legal wrong can be drawn, provided such findings are necessary to fulfil their investigative mandates.

In another case, *Phillips v Nova Scotia*,[8] the Supreme Court had the opportunity to address a number of *Charter* issues surrounding the coincidence of a public inquiry with criminal prosecutions. Two individuals, both corporate officers of a mining company implicated in a fatal disaster in Nova Scotia, resisted their compulsion as witnesses at a commission of inquiry investigating the disaster. They alleged that the publicity of their inquiry testimony could prejudice future jurors at their criminal trials. While the Court of Appeal for Nova Scotia accepted these claims and ordered a stay of the inquiry, the Supreme Court overturned this result. Sadly, its decision turned on a technicality: the witnesses had since elected for trial by judge alone, thus obviating the basis of their original claim. In an important concurring judgment, however, Mr Justice Cory opted to comment on the application of the *Charter* to witnesses in the applicants' position.

Justice Cory denied that the witnesses were entitled either to the stay of the inquiry or to the right not to testify: the high public importance of the inquiry, reflecting the community's pressing need for answers in the wake of a tragedy, warranted the uninterrupted pursuit of its mandate. The witnesses would benefit, however, from the inadmissibility of their testimony in any subsequent criminal proceeding, a protection enshrined in the *Charter*. The *Charter* also entitled them to protection against the "derivative" use of that testimony, meaning its use by police or criminal prosecutors to adduce evidence that would not have been discovered "but for" the witnesses' testimony. The witnesses might also petition the commissioner to ban the publication of inquiry evidence or findings, or for *in camera* hearings, should they be able demonstrate that such publicity would irreparably prejudice their rights to a fair trial.

While a minority opinion, Justice Cory's judgment is likely authoritative in the absence of further clarification from the Supreme Court (Ratushny 2009: 296). The decision implicitly rejects the most strident witness protections advocated by some of the law commission reports – notably, a prohibition against compelling the appearance or testimony of criminally accused witness. It also places important restrictions on the treatment of those witnesses, however, aiming to prevent the outcomes of public inquiries from affecting the outcomes of criminal trials. This may mark a distinction between Canadian commissions of inquiry and those of other jurisdictions. For example, Australia's *Royal Commissions Act 1902* (Cth) protects against the compelled testimony of criminally accused witnesses, but also stipulates that an inquiry may provide prosecutorial authorities with information or documents implicating the commission of a crime. In the Canadian context, the latter would likely be viewed as invalidly substituting an inquiry for a criminal investigation, and thus prohibited under the *Charter*. It would also violate the principle that inquiries not opine on matters of civil or criminal liability. In cases where inquiries bear a high risk of prejudicing a fair trial, or proceeding with criminal prosecution would unduly complicate the work of an inquiry, Canadian officials may be forced to choose between the two.

In addition to protections under the *Charter*, inquiry witnesses are entitled to procedural fairness in administrative law. Previously, standards of review in Canadian administrative law were dictated by a formal distinction between quasi-judicial and non-judicial administrative bodies. The latter were thought to be engaged in predominantly policy activities, and were accordingly afforded deferential review and limited enforcement of fairness requirements. Beginning with the Supreme Court's 1979 decision in *Nicholson v Haldimand-Norfolk (Regional) Police Commissioners*,[9] this approach has been replaced with a general duty of fairness applicable to all administrative bodies. Both the content of this duty, and the standard of review applicable, are determined by contextual factors. When an inquiry engages significant reputational or other risks for witnesses, a high standard of fairness is owed. This involves "not the same level [of fairness] as required at a judicial trial … [but a standard] within the upper end of the spectrum required for administrative tribunals" (Ratushny 2009: 289). Its features are likely to include the right to standing and to representation by counsel, and a strong duty of impartiality on the part of the commissioner. In the ordinary course, Canada's courts will afford deference to commissions of inquiry on matters of evidence, procedure, or other subjects within a commissioner's discretion. A failure to behave fairly, however, will be considered to violate the very jurisdiction of an inquiry, and is reviewable on a strict standard of correctness (Ratushny 2009: 301). Findings that arise from unfair treatment will be considered a nullity (Ratushny 2009: 286).

Evaluating commissions of inquiry

The impact of commissions of inquiry on public policy is difficult to assess in concrete terms. Some commissions have undoubtedly contributed to policy change, either by persuading governments of their recommendations or by building consensus and momentum for changes already afoot. Canada's adoption of North American Free Trade, universal healthcare, employment equity, and official bilingualism must each be credited, in large part, to the influence of commissions of inquiry (Ratushny 2009: 22). At the same time, the history of Canadian commissions of inquiry includes numerous instances of inquiries whose recommendations have not been adopted. Canada's federal government has not, for example, formally recognised a "nation to nation" relationship with its Aboriginal peoples, which the *Royal Commission on Aboriginal Peoples* recommended serve as the basis for expanded Aboriginal self-government.

The Hon Frank Iacobucci, a former Justice of the Supreme Court, has cautioned against evaluating commissions of inquiry solely based on their contributions to public policy: "Other institutions of government are designed to implement policy. If inquiries were so designed, they would lose most of their unique advantages, such as their detached independence from the political arena and bureaucratic politics, their flexibility and their ability to be self-determining within the terms of their mandate" (Iacobucci 1990: 28). In other words, some of the very features that make inquiries desirable – including their independence from the political imperatives of government – may lead them to recommendations that are not immediately palatable to government, or possibly even to the general public at a given point in time. A lack of immediate change resulting from an inquiry should not necessarily be considered a weakness. In some instances, it may be the marker of an inquiry that is ahead of its time.

Roderick Macdonald observes that when governments enact a new law or create a new policy, they are necessarily required to formulate a statement of an issue (what the issue "is") and their position in relation to it (Macdonald 1980: 388). He suggests that commissions of inquiry enable the suspension of issues in a more ambiguous state: "there are problems, issues *and solutions* which both the government … and the public … are either unable or unwilling to articulate at a given moment: this inarticulateness finds expression in a commission of inquiry" (Macdonald 1980: 388). A "legitimate" commission of inquiry, in Macdonald's view, is one that serves as a process by which its participants (both government and public) come to take responsibility for the definition of issues and for their respective positions in relation to those issues. Inquiries thus serve "to mediate urgent necessity and reflection; to redefine what is beneficial or harmful in society; to confirm, yet also challenge constituted authority; to diffuse feelings of hurt and rage in individual cases" (Macdonald 1980: 391). In this sense, the "point" of the inquiry is not so much the formulation of concrete policy proposals (at least not exclusively), rather, it is the intrinsic value of the process itself.

Following this line of thought, an inquiry succeeds not just by furbishing precise answers to questions posed in its terms of reference, but by generating new forms of understanding and dialogue across a range of perspectives. The accomplishments of some inquiries will be more profound in this respect than the accomplishments of others. Liora Salter (1990) notes that most inquiries rely heavily on the evidence and opinions of professional experts, whose views often reflect the prevailing debates and orthodoxies of their fields. This fact, together with the pressure on commissioners to formulate pragmatic recommendations, may limit the potential of inquiries to serve as sites of radical debate.

In rare instances, however, a particularly innovative inquiry brokers wider societal participation and gives weight to the perspectives of those often excluded from the policy process. Such inquiries can lead to truly transformative social change.

An illustrative example is provided by one of Canada's most celebrated commissions, the *Mackenzie Valley Pipeline Inquiry*, appointed in 1974 to investigate the potential impact of a proposed natural gas pipeline in Canada's Yukon and Northwest Territories. Commissioner Thomas Berger adopted what was then an unorthodox procedural approach. He combined formal evidentiary hearings involving the examination of expert witnesses, such as engineers, biologists, and economists, with less formal but broadly inclusive community hearings. The community hearings were held:

> [I]n each city and town, settlement and village in the Mackenzie Valley, the Mackenzie delta, and the northern Yukon – thirty-five altogether. At these community hearings, the people living in the communities were given the opportunity to speak in their own language and in their own way. Something like one thousand witnesses, many of them speaking through interpreters, spoke at these hearings. (Berger 2003: 17)

The community hearings proved influential. Berger concluded that the pipeline posed a threat to the livelihoods and territorial rights of the Dene, Inuit and Metis peoples living within the proposed development areas, and recommended a 10-year moratorium on development pending the resolution of outstanding Aboriginal land claims. The inquiry thus had a significant and immediate policy impact in that its central recommendation was adopted. It also had a more transformative social impact, however (Salter 1990: 178). The community hearings received wide media coverage throughout Canada, being simultaneously broadcast on public radio and documented in nightly television news. The result was to raise awareness about Canada's northern Aboriginal communities, their cultures and economic livelihoods, and their right to shape policy decisions affecting their future. The Berger Inquiry process, quite apart from its report, continues to be regarded as a watershed moment in building broad awareness of the status, agency and rights of Canada's Aboriginal peoples.

The Berger Inquiry also serves to underscore the importance of time in assessing the effects of a commission. In the intervening years since the report, several of the Aboriginal groups who participated in the commission have since settled outstanding land claims with the federal government. There is now a significant possibility that the pipeline development will proceed, with participation on the part of the Aboriginal communities affected. The long-term effects of the inquiry are thus still unfolding. This is instructive for the assessment of other commissions of inquiry. The fulfilment of inquiry recommendations depends very much on the political culture of the day and the influence of prevailing attitudes. The relationship between commissions of inquiry and social norms is not a simple one of cause and effect. It is complex and interactive, and mapping its full dimensions requires time.

Conclusion

The central aim of this chapter has been to provide an introduction to Canadian commissions of inquiry. Important differences may lie in the conduct of Canadian commissions of inquiry when compared with their Australian counterparts: active judges may be used more frequently as the heads of Canadian inquiries, for example, and stricter boundaries may be enforced between inquiries and other proceedings by the *Canadian Charter of Rights and Freedoms*. Yet Canada shares with Australia – and other countries – a common reliance on commissions of inquiry as an important means of addressing pressing public concerns and resolving important policy debates. Further comparative studies would no doubt benefit the conduct and appraisal of inquiries across jurisdictions.

Importantly, in appraising commissions of inquiry, we must be mindful that the adoption of their recommendations in public policy represents only one axis for evaluation. Quite apart from their immediate impact on policy, inquiries have the potential to reshape societal understanding of an issue and of the perspectives and experiences of discordant groups. They also have important intrinsic effects, both on the rights of individuals who may be adversely impacted by them, and on the expectations of those who view inquiries as an opportunity to seek recognition of their experiences, acknowledgment of an injustice, accountability from those in authority, or a range of other important values. Measuring success in these areas is no doubt a complicated task, but it is essential to properly recognising the distinct value of commissions of inquiry as civic institutions.

Canadian federal public inquiries mentioned in chapter: 1945-present

(in chronological order by prime minister, political party, inquiry, chair and year of appointment)*

William Lyon Mackenzie King (Liberal) 1935-1948
• *Royal Commission on Veterans' Qualifications* (Bovey: 1945) • *Commission to Inquire into the Purchase Price of Certain Land in the Township of Sandwich West, Ontario, Bought under the Provisions of the Veterans' Land Act* (Brodie: 1945) • *Royal Commission on the Halifax Disorders, May 7-8, 1945* (Kellock: 1945) • *Royal Commission to Investigate the Facts Relating to and the Circumstances Surrounding the Communication by the Public Officials and Other Persons in Positions of Trust of Secret and Confidential Information to Agents of Foreign Power* (Taschereau: 1946) • *Royal Commission on the Indian Act and Indian Administration in General* (Brown and Johnston: 1946) • *Royal Commission to Investigate Property Claims of Canadian Citizens of Japanese Origin Evacuated from Coast Areas of British Columbia in 1942* (Bird: 1947) • *Commission to Investigate Complaints made by Walter H. Kirchner, M.C., D.C.M., Secretary, Canadian Combat Veterans Association, Inc., Vancouver, British Columbia, Regarding Pension and Treatment Services with Respect to Certain Cases Concerning Which Mr. Kirchner had made Representations* (McCann: 1947)

Louis St. Laurent (Liberal) 1948-1957
• *Royal Commission on National Development in the Arts, Letters and Sciences 1949-1951* (Massey: 1949) • *Commission to Inquire into the Nature and Extent of the Damage Caused by the 1950 Floods in the Red River Valley in Manitoba* (Carswell and Shaw: 1950) • *Royal Commission on the Revision of the Criminal Code* (Martin: 1951) • *Commission to Inquire into and Report upon the Facts Concerning the Staking of Certain Areas of the Crown in the North West Territories and Yukon Territory* (Dispute between California Standard Co. and Sun Oil Co.) (Christie: 1951) • *Royal Commission on Patents, Copyright, Trade Marks and Industrial Designs* (Ilsley: 1954)
John Diefenbaker (Progressive Conservative) 1957-1963
• *Royal Commission on Energy* (Borden: 1957) • *Royal Commission of Inquiry into the Distribution of Railway Box Cars* (Bracken: 1958) • *Commission to Inquire into the Desirability of Establishing a New Band of Indians on Seabird Island, British Columbia* (Cassady: 1958) • *Royal Commission on Transportation* (MacPherson: 1959) • *Royal Commission on the Great Slave Lake Railway* (Manning: 1959) • *Royal Commission to Investigate the Unfulfilled Provisions of Treaties 8 and 11 as they Apply to the Indians of the Mackenzie District* (Nelson: 1959) • *Royal Commission on the Automotive Industry* (Bladen: 1960) • *Royal Commission to Inquire into Complaints received concerning certain activities of Station CHEK-TV, Victoria, British Columbia* (Stewart, Allison, Brown, Forsey, Marshall: 1960) • *Royal Commission on Government Organization* (Glassco: 1960) • *Royal Commission on Health Services* (Hall: 1961) • *Committee of Inquiry into the Unemployment Insurance Act* (Gill: 1961) • *Royal Commission on Taxation* (Carter: 1962) • *Royal Commission on Pilotage* (Bernier: 1962)

Lester Bowles Pearson (Liberal) 1963-1968
• *Royal Commission on Banking and Finance* (Potter: 1961) • *Royal Commission on Bilingualism and Biculturalism* (Dunton, Laurendau and Gagnon: 1963) • *Commission of Inquiry as to the Future of the Air Canada Overhaul Base at Winnipeg International Airport, and Related Matters* (Thompson: 1964) • *Commission of Inquiry into Crash of Trans-Canada Air Lines DC-8F Aircraft CF-TJN at Ste Therese de Blainville, P.Q. on 29th November 1963* (Challies: 1964) • *Commission to Inquire into and to Investigate the Charges of Irregularities in the Federal Election of 1963* (Nemetz: 1965) • *Commission of Inquiry into Freshwater Fish Marketing* (McIvor: 1965) • *Royal Commission of Inquiry into Working Conditions in the Post Office Department* (Monpetit: 1965) • *Commission of Inquiry into the Increases in Rates of Pay for Civil Servants in Group D* (Anderson: 1965) • *Royal Commission to Inquire into the Dealings of the Honourable Mr. Justice Leo A. Landreville, with Northern Natural Gas Limited* (Rand: 1966) • *Commission of Inquiry into Matters Relating to one Gerta Munsinger* (Spence: 1966) • *Royal Commission on Security* (Mackenzie: 1966) • *Royal Commission on the Status of Women in Canada* (Bird: 1967) • *Commission of Inquiry re Administration of Justice in the Hay River of the Northwest Territories* (Morrow: 1967)

Pierre Elliot Trudeau (Liberal) 1968-1979; 1980-1984
• *Commission of Inquiry into the Non-medical Use of Drugs* (le Dain: 1969) • *Commissioner on Indian Claims* (Barber: 1969) • *Airport Inquiry Commission* (Gibson: 1973) • *Mackenzie Valley Pipeline Inquiry* (Berger: 1974) • *Steel Profits Inquiry* (Estey: 1974) • *Commission of Inquiry into the Marketing of Beef* (Mackenzie: 1975) • *Air Canada Inquiry* (Estey: 1975) • *Royal Commission on Corporate Concentration* (Bryce: 1975) • *Commission of Inquiry into the Matter of a Crash of a Panarctic Electra Aircraft at Rea Point, Northwest Territories* (Stevenson: 1975) • *Royal Commission on Financial Management and Accountability* (Lambert: 1976) • *The Task Force on Canadian Unity* (Jepin and Robarts: 1977) • *Commission of Inquiry Concerning Certain Activities of the Royal Canadian Mounted Police* (McDonald: 1977) • *Inquiry into the Automotive Industry* (Reisman: 1978) • *Commission of Inquiry into Certain Allegations Concerning Commercial Practices of the Canadian Dairy Commission* (Gibson: 1979) • *Commission of Inquiry Related to the Security and Investigation Services Branch within the Post Office Department* (Marin: 1980) • *Royal Commission on Conditions of Foreign Service* (McDougall: 1980) • *Royal Commission on Newspapers* (Kent: 1980) • *Commission on Pacific Fisheries Policy* (Pearse: 1981) • *Royal Commission on the Economic Union and Development Prospects for Canada* (MacDonald: 1982) • *Commission on Equality in Employment* (Abella: 1983) • *Canadian Sentencing Commission* (Archambault: 1984) • *Royal Commission on Seals and the Sealing Industry in Canada* (Malouf: 1984

Joe Clark (Progressive Conservative) 1979-1980
• *Mississauga Railway Accident Inquiry* (Grange: 1979)
John Napier Turner (Liberal) 1984
• None appointed
Brian Mulroney (Progressive Conservative) 1984-1993
• *Commission of Inquiry on Unemployment Insurance* (Forget: 1985) • *Commission of Inquiry into the Collapse of the Canadian Commercial Bank (CCB) and the Northland Bank* (Estey: 1985) • *Commission of Inquiry Concerning Certain Matters Associated with the Westbank Indian Band* (Hall: 1986) • *Royal Commission on the Future of the Toronto Waterfront* (Crombie: 1988) • *Commission of Inquiry into the Use of Drugs and Banned Practices Intended to Increase Athletic Performance* (Dubin: 1988) • *Commission of Inquiry into the Air Ontario Crash at Dryden, Ontario (Canada)* (Moshansky: 1989) • *Royal Commission on National Passenger Transportation* (Hyndman: 1989) • *Royal Commission on New Reproductive Technologies* (Baird: 1989) • *Citizens' Forum on Canada's Future* (Spicer: 1990) • *Indian Claims Commission* (Dupuis: 1991) • *Royal Commission on Aboriginal Peoples* (Dussault and Erasmus: 1991) • *Canadian Transportation Accident Investigation and Safety Board Act Review Commission* (Hyndman: 1993)
Kim Campbell (Progressive Conservative) 1993
• *Commission of Inquiry on the Blood System in Canada* (Krever: 1993)
Jean Chrétien (Liberal) 1993-2003
• *Commission of Inquiry into Certain Events at the Prison for Women in Kingston* (Arbour: 1995) • *Commission of Inquiry into the Deployment of Canadian Forces to Somalia* (Létourneau: 1995) • *Commission on the Future of Health Care in Canada* (Romanow: 2001)

Paul Martin (Liberal) 2003-2006
• *Commission of Inquiry into the Actions of Canadian Officials in Relation to Maher Arar* (O'Connor: 2004)
• *Commission of Inquiry into the Sponsorship Program and Advertising Activities* (Gomery: 2004)
• *Miramichi and Acadie-Bathurst Electoral Boundaries Commission* (Daigle: 2004)
Stephen Harper (Conservative) 2006-present
• *Commission of Inquiry into the Investigation of the Bombing of Air India Flight 182* (Major: 2006)
• *Internal Inquiry into Actions of Canadian Officials in Relation to Abdullah Almaki, Ahmad Abou-Elmaati and Muayyed Nurreddin* (Iacobucci: 2006)
• *Commission of Inquiry into Certain allegations respecting Business and Financial Dealings Between Karlheinz Schreiber and the Right Honourable Brian Mulroney* (Oliphant: 2008)
• *Commission of Inquiry into the Decline of Sockeye Salmon in the Fraser River* (Cohen: 2009)

*This table was prepared using data from the Privy Council Office, available in its online archive of commissions of inquiry: http://www.pcobcp.gc.ca/index.asp?lang=eng&page=information&sub=commissions. At the time of writing, the archive was still in the process of construction and did not purport to contain a comprehensive inventory of all federal commissions of inquiry. Those commissions marked with an asterisk (*) were not referenced in the archive, but have been included here based on the author's personal knowledge.

References

Alberta Law Reform Institute, 1992, *Proposals for the Reform of the Public Inquiries Act*, Edmonton: Alberta Law Reform Institute

Alberta Law Reform Institute, 1991, *Public Inquiries*, Edmonton: Alberta Law Reform Institute

Berger, T., 2003, "Canadian Commissions of Inquiry: An Insider's Perspectives" in Manson, A., and Mullan, D., (eds), *Commissions of Inquiry: Praise or Reappraise?*, Toronto: Irwin Law, 13-28

Campbell, A., 2003, "The Bernardo Investigation Review," in Manson and Mullan, *Commissions of Inquiry*, 381-405

Canada, 2002, Commission on the Future of Healthcare in Canada, *Building on Values: The Future of Healthcare in Canada*, Ottawa: Commission on the Future of Healthcare in Canada

Canada, 1996, Royal Commission on Aboriginal Peoples, *Report of the Royal Commission on Aboriginal Peoples* Vols 1-5, [online] Government of Canada Web Archive, www.collectionscanada.gc.ca/webarchives/20071115053257/http://www.ainc-inac.gc.ca/ch/rcap/sg/sgmm_e.html

Canada, 1985, Royal Commission on the Economic Union and Development Prospects for Canada, *Report of the Royal Commission on the Economic Union and Development Prospects for Canada* Vols 1-3, Ottawa: Minister of Supply and Services

Canada, 1977, Mackenzie Valley Pipeline Inquiry, *Northern Frontier, Northern Homeland: The Report of the Mackenzie Valley Pipeline Inquiry* Vols 1-2, Ottawa: Minister of Supply and Services

Canada, 1967-70, Royal Commission on Bilingualism and Biculturalism, *Report of the Royal Commission on Bilingualism and Biculturalism* books 1-5, Ottawa: Queen's Printer

Canadian Judicial Council, 2010, *Protocol on the Appointment of Judges to Commissions of Inquiry*, Ottawa: Canadian Judicial Council

Hogg, P., and Bushell, A. A., 1997, "The *Charter* Dialogue Between Courts and Legislatures (Or Perhaps the *Charter of Rights* Isn't Such a Bad Thing After All)," *Osgoode Hall Law Journal*, 35(1),75-124

Iacobucci, F., 1990, "Commissions of Inquiry and Public Policy in Canada," in Pross, A.P., Christie, I., and Yogis, J.A., (eds), *Commissions of Inquiry*, Toronto: Carswell, 21-28

Le Dain, G.E., 1973, "The Role of the Public Inquiry in Our Constitutional System" in Arthurs, H.W., *et al*, (eds), *Law and Social Change*, Toronto: Osgoode Hall Law School, 79-95

Law Reform Commission of Canada, (LRCC), 1977, *Commissions of Inquiry*, Working Paper 17, Ottawa: Minister of Supply and Services Canada

Law Reform Commission of Canada, (LRCC), 1979, *Report: Advisory and Investigatory Commissions*, Ottawa: Minister of Supply and Services Canada

Macdonald, R.A., 1980, "The Commission of Inquiry in the Perspective of Administrative Law," *Alberta Law Review*, 18(3), 366-395

Manson, A., and Mullan, D., 2003, "Introduction," in Manson and Mullan, *Commissions of Inquiry*, 1-10

Morton, F.L., and Knopff, R., 2000, *The Charter Revolution and the Court Party*, Peterborough: Broadview Press

Ontario Law Reform Commission, (OLRC), 1992, *Report on Public Inquiries*, Toronto: Ontario Law Reform Commission

Ratushny, E., 2009, *The Conduct of Public Inquiries: Law, Policy, and Practice*, Toronto: Irwin Law

Roach, K., 2001, *The Supreme Court on Trial: Judicial Activism or Democratic Dialogue?*, Toronto: Irwin Law

Ruel, S., 2010, *The Law of Public Inquiries in Canada*, Toronto: Carswell

Salter, L., 1990, "The Two Contradictions in Public Inquiries" in Pross, *et al*, 173-5

Salter, L., 2003, "The Complex Relationship between Inquiries and Public Controversy," in Manson and Mullan, *Commissions of Inquiry*, 185-209

Witelson, T., 2003, "Declaration of Independence: Examining the Independence of Federal Public Inquiries," in Manson, and Mullan, *Commissions of Inquiry*, 301-36

Endnotes

1 The seminal statement of this principle was given by Justice Cory for a majority of the Supreme Court of Canada in *Canada (AG) v Canada (Commission of Inquiry on the Blood System)*, [1997] 3 SCR 440 at paragraph 34: "A commission of inquiry is neither a criminal trial nor a civil action for the determination of liability. It cannot establish either criminal culpability or civil responsibility for damages. Rather, an inquiry is an investigation into an issue, event or series of events. The findings of a commissioner relating to that investigation are simply findings of fact and statements of opinion reached by the commissioner at the end of the inquiry."

2 Part I of the *Constitution Act, 1982*, being Schedule B to the *Canada Act 1982* (UK.), 1982, c 11.

3 1846, 9 Vict, c XXXVIII

4 RSC 1985, c I-11, s 2. See also the discussion in Ruel (xxv-xxvi)

5 RSC 1985, c 31

6 These observations are admittedly speculative. Should either the rise of new forms of communication or the *Charter* have impacted the use of commissions of inquiry, one would expect to see this impact at the provincial level as well. I have confined my analysis in this chapter to data available with respect to the appointment of federal inquiries.

7 *Supra* note 1

8 [1995] 2 SCR 97

9 [1979] 1 SCR 311

20

Presidential commissions in the US political system

Kenneth Kitts

Introduction

The question of how to address controversies, crises, or traumas of national scope is certainly not unique to the government of the United States of America (USA). Indeed, social contract theory posits that the primary purpose of all governments is to provide law and order. When disruptions or threats emerge that threaten that order, it is normal for the public to demand answers and accountability. The challenge for those in power is to find the appropriate mechanism with which to respond. In the United States, these calls for action and accountability are processed by and through the Madisonian system of separated powers. It is a cumbersome system by design.

The framers of the Constitution were products of their time. Writing the document in 1787, soon after gaining independence from Great Britain, they were at least as concerned with guarding against governmental excess and abuse of power as they were with creating an efficient system for advancing the public good. In 1788, James Madison captured the issue brilliantly in Federalist No 51:

> If men were angels, no government would be necessary. If angels were to govern men, neither external nor internal controls on government would be necessary. In framing a government which is to be administered by men over men, the great difficulty lies in this: you must first enable the government to control the governed;

> and in the next place oblige it to control itself. (Hamilton, Jay and Madison 2006: 337)

In drafting the Constitution, Madison's solution to this challenge was to disperse governmental power along the lines of executive, legislative, and judicial authority, and then to ensure that each department would have the means necessary to "resist encroachments of the others". "Ambition," he wrote, "must be made to counteract ambition" (Hamilton *et al*: 337).

More than 200 years have elapsed since this constitutional order came into being. Even so, Madison and company cast a long shadow, and the dispersion of power the framers created continues to be the defining characteristic of American politics. This is the context in which US presidential commissions operate. It is an essential frame of reference for interpreting commission politics and the development of public inquiries in the US system of government.

The universe of US advisory commissions

Presidential commissions are only one of many types of ad hoc committees that exist within the universe of federal advisory bodies in the USA. Other bodies created within the executive branch are actually departmental committees, reporting not to the president but to a cabinet secretary or agency supervisor. These bodies typically deal with mundane, procedural questions far removed from matters that command national interest. Still others are interagency groups created to enhance policy coordination between two or more bureaucratic entities.

The complexity of the system is compounded by legislative involvement in public inquiries. Sometimes this takes the form of a special investigation conducted by a standing or select committee of Congress. The 1975 Church Committee hearings, so named for Senator Frank Church, into US intelligence activities stand as a good example of this type of probe. But these investigations are very political and frequently protracted. Even within Congress, this leads to calls to go outside normal channels in the search for answers to the most pressing questions on the public agenda. The result is that Congress has occasionally appointed its own blue-ribbon commissions. Perhaps the best-known examples of this type of group were the two Hoover *Commissions on the Organization of the Executive Branch* in 1947-49 and 1953-55.

Some critics find congressional commissions to be objectionable on grounds that lawmakers should be expected to perform the evaluative and investigative tasks that are delegated to the ad hoc body (Campbell 2002: xv). Others find value in the practice of asking "disinterested men of the highest probity" for assistance in dealing with issues "which congressional committees have neither the time nor the detachment to handle wisely and fairly" (Barth 1955: 215).

Because of this fragmentation, it remains exceedingly difficult to classify or even count federal advisory committees with precision. "No one knows," states a report by the General Accounting Office (GAO), "exactly how many miscellaneous boards, committees, and commissions exist at any given time" (GAO 1991: 17-6). Nor does GAO offer much hope that greater clarity will be forthcoming:

It is always helpful at the outset to define your universe. In this instance, however, we have been unable to discover or devise a satisfactory definition… Advisory committees are only one type of these miscellaneous bodies, albeit the largest. The impossibility of crafting a useful definition becomes apparent upon considering the key elements of function, creation, membership, and duration (GAO 1991: 17-5).

President Bill Clinton's *Task Force on National Health Care Reform* provides an excellent example of how difficult it can be to classify panels. The Task Force found itself at the centre of a federal court case in 1993, *Association of American Physicians and Surgeons v Clinton*. At issue was the legal status of committee chair Hillary Rodham Clinton. The duties of a First Lady, the court decided, made Clinton a de facto government employee. That decision, coupled with the fact that all other members of the panel were also executive branch officers, meant that the panel did not constitute a "public" advisory committee under statutory guidelines.

When the departmental, interagency and congressional panels are pared from the list of federal advisory bodies, there remains a small number – generally less than 5 per cent of the total – that may be loosely classified as presidential commissions. And loosely is indeed the operative word. Some groups are easy to classify as presidential by dint of being created by executive order, comprising members chosen by the president and reporting only to the White House. Other panels present more of an analytical challenge.

To aid in the process of classification, scholars have crafted a number of definitions to help identify the essential ingredients of a "true" presidential commission (Wolanin 1975: 7-9; Tutchings 1979: 11-12). Some widely accepted attributes are that the panel must be temporary in nature and must include at least one member from outside the executive branch, or the federal rolls generally, depending on the definition. But here the consensus ends.

Thomas Wolanin wrote in 1975 that a commission could not be considered presidential unless *all the members* were appointed directly by the president (Wolanin 1975: 7). However, that degree of White House control over commissions has become less common over time. The 1994-95 *Commission on the Roles and Capabilities of the US Intelligence Community* is indicative of the change. Of the 17 members appointed to that panel, President Clinton selected only nine. Along these lines, other commission scholars (Zegart 2004: 369; Zink 1987: xiii) have found it useful to account for the growing number of "national" or "presidential-congressional" panels that feature varying degrees of legislative input.

Table 1, at the end of the chapter, provides an overview of key investigative commissions in the US from World War II to the present. It is by no means an exhaustive list. The common thread is that each entry is tied to a major scandal or crisis that garnered sufficient national attention to warrant a response outside of normal bureaucratic or legislative channels.

The great diversity of responses to such controversies underscores that variety is the order of the day when it comes to public inquiries in the US. We see groups empanelled by the president, groups empanelled by Congress, and groups empanelled by joint action of the two branches. We even see a high-profile board of inquiry appointed by an agency director. Significantly, the overview also provides an opportunity to compare how two similar tragedies, the loss of two space shuttles – both to explosions, one in 1986 and the other in 2003 – gave rise to very different types of inquiry. This demonstrates that the emergence and trajectory of a public inquiry is situational. Politics, partisanship, and presidential preference play a large role in determining the contours of a blue-ribbon probe.

Presidential commissions as public inquiries

"Public inquiry" is not a commonly used term in the US political system. Instead, commission-based investigations in the US are normally referred to as just that – commissions – with the press sometimes applying its own explanatory modifiers such as "board of inquiry" or "blue-ribbon probe". In most instances the nomenclature used bears little or no relation to the panel's official designation, nor is it especially useful in helping to differentiate between various types of panels. Definitional chaos is still an unfortunate reality when it comes to commission-based inquiries in the US.

While commissions come in all shapes and sizes, Table 1 does suggest that presidential-variant commissions have predominated when it comes to the most high-profile events and investigations. The Japanese attack on Pearl Harbor and the Kennedy assassination gave rise to inquiries of this type, as did the Space Shuttle Challenger disaster and the incident at Three Mile Island nuclear facility.

To be sure, there are important exceptions to this investigatory rule. Significantly, the stock market crash of October 1929 did *not* give rise to a presidential commission, instead becoming the focus of a thorough probe by a Senate-hired attorney named Ferdinand Pecora. Congress also took the lead with the inquiry into the causes of the economic convulsion that began in 2007 by creating a *Financial Crisis Inquiry Commission* with all 10 members chosen by legislative leaders.

The commission created to deal with the terrorist attacks of September 11, 2001 deserves special mention due to the circumstances that surrounded its creation. The day after the attacks, a prominent Democratic lawmaker, Senator Robert Torricelli, stood on the floor of the US Senate and challenged President George W. Bush to "form a board of general inquiry to review the actions of the US intelligence community and the failures which led to this massive loss of life and compromise of national security". But as the days and weeks passed, Bush made no effort to empanel an inquiry. The break with tradition was not lost on everyone. David Rosenbaum of the *New York Times* (26 May 2002) noted that the president's stance represented a "reversal of normal form … usually, after a calamitous event of a political embarrassment, it is the White House that seeks a commission to investigate".

The reasons for Bush's obstinacy are debatable. Initially, the President and his lieutenants argued that a special investigation would tie up key officials and divert attention from the emerging war on terror. They soon brought forth a second argument that focused on protecting confidential information. Vice President Dick Cheney suggested that an inquiry would "multiply potential sources of leaks" of sensitive intelligence, and thus compromise the very security that it was intended to enhance. But any objective assessment of this question must also consider the fact that Bush's refusal to act was in line with his penchant for secrecy and determination to resist any development that could limit executive authority.

If Bush was the seemingly immovable object in this drama, the 9/11 families emerged as the irresistible will. The widows, parents and children of the victims found their voice, organised themselves, and mounted an effective lobbying campaign to get an inquiry established (Breitweiser 2006: 100-137). Congress took up the charge in the fall of 2002 and began to make plans for a commission of its own design. The bill that eventually made it into law was one of seven legislative proposals to create a board of inquiry to examine the 9/11 attacks (Kitts 2006: 133).

For Bush, the only thing worse than having to field questions from a group of his own creation would be to endure the same inquisition by a group of luminaries appointed by Congress. He thus reluctantly embraced the idea of a mixed national commission, for which he would share responsibility with Congress, in order to avoid being completely sidelined in the effort and to be able to exert some control over the commission's membership, mandate, and grant of authority. Bush signed the *National Commission on Terrorist Attacks Upon the United States* into law on 27 November 2002 – 14 months and 16 days after the worst terrorist attack in American history.

Although President Bush succeeded in achieving that influence, his delay carried a political price. Had he acted more expeditiously, he could have ended up with a far more compliant panel. He also could have avoided the suspicion and ill will caused by his year-long fight to prevent a blue-ribbon probe. Once the investigation was underway, Bush's attitude ranged from indifferent to defiant (Kitts 2006: 143-150). He risked any number of political confrontations with the commission. Conversely, the commission did not hesitate to take on the White House in public. That level of confrontation would have been highly improbable had the 9/11 Commission been more presidential in nature.

President Bush learned a hard lesson in commission politics with the 9/11 inquiry. And learn he did. In early 2004, when questions arose regarding the absence of weapons of mass destruction (WMD) in Iraq, he showed greater skill in handling calls for an investigation. He acted quickly to defuse the issue by appointing a more traditional executive-dominated panel to examine the WMD question, the *Commission on the Intelligence Capabilities of the United States Regarding Weapons of Mass Destruction.* The panel had no subpoena power, and all ten members were selected by the president without input from opposition leaders. Moreover, Bush granted the panel a generous period of 13 months to conduct its investigation. The schedule was politically convenient since the commission would not issue its report until well after the 2004 presidential election. In the end, the panel cited poor intelligence work, and not political interference from administration officials, as the main cause of the WMD failure. It was exactly the finding Bush needed to make the troublesome issue go away.

Commission politics and executive-legislative tensions

As mentioned in the introduction, commission politics in the US must be understood in the context of the Madisonian system of separated powers. The tension between the executive and legislative branches of government is exacerbated during periods of divided government when the normal contest of wills between the branches is heightened by an overlay of partisan pressures. In the first half of the 20th century, the president's party controlled both chambers of Congress more than 80 per cent of the time. Since 1950, however, divided government has become the rule rather than the exception with one-party control occurring less than 40 per cent of the time.

Partisan and inter-branch bickering over commissions has resulted in a standoff of sorts. Congress does not like being left out when a presidentially-appointed inquiry takes shape, yet there is nothing lawmakers can do to stop the president from using his star power to give a probe instant visibility. Conversely, presidents are free to use executive orders to launch blue-ribbon probes, yet they do not have the power to compel Congress to recognise the panel's legitimacy, or to equip it with the legal powers necessary to conduct a thorough investigation. In this environment, the political fight over commissions has, in recent years, moved to surrogate issues through which the two branches can continue to push for investigative primacy. Two of the more important issues with which to illustrate this dynamic are subpoena power and compliance with the *Federal Advisory Committee Act.*

The most common instrument by which presidents create investigatory commissions is the executive order. With an executive order, the president can set the panel's mandate, describe its composition, and set a timeline for completion of the probe and issuance of the final report. The president can even use his authority to require the cooperation of executive branch officials with the investigation, as President Ronald Reagan did in issuing the executive order creating a "Special Review Board" to examine the Iran-Contra affair. Even so, six executive branch officers refused to testify on their role in the Iran-Contra scheme, a list that included National Security Council staffer Oliver North, and former National Security Advisor John Poindexter. Commission Chair John Tower tried several different ways to secure their cooperation but each time was met with resistance. Reagan refused to push the issue (Kitts 2006: 110).

What is *not* within the scope of the president's authority is to equip the commission with the power to issue subpoenas. Subpoena power gives a commission the legal authority to compel attendance and testimony of witnesses and to require the production of documents or other material evidence that could have a bearing on the investigation. Most presidential commissions are not so equipped. Partly, this is due to the fact that many inquiries of this type focus on comparatively non-controversial matters of policy or administrative organisation and thus have no need for this power. Case-specific investigations of crises or scandals are less common. But even for commissions with a more investigative orientation, the conferral of subpoena power is dependent upon two separate steps: the President must ask, and Congress must grant.

The first condition is absolute. There is no case in the historical record of Congress forcing subpoena power on a presidential commission over a president's objection. The most obvious barrier to such a move would be that the president could exercise a veto over that legislative action. More to the point, however, is the fact that it is difficult enough to get sceptical lawmakers to grant subpoena power even when the president is behind the idea: absent his push, and it simply does not happen.

It is difficult to understand the logic by which a president would create a public inquiry and then cripple it by not petitioning Congress for subpoena power. Yet this does happen from time to time. President Reagan did not request subpoena power for the Tower Commission probe of the Iran-Contra scandal in 1986-1987. In this case, while noting the lack of subpoena authority in their final report, the commissioners maintained that the limitation "did not prevent the Board from assembling sufficient information to form a basis for its fundamental judgments". Similarly, President Bush did not act on subpoena power after creating the 2004 *Commission on the Intelligence Capabilities of the United States Regarding Weapons of Mass Destruction.* It is very likely that both presidents could have prevailed on the measure had they asked.

In cases where presidents do endorse a petition for subpoena power, the congressional response depends on the political winds of the time. In 1975, President Gerald Ford asked Congress to grant subpoena power to a commission of his creation on domestic spying by the Central Intelligence Agency. Representative Peter Rodino, chairman of the House Judiciary Committee, cited the lack of congressional input on the panel as a point of friction and fought successfully to deny the request. In 2010, a vote to give subpoena power to a presidential commission on the oil spill in the Gulf of Mexico sailed through the House by a vote of 420-1 before being derailed by Senate Republicans. By contrast, both the commissions dealing with the Pearl Harbor attack and the Kennedy assassination obtained subpoena power easily, with the latter panel enjoying the additional power of being able to grant immunity to reluctant witnesses.

A second surrogate issue for executive-legislative sparring over commissions is that of presidential compliance with the *Federal Advisory Committee Act* (FACA). FACA dates back to the early 1970s and was put in place to check the growth in the number of federal advisory panels and rein in the executive role in commission-based inquiries. Among other things, FACA requires that commissions have a clearly articulated mandate, that meetings be made public, that commission actions be duly recorded and communicated, and that commission membership be balanced with respect to differing political perspectives.

Coming as it did in an era when fears of an "imperial presidency" (Schlesinger 1973) were beginning to manifest, the FACA legislation carried a subtle commentary that presidents could not be trusted to mount inquiries without explicit statutory requirements for openness and accountability. Presidents from both political parties have bristled at these provisions.

Presidents Bill Clinton and George W. Bush prevailed in court when challenged to defend advisory boards they had established that, by their judgment, existed outside of FACA coverage (Mongan 2005: 914-920). More recently, President Barack Obama moved with great care in December 2012 to create a "task force" to look into the mass school shooting that occurred in Newtown, Connecticut. He went out of his way at a press conference to stress that his creation would not be "some Washington commission", then proceeded to structure an inquiry that, on technical grounds, stayed just beyond the boundaries of FACA.

As with Clinton and Bush before him, Obama has been challenged in federal court on his panel's non-compliance with the provisions of the Act. Whatever the legalities of his strategy, his actions in the wake of the shooting made perfectly good political sense. Avoiding FACA permitted him to move much faster and more nimbly than would otherwise have been the case. He was able to get the group up and running without having to go through a formal chartering process. He did not have to worry about including representatives from the gun lobby on the task force. And, when convenient, his delegates to the task force could simply exclude the press from selected committee meetings. All of this gave the president and his task force room for manoeuvre that would have been lacking had FACA provisions been observed.

Conclusion

The presidential scholar Harold Laski once observed: "The processes of government are very like an iceberg: what appears on the surface may be but a small part of the reality beneath" (Laski 1980: 2). Laski's observation is as true of presidential commissions as it is of the larger practice of government in the US. There is more to these curiously small and ad hoc bodies than meets the eye. The external face of a public inquiry can only hint at the amount of activity that takes place before the panel is established and, later, behind the scenes of the investigation.

Presidential commissions must be viewed through a political lens in order to understand these dynamics. The political pressures that swirl around commissions can be frustrating for those on the inside. But they nonetheless add richness to the story of American public inquiries. They also make it likely that scholars will continue to debate the extent to which public inquiries can perform effectively as agents of fact-finding and analysis. Whatever the outcome of that debate, presidential commissions and related types of inquiries are here to stay. They serve a useful role in allowing American leaders to respond when crises and political deadlock give rise to public demands for answers, accountability and action.

Table 1: Selected US investigative commissions of inquiry

Crisis/Event	President	Commission	Authorisation	Structure and Duration
Japanese Attack on Pearl Harbor (1941)	F.D. Roosevelt	Commission to Investigate the Japanese Attack of December 7, 1941 *Owen Roberts, chair*	Executive Order 8983 December 1941	5 members (all appointed by president) subpoena power = yes final report, January 1942
Assassination of President Kennedy (1963)	Johnson	President's Commission on the Assassination of President Kennedy *Earl Warren, chair*	Executive Order 11130 November 1963	7 members (all appointed by president) subpoena power = yes final report, September 1964
Urban Unrest (1965-1967)	Johnson	National Advisory Commission on Civil Disorders *Otto Kerner, chair*	Executive Order 11365 July 1967	11 members (all appointed by president) subpoena power = yes final report, February 1968
Revelation of CIA Domestic Spying (1974-1975)	Ford	Commission on CIA Activities Within the United States *Nelson Rockefeller, chair*	Executive Order 11828 January 1975	8 members (all appointed by president) subpoena power = no final report, June 1975
Three Mile Island Nuclear Accident (1979)	Carter	President's Commission on the Accident at Three Mile Island *John Kemeny, chair*	Executive Order 12130 April 1979	12 members (all appointed by president) subpoena power = yes final report, October 1979

Explosion of Space Shuttle Challenger (1986)	Reagan	Presidential Commission on the Space Shuttle Challenger Accident *William Rogers, chair*	Executive Order 12546 February 1986	13 members (all appointed by president) subpoena power = no final report, June 1986
Iran-Contra Scandal (1986)	Reagan	President's Special Review Board *John Tower, chair*	Executive Order 12575 December 1986	3 members (all appointed by president) subpoena power = no final report, February 1987
9/11 Terrorist Attacks (2001)	G.W. Bush	National Commission on Terrorist Attacks Upon the United States *Thomas Kean, chair*	Public Law 107–306 November 2002	10 members (9 appointed by congressional leaders, 1 by president) subpoena power = yes final report, July 2004
Explosion of Space Shuttle Columbia (2003)	G.W. Bush	Columbia Accident Investigation Board *Harold Gehman, chair*	Directive by NASA Administrator February 2003	13 members (all appointed by NASA Administrator) subpoena power = no final report, August 2003
Financial Crisis (2007)	G.W. Bush	Financial Crisis Inquiry Commission *Phil Angelides, chair*	Public Law 111–21 May 2009	10 members (all appointed by congressional leaders) subpoena power = yes final report, January 2011

Gulf of Mexico Oil Spill (2010)	Obama	National Commission on the BP Deepwater Horizon Oil Spill and Offshore Drilling *Bob Graham and William Reilly, co-chairs*	Executive Order 13543 May 2010	7 members (all appointed by president) subpoena power = no final report, January 2011

References

Annual Report of the President on Federal Advisory Committees, (1972-1998), General Services Administration. Washington, DC: Government Printing Office

Barth, A., 1955, *Government by Investigation*. New York: Viking Press

Breitweiser, K., 2006, *Wake-Up Call: The Political Education of a 9/11 Widow*. New York: Hachette Books

Campbell, C.C., 2002, *Discharging Congress: Government by Commission*. Westport, Connecticut: Praeger

General Accounting Office, 1991, *Principles of Federal Appropriations Law*, 2nd edition, Vol 1, July

Hamilton, A., Jay, J., and Madison, J., 2006, *The Federalist Papers*, New York: Cosimo

Kitts, K., 2006, *Presidential Commissions and National Security: The Politics of Damage Control*, Boulder: Lynne Rienner

Laski, H.J., 1980, *The American Presidency: An Interpretation*. Piscataway, New Jersey: Transaction

Mongan, M.J., 2005, "Fixing FACA: The Case for Exempting Presidential Advisory Committees from Judicial Review Under the Federal Advisory Committee Act," *Stanford Law Review*, 58(3), 895-934

Schlesinger, A.M., 1973, *The Imperial Presidency*, Boston: Houghton-Mifflin

Tutchings, T.R., 1979, *Rhetoric and Reality: Presidential Commissions and the Making of Public Policy*. Boulder: Westview

Wolanin, T.R., 1975, *Presidential Advisory Commissions: Truman to Nixon*. Madison: University of Wisconsin Press

Zegart, A.B., 2004, "Blue Ribbons, Black Boxes: Toward a Better Understanding of Presidential Commissions," *Presidential Studies Quarterly*, 34(2), 366-393

Zink, S.D., 1987, *Guide to the Presidential Advisory Commissions, 1973-1984*, Alexandria: Chawyck-Healey

21

Public inquiries – living up to their potential

Scott Prasser and Helen Tracey

As the preceding chapters have shown, public inquiries have proven a durable political instrument in Australian public life, mirroring their role in other Westminster systems of government. In Australia, they have over time enabled state and Commonwealth governments of all political persuasions to respond to social and economic change, to cope with the aftermath of major disasters and to deal effectively if not always expeditiously with political impropriety. Many a royal commission or public inquiry has helped to explain a catastrophic event, resolve a contentious issue, reveal wrongdoing or frame new public policy.

Some have gone under the radar; others have captured headlines from the day of their appointment to the day they disband on presentation of their final report. In their totality, as a major instrument of accountability and rational policymaking, they have been an indispensable tool for governments immersed in the difficult and messy business of solving complex public policy problems.

Adhocracy

Public inquiries have managed to maintain their relevance despite the greatly expanded role for government in people's lives which has led to a burgeoning of public sector agencies. In the 100-plus years since federation, the Commonwealth Public Service has grown from six departments of state to 18, with over 200 additional separate institutions and agencies answerable to Commonwealth ministers, covering just about every area of public activity. In this panoply of government agencies, there hardly seems room for the creation of new bodies, even temporary ones.

The expansion of state-funded institutions seems to belie predictions made over the past fifty years that bureaucracy as an organisational form would founder, because of its inability to adapt to rapid social change, and be replaced by adaptive, temporary bodies bringing together diverse specialists to solve new problems as they arise. Warren Bennis, in the 1960s, argued that each age produced a form of organisation appropriate to its own tempo, and foresaw that temporary organisations, in the form of task forces and transient teams, would be the order of the day for solving problems in post-industrial society. (Bennis 1996; Bennis and Slater 1968)

Alvin Toffler, in *Future Shock* (1970), acknowledged Bennis in also predicting a shift in power away from the permanent machinery of government to transient "throw-away" organisations. He labelled this new style of public administration "the new ad-hocracy" and considered it better equipped than traditional bureaucracy for the solution of non-routine problems. Like Bennis, he saw this development as a direct effect of rapid social change. Toffler expected these temporary structures, whose members would come together to solve a specific problem and then separate, to proliferate and supplant the regular structures of bureaucracy. The shift "from long-enduring to temporary forms, from permanence to transience ... from bureaucracy to Ad-Hocracy" was, he believed, an abdication by government of its responsibility and authority and a threat to democracy. This "constant generation and decay" of temporary, unaccountable organisations would "doom bureaucracy to destruction" (Toffler 1970: 130).

Other political analysts have similarly interpreted the growing use of ad hoc institutions, at least in the American context, as a symptom of government failure, a sign that the ordinary institutions of government were deficient and needed to rely on temporary and unaccountable bodies to generate policy, evaluate major blunders and resolve deadlocks (Bennis and Slater 1968; Rourke and Schulman 1989). In contrast to the rigidity of a bureaucracy that was no longer able to perform its many roles successfully, these "adaptive, problem-solving, temporary systems of diverse specialists" (Bennis and Slater 1968: 74) were better suited to respond to complexity and rapid change. At the same time however, their increasing use was seen to present "dangers of inadequacy, lack of accountability, and threats to democracy" (Rourke and Schulman 1989:131).

Waterman (1992) on the other hand argues that both adhocracy and bureaucracy are necessary and permanent. He believes that the duality is here to stay, that neither form will dominate, and that they will work in concert.

Waterman's view is certainly consistent with the Australian experience of public inquiries. While governments do resort to a public inquiry in part because alternative mechanisms are not as well suited to the task at hand, the appointment of ad hoc bodies in fact strengthens and adds legitimacy to government decision-making rather than displacing or diminishing the power of the bureaucracy or being incompatible with it. By bringing in expertise and concentrated effort when it is needed, in a body that can coexist comfortably with established agencies, public inquiries operate in a way that complements and adds value to their work.

The pertinent policy question is therefore not whether ad hoc inquiries undermine effective government as we know it, but how these temporary bodies are best used to deliver on their potential to underpin high quality policymaking and sound political decision-making. This is a particularly important question at a time when concern is increasing about the politicisation of the public service (Mulgan 2007), about a decline in the analytical and research capabilities of government departments (see chapter 7: Banks) and about the "dumbing down of democracy" through political game playing driven by the 24 hour media cycle and ever more polarised debate on important social issues (Tanner 2011).

Benefits

A well functioning democracy relies on governments having the confidence of the population. For democracy to thrive, people need to have trust that government is working for the common good, not simply serving sectional interests or seeking party political gain. People lose trust when a government appears to act in highly ideological and partisan ways, when political game-playing seems to dominate over substantive policymaking and efficient administration and when they observe complex social and economic issues consistently reduced to soundbites, "announceables", spin and marketing. By introducing substance and objective analysis to policy issues and having a clear focus on the national interest or common good, public inquiries play an important role in building confidence in public decision-making. As Banks observes, when the public no longer trusts government to produce effective policy solutions, the objective findings of an independent inquiry can fill the gap.

The appointment of a public inquiry as a prelude to determining policy or political action invariably goes some way towards countering any impression of partisanship or playing politics with an issue. Political decisions that defer to the authoritative advice of an independent public inquiry will generally be seen as proof, much needed, that politicians have taken the facts of the matter into account and acted accordingly. As a result, government will enjoy greater acceptance and legitimacy. In this way, public inquiries have the potential to shore up the standing of politicians at the same time as they improve the quality of policymaking and administration. Politicians ignore the advice of a public inquiry at their peril.

Being ad hoc rather than part of the established bureaucratic structure gives inquiries a number of advantages over alternate means of review and investigation. The temporary nature of inquiries means that they are flexible, responsive to the specific issue or incident, able to assemble the necessary specialists and well positioned to cut "across normal bureaucratic lines to capture opportunities, solve problems and get results" (Waterman 1992). They are "bespoke" instruments, able to be moulded to the task in hand, and dissolve once their commission is complete.

Being independent gives inquiries an advantage over that other much-used ad hoc source of advice, the consultancy or contracted arrangement. While consultants and contractors may well come with the expertise, flexibility of approach and resources that an inquiry enjoys, they lack the independence that is the key characteristic of an inquiry. Inquiries are not totally detached from government as they are appointed by the executive, but they are free from the constraints of day to day direction or detailed contractual arrangements and are able to consider matters as they emerge rather than as they are defined for them at the outset. In contrast to consultancies, they also carry out their commission in public and are expected to release their reports publicly.

It would be a mistake to confuse the ad hoc independent status of inquiries with being arbitrary or random. Inquiries are a purposeful organisational form, focused on solving a specific problem as formulated by the terms of their appointment or commission. Having this clear focus on a defined problem – a clear mission, clear scope, a set time frame to come up with an answer and a clear end point – is a real strength of the inquiry instrument over a bureaucratic agency. Having the luxury of dealing with a discrete problem and considering it from first principles is not common in public policymaking, which is more generally characterised by multitasking and incrementalism (Howlett 2011; Lindblom 1968). People assigned to an inquiry, without the distractions of other responsibilities and chosen for their expertise, are able to devote their efforts and considerable knowledge to the issue at hand. Whereas ongoing agencies operating within government and responsible to ministers, especially policy advisory bodies, are perceived to be attached to the status quo, often acting as partisan advocates for their policy area, inquiries come fresh to a problem with the expectation that they will be objective and analytical. They often do become eloquent in support of a particular policy direction and make resource-intensive recommendations similar to the demands of an expert statutory agency, but at least the ad hoc inquiry disbands with the presentation of its report rather than remaining a thorn in the government's side.

For all the potential influence of inquiries on public policy and the continuing heavy reliance on them by political leaders, the fear that they will supplant the established and accountable agencies of government is unfounded. Their temporary nature assures a peaceful and productive co-existence with ongoing institutions. Once they present their ideas and recommendations in a report, inquiries leave decisions on policy and action resting with elected politicians. This path to decision-making allays fears that policymaking will be reduced to a technocratic or instrumental process. Elected politicians are the final decision-makers. They will always need to find a balance between the evidence produced by an inquiry and the politics of the day. They too are responsible for communicating the messages arising from an inquiry, while the bureaucratic establishment continues to conduct the day-to-day activities of government, including the implementation of programs or policies agreed by government as a result of an inquiry. The ongoing institutions of democracy have the final say.

Costs

A universal concern with public inquiries is whether the benefits they offer over existing agencies outweigh their costs, which can be considerable. Many inquiries dealing with a single policy issue are lean and mean affairs, involving a small, often one-person review team relying on the resources of the public bureaucracy for secretariat support. Some more complex inquiries are also quite modest in their demands on the public purse. Philip Flood's four month *Inquiry into Australia's Intelligence Agencies* (2004) cost only $450,000 while Frank Brennan's *National Human Rights Consultation* (2008), which involved wide public consultation and commissioned research, budget was just under $500,000. The 1981 *Royal*

Commission into Activities of the Australian Building Construction Employees and Builders Labourers' Federation was a single member inquiry, with a small number of staff and a correspondingly moderate budget of $46,000. At the other end of the scale, the Trebeck Fuel Tax Inquiry (2001) cost $4.7 million and the Cole *Royal Commission into the Building and Construction* (2001) $76.6 million, costly but as nothing compared with the astonishing $434 million over four years budgeted for the 2013 *Royal Commission into Institutional Responses to Child Sexual Abuse.*

There is little evidence that governments can call on to demonstrate that the investment they have made in a public inquiry is well justified. Establishing the benefits calls for a qualitative judgement about the effectiveness of the inquiry in solving the problem at hand, over time, but also assessment of why it was preferable to appoint a new inquiry in the first place rather than opt for a review led by parliament or an existing agency within the bureaucracy or for a legal process.

Concerns

The public has good reason to be wary about the value of public inquiries. Commonly expressed concerns are that governments are motivated by political expediency in appointing them and that inquiries perform a mainly symbolic function, acting as a cloak for already determined government action or as a delaying or avoidance tactic. They can be used to bury an issue, to placate interested parties and advocacy groups, to divert attention from government and sheet home blame elsewhere, or as a whitewash for a scandal, misconduct or incompetence.

Certainly there are examples in the long history of inquiries which have deserved this kind of bad press. The clear political motives behind Thomas Cromwell's commission for the dissolution of the monasteries in 16th century England, to reduce the power of the church and fill the state treasury, set an early precedent both for a politically motivated inquiry and one with a long lasting impact. In more recent times, both the Costigan *Royal Commission on the Activities of the Federated Ship Painters and Dockers Union* (1980) and the Marks *Royal Commission into Use of Executive Power* (1995) in Western Australia (see chapter 4: Ransley) were widely regarded as politically motivated. The report of the first royal commission after federation, the S.S. Drayton Grange inquiry in 1902, was considered to be a whitewash, as were several inquiries since, including the Queensland *Royal Commission into Alleged Police Activities at the National Hotel* (Gibbs 1963), a precursor to the more effective Fitzgerald Inquiry (1987). Many policy inquiries over the years have been judged to be less than objective, simply a cover for giving government the policy solution that accorded well with its political agenda.

The many inquiries referenced in this book give a good overview of the highs and lows of the public inquiry instrument in practice. They open the way for attempting some generalisations about why inquiries have proved so durable, what makes them work or not work, whether they are worth the substantial investment in them and how their value can be improved.

Why so durable?

Inquiries can be seen as a victim of their own success. Over a long period, they have proved their value in matching public concern with official concern, gathering evidence and expert advice, listening to community views, giving people a hearing, uncovering the facts around an incident, even forestalling precipitate action. Numerous examples show how inquiries have lived up to their potential to make a significant difference to the quality of public life. They have dealt effectively, and sometimes repeatedly, with complex policy issues such as drought, education, defence, the arts and industry; they have helped resolve a policy dilemma, as in the *Independent Review of Economic Regulation of Domestic Aviation* (May 1985) and the *Review of the Future of Drug Evaluation in Australia* (Baume 1991); they have led to a better understanding of the causes of catastrophic events such as bushfires, floods and plane crashes, bringing relief by giving a hearing to people affected by them and helping prevent or mitigate the effects of similar incidents in the future; they have helped restore public confidence in the processes and personnel of government at both state and national levels through investigation of suspected impropriety, corruption or maladministration and have held individuals and organisations – doctors, officials, politicians and corporations – to account for wrongdoing; they have educated the public about important issues such as human rights, and in some cases, such as the Henderson *Commission of Inquiry into Poverty* (1972) and the Evatt *Royal Commission on Human Relationships* (1974), have been responsible for changing social attitudes; in many cases they have led to the creation of new structures within government, such as the panoply of integrity and permanent watchdog agencies created in Queensland following the Fitzgerald Commission (1989).

Despite having a number of more controllable alternatives, governments therefore continue to call on public inquiries for advice. One reason for opting for an inquiry is its flexibility of form and process. Inquiries are versatile. They vary in size, speed, style and scope and operate differently depending on the task in hand, how it has been defined and who has been appointed to follow it through. In addition to providing advice to government, they can serve a range of other purposes, such as raising the public profile of an issue, as was the case with the *Aboriginal Land Rights Commission* (Woodward 1973), or educating the public, as Frank Brennan's *National Human Rights Consultation* (2008) did. They are free to choose their approach, within the bounds of legislation, in the case of inquiries with royal commission powers, and procedural fairness, in the case of second tier inquiries. Thus Philip Flood was able to decide not to record or take a verbatim report of the evidence given to his inquiry, and Frank Brennan used Facebook and a blog and commissioned social research to gather and analyse people's views. The formality and legalistic processes of an investigative inquiry such as the bushfire inquiries described by Roger Wettenhall or an inquisitorial inquiry into political wrongdoing such as those described by Janet Ransley are clearly not suited to the policy-oriented inquiries which are the subject of Gary Banks' analysis.

Sometimes a government will choose an inquiry through impatience with the slowness of established bureaucratic agencies or suspicion about the loyalties of the public service. This is often the case when government changes after an election, especially if this comes after a long period out of office. Gourley attributes the appointment of the Coombs Commission and its generous remit in large part to the Whitlam Government's doubts about the capacity of the Canberra public service to respond to the policy directions of a Labor government after 23 years of conservative rule. A new government may also have an agenda for change which disturbs the equilibrium of existing agencies which might find it difficult to depart from past policies and precedents. A department that has spent considerable effort explaining and defending the policies of a previous government can easily be compromised in its capacity for objectivity and fresh ideas. Established agencies may also find it difficult to take a broad or long view of an issue, constrained as they are by their statutory responsibilities, their day-to-day administrative responsibilities and the need to deal with immediate problems. Issues that fall across the boundaries of different bureaucratic organisations are often more easily and effectively dealt with by a new ad hoc body than by interdepartmental arrangements.

The majority of inquiries, as we have seen, are driven by a policy imperative. Even investigative inquiries have a strong policy dimension, through their findings and recommendations. In their policymaking function, independent inquiries are vying with departments of state, the numerous permanent policy and advisory agencies within government, ministerial advisers, the parliamentary committee system and the increasingly common resort by government agencies to paid external consultancies and contractors. Here the competitive advantage of the public inquiry lies in its flexibility and objectivity. As a counterweight to an increasingly politicised and managerial public service, an independent ad hoc inquiry gives the appearance that government is genuinely and openly seeking advice. The inquiry has no previous involvement or fixed position and is expected to produce serious evidence-based and rational proposals. In this sense, inquiries have established themselves as ideal agents for policy change. They show government in a good light. Political decisions made on the basis of the recommendations of a public inquiry have greater credibility and acceptance than if they emerge from within government itself.

Risks

For all the benefits of the inquiry instrument over the host of alternatives available, a decision to establish an independent review of an issue is not without risk. Investigative inquiries especially can be politically perilous, and have been known to directly or indirectly bring down governments, or at least to be severely politically embarrassing. Janet Ransley identifies several inquiries, including the Fitzgerald Commission (1987) in Queensland, the Costigan Commission (1980) at the Commonwealth level, the WA Inc Inquiry (1991), the Woodward Commission (1990) in Victoria and the Jacobs Commission (1991) in South Australia which have had this effect. Even a policy inquiry can be politically hazardous if it produces radical, sweeping and expensive proposals for change without sufficient justification or when a simpler, more implementable and less expensive fix may be possible. The Gonski *Review of Funding for Schooling* (2010) may well be a case in point, although time will tell. Implementing and funding the reforms proved an immense challenge to the Gillard-Rudd Labor governments, and the Abbott Coalition Government initially signalled its intention to revisit the issue in a further review process to be undertaken in 2014, though this approach was quickly shelved in the light of the adverse public reaction to this proposal.

The work of an independent temporary body can take unexpected twists and turns and bring unpleasant surprises. Even if an inquiry is appointed as a stalling device, to delay making a difficult decision, eventually the time will come when the inquiry's report is in and the pressure on government to act returns. And even an inquiry that is set up to provide justification for a particular policy solution may prove intractable and head off in unexpected and unwelcome policy directions. There is always the danger that an inquiry will produce unpalatable or unaffordable recommendations, presenting government with a different kind of policy challenge.

Ignoring the advice of a public report, for whatever reason, leaves government open to political embarrassment. Non-implementation of findings is perhaps the most pressing problem public inquiries present to government. The goal of an inquiry is not its own end-product, its report, but policy change, in the national interest. It is an easy criticism to make of governments that they have invested heavily in an inquiry but failed to implement all, or even some, of its recommendations. Many inquiries have been wont to produce voluminous reports with large numbers of recommendations, presenting a particular challenge for policymakers. Mercifully, the 2000 plus pages and 337 recommendations in the five volumes of the Coombs Commission Report are at the extreme of report weightiness, at least in Australia. These hardly rate against some of the weighty tomes produced in other countries. The Warren Commission (1963), for example, investigating the assassination of President Kennedy produced an 889 page report with a further 26 volumes (about 18,000 pages) of evidence, yet even this did not bring resolution. The Warren Commission was criticised for its processes and the quality of its work, and its findings are still being challenged and re-examined, fifty years on.

Immediate acceptance and implementation is not necessarily a signal of good policy or good politics. It is clear from the story of the Coombs Commission, many of whose recommendations were gradually put into effect by successive governments, that a long-term view is needed to assess an inquiry's influence. Likewise, a seminal report such as the

Karmel Report, *Schools in Australia: Report of the Interim Committee for the Australian Schools Commission* (1972), has continued to shape school funding policies in Australia.

Implementation becomes a particular problem for governments which have too many policy inquiries on the go at the one time. For a period, while the inquiries are working to their different timetables, all remains quiet on the policy front, but then the reports begin to arrive. This can quickly become unmanageable and unaffordable, as the experience of the Whitlam government showed, even though many inquiry reports from this era lived on to shape policymaking decades later, probably because of the high quality of the reports themselves. The Rudd Labor Government elected in 2007 also created a whirlwind of inquiries – 40 in the first six months – which produced a large volume of advice on specific issues that was difficult to consider in a coherent policy framework. While an inquiry report can help government to rationalise and explain a particular policy approach and build public support for policy change, the appointment of too many policy inquiries will tax any government's management and political capability, diverting attention from important issues and inevitably resulting in much unfinished business.

The appointment of too many investigative inquiries brings a different danger – the value of an instrument whose authority derives from its use for significant matters may be debased by over-use, and public resources wasted. Political judgement is required to determine whether an independent investigative inquiry is warranted rather than a review by an existing body within the administration or recourse to the law. There is a tendency in the public and the press to call for a public inquiry or "judicial review" at the first suggestion of political or official wrongdoing, as was seen early after the election of the Abbott Coalition Government in 2013, when the misuse of expenses by Commonwealth parliamentarians caused a public stir. Opposition party calls for a public inquiry will often be no more than confected public concern, and the media, as Christian Kerr explains, dotes on the prospect of a political scandal. There are many existing avenues for checking and investigating to explore before the investment in a public inquiry would be warranted. Not every issue brought to public attention is likely to benefit from examination by an independent inquiry.

A far greater risk from the point of view of the public is that an inquiry will produce poor quality advice, which the government then feels bound to follow. Policy change, to be worthwhile and in the public interest, has to be an improvement on the existing situation, not just change for its own sake, and has to hold out the likelihood that it will achieve its objectives and solve identified problems. Much so-called reform fails this public interest test. In most cases, the policy changes recommended by a public inquiry will involve significant additional resources and the inquiry report will provide the evidence that this investment is likely to produce the desired outcomes. Some inquiry reports however, are less than convincing about the value and feasibility of the proposed changes. Either they are not implemented at all, as was the case with the Finkelstein Inquiry (2011), or they are implemented amidst considerable confusion and later found wanting, as with the Gonski Review (2010).

What can go wrong?

Given their flexibility and diversity of scope and purpose, it is hardly surprising to find that public inquiries vary greatly in their degree of effectiveness. Some, like the Coombs Commission on public administration and the Fitzgerald Commission in Queensland on police corruption, have had enormous impact on policies and administration over an extended period; others, like the 2005 Cole Inquiry into AWB and the 2010 Orgill Taskforce on the implementation of the Building the Education Revolution program, have been judged to be flawed and ineffective, or at least limited in their impact.

The potential of a public inquiry to serve the public interest lies in its capacity to inform debate, clarify facts, develop consensus and improve the quality of public life. Like good public policy, there are no hard and fast rules that will guarantee the success of an inquiry, nor is there any easy and obvious measure of effectiveness. Acceptance by government of an inquiry's recommendations, often seen as an indicator of success, is a blunt measure, and possibly flawed, if the recommendations themselves are unsound. Inquisitorial inquiries are sometimes judged on whether successful prosecutions follow, but this measure seems to presume guilt and to place greater weight on the inquiry's aim of laying blame than its broader purpose of uncovering the facts so as to avoid similar incidents in the future. A more qualitative judgement is required, assessing how well an inquiry achieves its policy objective, the nature of its processes and the soundness of its report and recommendations.

Both intrinsic and extrinsic factors come into play to make an inquiry effective. While the appointing government has an influence on effectiveness through the appointment of members, setting the terms of reference, allocating resources and often servicing the inquiry through a department of state, the report is ultimately the inquiry's own work. Once appointed, whether or not it does its job well and produces quality advice is largely in its own hands.

One dimension of the inquiry process that does not seem critical to effectiveness is the nature of the problem and its degree of difficulty. Inquiries heralded as great successes have dealt with more and less complex issues, from national security to individual misconduct. Over time, different inquiries with different approaches have addressed the same or similar problems, with quite different results, as Henry Ergas and Mark Thomson's overview of the numerous inquiries into aspects of defence efficiency shows.

Political context

The political environment in which an inquiry is established and carries out its business, including the way the inquiry manages that environment, is a critical influence on its effectiveness. The context is a combination of both the explicit task given to the inquiry, in its terms of reference, and implicit understandings about the problem, ie the hidden political agenda.

Having the right start, being well conceived in the first place, is critical to success. If the problem is poorly framed or tilted towards a specific solution, the result is likely to be distorted. Some inquiries are beset by controversy from go to woe, boding ill for the credibility of their conclusions. The fault can lie with the government's motivation in setting up the inquiry, the appropriateness of the issues being addressed, the qualifications of the inquiry's personnel or the way it goes about its work.

Some governments are more prone to rely on public inquiries than others, but a predilection for inquiries is more a matter of style – personal or political – than political leaning. The appointment of a plethora of inquiries can symbolise either a genuinely reformist, activist government with a real interest in policy innovation, or an indecisive government, unsure of policy directions and uncertain about relying on established bureaucratic channels. Certain issues may predominate the inquiry agenda of a particular government, reflecting either the government's reform priorities or the fact that a challenging issue – climate change is a case in point – is absorbing public attention.

A policy inquiry set up by and reporting to a government with a clear and coherent policy agenda is likely to have more impact than an open-ended review set up in an uncertain political climate. This is one explanation given for the difference in impact between the drought policy review initiated by the Hawke Labor Government in 1990, which occurred at a time when government had embarked on an extensive program of economic and agricultural policy reform, and that appointed by the Rudd Labor Government in 2008 which lacked the sense of being a genuine, open policy review within a clear political narrative.

Few political environments will remain constant over the full course of a review, especially if the inquiry is long-running. Over time, an inquiry can lose the interest of the appointing government, as occurred with the Fraser Coalition Government's *Committee of Inquiry into Technological Change in Australia* (Myers 1978) and the *Independent Public Inquiry into Domestic Airfares* (Holcroft 1980). A change of government will almost invariably affect the reception of an inquiry's recommendations. The Coombs Commission on public administration is a rare example of an inquiry reporting to a government of a different political persuasion whose recommendations were seriously considered. As Gourley describes it (chapter 12), the Fraser Government was less than enthusiastic at first, but went on to make "elaborate arrangements" for consideration of the report when it was completed eight months after the election, by which time the new government's initial suspicion of the public service had morphed into greater trust and reliance.

Many inquiries are appointed with quite a fanfare, creating high expectations of what they will produce in the way of solutions to complex problems. Setting up an inquiry in the first place increases the attention paid to an issue and, depending on the subject, especially if it is salacious or controversial, media coverage during the course of inquiry will serve to maintain public awareness and interest and raise expectations even further, often creating a political climate that is hard to manage once the report is handed down.

The political context also affects government decisions about resourcing and the time given to the inquiry to report. Refusing a request from an inquiry for additional time or resources is more likely to be a political than an economic decision, as Ransley notes in relation to the Gibbs (1963) and Cooke (1989) inquiries in Queensland, and can lead to a less than thorough examination of the issue, as Justice Phillip Evatt noted when the Hawke Labor Government denied his request for $9 million for a survey in the course of his *Royal Commission on the Use and Effects of Chemical Agents on Australian Personnel in Vietnam* (1983).

Degree of independence

The major source of the credibility of a public inquiry is its independence from government. A perception of government interference, through manipulation of terms of reference or inappropriate appointments or interference with procedural arrangements can jeopardise acceptance of an inquiry's findings, especially by a public with low levels of trust in government. It is tempting to dismiss the work of an inquiry if it is perceived as biased, or unbalanced.

A signal to the degree of independence of an inquiry is the extent to which it conducts its business in public. Whereas in earlier times the public nature of an inquiry may have been its major competitive advantage over a review by a government agency, public consultation is no longer the unique preserve of an independent inquiry. It is now expected in most policymaking. What distinguishes an inquiry is the public and transparent character of its deliberations in the process of fact-finding and reporting. Inquiries rely heavily on submissions, oral evidence and public consultation. The thoroughness, openness, objectivity and intelligence they bring to bear in conducting these processes are markers of an effective inquiry. The fact-finding process, at its best, has an educative as well as a data and information-gathering role, providing an opportunity for people to develop an understanding of other views and to move beyond fixed positions. The public report at the end of an inquiry is expected to present the evidence, analyse it objectively, weigh all sides, explore all possibilities and test alternative options before making recommendations.

Level of expertise

The quality of personnel is another important contributor to inquiry success. The accepted practice of using judges and legal professionals in investigative and inquisitorial inquiries, for their expertise in investigation and marshalling evidence and their independence from politics and the processes of government, has proven successful. Occasionally a concern is expressed that such appointments jeopardise the doctrine of separation of powers, but in most cases it is retired judges who are appointed to chair inquiries, thus avoiding any conflict of interest.

Very few investigative inquiries have come adrift through the failings of legal personnel. The Morris Commission (2005) into the overseas doctors' issue in Queensland health is a rare example of a commission that was disbanded before completion, because of "apprehended bias" of the commissioner. The argument was made at the time that Morris, as a QC, was skilled at legal processes but did not have the expertise of a judge in balancing and assessing the evidence (King 2005; Editorial, *The Courier-Mail*, 23 April 2005).

Policy inquiries tend to rely on the expertise of retired senior bureaucrats or academic specialists. Freed of the constraints of their former departmental responsibilities, senior bureaucrats can bring their considerable knowledge and experience to bear in providing objective and authoritative policy advice. Academics are similarly attuned to public policy settings whereas chairs from the corporate world, with their different skill set, may well struggle with the concepts and imperatives of public policy.

Some inquiries, like the Teague *Victorian Bushfires Royal Commission* (2009) and the Holmes *Queensland Floods Commission of Inquiry* (2011), have used a panel of members to bring a mix of expertise and a breadth of knowledge to the task. The challenge here is to achieve a size that is right for the task without being unwieldy, and to get a balance of experience and knowledge while avoiding representation of interests and without jeopardising the appearance of impartiality.

Process

There is a considerable literature about the importance of effective process in developing good policy (Edwards *et al* 2001; Althaus *et al* 2007; Banks 2009):

> Experience shows that good process is integral to consistently good policy. While some very poor policies have grown out of the most rigorous process, it is rarer for good policy to grow from a haphazard approach. (Bridgman and Davis, in Althaus *et al* 2007)

Good process, observing the concepts of due process, fairness and impartiality, is even more fundamental to the legalistic proceedings of an investigative inquiry. Inquiries can criticised for being biased, incompetent, inadequate, too secretive or insensitive, for misusing powers or for ignoring relevant information. Good process adds significantly to the credibility of findings and also serves to bring valuable information to public attention.

Volumes have been written about the attributes of good process, both for policymaking and for more legalistic proceedings. The "spirit of inquiry" (Bennis 1966), integral to an effective approach to solving complex policy problems and the essence of the public inquiry instrument, involves having clear steps for collecting views and information, using appropriate instruments for that purpose, objectively analysing the data gained, communicating the results of that analysis at reasonable intervals to clarify the issues, establishing benchmarks, identifying areas of disagreement and testing alternative conclusions. Transparency in evidence gathering is a particularly important feature of a good inquiry process. There is little policy-related evidence that is not contestable, and if there is no chance to test the results of research, because the processes are conducted behind closed doors or because public discussion is constrained, it cannot really be called evidence. As often as not, the evidence presented to a policy inquiry will be advocacy for a particular position: the secret of inquiry success therefore lies in effective analysis of the data. Not only does a lack of scrutiny of the evidence threaten the ultimate acceptance of a policy solution, it also misses the opportunity to educate the community about what is at stake in a policy issue.

Investigative inquiries are expected to seek out the truth in ways that are fair and follow due process, with an appropriate use of powers and safeguards. They are not adversarial in the way of litigation in the courts but they are still expected to rigorously, independently and dispassionately test the evidence presented, offering a more complete examination than is possible in the legal system.

Many investigative inquiries are set up under legislation which defines the powers available to them. The jury is still out on whether a statutory base for the second tier of inquiry is needed, as recommended by the Australian Law Reform Commission (ALRC 2009). The main purpose of a legislative base would be to clarify the powers of an inquiry. The concern is that this would be an unnecessarily heavy handed approach, making inquiry processes more legalistic, slow and costly. Given the variety of inquiry form and purpose, it would be difficult to draft legislation that would cover all types and it may detract from the versatility that is a major strength of the inquiry instrument. A similar risk attaches to the ALRC's proposal for an inquiries handbook to assist those setting up and running an inquiry. If a handbook ended up being interpreted as a set of rules rather than simply guidance, it would undermine a key advantage of these ad hoc, fit-for-purpose bodies.

Quality of report

The grand finale of all inquiries, the report, will be the basis for judging the quality of the inquiry process and the credibility of findings. Recommendations for action need to be well substantiated in the body of the report, counter arguments and counter claims should be discussed and conclusions need to be justified. Without this, the utility of the inquiry process, its capacity to inform, educate and analyse, is lost and public resources will have been wasted.

Conclusion

This chapter, and this book, have attempted to demonstrate how and why the public inquiry instrument, whether used for investigation or policymaking, has established itself as an invaluable and indispensable part of the apparatus of government. The independent public inquiry is an extra string to a government's bow, providing a temporary, fit-for-purpose body well suited to undertake a discrete task. Given the success of inquiries in resolving public problems over a long period, we would expect governments to continue to appoint them, and allow them to operate so that they deliver on their potential to make an ongoing contribution to sound public policy, accountability and integrity in public life.

Public inquiries mentioned in chapter

(in chronological order by year of appointment, with name of chair)

Commonwealth:

Royal Commission on the Transport of Troops Returning from Service in South Africa in the S.S. Drayton Grange and the circumstances under which Trooper Harold Burkitt, 2nd Australian Commonwealth Horse, who was in a serious condition of health, was not landed at Adelaide from the S.S. Norfolk (McLean: 1902)

Interim Committee for the Australian Schools Commission (Karmel: 1972)

Commission of Inquiry into Poverty (Henderson: 1972)

Aboriginal Land Rights Commission (Woodward: 1973)

Royal Commission on Human Relationships (Evatt: 1974)

Royal Commission on Australian Government Administration (Coombs: 1974)

Committee of Inquiry into Technological Change in Australia (Myers: 1978)

Independent Public Inquiry into Domestic Airfares (Holcroft: 1980)

Royal Commission on the Activities of the Federated Ship Painters and Dockers Union (Costigan: 1980)

Royal Commission on the Use and Effects of Chemical Agents on Australian Personnel in Vietnam (Evatt: 1983)

Independent Review of Economic Regulation of Aviation (May: 1985)

Review of the Future of Drug Evaluation in Australia (Baume: 1991)

Committee of Inquiry into Fuel Taxation (Trebeck: 2001)

Inquiry into Australian Intelligence Agencies (Flood: 2004)

Inquiry into Certain Australian Companies in Relation to the UN Oil-for-Food Programme (Cole: 2005)

National Human Rights Consultation (Brennan: 2008)

Building the Education Revolution Implementation Taskforce (Orgill: 2010)

Review of Funding for Schooling (Gonski: 2010)

Independent Inquiry into the Media and Media Regulation (Finkelstein: 2011)

Royal Commission into Institutional Responses to Child Sexual Abuse (McClellan: 2013)

States:

Queensland

Royal Commission into Alleged Police Activities at the National Hotel (Gibbs: 1963)

Commission of Inquiry into Possible Illegal Activities and Associated Police Misconduct (Fitzgerald: 1987)

Commission of Inquiry into the Activities of Particular Queensland Unions (Cooke: 1989)

Bundaberg Hospital Commission of Inquiry (Morris: 2005)

Queensland Public Hospitals Commission of Inquiry (Davies: 2005)

Queensland Floods Commission of Inquiry (Holmes: 2011)

South Australia

Royal Commission into the State Bank of South Australia (Jacobs: 1991)

Victoria

Royal Commission into the Tricontinental Group of Companies (Woodward: 1990)

Victorian Bushfires Royal Commission (Teague: 2009)

Western Australia

Royal Commission into Commercial Activities of Government and Other Matters, Western Australia (Kennedy: 1991) (WA Inc Royal Commission)

Royal Commission into Use of Executive Power (Marks: 1995)

Overseas:

President's Special Commission on the Assassination of President John F. Kennedy (Warren: 1963)

References

Althaus, C., Bridgman, P., and Davis, G., 2007, *The Australian Policy Handbook*, Sydney: Allen and Unwin

Australian Law Reform Commission, (ALRC), 2009, *Making Inquiries – A New Statutory Framework*, Report 111, Canberra: Commonwealth Government

Banks, G., 2009, *Evidence-based policy making: What is it? How do we get it?* Canberra: Productivity Commission

Bennis, W., 1966, *Changing Organizations: Essays on the Development and Evolution of Human Organization*, New York: McGraw-Hill

Bennis, W.G., and Slater, P.E., 1968, *The Temporary Society*, New York: Harper and Row

Edwards, M., with Howard, C., and Miller, R., 2001, *Social Policy, Public Policy*, Sydney: Allen and Unwin

Howlett, M., 2011, *Designing Public Policies: Principles and Instruments*, Abingdon: Routledge

King, M., 2005, "Morris commission passes RC test," *The Courier-Mail*, 30 April

Lindblom, C.E., 1968, *The Policy-Making Process*, New Jersey: Prentice-Hall

Mulgan, R., 2007, "Politicization of Public Service Advice," *Public Administration*, 85(3), 569-586

Rourke, F.E., and Schulman, P.R., 1989, "Adhocracy in Policy Development," *The Social Science Journal*, 26(2),131-142

Tanner L., 2011, *Sideshow: Dumbing Down Democracy*, Melbourne: Scribe

Toffler, A., 1970, *Future Shock*, London: Pan Books

Waterman, R., 1992, *Adhocracy*, New York: W.W. Norton and Company

About the authors

Nicholas Aroney is Professor of Constitutional Law at the University of Queensland. In 2012-13 he undertook with Ian Callinan QC a review of the *Crime and Misconduct Act* for the Queensland Attorney-General. His recent publications include: *The Constitution of a Federal Commonwealth: The Making and Meaning of the Australian Constitution* (2009).

Gary Banks is Dean and Chief Executive of the Australia and New Zealand School of Government and a Professorial Fellow at Melbourne University. He also chairs the Regulatory Policy Committee of the OECD in Paris. He was previously Chairman of the Productivity Commission from its inception in 1998 until 2012, and has extensive experience leading public inquiries into both social and economic issues. His current research interests centre on public governance and institutional influences on economic performance.

Stephen Bartos is Executive Director of ACIL Allen Consulting in Canberra and advises clients on economics, public policy, governance and risk. Prior to consulting, Stephen was Professor of Governance and Director of the National Institute of Governance at the University of Canberra and was previously Deputy Secretary of the Commonwealth Department of Finance and head of the Commonwealth's Budget Group.

Linda Courtenay Botterill is Professor in Australian Public Policy at the University of Canberra. Prior to her academic career, she spent 15 years in public policy practice in the Australian Public Service, in two ministerial offices and in two industry associations. She has written extensively on Australian rural policy and politics particularly in the areas of drought policy, the wheat industry and the role of the National Party.

Frank Brennan AO is a Jesuit priest, Professor of Law at Australian Catholic University and Adjunct Professor at the Australian National University College of Law and National Centre for Indigenous Studies.

He is an Officer of the Order of Australia (AO) for services to Aboriginal Australians, particularly as an advocate in the areas of law, social justice and reconciliation. In 2009, he chaired the Australian National Human Rights Consultation Committee. He was the recipient of the Migration Institute of Australia's 2013 Distinguished Service to Immigration Award.

Rosalind Croucher is President of the Australian Law Reform Commission and Professor of Law, Macquarie University (on leave while at the ALRC). Professor Croucher has lectured and published extensively, principally in the fields of equity, trusts, property, inheritance and legal history. In 2004 she was awarded an Honorary Fellowship of the Australian College of Legal Medicine and in 2013 Life Membership of the NSW Women Lawyers' Association.

Geoff Davies AO was admitted to the Bar in 1962, took silk in 1976 and from 1989 was the Solicitor-General for Queensland, the first member of the private Bar to hold that position. He served as President of the Queensland Bar Association 1987-1989 and in 1991 was appointed to the Bench of the newly established Court of Appeal of Queensland. In 2003 he was appointed an Officer of the Order of Australia (AO). Geoff retired from the Court of Appeal in 2005 and in the same year was appointed as Commissioner of the Queensland Public Hospitals Commission of Inquiry. He is presently a Judge of the Court of Appeal of Brunei Darussalam; an Adjunct Professor in the School of Law at the University of Queensland; and Chairman of Queensland Advocacy Inc.

Henry Ergas is the inaugural Professor of Infrastructure Economics at the University if Wollongong where his focus is on the economic, regulatory and public policy research program. He takes a special interest in the development and application of cost-benefit analysis and in the analysis of pricing and investment decisions in regulated infrastructure industries. Henry is a regular columnist in *The Australian* and Senior Economic Adviser at Deloitte Access Economics. He has held leading positions at the OECD, chaired the 1999 Australian Intellectual Property and Competition Review Committee and was a member of the Prime

Minister's Export Infrastructure Task Force in 2005 and the Defence Industry Policy Review in 2006.

Philip Flood AO was formerly Secretary of the Department of Foreign Affairs and Trade, High Commissioner to the United Kingdom and Ambassador to Indonesia. He was also Director-General of the Office of National Assessments and Director-General of Australia's Agency for International Development (AusAID). Philip has headed several public Inquiries, including the Inquiry into Australia's Intelligence Agencies that followed the Iraq War and an Inquiry into Immigration Detention Centres. Philip is author of *Odyssey by the Sea* (2005) and *Dancing with Warriors* (2011). He was awarded an Officer of the Order of Australia in 1992, the Bintang Jasa Utama (Indonesian Order of Merit) in 1993 and the Centenary Medal in 2003.

Paddy Gourley was employed in the Commonwealth Public Service Board and the departments of Industrial Relations and Defence from 1969 to 2000. Since then he has served on the boards of the Sydney Airport Corporation, the Great Energy Alliance Corporation and the Loy Yang Marketing and Management Company. He is a monthly contributor to the *Public Sector Informant*, a supplement to *The Canberra Times*.

Grant Hoole is a Canadian lawyer and academic, presently completing his PhD at the Faculty of Law, University of Ottawa, where his research focuses on commissions of inquiry. In 2012 he was an Endeavour Visiting Fellow at the Gilbert + Tobin Centre of Public Law at the University of New South Wales. He received his LLB/BCL from McGill University in 2006 and his LLM from the University of Toronto in 2010. He is a member of the Ontario Bar.

John Humphreys is a Visiting Lecturer of economics at the University of Queensland and the Managing Director of the Human Capital Project, a non-profit that operates in Australia and Cambodia. He has worked previously at the Australian Treasury and Centre for

International Economics, and has published books on trade, environment and tax reform. John is also a director of the Economic Society of Australia (Qld) and of the Australian Taxpayers Alliance.

Christian Kerr is a senior reporter with *The Australian* newspaper, a contributing editor to *The Spectator Australia* and a regular commentator on Australian politics, media and current affairs for local and international outlets. A co-founder of the website Crikey, he spent a decade working as a political staffer, serving as a political or communications adviser to two federal cabinet ministers and a state premier then acted as corporate relations manager for one of the country's biggest construction and infrastructure companies before embarking on a career in journalism.

Kenneth Kitts is Provost and Professor of Political Science at the University of North Carolina at Pembroke. His research focuses on presidential politics and the executive advisory system. He is the author of *Presidential Commissions and National Security* (2006).

Tony Makin is a Professor of Economics at Griffith University and Director of the Griffith APEC Study Centre. He has published widely on Australian and international macroeconomic policy issues and has previously served as an International Consultant Economist with the International Monetary Fund and as a senior economist in the Australian federal departments of Finance, Foreign Affairs and Trade, The Treasury and Prime Minister and Cabinet.

Scott Prasser has worked in federal and state governments in senior research and policy roles and is author of *Royal Commissions and Public Inquiries in Australia* (2006). He holds undergraduate and postgraduate qualifications from the University of Queensland and Griffith University.

Janet Ransley is currently Associate Professor and head of Criminology and Criminal Justice at Griffith University. She is the co-editor of *The Fitzgerald Legacy: Reforming Public Life in Australia and Beyond* (2010) and co-author of *Third Party Policing* (2005). Janet's current research interests include corruption investigation and prevention, policing effectiveness and criminal justice policy.

Charles Sampford (DPhil, Oxon), Director and Professor, Institute for Ethics, Governance and Law, a joint initiative of the UN University, Griffith, ANU, QUT and others. Charles was previously Foundation Dean of Law at Griffith University and Foundation Director of the Key Centre for Ethics, Law, Justice and Governance (the only Australian centre in law or governance to receive centre funding from the Australian Research Council) and held a Senior Fulbright to Harvard. He has written 120 articles and chapters and has completed 28 books and edited collections. Charles is also a Barrister and Company Director.

Alan Simpson is Senior Lecturer in the Department of Political Science and Public Policy at the University of Waikato, Hamilton, New Zealand. His publications include *The Constitutional Implications of MMP* (1998); *Referendums: Constitutional and Political Perspectives* (1992); chapters and articles on the Antarctic, Maori voting, voting in general elections, royal commissions and commissions of inquiry.

Graeme Starr has wide experience in government having worked as senior adviser to federal ministers and opposition leaders and headed major professional bodies. He has written extensively on politics and public policy and taught at several Australian and American universities. His recent publications include: *Carrick: Principles, Politics and Policy* (2012) and *Variety and Choice: Good Schools for All Australians* (2010). Graeme has undergraduate qualifications from the University of Sydney and postgraduate degrees from Carleton University, Canada, and West Virginia University, USA, where he earned his doctorate in Political Science as a Woodrow Wilson Dissertation Fellow.

Mark Thomson is a senior analyst at the Australian Strategic Policy Institute (ASPI). Mark joined ASPI in 2002 following a career in the Australia Department of Defence. His research interests include Australian strategic policy, defence economics, links between strategy and force structure, management of the Department of Defence and defence industry policy. Mark participated in the government's review of the Australian Defence Force Recruitment and Retention in 2005-06 and was a member of the Defence Industry Policy Review team in 2006-07. In 2008-09 he was a ministerial advisor during the development of the 2009 Defence White Paper.

Rodney Tiffen is Emeritus Professor in Government and International Relations at the University of Sydney. He is the author of eight books and over 60 scholarly publications mainly on media and politics. The second edition of *How Australia Compares* written with Ross Gittins was released in 2009. His latest book *Rupert Murdoch: A Reassessment* was published in 2014. Professor Tiffen worked with the Finkelstein Inquiry in 2011-12.

Helen Tracey has had a successful career in public policy, mainly in education with the Commonwealth Government, and has worked at the Public Policy Institute of the Australian Catholic University. She has academic qualifications in political science, public policy and education from the Australian National University and the University of London (Institute of Education).

Roger Wettenhall is Professor of Public Administration Emeritus and Visiting Professor in the Australian New Zealand School of Government Institute for Governance at the University of Canberra. He was editor/co-editor of the *Australian Journal of Public Administration* from 1989 to 1995, and now chairs the Institute of Public Administration Australia/University of Canberra Public Administration Research Trust Fund Management Committee. As well as his on-going interest in natural disasters, his main current research focus includes public and social enterprise, privatisation, public-private partnerships and non-departmental public bodies.

www.ingramcontent.com/pod-product-compliance
Lightning Source LLC
Chambersburg PA
CBHW050329270326
41926CB00016B/3376

* 9 7 8 1 9 2 5 1 3 8 2 4 5 *